Jaguar Books on Latin America

Series Editors

WILLIAM H. BEEZLEY, Neville G. Pen
American Studies, Texas Christian Un
COLIN M. MACLACHLAN, Professor and Chair, Department
of History, Tulane University

Addressing subjects as diverse as the region itself, the Jaguar Books on Latin America guide the reader through the myriad political systems, economies, and societies that comprise today's Latin America. Each volume in the series is edited by an eminent scholar in the field and gathers the most influential primary and secondary documents on a topic of central importance to the region's history and development. Together the Jaguar Books stand as a library of sources for teaching, as well as a useful reference for all those interested in Latin American culture, history, and current affairs.

Volumes Published

John E. Kicza, ed., *The Indian in Latin American History: Resistance, Resilience, and Acculturation* (1993). Cloth ISBN 0-8420-2421-2 Paper ISBN 0-8420-2425-5

Susan E. Place, ed., *Tropical Rainforests: Latin American Nature and Society in Transition* (1993). Cloth ISBN 0-8420-2423-9 Paper ISBN 0-8420-2427-1

Paul W. Drake, ed., *Money Doctors, Foreign Debts, and Economic Reforms in Latin America from the 1890s to the Present* (1994). Cloth ISBN 0-8420-2434-4   Paper ISBN 0-8420-2435-2

John A. Britton, ed., *Molding the Hearts and Minds: Education, Communications, and Social Change in Latin America* (1994). Cloth ISBN 0-8420-2489-1   Paper ISBN 0-8420-2490-5

Money Doctors,
Foreign Debts, and
Economic Reforms
in Latin America
from the 1890s
to the Present

Money Doctors, Foreign Debts, and Economic Reforms in Latin America from the 1890s to the Present

Paul W. Drake
Editor

Jaguar Books on Latin America
Number 3

A Scholarly Resources Inc. Imprint
Wilmington, Delaware

Scholarly Resources Inc.
104 Greenhill Avenue
Wilmington, DE 19805-1897

Library of Congress Cataloging-in-Publication Data

Money doctors, foreign debts, and economic reforms in Latin America
   from the 1890s to the present / Paul W. Drake, editor.
      p.   cm. — (Jaguar books on Latin America ; no. 3)
   Includes bibliographical references.
   ISBN 0-8420-2434-4. — ISBN 0-8420-2435-2 (pbk.)
   1. Economic assistance, American—Latin America—History.
2. Consultants—Latin America. 3. Latin America—Economic policy.
4. Economic stabilization—Latin America—History. 5. Debts, External—
Latin America—History. 6. Loans, American—Latin America—History.
I. Drake, Paul W., 1944–   . II. Series: Jaguar books on Latin America ;
3.
HC125.M584   1994
338.9'7308—dc20   93-34563
                                                             CIP

The paper used in this publication meets the minimum requirements of the
American National Standard for permanence of paper for printed library
materials, Z39.48, 1984.

To Violet Drake

About the Editor

Paul W. Drake holds a Ph.D. from Stanford University (1971). He is the Institute of the Americas Professor of Inter-American Affairs at the University of California, San Diego. He has been a visiting scholar at the Wilson Center, Washington, DC; Universidad de los Andes, Bogotá, Colombia; Universidad Católica, Valparaíso, Chile; Oxford University, Oxford, England; and the Instituto Juan March, Madrid, Spain. He is also a past president of the Latin American Studies Association.

His books include *Socialism and Populism in Chile, 1932–52* (winner of the Bolton Prize from the Conference on Latin American History), *Elections and Democratization in Latin America, 1980–85* (coedited with Eduardo Silva), *The Money Doctor in the Andes* (winner of the Bryce Wood Award from the Latin American Studies Association), *El Apra de la ideologia a la praxis* (coedited with Heraclio Bonilla), and *The Struggle for Democracy in Chile, 1982–90* (coedited with Ivan Jaksic). His research interests continue to focus on political and economic developments in South America.

Contents

INTRODUCTION

The Political Economy of Foreign Advisers and Lenders in Latin America

Paul W. Drake[*]

Today as yesterday the connection between foreign consultants and debts helps determine the economic restructuring and development of Latin America and has shaped the destiny of other countries reliant on external financing from wealthier nations. A recent example of the importance of these linkages occurred in 1991, when President George Bush told Russia that it could not obtain massive new loans until it sought the guidance of the International Monetary Fund (IMF). At the same time, a U.S. economist from Harvard, Jeffrey D. Sachs, counseled Russian president Boris Yeltsin on how to acquire foreign loans and construct a capitalist system.

Sachs had proved his mettle previously by designing sweeping reform programs for heavily indebted Poland and Bolivia. That activity paralleled visits to Poland and Bolivia sixty years ago by another U.S. academic economist, Edwin W. Kemmerer, who rewrote their economic legislation to placate foreign lenders. Such patterns have deep roots: earlier this century the U.S. government sent in economists along with marines to occupy client states in the Caribbean and Central America. There, intruders reformed financial practices in order to assure that foreign debts were paid on time. This essay explores the continuities and changes in these intricate economic relations from the 1890s to the 1990s.

*For comments on this essay, I am indebted to Michael Bernstein, Lisa Hilbink, Nils Jacobsen, and Richard Salvucci. I also want to thank Ms. Hilbink, my research assistant, for helping me find and edit the articles for this collection; her insight and judgment were invaluable.

The phenomenon of "money doctoring" has left a long trail that started well before the twentieth century and has extended far beyond Latin America. Economic consultants and monitors from abroad have been most important in the so-called Third World because of the economic and political instability suffered there and because of the receipt of foreign loans in those countries. Money doctors have conducted their operations on borrowers, not lenders. They have helped risky credit recipients attract loans in the first place, acquire subsequent loans to repay the old ones, and adjust or escape from some of those obligations during a debt crisis. As intermediaries between borrowers and lenders, debtors and creditors, these imported experts and supervisers also have supplied information, access, and security to foreign investors.

For over a century, foreign money doctors and financiers have played a crucial role in the economic history of Latin America. International economic sages, institutions, models, formulas, and exchanges have molded the region's role in the world economy. In turn, those external forces have transformed and been transformed by domestic structures and actors. This book focuses on the interactions of foreign advisers and lenders with other groups outside Latin America—participants such as governments, traders, investors, corporations, intellectuals, and so on. It also emphasizes their relations with agents inside Latin America—the policymakers, bankers, industrialists, agriculturalists, military, intellectuals, and workers. The impact of these interactions on economic reforms has depended upon the raveling and unraveling of transnational coalitions among foreign and domestic interest groups.

Untangling these alliances and results will reveal the political economy of international advising and lending. To understand money doctoring, this book will examine both its international and domestic political economy as well as the interface between external and internal forces. This introductory chapter will treat both facets, while the essay by economist Albert O. Hirschman concentrates on the internal aspects and that by historians Emily S. and Norman L. Rosenberg focuses on the external dimensions.

Debt Cycles in Latin American History

Time and again Latin America has ingested large foreign loans and then fallen short of their repayment. Each series of debt inflows and outflows has involved much larger dollar amounts than the previous round. In the main, these loan cycles have been determined by conditions in the international economy. A surplus of finance capital in the developed nations produces a spate of loans into Latin America. Thereafter, an international downturn halts the funding and triggers recessions and defaults. Over many years the debts are renegotiated and repaid at a reduced value.

Although these cycles have been disruptive, external loans, in and of themselves, have not necessarily been harmful or beneficial. Their impact has depended upon their timing, terms, and usage. They have promoted national development when their acquisition spurred growth, which facilitated their future repayment as a smaller percentage of the gross national product.

1820s–1920s

The first loan cycle occurred during Latin America's wars of independence, when naive Europeans invested in the fledgling countries. By the end of the 1820s most of the governments had defaulted; they were unable to revive the war-torn economies quickly and fund the new state apparatus, let alone repay external obligations. Some of these debt burdens hung over the young republics into the 1920s. Other loan spurts occurred in the 1860s, 1880s, and 1900s. Great Britain dominated the external economy, although France and Germany also had become prominent contributors before the end of the nineteenth century.

After Latin America's debt failures in earlier years, the United States sought to be cautious as it tried its hand at lending in the Caribbean and Central America around the turn of the century. It wanted to make sure that the Latin Americans repaid their loans punctually so that other foreign lenders would not intervene and U.S. investors could collect what was owed them. The United States encouraged loans because of their intrinsic profitability and because they underwrote purchases of U.S. goods.

In the United States at the end of the nineteenth century, it was widely believed that overseas outlets were needed for the country's excess products and capital. Washington's policymakers also hoped that loans could prime the pump for broader economic development in poor countries. They thought that U.S. dollars could help stabilize governments and their finances, again reducing temptations for foreign invasions. To increase the security of such lending, the United States began relying on money doctors.

1920s–1930s

Following the opening of the Panama Canal and the concluding of World War I, the United States replaced Great Britain as the dominant external economic power in most of Latin America. The Colossus of the North extended the hegemony it had established earlier in the Caribbean and Central America into South America. It brought the west coast into its orbit in the 1920s and the east coast in the 1940s.

Commercial expansion in the 1920s was fueled by the "dance of the millions." Private U.S. investors whirled through their first fiesta of massive lending to Latin American governments. These lenders competed avidly with each other and with Europeans to sign up voracious Latin American borrowers. U.S. private banks and financial intermediaries earned handsome commissions floating Latin American bond issues worth millions of dollars on the New York Stock Exchange. Through these channels, Latin America received the greatest influx of U.S. private finance capital prior to the 1970s.

In the 1920s, U.S. bankers and financiers sometimes arranged excessive loans because normally they were not committing their own money. Instead, they were marketing interest-earning securities to thousands of individual investors. Nevertheless, some banking houses bent every effort to try to investigate, fortify, and even control Latin American finances. They hoped to establish and protect long-term relationships with both borrowers in Latin America and bondholders in the United States. They sometimes relied on North American advisers to assess, prop up, or at least improve the image of financial conditions in the client country.

On the other side of the transaction, South American leaders employed foreign advisers to improve their access to loans at reasonable terms. Those governments knew that a reputation for fiscal disorder and loan defaults dissuaded many North Americans, who were new to international finance, from gambling their dollars on Latin American securities. The more checkered a country's credit record, the more valuable the certification from a money doctor. South Americans realized that Central American and Caribbean bonds sold at better terms in the New York market when their finances were directly supervised by U.S. officials. They instilled similar investor trust through inspections by U.S. bankers and economists.

Most of those Yankee dollars were spent on previous debts, administrative expenses, and, above all, on public works that substantially improved infrastructure. Reliance on U.S. capital made the Latin Americans generous to certain U.S. interests, and construction programs often awarded lucrative contracts to U.S. suppliers and builders. The defaults of the 1930s, however, left the borrowers with significant infrastructural gains at the expense of U.S. bondholders.

Until the Great Depression capsized the international lending and trading system, the major beneficiaries of the 1920s bond boom were Latin American governments and U.S. bankers, exporters, shippers, and builders. From 1931 to 1933 most governments imposed import· restrictions, established exchange controls, suspended foreign debt payments, and abandoned the gold standard. Although none of the countries repudiated its debts, only Argentina (under heavy British influence) and Haiti and the

Dominican Republic (under U.S. control) continued servicing their foreign obligations. Most of the countries eventually retired their outside debts by the 1950s at substantially reduced rates.

The 1930s depression made the costs of continued compliance with the rules of international finance overwhelmingly outweigh the benefits, leading the Latin Americans to disobey the hegemonic power, even though they did not discard its system. Reluctantly, they rejected the advice of foreign economists to balance their budgets, sustain the gold standard, and maintain external debt payments. As foreign loans and exchange evaporated, domestic pressures compelled governments to halt payments on foreign debt. Rather than employing money doctors to attract outside loans, Latin Americans used them to provide excuses when, because of bankruptcy, they were forced to declare a moratorium on foreign debt payments.

When country after country suspended payments, creditors found that neither sanctions against defectors nor rewards for loyalists had any impact. There were too many defaults and no lender of last resort; the international system contained no powerful external creditor, government, or multilateral institution with whom to negotiate or from whom to receive emergency loans. Since most of those debts were owed to thousands of scattered bondholders, no countervailing pressure or assistance could be supplied by the foreign banks.

U.S. banks individually tried to tide over Colombia and Peru, but the severity and longevity of the depression wrecked their efforts. Dedicated to laissez-faire and devastated by its own depression, the U.S. government refused to intervene significantly. In 1931, Princeton economist Edwin Walter Kemmerer did try to organize a rescue mission for the Latin Americans through the U.S. Federal Reserve system at a meeting of central banks in Peru, but that effort failed.

Most of the defaults occurred in the aftermath of the overthrow of existing regimes, whose legitimacy had rested on their ability to attract external funding by adhering to U.S. fiscal and financial norms. Most of those indebted governments happened to be civilian, constitutional republics. They were now replaced by military dictatorships, many of long duration. The result of the 1930s catastrophe, then, was default and dictatorship, whereas the result of the 1980s debacle would be debt and democracy.

In the 1920s–1930s cycle of debt infusion and hemorrhage, the U.S. government took essentially the same laissez-faire position it would take in the 1970s–1980s cycle of accumulation and collapse. In both eras, Washington officially argued that U.S. investors and Latin American debtors took their own risks in private transactions. The United States provided no legal guarantee of protection or assistance. Whereas the State Department closely supervised lending operations in the Caribbean basin in the opening decades of the twentieth century, it rarely interfered with deals in South America, a strategically less important region. It did deviate from this policy of abstention at times, however, especially at the end of the 1980s when it tried to arrange solutions between creditors and borrowers.

1970s–1980s

After decades during which public financing replaced private lending, conditions in the 1970s came to resemble those in the 1920s. Loans to Latin American governments mushroomed. Due in part to the recycling of petro-dollars from the Middle East through Western banks, money came increasingly from private rather than public agencies. Direct commercial bank credits—not bond issues in the stock market—became the principal instrument.

In the 1970s eager loan officers from the United States, Western Europe, and Japan shoveled billions of dollars to Latin American leaders, who were equally eager to obtain foreign financing in order to overcome economic stagnation, balance-of-payments bottlenecks, foreign-exchange shortages, inadequate investments, and political stalemates. The banks granted the bulk of these loans with little regard for creditworthiness, and most of the debts were incurred with a promise to repay in dollars at the variable interest rates of the day. In many countries, this windfall of loans benefited primarily financiers and speculators. Although governments devoted some of these funds to useful development projects, they expended others on military hardware of dubious necessity.

To acquire these loans or new ones to repay old notes, countries frequently had to obtain a checkup from the IMF. This gambit became increasingly necessary as debtors began facing difficulties in the latter part of the seventies. The Fund's blessing often required unpopular deflationary measures, such as reductions in government spending and in wages, along with exchange stabilization. Sometimes countries adopted similar orthodox policies on the recommendation of private U.S. academic economists. These advisers delivered their recipes to governments either directly or through their former students from Latin America. Many consultants worked for authoritarian rulers, who seemed capable of attracting and servicing massive loans, while enforcing tough stabilization programs.

As the 1970s progressed, further economic liberalization and more austere measures became necessary in order for Latin American countries to continue receiving and servicing their snowballing debts. They brought in more technocratic luminaries who would report that their governments were on the right track and therefore deserving of more loans. After a decade of debt-led development, Latin American borrowers became extremely vulnerable to the international recession in the early 1980s.

Just as the 1970s in Latin America echoed the 1920s, so the 1980s evoked comparisons with the 1930s. Once again, many of those countries rode a roller coaster of free-market policies and foreign loans to zoom up and then down with the world economy. When external financing dried up and interest rates soared, the hemisphere suffered the worst depression since the Great Crash. During 1982–1985, many countries were hit harder than in the 1930s as growth plummeted and unemployment ballooned. This miserable economic performance earned the 1980s the title of "the lost decade." As during the Great Depression, the economic cataclysm undermined or toppled governments. For many reasons, mostly military regimes took a tumble at this time, thereby ushering in a tidal wave of democratization.

During the depression of the 1980s, many analysts predicted that Latin Americans would have to choose between debt and democracy. They faced cruel trade-offs between allocating shrinking resources either to foreign obligations or to domestic investment and social needs. As it turned out, the decade was characterized by the maintenance of both debt and democracy, while the majority of Latin Americans endured a deteriorating standard of living. Neither default nor dictatorship swept the hemisphere. Most countries in the 1980s continued minimal service of their stupendous foreign debts, even though those burdens loomed much larger—absolutely and relatively— than in the thirties.

Governments used visits by the IMF, the chairman of the U.S. Federal Reserve Board, and U.S. academics to certify the rectitude of their policies. They employed such wisemen to reassert their worthiness for new private and public loans, which allowed them to maintain at least token payments on their external obligations. Governments also capitalized on these experts to justify belt-tightening to their citizens and to lobby for leniency from their bankers. They claimed penury, and they counted on money doctors to legitimize the reduction or suspension of their payments to foreign creditors. Meanwhile, the foreign banks hoped that these troubleshooters would protect their investments.

In contrast with the 1930s, big banks, multilateral institutions, and industrial governments kept almost all of the players in the international financial game in the 1980s. Rather than quickly resolved by nearly universal default, the debt crisis in the eighties lingered into the nineties. In large part, it persisted because the money was owed not to atomized bondholders but to huge banking consortia that kept debtors dancing along through pressure, threats, negotiations, and emergency credits until the end of the decade when their own exposure was drastically reduced. Bankers also succeeded by bargaining as a unified actor against individual countries afraid to form a debtors' cartel. In each iteration of the negotiations, the bankers kept Latin American governments hoping that they would receive more generous terms than their neighbors.

First World bankers, governments, and multilateral agencies all agreed with ruling groups in the indebted countries that full-fledged default would be an unacceptable blow to the entire international financial system. Neoliberal formulas for dealing with the crisis through unfettered market mechanisms reigned supreme. Latin Americans tightened their belts, pruned their governments, opened their economies, expanded their exports, and struggled to meet their external obligations. No alternative economic models or regimes could challenge the orthodox free-market canon, especially in light of the recent failures of populism and socialism. As a result, all sides muddled through the debt crisis of the 1980s until it became a secondary issue to the resumption of growth and development in the 1990s. That staunch faith in domestic and international market forces was reinforced by the preachings of money doctors.

Economic and Political Roles of Money Doctors

In a narrow sense, the most basic function of money doctors has been to transfer technology and institutions. Their job has been to bring new economic knowledge and techniques to the host country. Among other things, these fiscal physicians have been expected to teach the natives how to curb inflation, trim budgets, improve the balance of payments, and service the foreign debt. For the growth of capitalism in Latin America, adoption of more efficient foreign laws, agencies, and policies has provided an important boost. Such innovations have been especially influential when they have meshed with the legal and institutional infrastructure of the region's major trading partner.

The contribution of money doctors to this diffusion should not, however, be overstated. Most countries could have designed equivalent reforms without relying on advisers from abroad. Many of the recommendations of these consultants, such as the need to restrain fiscal outlays in order to rein in inflation, were public knowledge before their arrival. In technical terms, the transfer of technology usually has been quite small, and, despite appearances, it has not been the primary significance of money doctors.

More than conveying new knowledge, foreign economic advisers have constituted a political device for multiple actors in the lending and borrowing countries. Whatever their own motivations, these consultants have served three interrelated political purposes: 1) they have helped wealthier nations to expand their influence over poorer regions; 2) they have served the aims of political and economic contenders within the host countries; and 3) they have been used to justify and fund governmental growth.

Ever since the 1890s, Washington has recognized that nearly all U.S. advisers hired overseas can further its economic and strategic interests. However indirectly, U.S. health experts can induce foreigners to purchase U.S. drugs and medical equipment, military trainers can inspire them to buy U.S. arms and doctrines, agronomists to prefer U.S. seeds and farm machinery, engineers to favor U.S. construction firms and automobiles, artists to consume U.S. entertainment, educators to assign U.S. textbooks, and intellectuals to imbibe U.S. ideas. No matter how scientific, professional, and altruistic the agents, their presence has usually encouraged the adoption of the technologies, systems, products, and beliefs of the United States.

The installation of principles and practices copied from U.S. blueprints also has reduced uncertainties for international traders and investors. Incorporating these laws into the recipient countries has compensated for the lack of easily enforceable international regulations for transactions. In addition, U.S. leaders have hoped that technical missions would generally improve U.S. relations with the Third World. They have thought that buttressing economic growth and political equilibrium in such countries would reduce the dangers of disorder or, worse, revolution. Whether money doctors, disease eradicators, earthquake technicians, or Fulbright lecturers, these independent visitors have served as "chosen instruments" in the broader context of U.S. objectives to influence the rest of the world.

While experts have helped external powers penetrate and regulate less developed economies, their second function has been to serve the ambitions of political and economic contenders within the target countries. Competing domestic sectoral interests have capitalized on foreign missions to improve their standing vis-à-vis each other and foreign competitors. They have tried to captivate, coopt, or convert the foreign advisers and have used them and their reputations to tap international sources for credit.

Money doctors have had profound impacts on complex domestic groups, power relations, governments, and national developments within the recipient countries. In many cases, these advisers have promoted the concentration, urbanization, and institutionalization of Latin American economies along paths previously traveled by the United States. As a result, the republics have become more deeply integrated into twentieth-century world capitalism, their economies more articulated and differentiated as local elites respond to external opportunities. In many countries the availability of international credit has given the expanding urban sectors and governments gains over traditional landed elites.

Third, most host governments have employed foreign advisers to justify, rationalize, and fund the growth of their capabilities. They have become better able to collect revenues, assemble data, control expenditures,
organize and manage the bureaucracy, and obtain foreign loans. In the
afterglow of a renowned money doctor, the state is often better equipped to
negotiate with foreign and domestic capitalists. In many cases, its political
clout has been enhanced by the money doctor's backing or by using him as
a scapegoat for unpopular or unsuccessful policies.

Normally, money doctors have experienced the most success when
helping polish and legitimize proposals already favored by local elites. In
these cases, the adviser's primary role is to deliver and authenticate the
orthodox institutions and ideas of the era. Assuming first-class technical
expertise, the money doctor's secret for getting recommendations accepted
has been the existence of a winning coalition in the host country, as seen in
the Bolivian case study by Catherine M. Conaghan. Also helpful has been
the availability of foreign financial resources to reward governments for
good behavior.

Furthermore, money doctors have had better prospects when their
arrival coincided with the beginning of a fresh administration willing and
able to embark upon sweeping reforms. New leaders have used the missions'
reports to blame their predecessors for mismanagement and have taken
advantage of the advising teams' institutional reforms to recast and restaff
bureaucracies. In some cases, a money doctor's recommendations have
been more likely to be accepted and implemented under an authoritarian
regime; successful results from the implementation, however, are no more
guaranteed with a dictatorship than with a democracy, as the selection by
Karen L. Remmer shows.

Money doctors can increase a government's prestige not only abroad
but also at home. Faith in technocratic solutions to national problems,
especially when crafted by foreigners from more developed countries, has
been widespread in Latin America and elsewhere. Until the 1940s, experts
from the United States encountered few local technocrats capable of
challenging their recommendations scientifically. Despite nationalistic
resentments, many Latin Americans viewed outside technicians as above
local partisan divisions, more trustworthy and better trained than local
notables, and therefore able to discredit and override internal opposition to
authority and reforms.

Likewise, chances of success tend to be greater the more exalted the
expert. Although it is important for the adviser to boast impeccable scientific
and professional credentials, it is even more important that the consultant
come from a prestigious institution in a wealthy country. Almost regardless

of technical skill, an economist from the United States carries far more weight than one from Belgium, one from Harvard more than one from Slippery Rock.

Another contributor toward success has been the behavior of the missions. Money doctors and government officials usually operate behind closed doors, avoiding open discussions and press interviews (although Sachs has broken with this tradition by rallying support for his recommendations through public appearances). Until the results of their deliberations are ready to unveil, the mission members typically maintain an aloof air of scientific investigation and priestly secrecy. They claim to be devising highly technical solutions that are above the comprehension of common people and certainly above the quarrels of partisan politicians. Like military officers, they pose as apolitical decision makers, shielding their institutions, reports, laws, and programs from squabbles over influence and spoils. Handing down the completed projects suddenly from the heights of authority inspires awe—and also averts constant debate along the way. In some instances, such majestic policymaking has won quick approval for the proposals.

With few exceptions, high-powered money doctors have believed that their universal scientific principles can be applied everywhere. Almost all that is needed are strong and capable leaders. In the view of these economists, well-planned technical advances in institutions that are managed by apolitical, public-spirited experts can bring about improvements in any country, and there is little need to pay much attention to factors such as history, culture, social structure, or political situation. Given the "scientific" and "neutral" nature of their policies, they have expected them to be resistant to attacks from local politicians and vested interests.

Over the decades, the general content of the money doctors' policies, as well as their overall attitude toward them, has exhibited striking continuities. Time and again, their recommendations have trumpeted economic orthodoxy. Whether in the 1920s or the 1980s, foreign economic wizards have called for stable exchange rates, restricted emissions of currency and credit, corrections in the balance of payments, austerity in government to balance the budget and dampen inflation, and a general prescription of diet and discipline. The very predictability and simplicity of the pronouncements of most money doctors—not their novelty—have made them so attractive to governments as political instruments. Just as kings relied on priests to intone the appropriate benedictions, so presidents have trusted seasoned advisers to utter, with thundering solemnity, the proper platitudes.

In sum, as Albert O. Hirschman explains in his essay, foreign advisers have played several positive roles for host governments. They have riveted public attention on problems the government wanted solved, and, like a "random device," they have helped choose among competing solutions. They have sometimes introduced new ideas and often improved the details of reform packages. In addition, their stature has given reforms a neopositivist sheen of being purely technical and scientific, unpolluted by sordid politics. Finally, they have attracted foreign and domestic support for the government and its program.

Relying on foreign advisers, however, has its risks. Host governments have had little choice but to implement most of the missions' recommendations. After all, they invited the glittering teams with great fanfare, exposed their financial misdeeds to them, and staked their foreign credit rating and domestic political credibility on their success. In some cases, the missions' observations have proved embarrassing for the government, and in other instances the recommendations have been ill suited to local conditions, coming as they do from technocrats with little knowledge of the specific country on the operating table.

Furthermore, by its very nature technocratic decision making has its undemocratic aspects. It impedes the uninhibited consideration of all national opinions and interests, which are shunted aside in favor of the higher wisdom of the experts. Also, reliance on outside expertise has made some governments too dependent on foreigners, provoking a nationalistic backlash—a problem often encountered by the IMF.

Most foreign advisers, even those with soldiers by their sides, have found it much easier to get their recommendations accepted than to get them implemented properly or to see them achieve the results expected. Even when foreign appointees stay on as monitors, it has proved difficult to ensure that implementation adheres to legislative intent. Although some foreign formulas have worked predictably well, others have fit poorly with the legal, linguistic, cultural, political, and economic heritage of the Latin American countries.

Another problem has been that the foreigners' prestige has elevated certain ideas, institutions, and individuals to sacred, untouchable positions of power. Foreign consultants have tried to design more perfect reforms in Latin America than they could have at home, and some of their disciples and converts in the host country have become even more zealous and rigid than they themselves. In Selection 11, Patricio Silva describes such a case in the sanctification of the Chicago Boys in Chile.

In other cases, foreign models have not worked as expected because indigenous political and economic powers have subverted the reforms after the mission's exit. However technically sound, public financial institutions and their expert managers cannot be insulated effectively from politics; it is no more possible to create government agencies untainted by private and partisan pressures in Latin America than it is in the United States. Depoliticization seems especially unlikely in conflict-ridden economies of scarcity where the state plays a large role.

Moreover, some of the countries have had little interest in carrying through these foreign-inspired reforms as ends in themselves. In many cases, the primary audience for the reforms has been the lending rather than the receiving countries. After rubber-stamping the recommendations to please foreign investors, host governments have sometimes circumvented those promises in order to satisfy domestic political and economic pressures.

For centuries Latin American rulers have had to walk a fine line between external demands and internal expectations. Officials in colonial Spanish America, for example, told the Crown in Spain, "I obey but do not execute," to avoid implementing royal decrees unacceptable to local elites. In similar fashion, Brazilians in the nineteenth century labeled unconventional behavior designed to propitiate powerful foreigners "for the English to see." In the 1920s, Bolivians called legislation concocted more to curry foreign favor than to apply to local citizens "laws for export." In recent years, an analogous tactic has been the repeated signing and breaking of letters of intent with the IMF.

Theoretical Roles of Foreign Advisers and Lenders

Money doctoring can be understood from three different theoretical perspectives, defining it as a catalyst for either modernization, dependency, or hegemony. First, in the context of modernization theory, money doctors are agents of diffusion from developed to underdeveloped countries. They bring the latest attitudes and modalities from modern to traditional societies, and they pioneer scientific fiscal and financial institutions and operations. Their reforms have made it possible for high-risk countries to attract and utilize desperately needed foreign capital more effectively. By the same token, those loans have helped poor countries overcome capital, budgetary, and foreign exchange constraints. Thus, growth and development have accelerated, allowing the recipients to repay their debts out of a larger future treasury. This benevolent view assumes that the terms of the loans are not onerous and that borrowed funds are expended on productive purposes.

Second, in the framework of dependency theories, money doctors are depicted as providing the opening wedge for imperialist exploitation. Incorporating peripheral countries into an inferior role in the world capitalist system, these economic advisers impose foreign models and codes to subjugate the target countries and to facilitate the extraction of their surplus by international bankers, investors, and traders. Whether usurious or not, loans mainly grease the wheels of an inequitable world order that keeps the poorer countries and their poorer citizens in a subordinate position.

Although insightful, neither modernization nor dependency theories capture all the subtleties and complexities of money doctoring and foreign lending. Although foreign forces have made Latin American countries more dependent on the United States for models, loans, and trade, dependent development has proved capable of bringing about significant growth and structural changes that have expanded urban industries as well as the national state. Debt-led growth has entailed subservience to external powers, but it also has taken contradictory turns uncontrolled by U.S. interests.

Outside forces have been filtered through elitist domestic sociopolitical structures and groups that have pursued their own agendas within the constraints and opportunities presented by the international arena. On the one hand, an open economic model reliant on external credits has brought significant benefits—especially to upper-class Latin Americans—during upswings in the world economy. But it also has brought devastating disasters—especially to working-class Latin Americans—during downswings. The crucial issue has been to what extent Latin American countries could utilize foreign advisers and lenders to make the most of an inherently unequal relationship with the centers of world capitalism.

Third, through the optic of hegemony theories, money doctors can be analyzed as helping the United States establish, regulate, and maintain a stable international economic order. From this perspective, U.S. invasions in the Caribbean have forced those lilliputian countries to abide by U.S. economic models and induced their neighbors to follow suit. Examples in the Caribbean basin demonstrated that the potential for violence lurked behind the U.S. quest for economic concessions, its military methods enhancing its reputation as an emerging hegemonic power willing to use force. The specter of that option made some South Americans resist U.S. economic penetration out of fear that the flag would follow the dollar. Many more, however, welcomed North American investments with the hopes that their receptivity would avert armed intimidation.

By the 1920s, however, the U.S. government realized that landing marines was too costly, both internationally and domestically. Foreign as well as U.S. public opinion condemned classic colonialism and imperialism, and such tactics would be far more expensive in distant, stronger nations. Therefore, the new hegemon turned to peaceful, depoliticized mechanisms. It relied first on bilateral instruments like the Kemmerer missions and later on multilateral institutions such as the IMF. As it brought more and more states into its orbit, the U.S. system of economic domination acquired a reputation and an allure that rendered the use of direct force or incentives less and less necessary to enroll new members or retain older ones.

In the absence of easily enforced international laws, economic missions reduced risks for U.S. capitalists by duplicating U.S. procedures within the host countries. Like foreign corporations going behind tariff walls, these U.S. practices became internalized. While promoting capitalist conformity, economic emissaries also delivered information about foreign economies back to the hegemon.

For Latin Americans, these missionaries eased their entry into an international system wherein the United States appeared to guarantee stability and a chance at prosperity. In return for cooperation, the United States provided the "collective goods" of maintaining the international free flow of capital and commodities. Foreign loans induced Latin Americans to comply with U.S. rules; their entry fee consisted of accepting U.S. institutions and regulations, respecting foreign properties and obligations, and keeping their economies reasonably open. They were also expected to try to stabilize exchange rates, rectify the balance of payments, restrain government spending, and control inflation.

When the Latin Americans strayed from the path of virtue, they were reminded to get back in line. Once admonished, they repeatedly vowed to behave in the future, sometimes by adopting the recommendations of a private money doctor or by signing letters of intent with the IMF. These accommodations between the hegemon and lesser powers required extensively reiterated bargaining and negotiations over such issues as tariffs, exchange rates, and the rights of foreign investors. Both sides tried to minimize their costs and maximize their benefits. The only other options for the Latin Americans were to defect to an alternative economic regime, as Cuba did after the 1959 revolution, or to withdraw from the world system, as Paraguay tried to do in the nineteenth century.

From the 1920s to the 1960s, more and more Latin Americans feared that the United States was gaining far more than they did from the stability supplied by U.S. hegemony. Most of the ruling elites, however, especially from the 1970s to the 1990s, have continued to believe in a compatibility of interests. They have clung to the existing international system so long as their benefits appear to exceed their costs, even if the hegemon profits more than the underlings.

Within the subordinate states, these decisions to cooperate or clash with the hegemon have depended on the perceptions of the local ruling groups and governing coalitions. The United States, therefore, has sought to shape not only the international arena but also the decision making within the weaker countries. U.S. economists have helped convince Latin Americans to comply with the rules of the game and have worked to persuade the hegemon that their clients are behaving properly.

In contrast with dependency thinkers, the outlook of most hegemony theorists is that maintenance of law and order by a superpower can be relatively good for the subordinate as well as the superordinate participants in that economic system. Although not equally beneficial to all, the international regime is viewed as preferable to other alternatives. Of course, the consequences of U.S. hegemony have varied significantly with cycles in the world economy and with policies adopted by Latin American governments.

Evolution of Money Doctoring, 1890s–1990s

Colonization and Proconsuls

The United States first elaborated its brand of money doctoring in the empire it carved out of Spain's former possessions in the Caribbean and Pacific. After the Spanish-American War in 1898, the U.S. government dispatched economists along with troops to install U.S. economic as well as political institutions in the colonies and semi-colonies it had acquired. In Puerto Rico and the Philippines, U.S. economists replaced Hispanic with Anglo-Saxon economic legislation and codes. Here they learned the art of money doctoring and enacted most of the same reforms, including the gold standard, that they would later bring to South America.

From the 1890s to the 1920s security and economic motivations merged with U.S. interventions in putatively sovereign countries in the Caribbean and Central America. Most historians of these episodes have concentrated on military intrusion rather than financial control, even though the processes went hand-in-hand. The original justification for meddling in the Caribbean basin was to impose order so that non-American great powers would have no excuse for intervening with force—especially the excuse of collecting overdue debts. That concern led to U.S. involvement in fiscal and financial affairs to guarantee that sufficient revenues were available for debt servicing.

Intrusion in the economic management of foreign countries involved the installation of U.S. institutions and procedures. In extreme cases, U.S. officials were also imposed, for example, to collect customs receipts or regulate the money supply. Another outcome of intervention was that it became more convenient for the United States to have U.S. banks become the primary lenders to these republics, and it often arranged new loans to pay off dangling debts to Europeans. Those U.S. loans were secured by a variety of safeguards, including treaties, contracts, legislation, soldiers, and money doctors.

The United States carried out the most thorough financial sanitation in Cuba, Panama, the Dominican Republic, Haiti, and Nicaragua, countries that became protectorates under treaties conceding the right of U.S. intervention. Often borne by U.S. banks, U.S. financial influence also was felt strongly throughout the rest of the Caribbean basin. Eventually, U.S. economic tutelage reached into South America, usually carried by private practitioners and accompanied by the outward thrust of military and economic might.

Even in colonies or protectorates occupied by the U.S. military, U.S. interests were pluralistic as well as unified, conflicting as well as cohesive. They coalesced or clashed with equally diverse local elites, most of whom opposed the invasion but tried to take advantage of compatible U.S. objectives. U.S. government officials, soldiers, bankers, traders, and economists usually agreed on the proper financial and fiscal institutions even when they disagreed over exchange rates, tariff schedules, and tax burdens. For example, U.S. bankers might prefer to see Latin American governments spend scarce foreign exchange on debt servicing rather than on importing U.S. goods, and they would not mind a tax on other U.S. corporations to help with those debt payments. At the same time, Latin American business leaders might join with resident U.S. firms in opposing taxes on companies, preferring to spend foreign exchange to import capital goods. Money doctors had to tiptoe through this minefield of divergent economic interests.

Privatization and Kemmerer

In the opening decades of the twentieth century, the United States found it increasingly efficacious to export expertise through private agents rather than through government officials, as the Rosenbergs make clear in their historical overview. By favoring independent missions hired voluntarily by host countries, Washington avoided any appearance of complicity with advisers and lenders. This "hands-off" policy defused anti-interventionist criticisms at home and abroad. The State Department supported those missions, for example, with help to arrange the contract or with pressure from behind the scenes to heed their advice, but it did not officially sponsor them.

This privatized mode of operation suited the U.S. effort to export its beliefs of limited government and free enterprise. Indeed, the State Department knew that the same advice would be more acceptable from private economists than from representatives of U.S. government or business. Therefore, missions legally independent from Washington and Wall Street used persuasion in South America to replicate much of what U.S. officials had achieved through force of arms in the Caribbean basin: exchange stability, fiscal propriety, modern banking, efficient customs administration, reliable debt servicing, and an "open door" for equal treatment for foreign capitalists.

U.S. advisers of all kinds—military, medical, and sanitational—elbowed aside European competitors (although Latin Americans did continue to invite in a few Europeans in order to balance North American influence and to diversify their economic connections). From the 1890s through the 1920s, every Latin American country except Argentina and Brazil contracted U.S. financial consultants, and before World War II, Latin America had brought in more U.S. technocrats than any other world area. The most successful economic ambassador was Dr. Edwin W. Kemmerer, for whom the term "money doctor" was coined.

Between World War I and the Great Depression, Professor Kemmerer became a sort of one-man IMF. He was asked to reform the monetary, banking, and fiscal systems of Mexico, Guatemala, Colombia, South Africa, Chile, Poland, Ecuador, Bolivia, China, and Peru. Other countries, including Brazil, Panama, Argentina, and Romania, also considered inviting Kemmerer but did not follow through, some of them enacting versions of his reforms without his advice.

Kemmerer proposed virtually the same laws almost everywhere he went. He saw himself as a professional expert bringing universal, scientific advances to backward countries and their poorer citizens. In his view, technical enlightenment could create efficient institutions uncontaminated by politics and privilege. Kemmerer believed that he was using the gold standard to slay the dragons of exchange instability, inflation, and government overspending. Some of the fiscal reforms advocated by the U.S. Alliance for Progress in the 1960s, including improved tax collection and financial management, were foreshadowed by Kemmerer in the 1920s. Accompanied by a flood of finance capital from the United States, his reforms intensified Latin America's dependence on the Colossus of the North. At the same time, his programs accelerated the growth of urban capitalist sectors and institutions and expanded the extractive and distributive capacities of the central state.

Although many Latin Americans desired Kemmerer's economic remedies and institutions for their intrinsic worth, his hosts possessed ulterior motives. Above all, they hoped that his medicine would open up U.S. financial and commodity markets. They believed that access to the United States would satisfy their emergent urban groups and enhance their state's ability to cope with rising foreign and domestic forces. For the South Americans, Kemmerer's "seal of approval" allowed them to take some advantage of U.S. predominance and resources without becoming virtual colonies, like their neighbors in the Caribbean basin.

Despite significant differences in political and economic autonomy between the Caribbean and South America, a similar pattern evolved: more and more frequently, U.S. economic advice and models were adopted and accompanied by increasing reliance on U.S. trade, loans, companies, and entrepreneurs. In addition, a few of the U.S. specialists hired by the South Americans had gained experience in the forced financial cleanups of the Caribbean. The peaceful use of private instruments shielded the U.S. government from charges of imperialism, but at the same time it rendered the money doctors more independent and therefore more susceptible to manipulation by elites in the host countries. Like North Americans, Latin Americans tried to use these economic advisers to further their own sectoral or national interests.

Kemmerer frequently recommended not only legislation and policies but also administrators from the United States. Like IMF missions, his teams sometimes left advisers on the scene to provide guidance, to monitor performance, and to report back. Weaker, poorer, less creditworthy nations were most likely to accept the appointment of foreign officials to oversee such activities as taxation, customs collection, government accounting, central banking, and debt payment, despite patriotic resentment. More frequently than visiting consultants, these regular employees encountered stiff resistance from nationalists, politicians, and vested interests.

The Great Depression laid waste to Kemmerer's free-market policy prescriptions. Countries sought recovery through countercyclical, inflationary, inadvertently Keynesian measures. From the 1930s to the 1960s, Latin Americans expanded government agencies and deficit spending to push their economic systems toward more statist, nationalistic, and protectionist directions than Kemmerer would have approved. Nevertheless, his institutions—especially his central banks—survived as major instruments of national development. By the 1980s the essential features of his 1920s economic model came back in vogue. Resurrecting essentially laissez-faire doctrines, countries stabilized their currency and exchange rates, reduced government intervention, privatized public enterprises, slashed tariffs, opened their economies to international prices and competition, and relied on market mechanisms. Kemmerer would have been proud.

Institutionalization and the International Monetary Fund

After World War II, hundreds of economic experts inundated Latin America, coming mainly from the United States. They wrote reams of reports and recommendations for lending as well as borrowing governments, for unilateral, bilateral, and multilateral agencies. As external finance came to the region mainly from public entities, the analyses of these economists established conditions for granting billions of dollars in assistance from more developed to less developed regions of the world. Such economic advising became increasingly professionalized and institutionalized.

At the end of World War II, the victors institutionalized money doctoring in the International Monetary Fund. The IMF set out to restore the free-flowing international economy that had prevailed prior to the Great Depression. As a multilateral agency, its operations were ostensibly even further removed than Kemmerer's from obedience to U.S. policymakers, even though Washington obviously exerted a great deal of influence. Neither Kemmerer nor the IMF arrived in host countries as official delegations from formal or informal imperial governments. Both claimed reputations as apolitical international experts, invited voluntarily by host countries. Critics assailed both agents, however, as U.S. tools imposing bitter medicine on weaker nations.

In actuality, the IMF, like Kemmerer, normally helped design and implement policies that were really desired by Latin American as well as by North American elites. The Fund made its loans to clients conditional on their promise to carry out prescribed policies. Both Kemmerer and the IMF usually tendered similar recommendations: stabilize exchange rates, control currency emissions, restrict credit allocations, and discipline government budgets. Through those measures the Latin Americans sought better access to foreign loans, and, in this area, the IMF had more direct influence than Kemmerer—it could extend its own credits as well as certify creditworthiness to private lenders.

In contrast with the broadly acclaimed Kemmerer missions, the IMF has often aroused controversy and hostility. In Kemmerer's era, the host countries were less urbanized, mobilized, and politicized. Almost all Kemmerer needed was agreement among sectors of the upper class to win acceptance for his proposals. Inflation and stabilization policies were not yet embroiled in the fierce battles of highly articulate interest groups and social classes over scarce resources.

Whereas labor usually has been the enemy of the IMF's austerity proposals, trade unions typically applauded Kemmerer's efforts to stem the rising cost of living. In the 1920s, South American reformers normally lambasted inflation as a swindle perpetrated by agriculturalists, exporters, speculators, bankers, and a profligate government to skew income distribution in their own direction. By the 1960s, in contrast, reformers aligned with labor to excoriate stabilization programs as conspiracies by the affluent to maintain an inequitable distribution of income. Many Latin Americans criticized the IMF as the conservative bodyguard of foreign and domestic capitalists and demonized it as the enemy of the impoverished masses.

Import-Substitution and the New Academics

The IMF was not the only supplier of economic advising to Latin America after World War II. Other sources of technical assistance included the Interamerican Development Bank, the Export-Import Bank, the World Bank, the United Nations, the Agency for International Development, the U.S. Federal Reserve, and additional multilateral and bilateral agencies. Latin American governments supplemented financial advisers from the United States and Europe with experts from fellow Latin American countries, and they engaged in import-substitution, relying on national savants trained at universities in developed countries and endowed with creditworthy reputations in international financial circles. Thus, university exchange agreements provided another channel for the United States to export its economic technology.

Educated at the University of Chicago, the civilian advisers to Chilean dictator Augusto Pinochet (1973–1990) gained fame for dismantling the statist, protectionist policies that had accumulated since the Great Depression. The free-market proposals of the Chicago Boys sounded similar to those of Kemmerer and the IMF and evoked similar applause from the international financial community. Their government was one of the most successful at attracting foreign loans in the 1970s and then managing the debt crisis in the 1980s. After turning Chile into a neoliberal showcase for shrinking the state and opening markets, they inspired imitators throughout the hemisphere, contending that the same economic formula could fit every country, essentially regardless of history and culture.

The Chicago Boys represented the internalization of international money doctoring. Although native Chileans, their success still depended upon their links with prestigious foreign experts, institutions, and models. They identified with and drew sustenance and authority from not only the University of Chicago but also the IMF and major foreign banks. To what extent the Chicago Boys succeeded because, like many other money doctors, they worked with an authoritarian regime that could ram through their proposals has been subject to heated debate. There is no doubt, however, that a technocratic mode of policymaking has been congenial to military rulers and inevitably entails undemocratic methods, even when practiced by an elected government. The perseverance of an authoritarian style within a democratic regime has been quite common in Latin America.

Since the 1970s many countries with debt or development problems have turned to new academic money doctors, such as Jeffrey Sachs, for several reasons. Some governments have preferred the wider range of advice of these independents, some have wanted an opinion other than that always proffered by the IMF, and, in other cases, some do not want to use the IMF because they are effectively in default on their debt payments or their citizens are too hostile toward the Fund. Noncapitalist countries that do not belong to the IMF also have engaged the services of free-lance money doctors. In many cases, the problems set before these advisers have been broader and more severe than those usually dealt with by the IMF or the World Bank. Stanching hyperinflation or creating a market economy has been more challenging than stabilizing exchange rates.

One of the most famous new money doctors, who has advised on ways to stabilize macroeconomic variables, to ignite growth through free-market reforms, and to cope with the debt crisis, has been Harvard's Sachs. Other new academic advisers include Rudiger Dornbusch from the Massachusetts Institute of Technology and Albert Fishlow from the University of California, Berkeley. In addition to Bolivia and Poland, Sachs has advised Ecuador, Venezuela, Peru, Yugoslavia, and Russia. Although disagreeing with the IMF at times, Sachs, like most money doctors, generally has echoed its positions in favor of stabilization, government austerity, free markets, and free trade. In Bolivia, he supported one of the most stunning shock treatments ever to bring hyperinflation to a screeching halt. He departed from orthodoxy, however, by also recommending reduction of the country's foreign debt obligations.

Conclusion

Time after time, imported experts and supervisers have helped indigenous political forces restructure Latin America's economies, often to respond to foreign funders. Money doctors have served as effective political devices for borrowers as well as lenders and for vested interests in the receiving as well as the sending country. In most cases, they have functioned as intermediaries, negotiators, third-party observers, or enforcers for the shaky contractual relationship between international creditors and debtors. Both parties have tried to use such economic agents to improve their bargaining position; many times, the consultants and monitors have increased security for the lenders and credibility for the borrowers. As crisis managers, these economic authorities also have provided a linchpin holding together the world economy at fragile junctures.

So long as Latin America and other less developed areas covet financial assistance from more affluent lenders, money doctors probably will continue to proctor those transactions. As countries pursue modernization from a position of dependence upon wealthier nations, debt cycles are likely to recur. Although the provenance of creditors and monetary medics may change as U.S. hegemony declines, the remarkable continuities in the roles, behaviors, and impacts of foreign lenders and advisers can be better understood by examining the rich historical record. Studying the footprints of the money doctors also will shed light on the financial development of Latin America throughout the past century.

I

Colonization and Proconsuls

From the 1890s through the 1920s, U.S. economic advisers arrived along with troops in the Caribbean basin. Through its "proconsuls," the U.S. government became deeply involved in the foreign borrowing operations of the "protectorates" it colonized. Along with money doctors, U.S. "election doctors" made housecalls to try to inculcate democratic forms of government, installing U.S. political as well as economic institutions. Little pretense remained that these occupied countries were either politically or financially sovereign.

With the publication of their controversial book *Dollar Diplomacy* in 1925, Scott Nearing and Joseph Freeman supplied ammunition to critics who questioned these imperialist adventures. Of the four selections presented in this section on occupied countries, their contribution is the most critical. In the excerpt here, they concentrate on the interventions in the Dominican Republic and Nicaragua, tracing the intricate connections among U.S. policymakers, bankers, business executives, military personnel, and advisers. They also stress the linkages between economic and security interests and between economic and political controls over a country—exemplified, for example, when the United States denied funds to distasteful governments. Several of the economic surgeons mentioned by Nearing and Freeman practicing in the Caribbean and Central America also turned up later in South America.

The patterns that Nearing and Freeman describe in the Dominican Republic and Nicaragua were replicated in U.S. behavior toward Haiti. That tiny country also was forced to internalize U.S. financial and political institutions. The first essay on Haiti, published in 1927, is by Paul H. Douglas, who was to become the liberal Democratic senator from Illinois. As an economics professor at the University of Chicago, he shows that members of that institution have not always been as conservative as the Chicago Boys in recent years. Although critical of the occupation, Douglas notes that U.S. control did allow Haiti to acquire loans on better terms. His account is particularly revealing on the involvement of banking interests in the invasion and in the subsequent financial reforms.

Douglas's observations have the virtue of a firsthand account, since he visited the island in 1926 as a Quaker representative with a delegation from the Women's International League for Peace and Freedom. Their recommendation to withdraw from Haiti and return it to self-government, which was presented in a report to President Calvin Coolidge, was adopted as U.S. policy by President Herbert Hoover in 1930.

Another author who witnessed the Haitian occupation directly is Arthur C. Millspaugh, U.S. financial adviser and administrator in Persia (1922–1927) and in Haiti (1927–1929). As a representative of the United States, he was naturally more positive than Nearing, Freeman, or Douglas. Nevertheless, Millspaugh conveys a similar sense of the overpowering and overbearing U.S. economic presence. Haiti provided an extreme example of the surrender of sovereignty to foreign financial officials, an issue that was encountered with more subtlety by Kemmerer and the IMF. Haiti was also a glaring case of authoritarian rule by a U.S. financial czar. The excerpts from Millspaugh explain clearly how the United States imposed financial supervision on the Haitians through the treaty of occupation.

The Haitian experience exemplifies how most of the imported economic reforms were ultimately connected to the debt issue. In Haiti, the U.S. financial adviser insisted that resources be channeled to debt payments instead of to developmental projects. Regularizing customs collections, balancing the national budget, and cleaning up the banking system had many benefits, but they also were designed to assure that sufficient funds would be available to repay foreign loans. The same linkage reappeared with Kemmerer and the IMF.

All of these foreign agents displayed elaborate motivations and reasons for their reforms: to stabilize the budget, to rationalize taxes, to improve accounting, to protect banking reserves, to shore up exchange rates, to brake inflation, and to encourage investment. At the same time, they intended for most of their innovations to ensure that external debts would be serviced fully and efficiently. One of the few benefits Haitian elites expected from the takeover of their country was improved access to foreign loans.

Historians Emily S. Rosenberg and Norman L. Rosenberg provide a transition from public to private manifestations of money doctoring, from more coercive to more voluntary modes of operation. In their essay, originally published in 1987, they trace the evolution of that phenomenon under the auspices of colonialism, treaties, contracts, and professionalism. Although the mechanisms of financial mediation changed, the fundamental objective remained the same: to smooth the flow of international capital movements.

1 Scott Nearing and Joseph Freeman ◆ Dollar Diplomacy

The Strategic Importance of the Caribbean Area to the United States

Between spheres of influence like China and the Near East, and outright colonial possessions like the Philippines and Puerto Rico, stand the protectorates, which, though not owned by the United States, are under its political and economic control. Three of these protectorates—Santo Domingo, Haiti, and Nicaragua—have been acquired through armed intervention. All three are in the area around the Caribbean Sea, whose strategic and economic importance doomed it as an inevitable prey to American expansion.

The importance of the Caribbean region to the United States lies in its proximity, its commercial advantages as a source of raw materials and a market for manufactured goods, and as a strategic military addition to the Panama Canal. The opening of the Panama Canal raised the Caribbean "to a commanding position among the trade routes of the world."[1] Central America, President Woodrow Wilson declared, "is about to be touched by the great routes of the world's trade and intercourse running from ocean to ocean at the Isthmus."[2] In addition the Caribbean is the gateway to the Panama Canal, and expansionists have advocated turning it into an "American lake."[3]

The strategic importance of the Caribbean has impelled the United States to acquire naval footholds in that region. In addition to several good harbors on the Gulf of Mexico and the naval base at Key West, Florida, in its own territory, it has acquired ports belonging to the little republics to the south.[4] From Guantanamo, Cuba, the United States commands the Windward passage between Cuba and Santo Domingo; from Puerto Rico it controls the Mona passage; by turning Haiti and Santo Domingo into protectorates, the United States has acquired the Mole St. Nicholas in the former, and Samana Bay in the latter, as first-class naval bases. A treaty with Nicaragua gives the United States possession of the Great Corn and Little Corn Islands and the right to build a naval station on the Gulf of Fonseca. The Virgin Islands, acquired from Denmark in 1917, also offer facilities for an excellent naval base, while the Panama Canal itself forms the center of American naval power.[5]

From Scott Nearing and Joseph Freeman, *Dollar Diplomacy: A Study in American Imperialism* (New York: B. W. Heubsch, 1925), 122–71.

In addition to these strategic considerations, the outbreak of World War [One] forced the Caribbean countries to turn to the United States for economic relationships, not only in matters of trade but also for loans. "In several cases, our government has already taken a guiding hand in the negotiations. Conferences for the adjustment of the debt of Nicaragua, Haiti, and Santo Domingo have taken place, not in those countries, nor in the offices of New York bankers, but in the Department of State and the Bureau of Insular Affairs."[6]

One American authority has summarized the matter by describing the Caribbean area as

> a tropic belt similar to that which European nations have acquired long ago in other parts of the world. . . . They are so many natural markets lying upon one of the greatest commercial highways of the present and future—to and from the Panama Canal. From them come raw materials and secondary foodstuffs requisite for our factories and exchangeable for our basic foodstuffs and manufactured articles. They have become localities, also, for the investment of American capital under circumstances that may invite the exercise of political influence to a greater or lesser degree.[7]

The importance of the Caribbean economically and strategically has caused it to be called "the Mediterranean of the New World," and the countries around it "the American tropics." The necessity for expansion on the part of the United States, and the need for the rapidly accumulating capital of its financiers to find the nearest and easiest possible outlet, gave rise to a diplomacy which in one form or another has brought a number of the Caribbean countries under the direct control of the United States. As one historian has put it,

> Cuba is no more independent than Long Island. The island of San Domingo, with its two Negro republics, is no more independent than the State of New York. Nicaragua and Panama are only nominal republics, and nominal sovereignties. . . . If we are to have a Caribbean empire, we must get it by destroying the republican independence of the powers concerned. . . . We must make up our minds that if we acquire these islands we shall eventually have practically to annex the whole of Central America. . . .[8]

The Financial Conquest of Santo Domingo

The first of the Caribbean countries to suffer American military intervention and the practical establishment of a protectorate was Santo Domingo.

Armed intervention in Santo Domingo and its domination as an American protectorate becomes clearer when its position in the American empire is fully realized. When President [Ulysses S.] Grant proposed the annexation of the republic he declared:

The acquisition of Santo Domingo is desirable because of its geographical position. It commands the entrance of the Caribbean Sea and the Isthmus transit of commerce. It possesses the richest soil, the most capacious harbors, most salubrious climate, and the most valuable products of the forests, mines, and soil of all the West Indian islands. Its possession by us will in a few years build up a coastwise commerce of immense magnitude. . . . In case of foreign war it will give us command of all the islands referred to and thus prevent an enemy from ever possessing herself of rendezvous on our very coast.[9]

In 1893 the San Domingo Improvement Company, an American concern with offices in New York, bought the debt of 170,000 pounds sterling which a Dutch company had loaned to the Dominican government, and with it the right to collect all customs revenues to satisfy this claim.[10] In 1909 President [Juan Isidro] Jiménez of the Dominican Republic appointed a board of his own to collect customs. The American company thereupon appealed to the State Department at Washington to protect its interests, and after negotiations the Dominican government was induced to offer to buy the company's debt for $4,500,000. On January 1, 1903, representatives of both governments signed a protocol providing for this settlement and for a board of arbitrators to fix the details of payment. It was also agreed that in case Santo Domingo failed to pay, the United States was to appoint a financial agent to take over certain customs houses. This was the first economic hold on the little republic.[11]

Financial difficulties prevented Santo Domingo from paying its debts and reports were circulated that French and Italian vessels were on their way to the island to collect the debts by force.[12] Taking advantage of this opportunity, Secretary of State [John] Hay instructed the American minister, Thomas C. Dawson, to suggest to the Dominican government that it "request" the United States to take over its customshouses.[13] Pressed on all sides by foreign investors, [the Dominican government] had no choice but to make "the appeal."

On February 4, 1905, a protocol was drawn up between the two governments by which the United States was to act as bankrupt's receiver for Santo Domingo, taking over all its customshouses, administering its finances, and settling the claims of foreign and domestic creditors. Of the revenues which the United States should collect, 55 percent were to be used for paying bondholders and the remainder was to be turned over to the Dominican government for administrative expenses.[14] The Senate at Washington refused to ratify this drastic protocol, but President [Theodore] Roosevelt entered into an "executive agreement" with the president of the Dominican Republic which achieved the same results. Under this agreement the customs collectors were to be American and to have the support of American warships.[15] In that same year an American receiver-general named by President Roosevelt proceeded to collect customs "under the protection of the United States

Navy," and to issue bonds for the purpose of paying foreign creditors.[16] Roosevelt's tactics were severely criticized in and out of Congress, but finally the Senate decided to give the arrangement a coat of legality. On February 25, 1907, it ratified a revised treaty which provided: (1) that the president of the United States should appoint a customs collector for Santo Domingo and assistants; (2) that the United States government should afford them such protection as might be necessary; (3) that the Dominican government could not increase its debts or lower its taxes without the consent of the United States.[17] By the provisions of this treaty the American receiver-general was to issue twenty million dollars in gold bonds for paying off Santo Domingo's public debt. The sum total of revenues collected was to be applied as follows: First, to paying the expenses of the receivership; second, to paying the interest on the bonds; third, to the payment of the annual sums provided for the amortization of the bonds; fourth, to the purchase, cancellation, and retirement of the bonds; fifth, what was left was to be given to the Dominican government. The loan of twenty million dollars provided in the treaty was made by Kuhn, Loeb & Co. The treaty is still in force, and under its provisions the United States government is "to collect customs for fifty years" in order to pay interest to the New York bankers.[18]

American financial control of Santo Domingo was soon followed by interference with its political life. In 1911 the Dominican president was shot and a provisional government established. In the fall of the following year President [William H.] Taft sent two special commissioners to investigate the situation. They were to make the trip in a gunboat accompanied by 750 marines.[19] At the suggestion of the American commissioners the provisional president resigned. This interference by the United States led only to further revolutionary outbreaks.

An example of the workings of the Dominican treaty may be seen in the loan contract made in 1914 by the National City Bank of New York with the approval of the State Department by which the bank loaned Santo Domingo $1,500,000 at 6 percent. The contract specifically stated that the loan was made "in conformity to the Convention between the United States of America and the Dominican Republic ratified July 8, 1907, the payment of the principal and interest of which notes is secured by the pledge by the Republic of its customs revenues subject to an existing charge thereon securing the $20,000,000 Five per cent Customs Administration Sinking Fund Gold Loan of the Republic under and pursuant to the terms of the said convention," etc.[20] The $20 million loan which had first claim on the customs was the one issued by Kuhn, Loeb & Co.

The inauguration of Woodrow Wilson in 1913 did not change the attitude of Washington regarding government interference on behalf of

American finance. On September 9, Secretary of State [William Jennings] Bryan notified Santo Domingo that the influence of the United States would be exerted to discourage revolutions and to support the "lawful authorities." As revolutionary activities continued, the United States sent a warship, and Secretary Bryan notified the revolutionary elements that if they succeeded the State Department would not recognize them and would "withhold the portion of the customs collections belonging to Santo Domingo."[21] The American minister in Santo Domingo proceeded to arrange for new elections, and over the vigorous protests of the Dominican government, three American commissioners arrived on warships to watch the elections.[22] The following year the elections were again supervised by American commissioners.

Armed Political Control

American financial and political interference in Santo Domingo finally led to armed intervention. In April 1916, another insurrection took place in Santo Domingo, and this time, on May 4, 1916, U.S. Marines were landed. "Stealthily American battleships entered the roadstead of Santo Domingo City, and under cover of a score or more long-range, big-caliber guns the American admiral, with a large force of marines, landed on Dominican territory."[23]

President Jiménez resigned and the Dominican Congress elected Dr. Henriquez y Carvajal temporary president. The State Department refused to recognize this legally chosen president unless he signed a treaty with the United States which Washington had been pressing on Santo Domingo since 1915.[24] This treaty was even more drastic than the one forced on the republic in 1907, and was similar in nature and intent to the one forced by the Wilson administration on Haiti. It called for the control by American officials of the Dominican customs, treasury, army, and police. President Henriquez refused recognition by the State Department on such terms; whereupon, on October 17, following instructions from Washington, the American customs collector refused to pay the duly elected Dominican government the revenues to which it was entitled.[25]

A deadlock ensued. The entire country rallied around the president; political differences were forgotten, and officials performed their duty without pay as far as they could, owing to the refusal of the American officials to turn their salaries over to them until the treaty was signed. "The resistance to the American demands, though passive, was general."[26] This deadlock was finally broken by the flourish of American rifles. Captain H. S. Knapp, in command of the marines, declared martial law on November 29, 1916. He ousted the Dominican officials, dissolved the national legislature, forbade elections, and declared himself "supreme legislator, supreme judge, and supreme executor," established a regime of military force and courts martial, set up a rigid censorship, levied taxes, and increased the public debt.[27] This military dictatorship was, according to the official proclamation of martial law, set up under instructions from Washington because the "United States government . . . has urged upon Santo Domingo certain necessary measures which that government has been unwilling or unable to adopt."[28] Thus the United States frankly set up a military dictatorship for the purpose of forcing Santo Domingo to sign a treaty giving American investors complete control over the finances and administration of the republic.

The military dictatorship lasted until 1924. "A rear-admiral of the American Navy is military governor and exercises full executive and legislative functions, the Dominican congress being suspended. The posts of cabinet ministers are filled by officers of the American Navy and Marine Corps."[29] There is an American minister in Santo Domingo but naturally his duties are nominal. The military regime was to last until Santo Domingo was willing to sign the proposed treaty, thus allowing the United States to do "legally" what it had been doing by force. "The result of the operations of this arrangement," Secretary of State [Philander] Knox declared in 1912, when he tried to obtain the Senate's assistance in forcing a similar arrangement on Nicaragua and Honduras, "has been that the creditors now punctually receive their interest."[30]

As a result of the American occupation, the Dominican government was expelled,

> the government treasury was seized; the national congress was dismissed; elections were prohibited; thousands of marines were spread over the country and with unlimited authority over the natives; public meetings were not permitted; . . . destructive bombs were dropped from airplanes upon towns and hamlets; every home was searched for arms, weapons, and implements; homes were burned; natives were killed; tortures and cruelties committed; and Butcher Weyler's horrible concentration camps were established. . . . Repressions and oppressions followed in succession. When protests were made the protestants were fined heavily and also imprisoned, and when resistance or defense attempted bullets and bayonets were used. Criticism of the acts of the military government were not permitted . . . and those who violated the order were severely punished by fines and imprisonment. . . . The Dominican people have been "taxed without representation" and the money so raised expended recklessly and without in any way consulting them. . . . For five years this policy of suppression, repression, oppression and maladministration has continued.[31]

American Bankers and Armed Intervention

The direct connection between American investments and the military regime is indicated in a circular issued by Speyer & Co. and the Equitable Trust Co. of New York on June 20, 1921: "The United States Military Government of Santo Domingo issues in behalf of the Dominican Republic $2,500,000 Four Years Customs Administration 8 percent Sinking Fund gold bonds." The bonds, this circular said, will contain the following clause: "With the consent of the United States there is secured the acceptance of and validation of this bond issue by any government of the Dominican Republic as a legal, binding, and irrevocable obligation of the Dominican Republic, and the duties of the General Receiver of Dominican Customs as provided under the American-Dominican Convention of 1907, are extended to this Bond issue." The circular adds this sentence: "Until all these bonds shall have been redeemed the Dominican Republic agrees not to increase its public debt, nor to modify its customs duties without the previous consent of the United States Government; and its customs revenues shall continue to be collected by a General Receiver of Customs appointed by and responsible to the President of the United States."

This circular, explaining the reasons for an American customs receiver, also quotes a letter from Lieutenant Commander Arthur H. Mayo, U.S. Navy officer in charge of the Department of Finance and Commerce of the military government of Santo Domingo, which explains the purposes of the military regime. This letter is dated June 16, 1921, and is addressed to the Equitable Trust Co. and Speyer & Co.

> The Military Government will be withdrawn only upon the consummation of a treaty of evacuation between the Dominican Republic and the United States Government which shall contain among other provisions (a) ratifying all acts of the Military Government; (b) validating the above loan of $2,500,000 and (c) extending the duties and powers of the General Receiver of Dominican Customs until said Bonds shall have been paid.
>
> The Bonds are secured by a charge upon the customs and other revenues of the Dominican Republic.

Under the caption Purpose of Loan, the bankers' circular states: "The proceeds of this loan are to be used mainly for the completion of essential public works . . . and in part of the retirement of certificates of indebtedness. This work will be done under the supervision of American engineers, and such portion of the loan as is used for the purchase of supplies and equipment will be spent in the United States."[32]

A similar circular was issued in 1922 by Lee, Higginson & Co., declaring that: "Acting under Authority of the United States Government the

Military Government of Santo Domingo issues on behalf of the Dominican Republic $6,700,000 Twenty-Year Customs Administration 5.5 % Sinking Fund Gold Bonds. . . ." With the approval of the State Department the bonds stated that the military government of Santo Domingo guaranteed "the acceptance and validation of this Bond issue by any Government of the Dominican Republic as a legal, binding, and irrevocable obligation of the Dominican Republic." In a letter to Lee, Higginson & Co. reproduced in the bankers' circular, Lieutenant-Commander D. W. Rose, U.S. naval officer in charge of the Department of Finance and Commerce of the military government of Santo Domingo, again assured the bankers that during the life of the loan—which was to extend to March, 1942—the Dominican customs duties "shall be collected and applied by an official appointed by the President of the United States and that the loan now authorized shall have a first lien upon such customs revenues."[33]

A plan for the withdrawal of American marines from Santo Domingo was proposed by the Wilson administration in December, 1920, and a similar plan by the Harding administration on June 14, 1921. The plan made the military governor the provisional Dominican executive, and gave him the power to call elections. The Dominicans were to have this slight measure of autonomy provided they drew up an agreement with representatives of the American government ratifying all acts of the American military occupation, and entrusting the command and organization of Dominican forces to American officials.[34] These proposals were turned down by the people of Santo Domingo, who protested especially against the loans floated in their name by the American military government with American bankers, for which Santo Domingo paid interest varying from 9 to 19 percent.[35] On June 26, 1924, the Dominican Republic "ratified the treaty with the United States providing for the evacuation of the Dominican Republic by American military forces which have been stationed there since 1916. Simultaneously, it was announced from Washington that the withdrawal of the 1,800 marines in the Dominican Republic would be begun as soon as possible after July 10."[36] Later it was announced in the press that "General Horacio Vasquez and Federico Velásquez were formally inaugurated as President and Vice President, respectively, of the Dominican Republic on July 12. At the same time, the American flag was lowered from the fort and the Dominican emblem was hoisted. These acts brought to an end the military administration of the United States in the Dominican Republic."[37] Santo Domingo has thus been given a formal kind of partial independence in return for signing a treaty which makes it an actual protectorate. . . .

The Nicaraguan Protectorate

In Nicaragua, as in Santo Domingo and Haiti, the strategic interests of American diplomats and the financial interests of American bankers combined to produce first diplomatic and later military intervention. The strategic considerations centered around plans for a United States naval base at Fonseca Bay, and, more important still, a canal route across Nicaragua to supplement the advantages of the Panama Canal. The search for a canal route in Nicaragua is of long standing. . . .

On October 11, 1910, the State Department appointed Thomas C. Dawson, American minister to Panama and the expert who had arranged for American control of the customs of Santo Domingo, as special agent to Nicaragua. He was instructed that to "rehabilitate the finances and pay the legitimate foreign and domestic claims it would be advisable to negotiate a loan secured by a percentage of the customs revenues to be collected according to agreement between the two Governments, but in such a way as will certainly secure the loan and assure its object." Dawson was also instructed to seek a constitution providing "suitable guarantees for foreigners." He was to obtain liquidation of fixed claims, such as the Emery claim, and the adjudication of unliquidated claims. The State Department promised that when a plan for a loan to Nicaragua would be drawn up, it would "use its good offices to secure the conclusion of a contract based upon its terms between Nicaragua and some American financiers of high standing."

When Brown Brothers and Company learned of these plans they offered to the State Department to float the Nicaraguan loan. These bankers had entered into an agreement with the George D. Emery Company to collect their claim from Nicaragua, which had been settled for $600,000 in September, 1909, just before Zelaya fell. On February 2, 1911, Brown Brothers and Company wrote to Secretary of State Knox:

> We understand that the Government of Nicaragua is considering the advisability of obtaining a new loan for the purpose of refunding her present indebtedness and of providing for other governmental needs. We also understand that, in order to secure such loan upon advantageous terms, the Government of Nicaragua is desirous of enlisting the good offices of our own Government and of entering into engagements with it which shall furnish a satisfactory basis for such security as may be required. Should this information be substantially correct, we beg to say that, as bankers, we shall be glad to have the opportunity of negotiating for such a loan. Apart from our general interest in a matter of this kind, we beg to add that we are interested in the George D. Emery Co.'s claim against Nicaragua, under the protocol of September 18, 1909 and that we have, therefore, a peculiar interest in the readjustment of that country's finances.[38]

Secretary Knox replied that Brown Brothers would have an equal opportunity with other American bankers to bid for any loan Nicaragua might desire to secure.[39]

Meanwhile Dawson proceeded to carry out his instructions. On October 27, 1910, aboard an American battleship, the principal leaders of the Estrada revolution signed a series of agreements later known as the Dawson Pact. These stipulated that the United States would recognize the revolutionary government which it had assisted to seize power on the following conditions:

1. That a constituent assembly be chosen at once which would elect [Juan] Estrada president and Adolfo Díaz vice-president, for two years. Estrada could not succeed himself and no Zelayists could enter the administration.

2. That a mixed commission, satisfactory to the United States Department of State, be appointed to settle claims, including the Cannon-Groce indemnity.

3. That Nicaragua would solicit the good offices of the American Government to secure a loan to be guaranteed by a certain per cent of the customs receipts collected in accordance with an agreement "satisfactory to both governments."[40]

Dawson cabled these agreements to the State Department. He added that Nicaragua would embody them in a formal communication in which it would also request the United States to send a financial expert to work out a financial plan. The formal communication arrived in Washington soon afterward.[41]

Dawson's dispatch of October 28 informed the State Department that "a popular presidential election is at present impracticable and dangerous to peace." Therefore, as provided by the Dawson Pact, the Conservative Assembly elected November 27–28 unanimously chose Estrada president and Díaz vice-president. On January 1, 1911, President Taft formally recognized the Estrada government; three weeks later Secretary Knox instructed the new American minister to Nicaragua to carry out the provisions of the Dawson Pact. The dispatch added that Ernest H. Wands had been appointed by the United States government as financial expert. Secretary Knox forwarded copies of the Santo Domingo loan convention and of the proposed loan conventions with Honduras and Liberia, saying the Honduras convention would "answer all the requirements of the present case." He further instructed the American minister that "the Government of Nicaragua is to proceed at the earliest possible date to the signature of a convention with the United States which shall authorize the contemplated bankers' loan contract" to be secured by a percentage of the customs receipts. Knox also mentioned that the Nicaraguan minister to the United States, Salvador Castrillo, Jr., had requested his government to authorize him to sign the desired convention.[42]

For a time the Dawson Pact was kept secret, but the defeated Liberals in Nicaragua obtained a copy and published it.[43] The terms upon which General Estrada was supported by the United States aroused a storm of opposition in Nicaragua. Many patriotic elements saw in the Dawson Pact, with its provisions for a loan and American control of customs, the establishment of a virtual protectorate. American control of elections aggravated the situation. In February, 1911, the American minister in Nicaragua cabled to Secretary Knox that "the natural sentiment of an overwhelming majority of Nicaraguans is antagonistic to the United States, and even with some members of Estrada's cabinet I find a decided suspicion, if not distrust, of our motives." President Estrada, he added in another wire, dated March 27, was "being sustained solely by the moral effect of our support and the belief that he would unquestionably have that support in case of trouble."[44]

The Knox-Castrillo Convention of 1911

The chief object of supporting Estrada against the opposition of the Nicaraguan people was the floating of the loan and the control of customs to secure the loan. In April the Nicaraguan National Assembly determined to adopt a constitution guaranteeing the independence of the republic and directed against foreign control through loans. This constitution was opposed by the American representatives, and when it was adopted against their opposition, Estrada dissolved the assembly and called for new elections. The step was approved by the State Department at Washington. These proceedings resulted in protests which led to the resignation of Estrada in favor of Vice President Adolfo Díaz.[45]

But Diaz was no more popular than Estrada, and American support was necessary to keep him in office. "I am assured," the American minister wired the State Department on May 11, "the Assembly will confirm Díaz in the presidency according to any one of the . . . plans which the Department may indicate. . . . A war vessel is necessary for the moral effect."[46] On May 25 he wired that "rumours have been current that the Liberals are organizing a concerted uprising all over the country with the declared object of defeating the loan." The Liberals, he added, were "in such a majority over the Conservatives" that he hastened to repeat the suggestion "as to the advisability of stationing permanently, at least until the loan has been put through, a war vessel at Corinto." Secretary Knox replied that Díaz should not be permitted to resign and that a warship had been ordered to Nicaragua.[47]

While the struggle between the people of Nicaragua and the American representatives was in progress, Secretary Knox signed a convention with the Nicaraguan representative of the American-controlled government, at Washington. The Knox-Castrillo agreement of June 6, 1911, provided for the floating of a $15,000,000 loan to Nicaragua by American bankers and the control of Nicaraguan customs houses by the United States.[48] Nicaragua also pledged itself not to alter the customs duties without Washington's consent and to submit financial reports to the State Department.[49] At the same time, the State Department negotiated with the banking houses of Brown Brothers and Company, and J. and W. Seligman and Company for floating the loan, stipulating that the Knox-Castrillo convention should be made an integral part of the contract to be signed by the Nicaraguan government and the bankers.

The draft of an agreement for the $15 million loan was submitted by the bankers to Nicaragua on June 21. The loan was to be paid out by Brown Brothers and J. and W. Seligman, as bankers, to themselves as creditors of Nicaragua in the following way: to liquidate claims against Nicaragua; to establish a bank which the American bankers should administer; to improve the national railway, which they should control; and to build a new railway upon their own terms, a concession for which they were to obtain from Nicaragua and which they were to build with Nicaragua's money.[50]

The United States Senate refused to ratify the Knox-Castrillo convention, turning it down three separate times despite the special urging of President Taft.[51] Consequently, the loan agreement submitted by the bankers on June 21 could not go through. The following month, however, the bankers submitted another agreement which the American-controlled government of Nicaragua signed on September 1. Under this agreement Brown Brothers and J. and W. Seligman were to make a temporary loan of $1.5 million to Nicaragua.[52] The bankers agreed to reorganize the National Bank, taking over 51 percent of the stock, and allowing Nicaragua to keep 49 percent.

The loan convention (known as the "Treasury Bills Agreement") stipulated the following terms: (1) $100,000 of the loan was to be used as initial capital for the proposed bank; (2) the balance was to be used for reforming the currency of Nicaragua; (3) the bankers were to hire monetary experts to reform the currency, but Nicaragua was to pay for them; (4) the bankers were to deposit the sum used for reforming the currency—$1.4 million—with the United States Mortgage and Trust Company; (5) the loan was to be secured by a lien on the customs; (6) the customs were to be collected by an American nominated by the bankers, approved by the Secretary of State, and "appointed" by Nicaragua; (7) the customs were not to be changed without the bankers' consent.[53] The contract also gave the bankers a lien on the liquor tax, and reserved to the bankers the right "to solicit of the United States of America protection against violation of the present contract, and aid in enforcing its execution." The bankers and Nicaragua were to submit disputes to arbitration by the Secretary of State of the United States. Secretary Knox ordered the American chargé d'affaires to keep the Nicaraguan legislature in session until the loan agreement of September 1 was approved.

Correspondence between American agents in Nicaragua and the State Department at Washington continued to show that the United States was prepared to force political and financial control upon the little republic in the face of almost nationwide opposition. On July 12 the American chargé d'affaires notified Secretary Knox that "opinion generally expressed is that the United States Government has repudiated its policy of protecting Nicaragua against foreigners holding rights in ruinous concessions or contracts. . . . I strongly urge that no further action be taken until the assembly approves the loan contract." A month later he cabled that the "opposition to these loan contracts and concessions is becoming more determined."[54]

The State Department replied on September 30: "You are instructed that of the Nicaraguan matters under consideration by the Department, the ratification of the pending loan contract and the amendment of the decree establishing a claims commission are of the first importance and should be disposed of before attention is directed to other subjects." On October 5 the State Department [repeated] that "attention should be steadily directed to the loan and the claims commission matters; they are of the first importance and should be disposed of before consideration of political subjects, which should not be discussed unnecessarily." The Nicaraguan assembly approved the loan contracts on October 9.[55]

Under this agreement Secretary of State Knox appointed Colonel Clifford D. Ham as customs collector of Nicaragua. Colonel Ham was recommended by Brown Brothers and Company and J. and W. Seligman and Company as a person "worthy of our confidence."[56] From December 11 on, Colonel Ham collected the entire customs duties of Nicaragua. In December there also arrived in Managua Mr. Charles A. Connant of New York and Mr. Francis C. Harrison, formerly of the British Civil Service in India, to act as monetary experts for the bankers.

A Network of Loans

Juan Estrada was forced to resign because he sought to prevent the adoption of a constitution protecting Nicaragua's independence. His successor, Adolfo Díaz, supported by the "moral force" of an American battleship, continued Estrada's policy. While the loan contracts were being forced on Nicaragua, the assembly completed a new constitution. The chargé d'affaires . . . notified the State Department that this constitution provided that all government employees must be Nicaraguans except those on the Claims Commission, and that after adoption the constitution could be amended only by approval of two successive congresses. He asked that the signing of the constitution be postponed: he had "in mind the customs authorities who are not Nicaraguans," but Americans. President Díaz and General Mena, who controlled the assembly, promised that the constitution would not be promulgated until January 31. Secretary Knox insisted that the promulgation of the constitution be postponed until the arrival of the new American minister . . . on about January 18. [57]

The Nicaraguan assembly resented American interference. On January 12 it ordered the promulgation of the new constitution in a decree declaring that the "interposition of the Chargé d'Affaires of the United States carries with it, in effect, an insult to the national autonomy and the honor of the assembly."[58]

The new American minister's first act on arriving in Nicaragua was to study the new constitution and to notify the State Department of the provisions which he considered objectionable. He called the Department's attention to Article 2, which provided that "no compacts or treaties shall be concluded which are contrary to the independence and integrity of the Nation, or which in any wise affect its sovereignty." Article 55 provided that "Congress alone may authorize loans and levy contract by indirect measures."[59] The constitution also provided that foreigners must present their claims against the government in the same ways as Nicaraguans, and prohibited monopolies for the benefit of private individuals.

The new American minister called the State Department's attention to paragraph 14 of Article 85 as "most susceptible of adverse criticism." This section vested in the assembly the power to alienate or lease national property and to authorize the executive to do so "on conditions suitable to the Republic." It added that "the public revenues or taxes shall not be alienated or leased out."[60]

The constitution was promulgated with these clauses in it but the American bankers disregarded them in subsequent contracts and agreements. On March 26, 1912, they entered into an agreement with Nicaragua for a supplementary loan. Part of this loan—$500,000—was to be used by the monetary experts in stabilizing the exchange; the rest—$225,000—was to be used by the Nicaraguan government for current expenses. The loan was for six months at 6 percent, with an additional bankers' commission of 1 percent. It was to be secured by the customs revenues, second only to the 1911 loan; by a lien on all government railway and steamship lines; and by the claims of Nicaragua against the Ethelburga syndicate of London. Proceeds of any sale of railways or steamships or any agreement with the Ethelburga syndicate were to be used for the repayment of the loans under under this agreement. Anything left over was to be used for repaying the 1911 loan. This agreement also provided that Nicaragua should transfer all its railway and steamship lines to a corporation to be organized in the United States and to be tax free. The bankers were to have a one-year option to buy 51 percent of the capital stock of this new corporation for one million dollars. If the bankers exercised this option they were to lend the company $500,000 for extensions and improvements. The bankers were also to have an option on the other 49 percent; Nicaragua could not sell its share to anyone except the bankers until all the loans were paid up. Pending repayment the American bankers were to manage and control the railways and steamship lines exclusively and to choose the board of directors.[61] These loan negotiations were carried on jointly by the State Department and the bankers.[62]

Two months after this agreement was signed the American bankers signed an agreement with the Ethelburga syndicate of London. The Ethelburga bonds represented a loan contracted by the Zelaya government in 1909 for 1,250,000 pounds. By the agreement signed on May 25, 1912, the London balance, after interest and sinking funds had been paid off on the bonds, was transferred to the American bankers for account of Nicaragua. This balance amounted to about $1,195,000. The May 25 agreement was negotiated by the bankers in the name of Nicaragua. Under its terms the republic was to recognize the right of the American bankers and the London interests to "apply to the United States for protection against violation of the provisions of this agreement and for aid in the enforcement thereof." Among the provisions was that the bonds were to be secured by the Nicaraguan customs to be collected by Americans. The American bankers communicated with the State Department throughout the negotiations.[63]

On the same day that this agreement was signed with the Ethelburga bondholders the American bankers signed another agreement with Nicaragua supplementing the loan agreement of March 26. The March 26 loan was secured, in part, by the Ethelburga bonds. The supplementary agreement of May 25 provided that after interest and sinking funds on the bonds had been paid the balance should be used to repay loans made by the American bankers to Nicaragua.[64]

Bullet Diplomacy

Meantime the unpopularity of President Díaz increased. He was able to stay in power only because of American support. His opponents in the legislature were calling for an election. The American minister, with the approval of the State Department, informed them that before settling the political affairs of Nicaragua they should establish the proposed national bank and place the republic on a sound financial basis.

The Liberals refused to wait. On July 29 they proclaimed a revolution, seizing a large store of war materials, a part of the railway and steamers, and several customs houses. The American manager of the Bank of Nicaragua, Mr. Bundy Cole, wired to James Brown of Brown Brothers and Company, in New York, for protection. Brown Brothers and Company replied that the State Department advised them that Major Butler would arrive from Panama with American marines. On August 15, Major Smedley Butler landed with 412 marines, half of whom were quartered at the bank.[65] On September 4, 1912, the State Department notified the American minister at Managua that "the American bankers who have made investments in relation to railroads and steamships in Nicaragua, in connection with a plan for the relief of the financial distress of that country, have applied for protection."[66] The American marines at once took drastic action against the revolutionists. According to the report of the U.S. secretary of the navy for 1913, the following naval vessels with approximately 125 officers and 2,600 men participated in the subjugation of the revolution: *California, Colorado, Cleveland, Annapolis, Tacoma, Glacier, Denver,* and *Buffalo.* "The officers and men participated in the bombardment of Managua, a night ambuscade in Masaya, the surrender of General Mena and his rebel army at Granada, the surrender of the rebel gunboats of *Victoria* and *Ninety-Three,* the assault and capture of Coyotepe, the defense of Paso Caballos Bridge, including garrison and other duty at Corinto, Chinandega, and elsewhere."[67] The most notable event during the campaign was the assault and capture of Coyotepe which resulted in entirely crushing the revolution. The leader of the revolutionary forces surrendered to U.S. forces and was exiled to Panama aboard the USS *Cleveland.*[68] The part of the American minister in crushing the revolution consisted in sending notes to its leader, General Mena, to surrender the railroads which belonged to the American bankers. In this line of action he was assisted by the bankers' representatives.[69] Following the defeat of the revolutionists an election was held in which the American marines guarded the polls. On November 2, Díaz was reelected for a term of four years.

Exploiting Nicaragua

The expenses incurred during the revolution forced Díaz to apply to the American bankers for another loan. The terms on which the bankers offered to make the loan were protested by Díaz as harsh, but they were backed up by the State Department, and were incorporated in the loan agreement on November 4, 1912.[70] Under this agreement the bankers were to lend Nicaragua

$500,000 to be secured by the tobacco and liquor taxes, which were to be collected by the American-controlled Bank of Nicaragua. In addition the bankers were to get an option for the purchase of Nicaragua's 49 percent of the railroad stock for $1,000,000. The $500,000 loan was to be made from the funds realized by the Nicaraguan customs (collected by Americans) and the Ethelburga funds.[71] The Nicaraguan Congress refused to approve this agreement. After paying $350,000 on account under this agreement, the bankers stopped payments.

While the bankers were negotiating for an option on the entire railroad of Nicaragua, Wilson was elected president of the United States. On February 2, 1913, the American minister at Managua informed the State Department that the bankers would not

> advance another dollar nor entertain a new proposition until they are certain that the incoming administration at Washington will continue the present policy. This is deeply disappointing to President Díaz, who desires to reach a definite settlement of the financial question while the present Washington administration is still in office, as it thoroughly understands that question. Nevertheless President Díaz assures me he will not enter into a final loan contract, without previous consultation with the Department.[72]

To this Secretary Knox replied that "there is no foundation for the rumor that the incoming administration will change the present policy of the United States toward Central America," and instructed the American minister to confer with Mr. Bundy Cole, American manager of the National Bank of Nicaragua and representative of Brown Brothers and Company.[73]

With this assurance from the State Department, the bankers entered into a new agreement with Nicaragua on October 8, 1913.[74] The agreement stipulated the following:

1. The bankers were to exercise their option to buy 51 percent of the railroad stock for $1,000,000.

2. They agreed to lend Nicaragua $1,000,000.

3. They agreed to lend the railroad of which they would own 51 percent $500,000 for improvements and extensions.

4. The bankers also purchased 51 percent of the stock of the National Bank for $153,000.

5. They obtained a preferential right to buy the remaining 49 percent of both bank and railroad. Meantime they were to have custody of all the stock.

6. If Nicaragua defaulted, the bankers had the right to sell the bank and railroad stock six months thereafter.

7. The bankers' option on the concession for the Atlantic railroad granted in the 1911 loan agreement was cancelled.

8. The bank and railroad were each to have nine directors. Six were to be named by the bankers, one by the secretary of state of the United States, two by Nicaragua.

9. The collection of internal revenues was to be resumed by Nicaragua.

Of the $2,000,000 advanced by the American bankers to Nicaragua in payment for the railroad stock and as a loan, the republic was actually to receive only $772,424. The balance was used to pay off in full all previous loans, for replenishing the exchange fund, buying shares in the National Bank, and paying various charges to the bankers.[75] As a result of this transaction, not only had the American bankers collected all previous loans, but Nicaragua owed them $1,000,000, her Ethelburga balance was gone, and the bankers controlled and managed her railroad and bank.

During the negotiation of the October 8 agreement, the State Department was negotiating for a canal route through Nicaragua for which the republic was to receive $3,000,000. This sum was intended to make it possible for Nicaragua to repay her debts to bankers. The October 8 loan was made with the approval of the State Department.[76] A statement by Brown Brothers and Company and J. and W. Seligman and Company indicates that they had the pending canal treaty in mind. The statement reads, in part:

> Should the United States Senate . . . ratify the pending treaty with Nicaragua, providing for the establishment of a naval station on the Gulf of Fonseca and granting a perpetual right to build the Nicaragua Canal, the proposed payment to Nicaragua of $3,000,000 provided in the treaty as compensation, would put that Government in a position where it could liquidate the greater part of the local debt and claims.[77]

Buying the Canal Route

The treaty giving the United States the right to construct a canal across Nicaragua was signed on February 18, 1916. It is known as the Bryan-Chamorro Treaty. Under its terms the United States paid Nicaragua $3,000,000 in return for the following concessions: "1) The right to construct a trans-isthmian canal by San Juan and the Great Lake route or any other route in the territory of Nicaragua; 2) the control by lease for 99 years of the Great Corn and Little Corn islands and of a naval base in the Gulf of Fonseca; and 3) the U.S. option of renewing the lease on the naval base for another 99 years."[78]

The advantages of this treaty to the United States government have been explained by Colonel Clifford D. Ham, American customs collector in Nicaragua, to be that it forever eliminates "the danger of a foreign power seeking and obtaining those concessions"; that it promotes "better diplomatic and commercial relations" with Latin America; and that it would be "an important link in the chain, which we are attempting to forge, of preparedness and national defense, and the protection of our investment in the Panama Canal."[79]

That the Bryan-Chamorro Treaty was nothing less than a "proposed protectorate of Nicaragua by the United States" was clearly indicated in the official correspondence on the matter.[80]

One clause in the Bryan-Chamorro Treaty declared that nothing in it was intended "to affect any existing rights" of Costa Rica, Salvador, and Honduras. It will be remembered that in 1906 and 1907 the conflicting claims of several Central American republics to the territory comprised in the proposed Nicaraguan canal led to war, and subsequently to the establishment under the direction of the United States of the Central American Court of Justice. The court was hailed, at the time of its organization, as an inspiring example of international justice. The court was also invoked again and again by the Taft administration to settle Central American disputes.

During the negotiation of the Bryan-Chamorro pact Costa Rica and Salvador protested.[81] The naval base on the Gulf of Fonseca caused particular alarm.[82] When the treaty was ratified they appealed to the Central American Court of Justice, declaring that the treaty violated the rights. The court ruled that Nicaragua should maintain the status quo existing prior to the signing of its treaty with the United States; but both Nicaragua and the United States refused to abide by the decision of the court. Subsequently Nicaragua refused to re-join the court, and in 1918 the court was formally dissolved. The United States destroyed its own creation to suit its purpose by instructing Nicaragua to refuse to execute the award.

Since completing the financial and military conquest of Nicaragua in 1913, the American bankers and the State Department have maintained effective control. In 1918 the High Commission of the Republic of Nicaragua was appointed to supervise the expenditures of the republic. The commission consists of one Nicaraguan and two Americans, the latter chosen by the United States secretary of state.[83] The commission's reports are submitted to the Nicaraguan government and to the State Department.

In 1920 repairs were needed on the Nicaraguan railroad, controlled by Brown Brothers and J. and W. Seligman. The American bankers proceeded to float a $9,000,000 loan to Nicaragua. The purpose of this loan, they announced, was (1) to refund Nicaragua's external debt, including the

Ethelburga bonds; (2) to enable Nicaragua to buy "such stock of the Pacific Railways of Nicaragua as is held by interests other than the Government"; (3) to build a railway to the Atlantic coast.[84] The American bankers, of course, controlled the Ethelburga bonds and were the only interests "other than the Government" holding stock in the Pacific Railways. The loan largely came back to them with interest paid by Nicaragua.

In July, 1924, Nicaragua finished paying off its debt to Brown Brothers and J. and W. Seligman. As a result the Pacific Railways reverted to the republic. However, two Americans were appointed on the railroad's new board of directors. They were Joseph K. Choate and Jeremiah W. Jenks, who had been appointed to the High Commission.[85] In September of the same year Nicaragua bought the American bankers' share in the National Bank for over $300,000.[86] However, as in the case of the railroad, this formal transfer of the bank did not mean the end of American control. After President [Bartolo] Martínez assured Colonel Clifford D. Ham, American customs collector since 1912, that Nicaragua would maintain the gold standard, an American commission was appointed to revise Nicaragua's banking and financial laws. The commission consisted of Abraham F. Lindberg, formerly deputy customs collector in Nicaragua; and Jenks, already on the High Commission and the railroad's board of directors.

While the bankers exercised control over Nicaragua's economic life, the State Department and the American marines supervised Nicaraguan politics. Opposition to the American-controlled Conservative government, particularly the Chamorro faction, had not abated since 1913. An uprising took place in the summer of 1921, and the government declared martial law. Washington shipped ten thousand rifles, a number of machine guns, and several million rounds of ammunition. These enabled the Conservative government to retain control.[87] The Chamorro government was threatened by another uprising in the spring of 1922. The government arrested three hundred Liberals and declared martial law. The American marines threatened action and the Chamorro government was safe.[88]

As in Haiti, the presence of marines led to conflicts with the natives. In February, 1921, marines wrecked the offices of the Nicaraguan paper *Tribuna*, alleged to have criticised the American troops. The marines were not subject to martial law but were tried by a United States naval court, which sentenced them to two years' imprisonment.[89] In December of the same year marines and native police clashed in the streets; and in January, 1922, a fight between marines and native police resulted in the death of four Nicaraguans and the wounding of five. The United States Navy indemnified the families involved and court-martialled the guilty marines.[90] They were sentenced to ten years, but the sentences were later reduced. In August, 1925, the marines were entirely withdrawn from Nicaragua. They have been replaced, however, by a native constabulary trained and officered by Americans.

Notes

1. Academy of Political Science, "Proceedings," v. 7, p. 383.
2. U.S. "Congressional Record," v. 50, pp. 3803–4.
3. Academy of Political Science, "Proceedings," v. 7, p. 393.
4. G. H. Blakeslee, *Mexico and the Caribbean* (New York, 1920), p. 320.
5. Ibid., pp. 303–4.
6. Academy of Political Science, "Proceedings," v. 7, p. 390.
7. Blakeslee, *Mexico and the Caribbean*, p. 187.
8. Academy of Political Science, "Proceedings," v. 7, p. 423.
9. S. G. Inman, *Problems in Pan Americanism* (New York, 1921), p. 273.
10. C. L. Jones, *Caribbean Interests of the United States* (New York, 1919), p. 110 ff.
11. U.S. "Treaties, Conventions, etc.," v. 1, p. 414.
12. U.S. "Foreign Relations," 1905, p. 334.
13. Ibid., pp. 298, 334, 342.
14. U.S. "Foreign Relations," 1905, p. 342.
15. Jones, *Caribbean Interests of the United States*, p. 110 ff.
16. J. H. Latané, *The United States and Latin America* (New York, 1920), p. 279.
17. U.S. "Foreign Relations," 1907, pp. 307–9.
18. U.S. "Foreign Relations," 1907, pp. 307–9; Jones, *Caribbean Interests of the United States*, p. 118.
19. U.S. "Foreign Relations," 1912, p. 367.
20. Ibid., 1913, pp. 459–60, 465–6.
21. U.S. "Foreign Relations," 1912, pp. 425–7.
22. Ibid., pp. 441–53.
23. U.S. "Haiti Hearings," p. 49; *Current History Magazine*, v. 15, p. 893.
24. Ibid., p. 894; U.S. "Haiti Hearings," p. 93.
25. U.S. "Haiti Hearings," p. 93.
26. Blakeslee, *Mexico and the Caribbean*, p. 208.
27. U.S. "Haiti Hearings," pp. 51–2.
28. Ibid., pp. 93–4.
29. Blakeslee, *Mexico and the Caribbean*, p. 208.
30. U.S. "Foreign Relations," 1912, p. 1089.
31. U.S. "Haiti Hearings," pp. 50–1.
32. Speyer & Co., and Equitable Trust Co., "Circular," June 20, 1921.
33. Lee, Higginson & Co., "Circular," March, 1922.
34. *Current History Magazine*, v. 15, p. 895.
35. Ibid.
36. Ibid., v. 20, p. 845.
37. Ibid, p. 1011.
38. U.S. Sen. For. Rel. Com., supra, Part VI, pp. 170–71.
39. Idem.
40. U.S. "Foreign Relations," 1910, pp. 763–4.
41. Ibid., pp. 765–7; Ibid., 1911, pp. 625–7, 652–4.

42. Ibid., 1910, pp. 765–7; Ibid., 1911, pp. 649–52.

43. U.S. Sen. For. Rel. Com., "Hearings on Nicaraguan Affairs," 1913, p. 15.

44. U.S. "Foreign Relations," 1911, pp. 655–6.

45. Ibid., pp. 657–8, 660.

46. U.S. "Foreign Relations," 1911, p. 661.

47. Ibid., 1911, pp. 661–2.

48. Ibid., 1913, p. 1040.

49. Ibid., 1912, pp. 1074–5; Blakeslee, *Mexico and the Caribbean*, p. 246.

50. U.S. Sen. For. Rel. Com., "Hearings on Nicaraguan Affairs," 1913, Part VI, pp. 174–202.

51. U.S. "Foreign Relations," 1912, p. 1076.

52. Ibid., pp. 1078–9.

53. U.S. Sen. For. Rel. Com., "Convention between the U.S. and Nicaragua," Part VI, pp. 205–6.

54. U.S. Sen. For. Rel. Com., "Convention between the U.S. and Nicaragua," Part VI, pp. 636, 639.

55. Ibid., pp. 667–70.

56. U.S. "Foreign Relations," 1912, p. 1079.

57. Ibid., pp. 993–6.

58. Idem.

59. U.S. "Foreign Relations," p. 997.

60. Ibid., pp. 997, 1003.

61. U.S. Sen. For. Rel. Com., "Convention between the U.S. and Nicaragua," Part VI, pp. 210–16.

62. U.S. "Foreign Relations," 1912, pp. 1093–1100.

63. Ibid., pp. 1081–2, 1100–1; U.S. Sen. For. Rel. Com., "Convention between the U.S. and Nicaragua," Part VI, pp. 234–5, 239–49.

64. U.S. Sen. For. Rel. Com., "Convention between the U.S. and Nicaragua," Part IX, pp. 400–1.

65. Ibid., Part XIII, pp. 504–10.

66. U.S. "Foreign Relations," 1912, p. 1043.

67. U.S. Navy, "Annual Report," 1912–13, p. 38.

68. U.S. "Foreign Relations," 1912, pp. 1053–4.

69. U.S. Sen. For. Rel. Com., "Convention between the U.S. and Nicaragua," Part X, pp. 424–6.

70. Ibid., Part VI, pp. 255–6.

71. U.S. Sen. For. Rel. Com., "Convention between the U.S. and Nicaragua," Part VI, pp. 258–61; Ibid., Part VIII, 400–7.

72. U.S. "Foreign Relations," 1913, p. 1035.

73. Ibid., pp. 1036–67.

74. U.S. Sen. For. Rel. Com., "Convention between the U.S. and Nicaragua," Part VI, pp. 261–4.

75. U.S. Sen. For. Rel. Com., "Convention between the U.S. and Nicaragua," Part VI, p. 280; U.S. "Foreign Relations," 1912, pp. 1094–1102.

76. Ibid., 1913, pp. 1052, 1057.

77. U.S. "Foreign Relations," 1912, p. 1063.

78. Blakeslee, *Mexico and the Caribbean*, p. 306.

79. "Review of Reviews," v. 53, p. 185.

80. U.S. "Foreign Relations," 1913, p. 1027.

81. U.S. "Foreign Relations," 1913, pp. 1022, 1025.

82. Ibid., p. 1027.
83. Moody's "Analyses of Investments; Governments," 1925, p. 538.
84. *Commercial and Financial Chronicle*, New York, Dec. 18, 1920, p. 2372.
85. *Wall Street Journal*, July 14, 1924.
86. *Commercial and Financial Chronicle*, New York, Sept. 13, 1924, p. 1236.
87. *New York Times*, Dec. 2, 1921.
88. Ibid., Apr. 7 and 25, May 23, 1921.
89. Ibid., Feb. 10 and 27, 1921.
90. U.S. Congress, 68:1, "Sen. Doc." 24.

2 Paul H. Douglas ◆ Occupied Haiti

For over a year prior to the formal American intervention in July, 1915, the government of the United States had been attempting to negotiate a treaty with the Haitian republic which would have placed the collection of the Haitian customs in the hands of the American government. Special commissions were sent to Haiti during the first part of 1915 to secure such an agreement but failed to secure the acceptance of the proposal by the Haitian government. The probable reasons for such a demand are not very clear, since practically all of the external debt was held in France, while the Haitians had, moreover, met virtually all of the interest payments and were only in default for some of the amortization payments. The only justifiable excuse for such a request would have been to forestall any attempt at financial intervention on the part of France.

There were, however, two other sources of economic friction between the Haitian and the American governments; namely, the disputes between the Haitian government and the National Bank of Haiti, and that with the National Railroad Company.

The bank had been apparently anxious for some time to secure American control over the Haitian customs, since a message from the United States minister in Haiti to our State Department in July, 1914, stated that the bank was planning to refuse to renew the budgetary convention, in order that the Haitian government should be rendered financially helpless and be compelled to ask for American assistance. The salient passages in this communication are:

> If then, at the end of the fiscal year, on September 30, the bank shall not have renewed the convention, the government will find itself without funds of any sort, and with no income, and undoubtedly will find it most difficult to operate. The statement that the government, in the absence of a budget convention, will be without income is based upon the fact that under the terms of the Loan Contract of 1910, the bank is designated as the sole treasury of the government, and as such receives all moneys of the government, and further, is empowered to hold such moneys intact until the end of the fiscal year, which, in this particular case, would be September 30, 1915.
>
> There is nothing in the loan contract providing for advancements by the bank, and the convention budgétaire has been in the nature of an accommodation extended by the bank. As before stated, the suspension of the convention

From *Occupied Haiti*, ed. Emily Greene Balch (New York, 1972), 15–52. Reprinted by permission of Garland Publishing.

budgétaire most likely would bring the government to a condition where it could not operate.

It is just this condition that the bank desires, for it is the belief of the bank that the government when confronted by such a crisis, would be forced to ask the assistance of the United States in adjusting its financial tangle and that American supervision of the customs would result.[1]

The clear implication of this was that the bank intended to impound the governmental receipts for the entire year from September 30, 1914, to September 30, 1915, and to advance them nothing from these moneys in the meantime. The bank claimed in defense of this position that they were not obligated by the agreement of 1910 to pay out the revenues as received.

On October 1, the American minister reported that the bank had refused to renew the convention and that the government was planning to issue paper money in order to meet expenses. The bank protested against this projected issue. Continual trouble with the bank and the expense caused by another revolution during the last week of October led the government to try to get possession of the balance of a $2,000,000 fund which the government had deposited in the bank for the purpose of redeeming the paper currency. This redemption had been postponed, and the balance of the earmarked funds had, apparently, been at least partially employed by the bank, and by its chief owner, the Banque de l'Union Parisienne, in its ordinary banking business, without paying interest to the government.

The government wished to secure possession of this balance, but the bank claimed that since this money was earmarked for the specific purpose of redeeming the paper money they could not, in their position as trustee, permit the government to use it.

In December, 1914, the Haitian government tried to use force to secure possession of these funds, but at the request of the bank the United States cruiser *Machias* was sent to Port-au-Prince. Marines were landed and $500,000 of the reserve was transferred from the bank to the *Machias* and taken to New York, where it was deposited with the National City Bank. In 1919 this was returned with 2 percent interest. This was a higher rate than would have been obtained had the money been left in the vaults of the Haitian bank, but it was considerably less than the market rate for such long-time deposits.

The second dispute was with the National Railroad of Haiti. This company in 1910 secured a concession from the Haitian government for a railroad from Port-au-Prince to Cap Haitien, which was to be composed of twenty-one sections. The Haitian government in turn agreed to guarantee 6 percent interest on the cost of constructing the road up to a maximum of $32,500 a mile. The man who engineered this contract through was an American adventurer by the name of James P. MacDonald, who originally seems to have been acting on his own responsibility. Three unconnected spurs of the railroad were built at a total alleged cost of approximately $3,600,000. The Haitian government, after making one or two interest payments in 1913, refused to make further payments on the ground that the railroad, by failing to construct the agreed-upon number of sections, had failed to fulfill its contract.

Mr. [Roger] L. Farnham, who was president of the railroad and an employee and later a vice president of the National City Bank, replied, on the other hand, that it had been the revolutions which had prevented further construction, and that consequently the company was not responsible for the failure to complete.

During the latter part of 1914 and the first part of 1915, the correspondence of the United States Department of State shows it to have been exerting its influence in favor of the National Railroad, the bonds of which were owned in France and in the United States, but which was managed in the United States by representatives of the National City Bank.

During the months of June and July, 1915, a revolutionary movement developed in the North against President Guillaume Sam, and several towns were seized by the revolutionists. On July 27, a popular uprising in Port-au-Prince itself drove the president from the presidential palace to the French legation, where he sought sanctuary. A large number of the president's political opponents were confined in the national prison, and the commander of the prison . . . then murdered no less than 164 of them. This so infuriated the populace of the city, who believed that the massacre had been committed by the order of the president, that a mob invaded the French legation, murdered Guillaume Sam, and, tearing his body to pieces, marched through the streets of the city with the dismembered parts.

At this juncture, the USS *Washington* arrived under the command of Admiral [William B.] Caperton. A force of sailors and marines was landed, and the city was policed. Revolutionary bands were disarmed and order was restored.

But the American forces did not retire when this had been acccomplished. They interested themselves in the election of a president by the National Assembly, and the candidate favored by the Americans, Philip Sudre Dartiguenave, was chosen by that body. American influence seems actively to have been used in his favor.

Almost immediately after his election, the American State Department urged upon the Haitian government a treaty which not only provided that the collection of customs should be in the hands of an American appointed by the president of the United States, but that a financial adviser should also be appointed by the United States. A gendarmerie manned by Haitians, but officered by Americans appointed by the United States, was also provided for in the treaty, and, in addition, American control over sanitation and public works was also demanded.

The excuse which is generally given for the American occupation of Haiti is that it was necessary to prevent foreign intervention. Thus Secretary Robert Lansing, in his letter to the McCormick Committee, declared that it was "designed to prevent the Germans from using Haiti as a submarine basis," yet virtually all of the German cruisers had been swept from the seas by the summer of 1915.[2]

There is little or no evidence to indicate either that this would have been possible or that any steps had been taken by the Germans in this direction. Americans in Haiti, on the other hand, say that our intervention was necessary to prevent the French from actively interfering. This again ignores the fact that the French were so burdened with military problems in 1915 as to prevent their turning their energies to Haiti. A small force of French sailors were, it is true, landed at Cap Haitien in June, to protect property, but they quickly withdrew in complete amity with the Americans when Admiral Caperton arrived on July 1, or over three weeks before the intervention in Port-au-Prince.

It seems, therefore, that there was virtually no danger of foreign intervention, and that if the authorities in Washington believed that there was, the cause was in the state of their nerves rather than in any actual menace.

Admiral Caperton seized the custom houses and began to collect the revenues, which he then deposited in the National Bank of Haiti, from which the services of the government deposits had been taken earlier in the year by the Haitian government.

The treaty was approved by the Haitian cabinet in the early part of September, 1915, but there was a great deal of opposition to it in the National Assembly, and a delay ensued.

In order to force ratification, Admiral Caperton then shut off the payment of salaries to the government officials. These were resumed in October, but the question of unpaid back salaries was to be adjusted *after* the Haitian Senate should fianlly vote upon the ratification of the treaty. In this way financial pressure was still continued. On the eve of the final vote, the U.S. government warned the Haitian president that if the treaty were not ratified, the United States "has the intention to retain control in Haiti until the desired end is accomplished, and that it will forthwith proceed to the complete pacification of Haiti."

Subjected to these threats, Haiti ratified the treaty, November 11, 1915, but accompanied this by a series of interpretive resolutions which the United States later refused to recognize. It was ratified by the United States, and proclaimed May 3, 1916. Under its provisions the United States has taken control of the following services—finance, gendarmerie, public works, agriculture, health and sanitation, although the authority to do so in the case of agriculture and health is far from clear. Whether by oversight or design the Departments of Justice and Education and the Post Office were left in Haitian hands, a fact that one often hears regretted by Americans in Haiti.

As the treaty was forced through under duress it is difficult to maintain that Haiti is morally bound by its provisions.

Article XVI states that the treaty shall remain in force for ten years, (that is, to May 3, 1926), and for a second term of ten years, "if, for specific reasons presented by either of the high contracting parties, the purpose of this Treaty has not been fully accomplished."

Within less than a year, on March 28, 1917, the treaty was extended under this clause to May 3, 1936, by M. Louis Borno, then foreign minister, and now president of Haiti; and Mr. [Arthur] Bailly Blanchard, American minister in Haiti. Haitians claim that this extension is invalid both because, as they hold, the agreement does not authorize an extension before there had been time to try out the treaty, and because the extension *has not been ratified* either by the United States Senate or by the Haitian National Assembly, which, as we shall see, was dissolved before it finally took action.

They hold that as the consent of the National Assembly was necessary for the ratification of the original treaty, it was also necessary for the extension, and that consequently the Haitian nation cannot be said to have requested a renewal and that, therefore, the terms of the treaty do not extend beyond May 3, 1926. Yet it is upon this, at the best, disputed agreement that the authority of the American occupation now rests.

In 1916, the National Assembly was dissolved by the American officers of the Haitian Gendarmerie. They were acting on the immediate orders of President Dartiguenave, but in view of the general control exercised by the American occupation, it seems undeniable that this dissolution was carried through with the consent, and possibly at the suggestion of the American representatives.

New elections for the National Assembly were conducted in January, 1917, under the supervision of the gendarmerie. When the National Assembly met, it was presented with the draft of a new constitution which had been drawn up by the then assistant secretary of the U.S. Navy, Franklin D. Roosevelt. One clause of this constitution gave to foreigners the right to hold land. This right had previously been consistently refused by the Haitians, who had been afraid that if foreigners were permitted to own land, they themselves would be speedily reduced to a condition of economic servitude. Largely because of this provision as to ownership of land, the National Assembly refused to ratify the constitution.

Acting through President Dartiguenave, the American occupation then proceeded a second time to dissolve a Haitian Congress, and Major Smedley D. Butler, U.S. Marine Corps, who as head of the gendarmerie had also the Haitian rank and pay of a major general, was sent with other officers to accomplish the act. These officers carried out their instructions, fully armed. The doors of the National Assembly were then locked in order to prevent the Assembly from entering the chambers again, and since then no Haitian Congress has been allowed to convene.

Since the Americans had thus dissolved the National Assembly, it was necessary to submit the constitution to some other body, if legal ratification was to be secured. It was accordingly decided to have the constitution voted on by the people in a special election.

On June 12, 1918, this plebiscite was held. The constitution was naturally a somewhat elaborate document, and its several provisions of fundamental importance to the country. Voters were, however, given only a short time to study it, and were required to approve or disapprove of it as a whole. Gendarmes, officered in the main by Americans, were in charge of the ballot boxes and of the whole conduct of the election.

Owing to the illiteracy of the electorate, the voters were not required to mark a ballot, which most of them could not have read.

From the testimony taken on the subject by the Senate Committee of Inquiry . . . it appears that there were prepared two sets of ballots, distinguished by their color; the white to signify approval, the pink disapproval, and that the voters were given the white ballots only. The colored ballots were in charge of a gendarme whom they could ask for them, if they chose. Pressure was used to get out a large vote. Under the circumstances it is not surprising that the constitution was declared to have been approved by a vote of 98,294 to 769. . . .

It is obvious that as a matter of fact the real power in Haiti is exercised, not by the Haitian officials, but by the American occupation. A body of U.S. Marines is stationed in the Republic, most of whom are quartered behind the president's palace. The presence of these American marines is not specifically authorized in the treaty, and hence, even if that instrument should be accepted as binding, is of more than doubtful legality.

The only possible authorization is that phrase in the treaty which states that "the United States will lend an efficient aid for . . . the maintenance of a government adequate for the protection of life, property and individual liberty." It seems that at any rate the United States government should not have the exclusive power of interpreting the meaning of this phrase.

The United States also effectively controls all legislation in this "sovereign and independent" state. Proposed laws must be submitted to the American legation and to the American High Commissioner before they can be enacted by the Council of State, now acting in lieu of an elected National Assembly.

If the High Commissioner has any serious objection to a law, it is apparent that he can prevent if from being enacted. The occupation is thus essentially supreme. Up until 1922 the ranking officer of the United States Marines in Haiti was also the representative of the American government, and although the lines of authority between the American commander and the American minister to Haiti were not always clear, the military character of the occupation was quite evident.

In 1922, however, Brigadier General John H. Russell, U.S. Marine Corps, was appointed by the president as High Commissioner to Haiti, and since then no Minister to the country has been appointed. General Russell is, therefore, at once the representative of the State Department and of the Navy, and even though he makes the legation his headquarters and appears primarily as a civilian, our occupation is nevertheless a thinly disguised military control.

Thus the American powers over Haiti are in reality almost complete. American approval is needed for the enactment of laws, the revenues of the country are collected under the supervision of Americans, and the budget is drawn up by the American financial adviser. The financial adviser scrutinizes all vouchers and withholds payments that he believes to be not in conformity with the principles of the budget or with efficient administration. The control over the gendarmerie is in American hands, as are also the services of Health and Public Works, and Agriculture. Only Justice and Education are outside of American control.

It is the present custom of the financial adviser to refuse to pay such court awards against the state as he believes to be unjust. The gendarmerie, controlled as it is by Americans, would naturally refuse to arrest him for refusal to obey the rulings of the courts. There can be little question that the financial adviser has saved the Haitian state a considerable amount of money by his refusal to make the payments which the courts have ordered him to make. Nevertheless, the principle established is not a happy one, and the legal relationships should be cleared up as quickly as possible. . . .

The American occupation would, undoubtedly, like to have the treaty amended so that they might secure control of the courts, and of education, in addition to the other branches of the administration which they now have in their hands. Such a change would, undoubtedly, be bitterly resisted by the Haitians, and any extension of the treaty which contained these terms could probably be secured from the Haitian government only under duress.

One of the most frequent complaints that one hears in Haiti is of the exclusion of Haitians from the more important administrative posts, which are filled by Americans, and the sharp contrast between the small salaries received by Haitian administrative officials and those received by the foreigners. The Americans are in many cases officers of the Marine Corps, in receipt of their regular salaries from the United States as such. Their services are lent to the government of Haiti, which pays an additional salary. This Haitian salary may be low by American standards; it may be a very small price for the service rendered, which is also being paid for in part by the United States.

Nevertheless the fact that American officers receive salary from two sources, and the feeling that the facts are not fully or commonly known cause criticism. The total sum paid annually from Haitian tax money to American officials is approximately $425,000, as compared to approximately $2,850,000 paid to Haitians in its service. The payment to Americans forms, therefore, 13 percent of the total expenditures paid to its personnel by the Haitian government. The additional amounts paid by the United States, as explained above, to the members of its naval and marine force who are loaned by the Haitian government, are approximately $495,000 a year, which is 17 percent more than is paid by the Haitian government to all Americans in its service.

The total paid to American officials is, however, divided among a much smaller number of people than that which goes to Haitians, and the individual salaries of the Americans are very much higher.

The financial adviser and general receiver is paid $13,500 a year, and the director of internal revenue is paid $7,500 a year. The director of the Agricultural Technique Service is paid $10,000 a year. The salaries of these men and also of the other Americans who are in the agricultural and financial services are entirely beyond those paid by the Haitian government to Haitian officials, apart from the president.

The leading Americans in the Department of Public Health and the gendarmerie receive grants from the Haitian government of from $150 to $250 a month. These grants in combination with their American pay are sufficient to bring their total salaries in some cases up to $7,500 a year.

It is not quite easy to say what the occupation costs the United States financially. The total yearly amount may be put perhaps at between $1,000,000 and $1,250,000. But of this a considerable part (perhaps between $500,000 and $750,000) is the expense of maintaining the marines in Haiti, and if these men would be maintained elsewhere if not there, it cannot be said that the occupation costs the American taxpayer the whole of the first mentioned sum. . . .

A. S. Maumus, who was appointed receiver of customs at the insistence of Mr. William Jennings Bryan in 1916, was not able to revise the Haitian finances in order that the tax burdens might be more equitably distributed. The various financial advisers that were appointed did no more than the receiver of customs, and one of them was absent in the United States for most of the time during which he served.

With the coming in 1924 of Dr. [William Wilson] Cumberland, who was appointed to fill the positions of both general receiver and financial adviser, the financial policy of the republic was placed on a more solid foundation. For the first time, an intelligible system of accounts was worked out and an accounting system devised which not only shows the expenditures and income of the government but also assists in checking fraudulent expenditures.

In addition, an attempt was made both to revise the customs law and to develop internal revenues as a means of making the country less dependent financially upon the volume of its export trade. This is particularly necessary in a one-crop country, such as Haiti, where an accident to the principal crop may severely cripple the finances of the government. At the time when Dr. Cumberland assumed office, revenues from internal sources composed less than 10 percent of the total receipts of the government, but these have been gradually increased, and it is the hope of the administration ultimately to draw approximately half of its revenues from internal sources. The public revenues will thus be more independent of the coffee crop.

Dr. Cumberland and his assistants have also revised the tariff law which, as has been stated, bore far more heavily upon the peasants than upon the well-to-do classes of the city. A preliminary draft has been prepared which, however, has not yet been enacted into law. This draft increases the duties upon such luxuries as perfume and imported liquors, and decreases both the import taxes upon necessities and the export taxes upon commodities which are raised by the peasants. . . .

On October 3, 1919, a so-called Protocol between the United States and Haiti was signed at Port-au-Prince, the provisions recognizing certain claims as binding upon the Haitian government, and setting up a claims commission to deal with others. In Article VI of this instrument the Republic of Haiti "agrees to issue . . . not later than two years after the date of the signature of this Protocol a national loan of 40 million dollars gold."

The external loans of 1876, 1896, and 1910 had been floated by the Haitian government in France, and these bonds were in the possession of French holders. The 1910 loan especially had been floated on terms which were very advantageous to the Banque de l'Union Parisienne, which had acted as the fiscal agent for the Haitian government. Owing to the postwar depression of the French franc, it became evident that the Haitian government would be able to save money by floating a new dollar loan in the United States and paying off the franc loans which were held in France.

The loan authorized in 1919 by the Haitian government was to provide for the refunding of the external and internal loans, for the settlement of claims against the government, and for public improvements. In 1922 when the value of the franc was approximately 9 cents instead of its normal exchange value of 19.6, a loan of $16 million was floated in the United States. This loan was to draw interest at 6 percent, and was to be amortized in not fewer than thirty years. By the Protocol between Haiti and the United States, the control over Haitian customs was given to the United States during the life of the loan. This, in other words, would mean that the United States control over customs might last until 1952, instead of 1936, as was authorized by the Treaty of 1916 and the proposed renewal of 1917.

After some negotiations, various banking houses were finally asked to bid upon the issue and the best bid was made by the National City Bank, which offered 92.1 for the bonds. This amounted to approximately 6.5 percent interest, which is a lower rate of interest than most Central American countries would be able to secure on their own credit. There can apparently be little doubt but that the guarantee on the part of the American government to collect the customs and to deduct the interest upon the foreign loan lowered the rate of interest which the Haitian government would otherwise have been compelled to pay. The loan is, as a matter of fact, being amortized at a more rapid rate than is formally called for, and if the present rate of redemption is continued, it will be completely amortized by approximately the year 1942, instead of by 1952.

It should be noted that approximately only half the French bondholders have accepted payment in paper francs, and that the remainder are holding out for a payment in gold francs. If they should be successful in obtaining such a payment, it would of course enormously increase the financial burdens of the Haitian people.

This claim of the French bondholders is, however, weakened by the fact that it has been the inflation policy of the French government that has caused the depreciation of the franc. To redeem the bonds in gold francs would be to give to the holders a preferential treatment which has not been accorded to those who own French governmental bonds. From the proceedings of the Haitian Congress in 1910, it appears, moreover, that they definitely rejected the idea of redeeming the bond issue in terms of gold francs.

Many Haitians criticize Mr. McIlheny for not waiting for the franc to depreciate further before refunding the French loan. Had this been done, the savings effected would have been still greater. It is perhaps hardly fair to blame Mr. McIlheny for failing to foresee the continued issue in France of paper money, particularly in view of the rise in the value of the franc in the years 1920 and 1922. . . .

The Protocol of 1919 between the United States and Haiti, which authorized the $40 million loan and which established a claims commission, also provided that the interest upon the $3,545,000 of bonds of the National Railway of Haiti, which were guaranteed by the Haitian government, should be recognized as a legitimate charge upon the Haitian government and should not be passed upon by the claims commission. The accrued interest upon these bonds was not met until 1922, and during this time the price of these bonds on the Paris Bourse fell much below par, and were below sixty in 1920. Since this quotation was in terms of paper francs, the depreciation in terms of American money was even greater.

It might have been possible for the then financial adviser to have purchased a considerable amount of the bonds on the market at this low rate, and thus have saved the interest and principal which the Haitian government would otherwise have been compelled to pay. Some savings could, undoubtedly, have been effected by making such purchases because the value of the entire bond issue in terms of American money was little, if any, under $800,000.

The financial adviser did not, however, purchase the bonds on the open market, but instead, in 1922, paid out approximately $2 million to meet the accrued interest, which had been accumulating since 1914.

In the following year a reorganization of the railway was carried through whereby the bondholders of the National Railway exchanged their bonds at 25 percent discount for 6 percent Series B bonds of the Republic of Haiti. In this way they became direct creditors of the Haitian government rather than of the National Railways.

The bondholders were induced to give up $600,000 of the accrued interest which had been turned over to them for the purpose of extending the line of the National Railway into the interior, to tap territories which it was thought would yield increased operating income. Taken all in all, the program of reorganization which was carried through reduced the ultimate liabilities of the Haitian government for the railway, including interest and amortization from $13 million to $8 million. The railroad will therefore cost the Haitians, from first to last, $8,330,000.

It is probable that had there been no foreign intervention in Haiti, the Haitian government would have refused to meet the interest upon the bonds, and, therefore, the Haitian people would not have been compelled to pay out any appreciable sum for it.

Some Americans defend the official policy towards the railroad on the ground that once the contract was made in 1910, it was the duty of the Haitians to live up to it, and that the Americans were justified in teaching the Haitians to respect the sanctity of contracts. This overlooks the fact that a contract which is tainted with fraud and corruption at its source, as this contract was, is neither legally nor morally binding. It is in fact not a contract at all, for this requires good faith.

It is precisely on such grounds that the U.S. Supreme Court invalidated the lease of the naval oil reserves to E. L. Doheny through the secretary of the interior. . . . The plea that the innocent holders of the bonds should be protected also plainly overlooks the fact that the innocent holders of any form of stolen property do not have any legal claim to the property of this description which they hold. To admit such a right would of course prevent any injured person from recovering property corruptly taken from him. If these innocent holders are to be indemnified, the obligation rests upon those who sold them the bonds, knowing as they presumably did the conditions under which the contract was secured, rather than upon the Haitian people, who had taken no part in their own betrayal.

The railroad itself has been an almost complete financial failure. Constructed as it was in three disconnected sections, the most important of which paralleled the seacoast, and hence was exposed to water competition, its revenues have been almost ludicrously slight. From 1914 to 1922 its total gross revenues did not average over $85,000 a year. This was less than half of the operating expenses, if depreciation is taken into account. If the interest charges of approximately $212,000 a year are added to this, it will be seen that the gross revenues only amounted to approximately one fourth of the total cost of the railroad.

It must also be added that the road has paid unnecessarily high salaries to its president, Mr. Roger L. Farnham, and to New York attorneys. Mr. Farnham while receiver was paid $24,000 a year, while Sullivan & Cromwell, attorneys for the receivership, were paid $20,000 a year. It is known that Mr. Farnham's present salary is approximately $18,000 a year. Yet, Mr. Farnham is in New York most of the year, and apparently devotes little of his energies to the actual conduct of the railway, which is clearly of so small and insignificant a character as to render unnecessary the services of so high-priced an official.

Since the Haitian government is compelled to make good any failure of the road to earn interest upon the bonds, it would seem that in self-protection it should have the power to control operating expenses. Otherwise, it would always be possible to pad the operating expenses and compel the government to meet the interest on the bonds. It should, therefore, take active steps to reduce the salary which is now being paid by the railroad to Mr. Farnham.

Who then has made a profit from the railway? It is not denied by anyone that the National City Bank now holds approximately 70 percent of the railway bond issue. Since these bonds were originally sold in France, the inevitable conclusion seems to be that they were purchased by some one from their French holders and passed either directly or indirectly into the hands of the National City Bank. In view of the prices at which the bonds were selling on the Paris Bourse, ranging between twenty-five and thirty in terms of dollars, it is patent that someone has made a large profit upon the transaction, which in the aggregate is probably between $2.5 and $3 million. . . .

A number of internal loans were floated from 1911 to 1914 to finance the carrying out of various revolutions. These loans were in part forced upon Haitian citizens, and in part were advanced by German merchants at exceedingly high rates of interest. In one case, the loan was floated at a rate of forty-eight, or for every forty-eight dollars advanced, the government agreed to repay one hundred dollars. As has been stated, interest upon these internal loans was not paid until 1922.

Since then they have been redeemed by the Haitian government in the following ways: (1) cash up to one third of their face value has been paid to the holders, and (2) Class B Haitian bonds drawing 6 percent have been issued in exchange for the other two thirds. A number of persons and institutions undoubtedly have made a considerable profit by buying up this internal loan at a low rate from its holders before back interest was paid and the bonds redeemed.

The Protocol of 1919 provided for the creation of a claims commission which would pass upon all claims which existed prior to 1916. One member of this commission was to be appointed by the Haitian secretary of finance, one by the United States secretary of state, and the third, who is not to be a citizen either of Haiti or of the United States, by the financial adviser. It will thus be seen that two of the three members of the claims commission were really appointed by the American government. The commission was somewhat slow in getting under way, but it has since been working at a more accelerated pace, and it has now passed on most of the claims. The total amount of claims awarded thus far amounts to approximately $2.8 million, while the amounts disallowed equal $21 million.

There has, on the whole, been little criticism of the work of the claims commission, and it seems to have tried to safeguard the legitimate financial interests of the Haitian government. Thus claims by the National Railway for alleged damages caused by the revolutionary disorders during the years 1911–1914 have been, in the main, rejected, as have certain other exorbitant claims advanced by foreign nationals. The awards of the commission are paid one third in cash and two thirds in Class B 6 percent bonds. . . .

The contract which the Haitian government made with the Banque Nationale de la République d'Haïti in 1910 was drawn for fifty years. It granted to the bank (1) the exclusive service of the treasury, and (2) the monopoly of note issue.

The National City Bank first purchased the interests of the three other American banking firms (that is, Speyer & Co., Hallgarten & Co. and

Ladenburg, Thalman & Co.) and after the war bought the interests of the Banque de l'Union Parisienne for approximately $1.4 million. In view of the changed ownership of the bank, a new contract was drawn up in 1922 by the Haitian government with the assistance of the State Department and the financial adviser.

In certain respects the conditions were altered in favor of the Haitian government. The commission which the bank had formerly collected for acting as the fiscal agent of the government was reduced from 1.5 percent upon receipts and expenditures to 1 percent. The profit upon the issuance of subsidiary coinage was also given to the government.

The contract of 1922, like the contract of 1910, was, however, silent upon the question as to whether the bank should pay interest to the government upon the deposits which the government had with it. This was not a matter of appreciable importance during the period of Haitian independence, because the government rarely had a surplus, but it was important during the period of American control when a surplus of $4 million was accumulated to meet possible decreases in revenue resulting from bad coffee years. The two Haitian ministers of finance under whom the contract was negotiated, Messrs. J. C. Pressoir and Louis Ethéard, declare that they were the ones who refused to allow the bank to pay interest. They justify their action on the ground that if the bank paid interest it would then loan out the deposits again to borrowers, whereas if no interest were paid, the Haitian officials would be able to call for the money at any time that they wished!

This misapprehension of the principles of modern banking seems almost inexcusable. It is in part explained, however, by the difficulty which the Haitians feel they had in securing possession in 1914–15 of the funds which were earmarked for the redemption of paper money. The desire to be able to lay their hands on the money at any moment led these two ministers of finance to regard the modern bank as analogous to a safety deposit vault and to misunderstand the way in which banks, by keeping their assets liquid, can meet the demands of their depositors.

While the ignorance of the Haitian ministers of finance of the elementary principles of banking was lamentable, it must be added that the National City Bank and the American officials must bear some share of the responsibility in the matter. A high standard of business ethics would, it would seem, have led the bank to be unwilling to take advantage of the ignorance of the Haitians. It would also seem that the principle of trying to protect the interests of one's customer should have led the National City Bank to offer voluntarily to pay interest.

Certainly while the American officials did not propose that the City Bank should be given the deposits without interest, their obligations as trustees should have made them prevent the final capitulation to the interest of the bank. The result of this unfortunate provision is that no interest at all is paid upon the deposits of the Haitian government with the Banque Nationale de la République d'Haïti, which now amount to approximately $1 million. The financial adviser has, it is understood, transferred some $3 million of the surplus to the National City Bank in New York, where the rate of interest paid is commonly understood in Port-au-Prince to be 2.5 percent.[3] The market rate of interest, however, in New York on such deposits as these, which need not be subject to call, is approximately 3.5 or 3.75 percent.

The Banque Nationale de la République d'Haïti and the National City Bank are, therefore, paying approximately $80,000 less interest annually than the government could secure at ordinary commercial rates. It would seem, therefore, that every effort should be made by the government to recover this amount. If the National City Bank refuses to pay the market rate, then it would seem that an effort should be made to interpret the contract so that the surplus funds might be deposited with other banks, which would pay the going rate of interest. It is believed that the contract does not grant to the Banque Nationale de la République d'Haïti exclusive right to all government deposits as the phrase "exclusive service of the treasury" might be interpreted as not analogous with an exclusive right to retain all deposits.

The bank also makes a small amount of profit, undoubtedly, on the 1 percent commission that is given it for handling government funds. It may also derive profit from the monopoly of note issue. It is able to make commercial loans by loaning bank notes as well as by creating deposits. Commercial loans are, as a matter of fact, generally made by giving the borrower bank notes rather than by creating a checking account for him. The ordinary rate of interest on these loans is approximately 9 percent.

The bank has to maintain against these bank notes a reserve of only one third in American money. Half of this, however, may be on deposit outside of the country, where it may, of course, be loaned out, and consequently draw interest. A reserve of 16.7 percent is, therefore, the maximum that is legally required. But this reserve, it will be noted, need not be in gold, but in any type of lawful American money. Federal Reserve notes can, consequently, be used as a reserve, but these are also in part based upon commercial paper and arise out of commercial transactions in the United States. It is, therefore, theoretically possible for the Banque Nationale de la République d'Haïti to make not far from ten dollars' worth of commercial loans upon a gold security of approximately one dollar.

In practice, however, the bank has maintained a much larger cash reserve than the legal requirements, this reserve in late years having amounted to over 65 percent of its note issue. The profits which have been realized upon this item are not, therefore, as great as those which are theoretically possible.

Some even believe that because of the expense of printing, handling, and retiring paper currency of such small denominations, no profit at all is made. If any profits are made, the only share which the government receives is a payment of 1 percent on all circulation above 10 million gourdes ($2 million). At the present time, the Haitian money in circulation amounts to approximately 15 million gourdes ($3 million). It would have been highly desirable to have drawn the original contract so that the share of the Haitian government in such profits as the bank may sometimes secure from the note issue would have been larger. . . .

Notes

1. See *Foreign Relations*, 1914, p. 346.
2. See Report of McCormick Committee, Senate, 67th Congress, Second Session, Report No. 794, pp. 31–37.
3. See Annual Report of the Financial Adviser-General Receiver, for year October 1923–September 1917, p. 77.

3 Arthur C. Millspaugh ◆
Haiti under American Control, 1915–1930

The Haitian-American treaty as finally concluded was wider in scope than the project of July 2, 1914, which, it would seem, was intended to relate exclusively to fiscal administration. At that time it was contemplated that the appointment of a financial adviser should be discretionary with the president of the United States, unless the Haitian government should request the appointment of this official, and the financial adviser should "generally exercise the functions of a comptroller of accounts." The draft of August 12, 1915, represented a significant advance in definiteness and amplification. Instead of signing and ratifying this project without modification, as the United States government wished, Haitian officials, of whom Foreign Minister M. Louis Borno was probably most influential, succeeded in drawing the Department of State into negotiations which resulted in the vague and ambiguous phrasing of certain provisions which had previously been clear and specific. Nevertheless, in many respects the instrument as signed was essentially the same as the draft of August 12.

Article I of the treaty stipulated that the United States "will, by its good offices, aid the Haitian Government in the proper and efficient development of its agricultural, mineral and commercial resources and in the establishment of the finances of Haiti on a firm and solid basis." This article had not been in the original draft and was suggested by Foreign Minister Borno, evidently with an eye to loans and investments of capital. The treaty went on to provide that the president of Haiti should appoint, upon nomination by the president of the United States, a general receiver, his "necessary" aids and employes, and a financial adviser. Nothing was said of the possible dismissal of these officials. The powers of the financial adviser were rendered ambiguous, by providing that he "shall be an officer attached to the Ministry of Finance, to give effect to whose proposals and labors the minister will lend efficient aid." The financial adviser's duties were enumerated but they apparently related to inquiry and recommendation, with possibly one exception—that which bound him to "aid in increasing the revenues and adjusting them to the expenses." The Haitian government agreed to "provide by law or appropriate decrees for the payment of all customs duties to the general receiver, and [to] extend to the receivership, and to the financial adviser, all needful aid and full protection in the execution of the powers conferred and

From Arthur C. Millspaugh, *Haiti under American Control, 1915–1930* (Boston: World Peace Foundation, 1931), 54–130.

duties imposed herein"; and the United States on its part agreed to "extend like aid and protection." It was prescribed that the Haitian government, "in cooperation with the financial adviser," should "collate, classify, arrange and make full statement" of the debts of the republic. The general receiver should apply all his collections and receipts, first, to the expenses of his office and that of the financial adviser, second, to the interest and sinking fund of the public debt, third, to the maintenance of the Haitian constabulary, and the balance to the Haitian government for current expenses; but expenses of the receivership and of the financial adviser should not exceed 5 percent of customs revenue, unless by agreement of the two governments. It was stipulated that the general receiver should make monthly reports to "the appropriate officer of the Republic of Haiti and to the Department of State of the United States."

Haiti agreed not to increase its public debt "except by previous agreement with the President of the United States," nor to "contract any debt or assume any financial obligation" unless a surplus of ordinary revenues were available for the interest and sinking fund of the new obligation. It was also provided that Haiti would not, without a previous agreement with the president of the United States, modify the customs duties so as to reduce customs revenue, but would "cooperate with the financial adviser in his recommendations for improvement in the methods of collecting and disbursing the revenues and for new sources of needed income."

As a measure "necessary to prevent factional strife and disturbances," the Haitian government obligated itself "to create without delay an efficient constabulary, urban and rural, composed of native Haitians," to be "organized and officered by Americans, appointed by the President of Haiti, upon nomination by the President of the United States."

The Haitian government agreed "not to surrender any of the territory of the Republic of Haiti by sale, lease or otherwise, or jurisdiction over such territory, to any foreign government or power, nor to enter into any treaty or contract with any foreign power or powers that will impair or tend to impair the independence of Haiti." Provision was made for the execution of a protocol for the settlement of foreign claims against Haiti.

Article XIII is of particular interest as in conjunction with Article I if included within the scope of the treaty the development of the natural resources of the country; and to this end the Haitian government agreed "to undertake and execute such measures as in the opinion of the high contracting parties may be necessary for the sanitation and public improvement of the republic, under the supervision and direction of an engineer or engineers" to be appointed like other Americans in the Haitian service.

The term of the treaty was to be ten years; but it might be extended for an additional ten years if, "for specific reasons presented by either of the high contracting parties, the purpose of this treaty [had] not been fully accomplished."

The final substantive article gave to the high contracting parties "authority to take such steps as may be necessary to insure the complete attainment of any of the objects comprehended in this treaty; and, should the necessity occur, the United States will lend an efficient aid for the preservation of Haitian independence and the maintenance of a government adequate for the protection of life, property and individual liberty."

Haitian diplomacy and, perhaps, a desire in the Department of State "to show every possible consideration for Haitian sensibilities,"—with probably a lack at Washington of a clear and comprehensive understanding of social and economic conditions in the republic—had produced a treaty which, in the light of the apparent determination of the United States at that time to accomplish its purpose in Haiti, would require supplementary agreements and many interpretations. Whether the financial adviser could prepare the budget or control ordinary governmental expenditures was far from clear. Whether American officials in Haiti were to be responsible to the president of the United States who nominated them, to the president of Haiti who appointed them, or to the Haitian minister with whom they were to work was not specified. The financial adviser was to be "attached to the Ministry of Finance," but the general receiver and the financial adviser were evidently vested with functions the exercise of which depended entirely on their own judgment. There was no suggestion in the treaty that Americans engaged in the finances, the constabulary, sanitation, or "public improvement" should by themselves form a unified organization. Nothing was said in the treaty about the presence of American forces in Haiti, about education, or about the judiciary, and American supervision of agricultural development was, if intended by either government or both governments, left largely to inference. . . .[1]

On the signing of the modus vivendi both Admiral [William B.] Caperton and Minister [Arthur Bailly] Blanchard recommended an immediate loan of $1.5 million but they were informed that the loan could not be arranged until after the arrival of the Haitian Commission in Washington and the settlement of difficulties with the National Bank.[2] Admiral Caperton on December 6 again urged a loan as "vital and imperative," stating that salaries and other obligations amounting to $500,000 should be paid before December 20 or "Government prestige [would] be lost among Haitians and serious conditions [would] result;" but the State Department was now "averse to [a] loan being made unless assured it [would] be properly disbursed.[3] Minister Blanchard on December 11 strongly supported the admiral's recommendations, but the State Department five days later wanted to know how the money would be used.[4] It was then arranged that this amount should be disbursed under the control of a naval paymaster, but it next appeared that the bank would not advance the money unless its contractual rights were restored.[5] Minister Blanchard thereupon telegraphed the items of the Haitian budget, which showed more than $600,000 in arrears, and on December 20 Admiral Caperton requested authority to use surplus customs receipts for pressing demands.[6] Nine days later the Department of State telegraphed that, according to its calculations, the deficit was only $65,000, and that it was "not prepared to consent to the use of an advance of $500,000 . . . for the purposes contemplated" in the Haitian budget and would not approve an increase of the foreign debt of Haiti for any such purposes. Nevertheless, in view of the "alleged urgency" of the matter the minister was directed to report immediately the sum absolutely necessary to defray salaries for November and December.[7]

As the year ended Admiral Caperton was instructed to use $50,000 of Haitian funds for payment of salaries, this sum is to be paid directly to the employees.[8] In January, 1916, the departments at Washington wanted Haitian expenditures kept down to $100,000 a month: Admiral Caperton was to use his discretion in disbursing funds and was "not bound to be governed by the budgetary law in making these disbursements."[9] Strict control of expenditures stopped much petty graft and pleased those who now received their salaries.[10] But it also forced the discharge of employees, and the Haitian legation at Washington reminded Secretary [Robert] Lansing that in throwing "numberless citizens" on their own resources the Haitian government "had relied to a certain extent on the industrial and agricultural works that were to be started in the country by American capital.[11]

At the time of the intervention, amortization of the 1875 debt was in arrears from 1903 and amortization of the 1896 debt was in arrears from 1914. Default in payment of interest first occurred after the intervention, funds not being transferred to Paris to meet the interest maturity of November 15, 1915. Admiral Caperton in March, 1916, appears to have transferred funds to Paris for the payment of overdue interest, but in an amount insufficient to pay the interest on any one of the loans, and no payments of interest were made until the debt service was resumed in 1920, when all arrears both of interest and amortization on the foreign debt were paid.[12] At this time the market for Haitian coffee was closed by French war restrictions and the shortage of ocean transportation. Haitian exports and revenues decreased, and had Admiral Caperton met the entire debt service little would have been left for the current expenses of the Haitian government.

An agreement was at last signed on July 10, 1916, between the Haitian Commission and the representatives of the National Bank of Haiti, with a provision that on approval of the agreement by the Haitian legislative body the bank would advance $500,000 to the government.[13] Flotation of a loan seems also to have been delayed by the desire of the National City Bank to acquire sole control of the National Bank of Haiti. This desire was gratified in February, 1920, the State Department having insisted on certain changes in the contract which were advantageous to Haiti.[14]

A protocol was signed at Port-au-Prince on October 3, 1919, providing for the settlement of foreign claims against Haiti by a claims commission. For the funding of the obligations so adjudicated, for the refunding of other debts of the Haitian government, and for constructive expenditure Haiti agreed to issue within two years a thirty-year loan of $40 million. It was further agreed that the service of this loan should be a first charge on the internal revenues of Haiti and a second charge on the customs receipts. Although in Article I it was "clearly understood that this protocol does not in fact or by implication extend the provisions of the treaty," it was agreed in Article VI that the terms and dates of issue of the loan should be fixed "in accord with the financial adviser," in Article VII that any balance remaining after foreign and domestic indebtedness had been taken care of should be applied, "in accord with the financial adviser," either to public works or to the service of the loan, and in Article VIII it was agreed that, after the expiration of the treaty and during the life of the loan, the collection and allocation of the hypothecated revenues should be under the control of an officer or officers appointed by the president of Haiti upon nomination by the president of the United States.

Aside from the establishment of control over revenues, the budget and expenditures, already mentioned, and the conclusion of difficult and tedious negotiations relative to the bank and the loan, there was little noteworthy financial progress during this period. . . .

The financial adviser and the Haitian government could not agree on a plan for the reorganization of internal revenues; but certain internal taxes formerly unenforced were now collected and total internal revenues were more than tripled.[15] Maintaining that the burden of the Haitian tariff rested too heavily on the peasantry, one of the U.S. officials favored reduction or elimination of export duties. But no tariff reform was possible until debt refunding had removed pledges from specific revenues, and the State Department disapproved a Haitian law reducing export duties on coffee.[16] Abuses in the customs service had largely ceased, and a law to assist in the control of smuggling was passed.[17] There was little improvement in accounting. Nevertheless, the public debt had been reduced and government receipts in general were showing a tendency to increase. . . .[18]

An important question of jurisdiction arose in connection with the fiscal control of the financial adviser-general receiver. The general receiver was given powers in the treaty which he was apparently intended to exercise without orders or instructions from any quarter, and was to report monthly to the minister of finance of Haiti and to the Department of State of the United States. The financial adviser was to "enlighten both Governments with reference to all eventual debts," but he was to "recommend improved methods of collecting and applying the revenues" and make other recommendations to the minister of finance. Both governments pledged themselves to extend to the receivership and to the financial adviser aid and protection in "the execution of the powers conferred and duties imposed." Although the financial adviser sought and accepted instructions from the Department of State, it is not clear that he was legally obligated to do so; but in practice every other financial adviser followed his example in this respect. On the other hand, two financial advisers strenuously disputed the right of the high commissioner, without a decision from the Department of State, to approve claims, appropriations or expenditures, when these were disapproved by the financial adviser. From February, 1924, to the fall of 1928, the high commissioner and the financial adviser through cooperation and consultation were generally in agreement on financial matters and neither approved an appropriation without concurrence of the other. In fact, it was the financial adviser rather than the high commissioner who was looked to for final decisions in financial and economic questions, and who was most frequently accused of dictatorship by Haitian critics. It is understood that following the resignation of the financial adviser-general receiver in January, 1928, after a controversy with General [John H.] Russell, the latter was instructed by the Department of State to approve no expenditure proposal disapproved by the financial adviser until it had been submitted to the department with the views of the financial adviser. . . .

Economic rehabilitation depended on various factors, and among these were establishment of confidence in the minds of Haitian producers and foreign investors, reorganization of taxation, and constructive expenditure by the government. Peace, order, and fiscal honesty had done much to create confidence. Tariff revision was one of the obvious first steps in the reorganization of an archaic revenue system, but customs duties, encumbered with guarantees of loans, could not be modified until the debt had been refunded. Flotation of a refunding loan had been delayed by the unsettled controversy with the National Bank and by a complication of clogging conditions.

At the time of his appointment the high commissioner was instructed to press vigorously the matter of obtaining Haitian legislative authorization for a loan. After oral conversations he wrote the minister of foreign affairs on April 15, 1922, requesting the Haitian government to name a member of the claims commission and suggesting that the financial adviser, then in Washington, be given full powers to negotiate a loan. It appeared to the Haitian government that the protocol of October 3, 1919, which was to be in effect two years, had now lapsed; and other objections were raised to the proposals of the high commissioner.[19] After Mr. Borno became president, however, difficulties were removed, and a loan of $40 million was authorized by laws of June 26, 1922, and October 27, 1922.[20]

In the same year, the Series A loan, amounting to $16 million, was floated by means of sealed bids solicited by representatives of the Haitian government at Washington under the auspices of the Department of State. The best bid was made by the National City Company of New York which offered 92.137. The bonds were sold to the public at 96.50. Stipulations of the loan contracts provided for equal monthly payments to be made to the fiscal agent, such payments to be sufficient to meet interest requirements at 6 percent and to create a sinking fund adequate to repay the loan in a thirty-year period. An interesting feature of the loan was a provision that when the revenues of Haiti should exceed $7 million, specific percentages of any excess up to $8 million must be used for the establishment of a market fund for additional amortization, provided bonds were purchasable in the market at or below par. Principal and interest were payable in dollars in New York. The loan was secured by a first lien on all Haitian revenues and was further protected by a provision that, during the life of the loan, revenue administration should be in charge of an American.[21]

With the proceeds amounting to $15,039,945.04, claims of the National Bank and National Railroad were immediately paid and a sum of $6,037,650.00 was used for refunding the three French loans, which in 1915 at the then rate of exchange had stood at $21,470,617.99.[22]

In the meantime, the claims commission had been appointed, began its public hearings in April, 1923, and before the end of the year 73,269 claims amounting to $38,394,146.44 were presented to it.[23] While judicial astringents were being applied to this long-festering mass of pecuniary exaggeration, the Council of State authorized an issue of $5 million in Series B bonds to refund the unpaid balance of previous internal loans and to fund that portion of the awards of the claims commission which were to be payable in bonds.[24] The commission completed its work in June, 1926, awarding a total sum of $3,495,836.54, less than 9 percent of the amount demanded by claimants. In the meantime, the Series B loan had been floated through the National City Company of New York on the same terms as the Series A loan with respect to rate of interest, period of maturity, security, and administration, except that Series B bonds were payable in Haiti and were subject to the Haitian income tax of 10 percent. Of Series B bonds, an amount of $765,958.06 remained unissued, so the actual loan was for $4,234,041.94.[25] Thus, with a few exceptions, all of the outstanding claims against Haiti were settled and either paid out of the Series A loan or funded with Series B bonds.[26]

A substantial amount still remained from the proceeds of the Series A loan; and of this $300,000 was used for amortization and the balance, $2,411,736.95, was allocated for public works.

An effort was now made to solve the problem of the National Railroad. It will be recalled that this enterprise had received from the Haitian government a guarantee of 6 percent on outstanding railroad bonds amounting to $3,544,581.60 and a sinking fund guarantee of 1 percent, obligating the Haitian government to pay yearly $248,120.71.[27] General Russell declared the National Railroad to be "a profitless railroad running through an unproductive area of the country"; but it was the opinion of the financial adviser that upon the completion of the railroad "profitable operation [would be] possible with great economic benefits."[28] In any event, the concern was in the hands of a receiver and it was eminently desirable to relieve the government, so far as possible, of the financial burden which it had unwisely assumed, and, at the same time, to enable the railroad to become, if possible, a paying enterprise.

All arrears of interest and amortization on the railroad bonds, amounting to $2,160,856.90, were paid to the receiver of the railroad in the spring of 1923 out of the proceeds of the Series A loan. Before making payment to the bondholders, however, the receiver obtained the agreement of a large majority of them to the exchange of their railroad securities for new bonds of the Haitian government, to be issued in an amount equal to 75 percent of the value of the railroad bonds. As soon as this agreement had been reached, a plan for reorganizing the railroad was worked out with the Department of State, the high commissioner, and the financial adviser, in consultation with President Borno.

According to this plan, which was approved by the Council of State on December 27, 1923, railroad bonds were to be exchanged for Series C bonds on the Haitian government, the railroad company to assume responsibility for the interest and amortization of this debt as soon and so far as its net income would permit.[29] A part of the cost of new construction was to be paid by the Haitian government by means of Series D bonds; but there was added, on the suggestion of the Department of State, a proviso that the Series D bonds should be issued by the Haitian minister of finance, in accord with the financial adviser, after authorization of the Council of Secretaries of State only when, "according to the opinion of these functionaries, the financial condition of the state permits it to assume this new charge."[30] For all funds furnished by it for new construction the Haitian government was to receive preferred stock and was to have representation on the board of directors. The plan also gave the government an extensive right to supervise and control the issue of new bonds and stocks, as well as the management and operation of the road.

Series C bonds were authorized by the Haitian government in an amount of $2,660,000. The Metropolitan Trust Company of New York acted provisionally as fiscal agent for the exchange of railroad bonds for Series C certificates. With respect to interest rate, maturity, and security, this loan was identical with the Series A loan, and the National City Company was likewise appointed fiscal agent for its permanent administration. Due to the failure of certain holders of railroad bonds to effect exchange, it was possible to cancel an amount of $1,839.20 in Series C bonds.[31] By the plan of reorganization, Haiti was saved a substantial sum of money and practically relieved of any further financial involvement in the railroad.[32]

The plan did not, however, put the railroad on a paying basis. In order to solve this phase of the problem, the receiver of the railroad proposed a new contract by which the road would have become essentially a private enterprise, relieved of any contingent responsibility for the service of the Series C bonds and freed of any government control of financing, rates, operation, and construction. The government, giving up its representation on the board of directors and its right to share in profits, was freed of the obligation, such as it was, to issue Series D bonds. These proposals were considered by the financial adviser-general receiver, the high commissioner, and the State Department at intervals during almost three years; and finally in the latter part of 1928 a project was approved by the department and presented by the high commissioner to President Borno. The latter rejected it. In 1929, a new contract was negotiated by the financial adviser-general receiver, accepted by President Borno, and submitted to the Council of State but was not approved by that body.[33]

From 1923 to 1930, there were three financial advisers, and each followed more or less consistently the policy of reducing the debt more rapidly than was prescribed by the amortization schedules of the loan agreements.[34] At the same time, each pointed with pride to a growing cash reserve.

The financial adviser-general receiver reported at the end of 1923–24 "one of the largest sums expended for actual debt reduction, as contrasted with the liquidation of obligations in default, which Haiti [had] ever made in a year"; and in each of the next three years an increased amount was paid on the debt.[35] In 1924–25, 28 percent of revenue was devoted to the service of the public debt and in 1925–26, 23 percent. Although the financial adviser-general receiver believed that the debt was "well within the resources of the population" his policy was to reduce it "as rapidly as possible, consistent with the proper conduct of the ordinary activities of the Government."[36] At the end of 1925–26, the Series A loan had been diminished at about double the rate originally contemplated; and in 1928 it appeared possible that the entire funded debt might be liquidated as early as 1943.[37]

American fiscal control had resulted in 1923–24 in accumulating an unobligated cash surplus of approximately $1.4 million, the largest which had ever been on hand in the history of Haiti.[38] In justifying maintenance of a large cash reserve, Dr. W. W. Cumberland explained in 1924 that the treaty of 1915 prohibited the creation of obligations against the Haitian treasury without the approval of the president of the United States, and the law of Haiti limited expenditures to the revenues actually realized. "In view of these circumstances," he argued, "sound financial policy necessitates the accumulation of a substantial cash balance if the ordinary services of the Government are to continue without interruption." Moreover, "in the case of Haiti, a strong treasury position should not result in lavish expenditures. . . . Accordingly, a treasury surplus is as legitimate and as essential on the part of the Haitian Government as it is on the part of a well-managed corporation." Furthermore, a reserve was designed to meet fluctuations both of income and of expenditure, and in Haiti there were wide variations of revenue from year to year and from month to month. But it was Dr. Cumberland's conclusion in 1924 that the cash balance was then "as large as needs to be carried in normal times."[39] Nevertheless, the reserve increased each year, and at the end of 1927–28 it had grown to almost $4 million.[40] At that time the financial adviser-general receiver observed that no one "would seriously contend that it need be maintained indefinitely" in that amount; but during the two following years it was kept at an even higher figure.[41]

Growth of the surplus after 1926–27 was largely due to the increasing difficulty of rapid debt reduction. Amortization beyond the terms of the loan contracts could only be effected by purchases of bonds in the market at or below par. Series A bonds in October, 1924, were selling on the New York exchange at 92; but they rose during the following year to 97 and in 1928 were above par. Series B internal bonds, which had been quoted as low as 50, sold in 1928 above 90.[42] In 1927–28, when revenues were unprecedentedly large, only a little more than a million dollars could be devoted to debt reduction.[43] It was now the somewhat guarded opinion of the financial adviser-general receiver that the repayment of the debt in accordance with the loan requirements would be "sufficiently rapid"; and, without implying that the debt was "burdensome," he believed that in view of Haiti's peculiar needs debt charges approached the maximum which could be borne without "unduly postponing development."[44]

After criticizing the practice of debt retirement in excess of requirements, Financial Adviser-General Receiver S. de la Rue announced in March, 1930:

I therefore wish definitely to state that my policy with regard to the public debt contemplates retirement of present loans only to the extent that contractual obligations require. Surplus funds accumulating in the treasury will be diverted as soon as possible for use in extending the various activities of the governmental services, and in amplifying and improving as fast as may be expedient the roads, harbors, buildings and public enterprises.[45]

The public debt of Haiti was reduced from about $24,210,000 on September 30, 1924, to $16,541,000 on September 30, 1930. Were the cash surplus deducted the net debt of Haiti on the latter date would have been about $12,565,000.

Many circumstances need to be considered in judging this aspect of American financial administration; but it is clear that the handling of the debt and the reserve by the financial adviser-general receiver diminished by a substantial amount the funds that might have been used for other purposes. Such diminution may not have been an unmixed evil, for both Haitians and Americans sometimes requested funds for purposes which might well seem to a prudent financial administrator less constructive and less productive than debt reduction.

Because of absence of land and excise taxation in Haiti, the revenue structure remained decidedly lopsided. Almost 90 percent of government income in 1924–25 was derived from customs duties, although the financial adviser-general receiver believed that internal revenue should equal or perhaps exceed that from external sources.[46] Not only was revenue too largely dependent on foreign trade, which in turn was dependent on Haiti's shipments abroad, but a single product, coffee, comprised almost four fifths of the total value of Haitian exports.[47] Prior to 1919–20, receipts from export duties often exceeded those from the import schedules; and from 1923 to 1929 customs revenue from exports was almost one half that from imports.[48]

The financial adviser-general receiver in 1925 showed that the burden of taxation, state and local, was approximately $4.20 per capita, "probably the lowest in the Western Hemisphere"; but wealth and income were so pathetically meager in Haiti that the revenue of the central government absorbed perhaps as much as 20 percent of the annual income of the people, a very high ratio since "the margin of the Haitian population above the necessities of existence is discouragingly small." "In the absence, therefore, of the development of additional sources of wealth and income," he believed that "no attempt should be made to increase the revenues of the Government, except the institution of such fiscal charges as will stimulate production."[49] Revenue reorganization, as proposed by Americans in Haiti, had in view, therefore, a change in the type of taxation and a shifting of its incidence, but with no increase of the tax burden relative to national income.

An internal revenue project, apparently drafted in 1919, was pressed by the high commissioner in April, 1922; and in his report for 1923 he expressed the opinion that the tariff could not be "safely revised" until after an internal revenue law had been put into operation.[50] Early in that year, a committee consisting of the minister of finance, the financial adviser and the general receiver had prepared a draft providing for a tax on sales. This feature was highly unpopular and was abandoned; and, later in the year a new project was produced, aiming merely to create machinery under the general receiver for the collection of internal revenues.[51] This project experienced delay, objections, and prolonged discussion in the Council of State but was passed on June 6, 1924, shortly after the financial adviser-general receiver had agreed to an increase in the salaries of the councillors. The law created a Bureau of Internal Revenue under an American director responsible to the general receiver; but no new internal taxes were imposed until 1928. Nevertheless, administrative improvement resulted in a gradual increase of revenue from existing sources.[52]

From the beginning of the receivership tariff revision was recognized to be necessary and was urged by the general receiver.[53] Even before the enactment of an internal revenue law, work was begun on the revision of what was called "one of the worst tariffs in existence."[54] The project was studied by the Department of State and Commerce at Washington and published in Haiti in May, 1925, and hearings were given to the merchants of the country.[55] It was voted by the Council of State on July 26, 1926.[56]

The new law not only placed higher duties on luxuries as compared with necessities but it also imposed protective duties on certain articles which, it was thought, could be produced in Haiti. A high duty, for example, was placed on tobacco, of which little was raised in Haiti.[57] The tariff contained no free list, but in a law of July 25, 1928, certain agricultural implements and machinery, books, printing presses, and printing apparatus were exempted from taxation.[58] In the following year, additional articles were exempted with a view to encouraging education and agriculture.[59]

The new tariff aimed to maintain customs revenues at their former level and did not eliminate or reduce export duties, the most important of which were on coffee. The financial adviser-general receiver in 1925 noted "considerable evidence to the effect that the export duties of Haiti [had] had a retarding effect on agriculture"; and, though the export duties constituted "more of a psychological than a fiscal problem," he was disposed to consider "how those taxes [might] be reduced or abolished, provided equal revenue could be obtained from other sources."[60] General Russell, however, in his report for 1926, pointing out that the burden of export taxation was borne by the peasant, declared that "one of the principal objects in refunding the public debt of Haiti [had been] . . . to permit, when the time was opportune, the elimination or reduction of these obnoxious taxes and burdens that had so unwisely been imposed upon the mass of the Haitian people"; and to this end he emphasized the necessity of an "internal revenue tariff" which was then in preparation.[61] Dr. Cumberland came back to the question in 1927; and, with reference to the suggestion that "relieving coffee from present fiscal contributions would over a period of years tend to encourage production," he declared that this was "theoretically true, but when applied to Haiti [could] be accepted only with misgiving," for the reason that "coffee grows in a manner not far removed from the wild state" and extremely attractive prices which had then prevailed for some years had "failed to stimulate the peasants of Haiti to increase their production." On the other hand, he declared that it was difficult for Haitian producers "to hold their place in the world market so long as they [had] to pay export taxes, while their competitors [were] not faced with similar fiscal burdens."[62]

It was not, however, until July, 1928, that discussion of export taxation yielded concrete results. At that time export duties on crude salt were reduced and on bananas wholly removed.[63]

The high commissioner in 1923 was planning for a tax on the production of alcohol, and two years later the financial adviser-general receiver urged a tax on both production and consumption of this beverage, repeating his recommendation in 1926.[64] An excise tax law, placing moderate imposts on both alcoholic beverages and manufactured tobacco, was passed on August 14, 1928. This law not only marked a step toward the establishment of modern and productive internal taxes but also contained a provision which empowered the president, on the recommendation of the minister of finance in accord with the financial adviser, to suspend after October 1, 1929, wholly or partly any of the export duties, provided that the revenue so lost should not exceed receipts from the new excise taxes.[65]

Rum was the drink of the people; and on account of the presence of perhaps two thousand small stills in the country and the peasant's habit of purchasing his smoking tobacco by the leaf from tubs, the law was difficult to put into operation. As it was probably the only internal tax that had ever been felt by a large portion of the population, it was widely misunderstood and as widely misrepresented.[66] Nevertheless, it produced during its first full year of operation nearly a half million dollars and brought the total of internal revenue to three times what it had been in 1920–21.[67] In consequence, President Borno, in an executive order of September 7, 1929, reduced the export duty on the highest two grades of coffee, and about a year later on the third grade as well.[68]

The financial adviser-general receiver declared in 1925 that a tax on landed property was "the most needed reform in the revenue structure of Haiti"; and that a "moderate land tax" would stimulate the productive utilization of land and would discourage the holding of uncultivated land for speculative purposes. Two years later he expressed the opinion that land "should supply the principal resources of the treasury," and policies were being formulated "for expanding internal revenues by means of land taxes."[69] A project of law for a small tax on real estate, with a double imposition on unimproved or uncultivated land, was drafted in 1928;[70] but the high commissioner declared that "the imposition of a land tax lies in the future," because of the ignorance of the peasants and the absence of proper land laws, land surveys, registration offices, and means of settling titles.[71]

Notes

1. *Hearings*, p. 68–69, 86–87. The Department of State on August 22, 1915, said that it "would not be unsympathetic toward any proper effort which might be made . . . to establish a good school system. . . ." *For. Rel., 1915*, p. 436. On September 16, 1915, Minister Borno wrote to the American chargé giving the Haitian government's interpretation of Articles II, V, and VI of the treaty; and in replying on September 20 Chargé Davis took occasion to call attention to the words "will lend an efficient aid" in Article XIV, explaining that this "undertaking by the United States Government naturally implies the lending of its armed force should internal strife or uprising endanger the existence of the Government" and that "the United States considers it its duty to support a constitutional government and aid the people of Haiti in maintaining domestic peace throughout the country." *Ibid., 1915*, p. 454–455.

When the Chamber of Deputies ratified the treaty, it did so with an "interpretative commentary," expressing the view that the president of Haiti could dismiss the general receiver for malfeasance in office and the "delinquent could even be amenable to an action" under Haitian law; that the customs force is "exclusively and directly" appointed by the president of Haiti; that the financial adviser is no longer a "comptroller placed above the executive and legislative powers" but "is nothing but an official attached to the Ministry of Finance where he collaborates with his work and advice"; that the financial adviser "confines himself to pointing out, enlightening, recommending, suggesting, prompting"; that the Hague Tribunal would be the competent jurisdiction to decide disputes in the execution of the treaty. *Ibid., 1916*, p. 322–325. The interpretative commentary was sent to the Department of State with the exchange of ratifications on March 15, 1916. On April 5, 1916, Secretary Lansing pointed out to the Haitian legation at Washington relative to the interpretative commentary that, "as this paper was not before the United States Senate at the time it gave its advice and consent to the ratification of the treaty by the President, it is impossible to consider the views expressed therein as having any binding force on the Government of the United States." *Ibid.*, p. 325–326.

Ratifications were exchanged on May 3, 1916, on agreement that any provision, on which the interpretative commentary should be found not in accord with the English text of the convention, should be construed and interpreted in accordance with the clear language of the English text. *Ibid.*, p. 327.

2. *For. Rel., 1915*, p. 531; *For. Rel. 1915*, p. 53–54; *Hearings*, p. 400; *For. Rel., 1915*, p. 325.

3. *Hearings*, p. 402.

4. *For. Rel.*, 1915, p. 533.

5. *Hearings*, p. 403; *For. Rel., 1915*, p. 533–534.

6. *Ibid.*, p. 534; *Hearings*, p. 404.

7. *For. Rel., 1915*, p. 536–537.

8. *Ibid.*, p. 537–538.

9. *Hearings*, p. 409–410; *For. Rel., 1916*, p. 339–340.

10. *Hearings*, p. 410–411, 620–621; *For. Rel., 1916*, p. 341–342, 345–349.

11. For. Rel., 1916, pp. 345, 355.

12. *Hearings*, p. 414–419, 1393–1394; *For. Rel., 1916*, p. 351. The general receiver was instructed in February, 1922, to resume payment of interest on the funded internal debt, but postponed action on request of the Haitian government. *Hearings*, p. 1352.

13. For text see *For. Rel., 1916*, p. 358–359.

14. *Hearings*, p. 1418–1426.

15. Internal revenues were $109,878.38 in 1915–16 and $360,102.42 in 1920–21. *Hearings*, p. 1352–1353, 1399–1400.

16. *Ibid.*, p. 1351, 1396, 1400–1401; *Documents Diplomatiques*, p. 164.

17. *Hearings*, p. 1395; *Report of Receivership of Customs*, 1917–1918, p. 5.

18. "It may be frankly admitted that the financial results of the earlier years of American participation in Haitian administration were not particularly favorable, but this fact was due to causes over which neither Haiti nor the United States had control, namely, the European war." *Report of Financial Adviser-General Receiver, 1923–24*, p. 57; *Hearings*, p. 1228–1233.

19. *Hearings*, p. 1521–1525. It may be suspected that, if there was loss of interest in the loan on the part of Haitian politicians, it might have been due in some degree to that provision of the protocol of October 3, 1919, which stipulated that any surplus remaining after the liquidation of the foreign and domestic debt should be applied by the Republic of Haiti to public works or to the loan service "in accord with the financial adviser." Sen. Doc. No. 135, p. 7.

20. *Report of Financial Adviser-General Receiver, 1923–1924*, p. 82.

21. The loan "was in large part floated for the purpose of refunding the foreign debt of Haiti because that debt was principally in French francs and because francs could be obtained at a substantial discount." *Report of Financial Adviser-General Receiver, 1923–1924*, p. 82.

22. *Report of American High Commissioner, 1923*, p. 2; *Report of Financial Adviser-General Receiver, 1923–1924*, p. 82–83.

23. *Report of American High Commissioner, 1923*, p. 2, 40; *ibid., 1926*, p. 6.

24. *Ibid.*, p. 39.

25. *Report of Financial Adviser-General Receiver, 1923–1924*, p. 84–85; *1926–1927*, p. 92; *1927–1928*, p. 105–106.

26. *Report of American High Commissioner, 1924*, p. 6; *1925*, p. 8–9; *1926*, p. 7–8; *Reports of Financial Adviser-General Receiver, 1923–1924*, p. 97–98; *1924–1925*, p. 95–97; *1925–1926*, p. 92–95.

27. *Report of American High Commissioner, 1923*, p. 2, 39–40; *Report of Financial Adviser-General Receiver, 1923–1924*, p. 87.

28. *Report of American High Commissioner, 1923*, p. 2, 40.

29. *Ibid.*, p. 2; *Report of Financial Adviser-General Receiver, 1923–1924*, p. 88.

30. The plan of reorganization contemplated the construction of a new line through the Artibonite Valley, a region which, in the opinion of the high

commissioner, promised "to be perhaps the most bountiful portion of the country."
Report of American High Commissioner, 1923, p. 3.

31. *Report of Financial Adviser-General Receiver, 1926–1927*, p. 27; *1927–1928*, p. 107.

32. *Ibid., 1923–1924*, p. 85–89.

33. *Ibid., 1924–1925*, p. 98, *ibid., 1925–1926*, p. 95. A newly constructed line in the Artibonite Valley was opened in December, 1925; but by this time automobile buses as well as coastwise vessels were competing with the railroad and its future did not look bright. *Ibid., 1925–1926*, p. 95.

34. Mr. McIlhenny resigned as financial adviser on October 11, 1922, and was replaced by Mr. John S. Hord, who in turn resigned during the following year. After an interregnum during which the general receiver, Mr. A. S. Maumus, acted as financial adviser, Dr. W. W. Cumberland, previously superintendent of customs in Peru, took the position of financial adviser-general receiver, in January, 1924. On the resignation of Dr. Cumberland in 1927, Dr. A. C. Millspaugh, who had served as administrator general of the finances of Persia, was appointed financial adviser-general receiver, and on the latter's resignation in January, 1929, the position was filled by Mr. S. de la Rue, who had been financial adviser of Liberia.

35. $561,579.18, *Report of Financial Adviser-General Receiver, 1923–1924*, p. 86; the amounts were: 1924–25, $1,163,447.48; 1925–26, $1,384,836.90; 1926–27, $1,720,044.84. In the latter year debt reduction was due in part to the cancellation of unissued Series B bonds. *Ibid., 1924–1925*, p. 82; *ibid., 1925–1926*, p. 79; *ibid., 1926–1927*, p. 90, 95.

36. *Ibid., 1925–1926*, p. 84–85.

37. *Report of Financial Adviser-General Receiver, 1925–1926*, p. 80; *ibid., 1927–1928*, p. 109.

38. *Ibid., 1923–1924*, p. 70.

39. *Ibid.*, p. 78–79; *1924–1925*, p. 80.

40. *Ibid., 1927–1928*, p. 103.

41. Amount of cash balance at end of last seven fiscal years:

September 30,	1924	$1,399,800
"	" 1925	1,273,600
"	" 1926	2,331,800
"	" 1927	2,496,200
"	" 1928	3,874,800
"	" 1929	4,072,200
"	" 1930	3,976,600

Financial Adviser-General Receiver, *Monthly Bulletin*, September, 1930, p. 5.

42. *Report of Financial Adviser-General Receiver, 1923–1924*, p. 87; *ibid., 1924–1925*, p. 87; *Report of American High Commissioner, 1925*, p. 13. Both issues declined for various reasons in 1929 and 1930.

43. $1,053,748.00. *Report of Financial Adviser-General Receiver, 1927–1928*, p. 105.

44. *Ibid.*, p. 109. For a Haitian view of the general question see Beauvoir, Vilfort, *Le Contrôle finançier du Gouvernement des États-Unis d'Amérique sur la République d'Haïti*, Paris, Recueil Sirey, 1930.

45. *A Review of Finances of the Republic of Haiti, 1924–1930*, March 3, 1930, p. 30–31; *infra*, p. 186.

46. *Report of Financial Adviser-General Receiver, 1924–1925*, p. 51.

47. *Ibid.*, p. 30; *ibid., 1927–1928*, p. 23–27.

48. *Ibid., 1927–1928*, p. 55.

49. *Ibid., 1924–1925*, p. 58–59.

50. *Hearings*, p. 1521–1525; *Report of American High Commissioner, 1923*, p. 13.

51. *Report of American High Commissioner, 1923*, p. 4.

52. Internal tax receipts, amounting to $379,434.34 in 1920–21, had risen to $559,174.10 in 1923–24; and in 1926–27, the last fiscal year before new internal taxes were collected, receipts stood at $830,657.59. *Report of American High Commissioner, 1924*, p. 8–10; *Report of Financial Adviser-General Receiver, 1923–1924*, p. 51–52; *ibid., 1927–1928*, p. 55.

53. *Report of Receivership of Customs, 1916–1917*, p. 10; *ibid., 1917–1918*, p. 8; *ibid., 1918–1919*, p. 9–10; *ibid., 1919–1920*, p. 8; *ibid., 1920–1921*, p. 4; *ibid., 1921–1922*, p. 4.

54. *Report of Receivership of Customs, 1916–1917*, p. 17–18; *Report of Receivership of Customs, 1919–1920*, p. 8; *Report of Financial Adviser-General Receiver, 1924–1925*, p. 37–38.

55. *Report of Financial Adviser-General Receiver, 1923–1924*, p. 36–39; *1924–1925*, p. 37–40; *1925–1926*, p. 30–31; *Report of American High Commissioner, 1925*, p. 2.

56. *Report of Financial Adviser-General Receiver, 1925–1926*, p. 31.

57. *Ibid., 1927–1928*, p. 59. A few changes in the tariff were made on July 25, 1927. *Ibid., 1926–1927*, p. 32.

58. *Ibid., 1927–1928*, p. 35.

59. *Ibid., 1928–1929*, p. 41.

60. *Ibid., 1924–1925*, p. 39.

61. *Report of American High Commissioner, 1926*, p. 13–14.

62. *Report of Financial Adviser-General Receiver, 1926–1927*, p. 53, 56.

63. *Ibid., 1927–1928*, p. 35–36, 56.

64. *Report of American High Commissioner, 1923*, p. 4, 6; *Reports of Financial Adviser-General Receiver, 1924–1925*, p. 65; *1925–1926*, p. 60–61.

65. *Ibid., 1927–1928*, p. 57–58, 67–68.

66. *Report of Financial Adviser-General Receiver, 1927–1928*, p. 67–68, 147–148.

67. Excise-tax receipts in 1928–29 were $452,763.67 and in 1929–30, $546,495.75. *Ibid., 1928–1929*, p. 55; *Monthly Bulletin*, September 30, 1930, p. cc.

68. *Report of Financial Adviser-General Receiver, 1928–1929*, p. 41–42; *Monthly Bulletin*, July 1930, p. 12.

69. *Report of Financial Adviser-General Receiver, 1924–1925*, p. 63; *ibid., 1926–1927*, p. 65.

70. *Ibid., 1927–1928*, p. 68.

71. *Report of American High Commissioner, 1929*, p. 19–20. "A tax upon landed property is as yet far in the future." *Report of Financial Adviser-General Receiver, 1928–1929*, p. 71.

4 Emily S. Rosenberg and Norman L. Rosenberg ◆ From Colonialism to Professionalism: The Public-Private Dynamic in United States Foreign Financial Advising, 1898–1929

Throughout the twentieth century, North Americans have loaned money and given financial advice to capital-poor, less industrialized nations. Since World War II highly visible government agencies and multilateral bodies such as the International Monetary Fund and the World Bank have organized and extended much of this economic assistance. But from 1898 to the onset of the Great Depression of the 1930s, North Americans experimented with other methods, especially nongovernmental ones, designed to bring financial order to so-called backward states. Such advisory efforts have received little systematic study: even basic information on pre-World War II financial advising has never been compiled, assessed, or interpreted. Although loan conditionalities and the role of foreign economic expertise loom as major, controversial issues in U.S. relations with Third World nations, little historical literature traces or explains previous financial advising relationships between non-European foreign nations and public and private institutions in the United States.[1]

This essay analyzes the forms that United States foreign financial advising took during the transitional period from 1898 to 1930, after territorial colonialism had ceased to seem a viable way of imposing financial arrangements, but before the advent of post-World War II international financial institutions. It focuses on Latin America in order to develop a structural framework for understanding the different relationships from which North American financial advisory missions to various nations drew authority and legitimacy. Four categories, which form a continuum, provide the analytical framework: colonialism, treaty, legal contract, and professionalism.

The four arrangements exemplify, in the international field, a change from colonial "status" to liberal capitalist "contract," a rough analogue to an earlier shift in the definition and conceptualization of personal relationships within the emerging domestic order of industrial capitalism. They also reflect predominant themes in U.S. history since the mid-nineteenth century. New hierarchical forms of socioeconomic organization emerged that, unlike older, paternalistic arrangements based on status, seemed to be legitimated

From the *Journal of American History* 74 (June 1987): 59–82. Reprinted by permission of the authors and the *Journal of American History*.

by mutual consent. Economic relationships became depoliticized as the private authority of contracts and experts substituted for a popular political process. The increasingly corporativist or "associationalist" nature of U.S. government policies meant the delegation of "public policy" functions to the "private" sector and the consequent blurring of distinctions between the two realms.

An analysis of financial advising helps to answer the perplexing historical question: Why did the United States relinquish formal territorial colonialism so quickly? The answer, this essay suggests, lies less in some anticolonial commitment or exceptional past history than in the availability of neocolonial substitutes. Familiar with a domestic order in which economic relationships were expressed through contracts and were increasingly rationalized by professional expertise and financial managers, North Americans dealing with people in less powerful states developed international economic relationships structured by similar arrangements. In both the colonial (status) and postcolonial (contract) mentalities, some states were seen as natural dependencies of the United States; basic issues remained the same: how to express, structure, and justify paternalism.

In tracing the changing forms and structures of financial supervisory relationships, it is useful to draw perspectives from practitioners of a range of disciplines: from sociologists who have analyzed the rise of professionalism; from legal scholars who have critically dissected formal legal doctrines; and from historians, political scientists, and economists who have studied individual advisory missions. Because financial advising was nearly always connected with foreign lending, the study of advising also necessitates examination of loan negotiations—both the actual texts of foreign loan contracts and prospectuses and the documentary records of international negotiations. This study rests on an examination of all of the loans or attempted loans that were associated with advisory missions between 1898 and 1929 and looks at the circumstances and conditions of each.[2]

Colonialism

The American government originated advising efforts. After 1898 the Bureau of Insular Affairs hired economists and administrators to sweep away the legacies of Spanish control and to institute modern fiscal practices in Puerto Rico and the Philippines. North Americans moved the new colonies onto gold-exchange standards; they rationalized the tax systems by bringing "scientific" tariffs into the customs administrations and by introducing new types of levies; they launched new, more centralized, banking systems; and they experimented with methods of providing more flexible credit (agricultural banks, for example) and of encouraging savings. Besides these substantive changes, U.S. colonialism introduced new systems of accounting and stricter supervision over tax-collecting agencies.[3]

Many of the colonial financial administrators hired by the bureau were economists who had crusaded for a domestic gold standard in the 1890s and who advocated a flexible and centralized banking system for the United States (ultimately embodied in the Federal Reserve Act of 1913). The most important were Jacob Hollander in Puerto Rico and Charles Conant, Jeremiah Jenks, and Edwin W. Kemmerer in the Philippines. All had close ties to the financial community and shared its desire to stabilize, centralize, and professionalize the financial system at home and abroad.[4]

Having gained confidence and experience bringing gold-based financial systems to the two colonies, such economists easily believed that their expertise in financial reorganization could benefit other unfortunate silver-standard nations as well. In 1903 Congress appropriated funds to create a Commission on International Exchange, which advised Mexico, Panama, and China on the process of adopting a gold-exchange monetary standard. Conant and Jenks, the principal members of the commission, probably deserve designation as the founders of the profession of international financial advising. But the commission, which did its work in 1903–4, had only mixed success; thoroughgoing rehabilitation of "backward" countries depended on a more substantial presence of American imperial power. Yet American public opinion and Congress, soured by the bloody war to subdue the Philippines, had turned against territorial imperialism. Just when some people were beginning to develop the expertise and credentials for careers in foreign economic administration, the possibility that the United States might need a large corps of colonial civil servants dimmed.[5]

Treaty (or Convention)

In 1904 the Dominican Republic became a laboratory for working out new means of reforming the "backward" financial practices of foreign nations. In devising what policymakers subsequently viewed as the "Dominican model" of rehabilitation, the State Department worked closely with investment bankers. Investment banking had grown rapidly in the late nineteenth century, primarily as a result of domestic railroad financing, and industry leaders were starting to show an interest in foreign fields. The Dominican model became the first major example of a new partnership between bankers seeking higher foreign interest rates and the activist, promotional bureaucracy taking shape within the administration of President Theodore Roosevelt.[6]

Deeply in debt to European bondholders and threatened by warships, the Dominican Republic seemed of strategic importance to Roosevelt because of its proximity to one of his pet projects, the Panama Canal. In his 1904 corollary to the Monroe Doctrine, directed at the Dominican situation, Roosevelt announced that when states of the Western Hemisphere conducted their economic affairs irresponsibly enough to raise the possibility of European intervention, the United States would assume the role of an "international police power." Together with this stick of gunboat diplomacy, Roosevelt also extended a carrot to Dominican leaders: the U.S. government would send a financial adviser who could work with the Dominican government, the Department of State, and North American investment bankers to devise a program for refunding the defaulted debt by a new loan.

The subsequent plan for the Dominican Republic, worked out by Hollander, a political economist from Johns Hopkins who had recently reorganized the finances of Puerto Rico, involved two separate documents. One was a convention between the United States and the Dominican Republic, under which the Dominican customs collections, the major source of government revenue, would be administered by a U.S. receiver appointed by the secretary of state (but paid by the Dominican Republic). The other document was a loan contract between the Dominican government and the investment banking house of Kuhn, Loeb and Company. The bankers were able to offer buyers Dominican bonds with a much higher rate of interest than domestic bonds paid, and the Dominican bonds were virtually guaranteed by the U.S. government because the convention provided that customs revenues would service them.

The convention and the contract were interdependent. The Dominican government accepted the foreign receivership in order to get the loan; the bankers extended the loan only because the convention's guarantee of government involvement minimized the risk; and policymakers used the loan to force a financial rehabilitation that would, they felt, advance the strategic concerns of the United States in the Caribbean. Such corporate-government cooperation seemed to offer the possibility of guiding a dependent state through fiscal reform without burdening the United States with political sovereignty. After initially balking at assumption of such responsibility by the U.S. government, Congress passed the Dominican Convention in 1907.[7]

From 1908 to 1912, the administration of William Howard Taft made the dollar diplomacy put together in the Dominican Republic the cornerstone of its foreign policy. Taft promised U.S. voters that he would foster stability in critical areas by substituting "dollars for bullets," by sending bankers with loans rather than battleships with marines. By 1911 Secretary of State Philander Knox—a lawyer with close ties to the investment banking community—had readied convention-loan packages on the Dominican model for Nicaragua and Honduras. Similar plans for Guatemala and Liberia were on the drawing boards; others were under discussion. Investment bankers, eager to cash in on high rates of interest that were virtually government insured, courted policymakers and maneuvered to get their firms included in the loan/receivership plans.[8]

Efforts to follow the Dominican model temporarily stalled. To congressional critics, it appeared that a treaty commitment to tax collecting and debt servicing in a foreign country could lead to the political, and even military, commitments that most of their constituents wished to avoid. Many congressional opponents, carrying on the legacy of populism, distrusted such executive branch maneuvering, power, and alliance with large banking establishments. The conventions stipulating North American-run financial receiverships for Nicaragua and Honduras failed to pass Congress in 1911, and the other, similar projects ground to a halt.[9]

The strategic situation created by World War I, however, led the Senate to accept the establishment of an economic advisory structure in Nicaragua in 1917. And after the military occupation of Haiti, the Senate ratified a treaty with Haiti that brought American financial advisers to that country as well.[10]

During the late teens, American financial advisers were also sporadically involved in both Cuba and Panama, though no documents explicitly granted them authority. The protectorate agreements signed with both countries in 1903 implied strong advisory roles in their financial affairs, but the countries maintained at least theoretical control over their customshouses and expenditures (except when under military occupation).[11]

Before the end of World War I, then, Congress had ratified the presence of U.S. financial advisory structures in Cuba, Panama, and the Dominican Republic, Nicaragua, and Haiti. If imperialism is a process by which one state assumes sovereign powers over another, setting up a dependent relationship, relations between the United States and all of these countries can be included under the term, even though they were not formal colonies of the United States. The congressionally acknowledged dependencies all lasted into the 1930s and 1940s, when each was gradually phased out in favor of less formal relationships of structural dependency.[12]

Contract

If a variant of old-fashioned imperialism dominated the relations of the United States with many Caribbean countries up to World War I, new methods of achieving U.S. hegemony also began to emerge. There was a clear shift from essentially imperialistic, treaty-enforced dependency status to what might be called "colonialism-by-contract." It involved a supervisory relationship, sponsored by the U.S. government but included as a provision in a "private" loan contract signed between an international investment banking firm located in the United States and a foreign government. Supervision established as a "private" contractual obligation (an arrangement that contemporaries termed "loan control"), rather than a public, treaty obligation, did not involve messy congressional processes and thus did not easily become the subject of public scrutiny and debate. Before discussing the specifics of this shift, which recalls Sir Henry Maine's well-known distinction from "status" to "contract," it is useful to locate the process within broader trends in legal culture and political economy.[13]

The legal historian Morton J. Horwitz has written that "one of the central goals of nineteenth century legal thought was to create a clear separation between . . . public law and the law of private transactions," such as contracts. The emerging legal profession sought to "separate law from politics" and to create "a neutral and apolitical system of legal doctrine and legal reasoning" free from what were thought to be the unpredictable tendencies of democratic politics. Yet, he observes, the public/private distinction emerged at the time when "large-scale corporate concentration became the norm" and "private power began to become increasingly indistinguishable from public power."[14]

Horwitz's analysis illuminates international loan contracts containing advisory obligations (often negotiated with State Department encouragement). Such contracts clearly reflected "public" purpose and involvement. But the sharp divisions between public law and private law helped to mask the government's behind-the-scenes role and to legitimate close advisory ties as the result of "free" private marketplace transactions. Supervisory responsibilities that had troubled Congress when they were presented as "political" and "public" conventions raised fewer objections when they involved application of the "science" of law (and economics) within a "private" contract.

The analysis of Robert Gordon, also a legal scholar, provides other insights into the international contracts of the early twentieth century. Lawyers, he writes, tend to have a "deeply ingrained suspicion of the notion that they should be depicted as a species of intellectuals producing ideology. . . . Naturally they think of themselves as practical persons occupied with practical affairs. . . . [But] a legal document . . . is a kind of political constitution." It embodies assumptions about representation and who may exercise power over whom; about decision-making discretion and delegation; and about entitlement and responsibility for gains and losses. Contract law is intricately bound up with power; it both expresses and reinforces power relationships. Yet, while the deeper structure of contracts is overtly political and ultimately ideological, the rhetoric of contract law helps disguise such realities. In the international arena, power enforced by gunboats seems oppressive, arbitrary, and highly political; contracts seem products of mutual consent, enforced by neutral, apolitical processes.[15]

The history of a number of international loan contracts indicates that the hitherto "public" extension of U.S. imperial control shifted into the "private" sphere when contracts replaced treaties as the mechanisms to introduce and to legitimate economic supervision over potential dependencies. In these cases, contracts reinforced, though they altered, a neocolonialist, hierarchical order in which people with money and presumed expertise held critical financial power over debtor nations.

Nicaragua became the first example of this development. The proposed Nicaraguan Convention of 1911 provided for a North American collector of customs appointed by the U.S. State Department. After Congress rejected this convention, bankers proceeded with a smaller loan to Nicaragua. The contract required a North American customs collector suggested by the bankers and approved by the State Department.[16] For Nicaragua, the reality of both arrangements was the same; in either case an American designated by the State Department became the tax collector. But moving this supervisory provision out of a convention and into a contract was of domestic importance in the United States. Few citizens in the United States were interested in the details of "private" loan contracts, and those who were had no control over their contents. Indeed, the North Americans most directly concerned about foreign bonds—people with money to invest—would only applaud the bankers' attempts to spread efficient revenue collection and to secure bond earnings with the help of supervisors designated by the U.S. government.

Although in 1916–17 Congress did accept a more formalized and "public" supervisory relationship with Nicaragua (under the Bryan-Chamorro Treaty and the Financial Plan of 1917), the rehabilitation of foreign economies through loan controls in private contracts remained an important option for policymakers. For example, the 1912 receivership in Liberia reflected this pattern; the international banking consortium that Taft supported for China proposed loans in return for supervision; and banking consortia formed for Mexico and China in 1918 under Woodrow Wilson did the same.[17]

After the war, as policymakers sought to secure firmer positions of strategic and economic influence in Central and South America but confronted congressional suspicion of international commitments, arranging controlled loans became a major priority. Boaz Long of the Division of Latin American Affairs, for example, wrote in February, 1918, that establishing formal protectorates "would not be possible under present day conditions" but that "something along the lines of those used in the Haitian situation (financial control), might produce the favorable effects desired." Long recommended the following plan to promote United States-dominated stabilization and development:

> a) We must improve their national credit standing before the world. Refinance Central American countries, one by one, as rapidly as possible, along lines that would tend to cause their business and banking transactions to be handled largely through the United States.
>
> b) Before undertaking rehabilitation we should, looking to this end, cause to be established now in the capital of each Central American Republic a bank. This might be a branch of any American bank, or banks. . . . It should be organized with sufficient capital to engage in the larger transactions and have specially in mind the training of its personnel so that it might be in a position successfully to undertake the financial rehabilitation of the country when the time became opportune.[18]

Between 1919 and 1923, in line with these recommendations, the State Department worked with North American foreign financial advisers and investment bankers on many controlled loans. Especially during 1922 the State Department was remarkably active in promoting and hammering out with bankers the details of supervised loans, which were projected for most Latin American governments and for many outside Latin America as well. State Department officials regarded loan controls as a means to advance U.S. strategic, economic, and humanitarian interests by introducing North American-guided financial stability to the region. Dana G. Munro of the Division of Latin American Affairs wrote in 1922 that the policy of using loans "to insist much more strongly upon desired reforms" aimed "to obtain . . . political and financial reforms which will make for greater stability of government and which will provide a safe field for American commerce and investment."[19]

A summary of the conditions surrounding the loan negotiations with Guatemala, Honduras, El Salvador, Bolivia, and Peru will demonstrate the State Department's desire to use controlled loans to carry out foreign-policy objectives. It will also highlight some of the difficulties of such dollar diplomacy and suggest why loan controls proved relatively short-lived.

In 1919, at the State Department's suggestion, the Guatemalan government hired Edwin W. Kemmerer to recommend remedies for the country's monetary and financial ills. Kemmerer's career and economic views had a pervasive influence on financial advising in Latin America during the 1920s. Kemmerer had studied with Jeremiah Jenks at Cornell and later, from 1903 to 1906, implemented Charles Conant's currency reform for the Philippines. Following his experience in the Philippines, Kemmerer launched an academic career that took him to Cornell and to Princeton. In 1916 he published *Modern Currency Reforms* and in 1917 advised the Mexican government of Venustiano Carranza on an anti-inflationary currency program. After the war, he established his reputation in the government as a leading expert on Latin American financial reform, advised the banking house of Dillon and Read, undertook financial missions to more than a dozen foreign nations, and advocated conservative Republican economic policies at home. He served as president of the American Economic Association in the mid-1920s.

Kemmerer shared the economic views of Jenks and Conant, including a belief in the quantity theory of money and a firm commitment to spreading a gold-exchange currency standard maintained, in each nation, by a national bank. True to the agenda of most turn-of-the-century academic economists, he saw inflation and inconvertible currencies as the primary evils within the world economic system. Unlike the post-World War II generation of economic advisers, Kemmerer spoke little of promoting "development" or "modernization." Instead he sought primarily to promote gold-based convertible currencies as the basis for a self-adjusting and self-regulating international economic trading and investment order [see Selection 5, this volume].[20]

In his 1919 report on Guatemalan finance, Kemmerer traced the country's economic ills to its inflation-ridden paper currency, which created opportunities for graft and self-interested manipulation. He predictably recommended creation of a strong national bank and introduction of a gold-exchange currency reform. These measures, of course, necessitated an infusion of foreign (U.S.) capital for use in promoting stabilization. The State Department asked its minister in Guatemala "to receive permission from President [Juan] Estrada to show [Kemmerer's] report to various American interests in order to sound them [out] with regard to possibility of their participation in proposed national bank." State Department officials subsequently tried to devise a controlled loan/fiscal rehabilitation package, but the Guatemalan government always balked at foreign supervision. The plans never succeeded.[21]

The State Department's effort to secure a controlled loan for Honduras likewise failed, but the attempt was important, as in Guatemala, because it demonstrated a continuing policy and because it involved Arthur N. Young as the foreign adviser. Young, a former student and close friend of Kemmerer, worked in the Office of the Foreign Trade Advisor when the State Department recommended his services to Honduras. Young stayed in Honduras for more than a year, in 1920–21, and fashioned a comprehensive rehabilitation plan that so impressed the State Department that they subsequently offered him a job as economic adviser in the department. He held that governmental position from 1922 to 1928, until he began a lengthy stay as an economic adviser to the government of China.

Strongly influenced by Kemmerer's views and work, Young offered ambitious recommendations for Honduras that went beyond those his mentor had made for Guatemala. Young's one hundred-page memorandum on the "State of Financial Reforms in Honduras" (May 31, 1921) called for U.S.-sponsored financial reform as a bulwark against political instability and British intervention. It analyzed the deplorable state of the finances of Honduras (in default to British creditors since 1873 and beset by chronic budget deficits and graft) and, like Kemmerer's plan, it proposed monetary and banking reform to bring Honduras onto a stable gold standard. Young then went on to scrutinize public expenditures, calling for reduced outlays and new procedures to eliminate corruption; he studied sources of revenue and suggested specific tax reforms; he examined financial administration, particularly the need to reform customshouses; and he recommended consolidation of the internal and foreign debt. In short, he sketched a comprehensive fiscal transformation similar to the one that U.S. officials had been trying to effect in their colonies of Puerto Rico and the Philippines.[22]

The key to Young's program—as to Kemmerer's—was extension of a loan by U.S. bankers. The loan would consolidate debt, finance currency reform, and help instill discipline in expenditures and in administrative practices. Yet bankers were interested in lending only if some loan control would minimize their risk. Thus, in early 1922, Young, now back in Washington as economic adviser to the State Department, proposed granting Honduras a loan on the model of one that the department was supporting for the government of El Salvador.[23]

In El Salvador, Minor Keith of United Fruit was trying to interest American bankers in extending a controlled loan. Keith proposed, and the State Department accepted, an ingenious arrangement providing for an exchange of notes between the two governments. The note of October 20, 1921, from the minister of foreign affairs of El Salvador assured the United States that, in connection with the pending loan and stipulated in its contract, a director of customs would be appointed in the following manner: The bankers would nominate two persons to be director of Salvadoran customs, one of whom would then be selected by the Salvadoran government, channeling the appointment "through the office of the Secretary of State of the United States." In case of an interpretive dispute between the bankers and El Salvador, the secretary of state would refer the matter to the chief justice of the United States for a binding settlement.[24] Secretary of State Charles Evans Hughes's return note stated that the United States was gratified by the assurances and would carry out the stipulations. Apparently Hughes saw no question of either constitutional or ethical impropriety in providing official sanctions for a bank's appointment or in pledging the chief justice of the United States to settle potential disputes between the bankers and El Salvador. With this evidence of U.S. government involvement, accomplished in an exchange of notes that did not require congressional ratification, Keith was able to convince bankers to make the loan. The Loan controls indirectly authorized by the Department of State, Keith believed, would help safeguard his fruit company's interests; and he himself (and his lawyer Lester Woolsey, who had been the State Department solicitor during the Wilson administration) stood to profit from a complicated plan for refunding old British bonds.[25]

Young, who became economic adviser to the State Department during the period that this exchange of notes took place, initially viewed the Salvadoran loan as a possible model for Honduras and elsewhere. But the State Department's pleasure about the new arrangement was short-lived. After the exchange of notes, Keith changed bankers, substantially altered the loan contract, and significantly raised the profits to be earned by himself and by the bankers. Secretary Hughes tried to convince Keith and Woolsey that the profit on the loan was "unconscionable" and should be lowered. But, when Keith refused to ameliorate the terms, Hughes concluded that Keith might have a legal case against the department if it withdrew support from the exchange of notes because his negotiations had presupposed the department's role. Repudiation of the loan after such heavy previous involvement, State Department officials agreed, would prove too embarrassing. The department unhappily acquiesced and approved the loan that its officers now privately viewed as offensive and exploitative.[26]

Even worse problems followed. Despite the State Department's request that the exchange of notes remain confidential, as they had technically pertained to a previous, less exploitative version of the loan contract, the brokerage firm selling the bonds, F. J. Lisman and Company, published a greatly exaggerated version of the State Department assurances. Lisman's public prospectus for the Salvadoran bonds claimed that the exchange of notes made any violation of bondholders' rights a "direct breach of covenant and treaty." The prospectus also plagiarized material from a book by Dana Munro and contained inaccuracies. State Department officials, furious at Lisman, had to respond to a flurry of criticism that resulted from the public's understandable confusion over the department's role. The prospectus, after all, asserted a treaty commitment even though Congress had never been consulted in any way. Munro wrote to Francis White of the Latin American Division, "We cannot well afford to permit the Department to be placed in a position of helping to advertise a loan of this character." Yet that was just what had happened.[27]

The Salvadoran loan negotiations revealed the central dilemma of dollar diplomacy in the early 1920s. Influential public opinion outside government and financial circles, both in the host country and domestically, opposed the overt involvement of the State Department in loans. In part, critics feared that any official guarantee might lead to military intervention; in addition, many held a profound distaste for government's cozy relationship with bankers, a relationship that often seemed to imply a public guarantee for private profits. Yet bankers and brokers could not sell the bonds of risky countries unless they could advertise some convincing security. Any mention of the U.S. government—playing any role—assisted bond sales. The "exchange of notes" accompanying the Salvadoran contract had been crucial in attracting bankers' support. In short, the State Department's dilemma involved minimizing conspicuous involvement while maximizing some kind of security for the loans its officials considered essential to the process of bringing "stability" to Central and South America.

A simultaneous controversy over a controlled loan for Bolivia further illustrated the difficulties of maintaining a legalistic public/private distinction in face of the reality of the cooperative effort implied by the strategy of dollar diplomacy. State Department officials, especially Munro (Kemmerer's neighbor and family friend), had worked with Equitable Trust Company on a controlled loan for Bolivia during 1921–22. The foreign trade adviser had stated that the project seemed satisfactory, and the State Department even had its minister in Bolivia urge the Bolivian president to sign the loan contract.[28]

The contract immediately created a storm of protest in Bolivia. The large $33 million loan provided a handsome profit for the bankers (a nine-point spread between the cost of the loan to the bankers and to the public), far exceeded the capacity of Bolivian revenues to pay, and placed the collection and administration of Bolivian revenues in the hands of a three-person Permanent Fiscal Commission controlled by United States bankers. Faced with outright domestic revolt, the Bolivian president backed off, declaring the loan unconstitutional and joining his opposition in condemning the bankers for taking advantage of his poor country.

As outcries against the Bolivian loan mounted throughout Latin America, the secretary of state asked the department's solicitor for a detailed study of the Bolivian loan. The solicitor reported that it placed an extremely heavy burden on Bolivia and also violated Bolivian law. He concluded "that, in the long run, it is to the disadvantage of the United States foreign banking institutions . . . to take advantage of the financial exigencies of Latin American countries by imposing heavy and unreasonable burdens upon them. That seems to have been done in the present case." As in the case of the Salvadoran loan, State Department officials kept the lid on this in-house condemnation and concluded that they should take no public action in support of Bolivia and against the contract that they had, after all, previously approved.[29]

The department's implicit support for the bankers' position in a loan that even the department privately conceded was outrageously exploitative drew heavy criticism in Latin America and in Congress and the press at home.[30] The embarrassing controversies raised by the State Department's relationship to controlled loans in both El Salvador and Bolivia dampened enthusiasm for such arrangements.

The dilemmas persisted. Kemmerer, Young, Munro, and many other postwar economic foreign policymakers believed that the extension of U.S. private bank credits could—and should—be used to force the kind of economic rehabilitation, supervised by North Americans, that seemed to them in the interests of the American government and of foreign nations. Yet how could the department follow, encourage, and ultimately approve loan negotiations that would introduce North American financial supervisors, while maintaining the fiction that they were "private" loans for which the government took no responsibility? And how could U.S. bankers and policymakers reap the supposed benefits of loan controls without risking a backlash of resentment? In short, how could a public/private distinction be maintained in face of the contrary reality of cooperative endeavors?

Professionalism

While contractual loan controls were proving troublesome in the case of El Salvador and Bolivia, a new adaptation in financial rehabilitation efforts began to emerge. The Peruvian and Colombian governments sought to establish "voluntary" relationships with U.S. professional advisers. These governments feared domestic opposition to formal supervisory arrangements under loan contracts, yet they realized that bankers would never negotiate without some sign of lessened risk. Employing North American experts in key advisory positions, even before a loan was extended, became a means of attracting capital while preserving national sovereignty from assault.

In 1921 President Augusto B. Leguía of Peru learned that Guaranty Trust Company was prepared to extend a loan to Peru, if the Peruvian government would approve someone nominated by the State Department as a collector of customs. Leguía thus requested that the State Department advance a name immediately, so the appointment would appear to be a "sovereign act." Arranging financial supervision prior to the loan, he informed the U.S. minister, would head off criticism by those who "are sensitive about sovereignty." The minister asked the State Department to appoint a man "of financial strength who can see into the future . . . to come into Peru and make the second Conquest."[31]

Secretary of State Hughes advanced the name of William Wilson Cumberland, the department's foreign trade adviser who, like Young, was a

former student and friend of Kemmerer. Guaranty Trust then informed the
assistant secretary of state that the company would be interested in a loan
only if Peru granted Cumberland broad powers. Consequently, when Peru
offered Cumberland the position of administrator of customs, he and the
bankers insisted that the job include more authority than the title implied.
Cumberland subsequently came to Peru with three American assistants and
with full authority to revise the system of revenue collection, to propose
changes in import and export duties, to control hiring, firing, and promotion
in the customs service, to be consulted in advance on all government
financial policy, and to become director of any future national bank. He did,
in fact, establish a central bank in Peru and served as its director until
1924.[32]

Despite Cumberland's presence, years of complicated negotiations with
various bankers produced no immediate loans for Peru. The frustrations of
his job convinced Cumberland that the only hope for Peru was the kind of
firm control, backed directly by the U.S. government, that had been
established in Nicaragua.[33] He gratefully left Peru in 1924 to become
financial adviser and general receiver for the Republic of Haiti, where his
power rested on U.S. military forces and on treaty obligations.

Colombia was more successful in using professional U.S. advisers to
attract loans. In loan negotiations between Colombia and Blair and Company,
the bankers expressed willingness to lend if Colombia would engage a
financial expert suggested by the Department of State. Before signing the
$5 million Colombian loan of 1922, the Colombian government therefore
requested a nomination from the secretary of state, who submitted
Kemmerer's name. Colombia hired a five-person financial mission, headed
by Kemmerer, to recommend financial reform. The Kemmerer commission
to Colombia in 1923 was the first of several similar missions; subsequent
ones visited Chile, Bolivia, Ecuador, Peru, and other nations outside the
hemisphere.[34]

The mission to Colombia proved highly successful. Kemmerer drew up
a set of comprehensive recommendations, covering money and banking,
public finance, taxation, and administration. The Colombian legislature
passed the commission's recommended laws in each of these areas, and two
of the mission's members stayed on as more permanent advisers, paid by the
government of Colombia. Kemmerer himself acquired a legendary image
when, in one weekend, he dramatically interrupted a run on Colombia's
banking system by opening the new central bank months earlier than scheduled. When Kemmerer returned to the United States and began extolling
Colombia's future under his reforms, bankers began flocking to Colombia
to extend credit, and Colombian bond prices rose.[35]

Colombia, by pursuing a professional relationship, rather than overt loan controls through either treaty or contract, seemed to have achieved a major success for everyone. The Colombian government found that money suddenly became easy to borrow; bankers found Colombian bonds easy to sell; Kemmerer found his services as a "money doctor" in great demand; the State Department applauded the spread of fiscal reform and the influx of U.S. economic power.

After 1923, then, financial advising and supervision increasingly came to be a professional arrangement that seemed thoroughly depoliticized and separated from public policy. U.S. bankers, brokers, and investors grew increasingly eager to lend money at the more profitable rates offered abroad, and that gradual change in U.S. capital markets also accelerated the trend toward the use of private advisers rather than State Department-mediated loan controls. As capital for foreign loans became more available, visible State Department involvement became less necessary as a prerequisite to U.S. foreign lending. The advisory missions continued to express public purposes; removing advising out of the realm of politics and into the realm of expertise suited the needs of all parties: host government, bankers, economists, and the State Department. The convergence of interest that led to the formation of such professional relationships deserves closer scrutiny.

Countries seeking loans viewed employment of American advisers as a means of attracting capital while avoiding politically unpopular loan controls. Opposition groups, who found it easy to attack financial advisers forced by American bankers or appointed by the State Department, had a more difficult time leveling charges of imperialism against someone, like Kemmerer, hired as an academic expert in international economics. Indeed, Kemmerer cultivated his image as a detached and disinterested man of science. His refusal to make statements to the local press during his stay in a host country, for example, endowed his mission with an aura of technical superiority, above the hullabaloo of public debate. His mission's long working hours—often twelve hours a day—impressed hosts with the professionals' seriousness and dedication. The staggeringly high fees Kemmerer charged reinforced notions about the great value of his advice and made his recommendations difficult to ignore or repudiate. Finally, Kemmerer's aloofness from the local U.S. embassy gave the impression that he was not an agent of governmental policies. Although large numbers of people within the "Kemmererized countries" (Colombia, Chile, Bolivia, and Ecuador) criticized his reforms in the economic hard times of the 1930s, his reputation was unassailable during the 1920s. Kemmerer and the associates he typically left behind did (except in Ecuador) open the way to substantial loans and better bond ratings.[36]

Bankers promoted Kemmerer commissions because bond buyers liked to see evidence of U.S.-directed fiscal reordering on loan prospectuses. A Kemmerer mission buoyed bond prices. After the Colombian mission, the banking house of Dillon and Read quickly arranged to put Kemmerer on a retainer for his advice, and until the end of the decade Dillon and Read encouraged him to take missions to countries in which they wished to invest or in which prices on bonds the house had issued were lagging. The relationship between Kemmerer and Dillon and Read was secret; it might have tarnished the professional, objective image that underlay Kemmerer's success.[37]

The State Department likewise supported the Kemmerer missions. In 1923, while Colombia was offering a model of the use of professional advisers to attract foreign capital, the State Department was trying to explain away its role in the embarrassing Salvadoran and Bolivian loans and was agonizing over how to devise controlled loans for Honduras and Guatemala. The reforms recommended by the Kemmerer missions were those the State Department favored. Kemmerer, after all, had close personal ties to many State Department officials and had been a mentor to the postwar policymakers who sought to promote rehabilitation and stability through U.S.-directed financial reform. The department was consequently pleased to see him develop a depoliticized approach to expanding American investment capital and influence in the hemisphere.[38]

After 1923 the trend toward the use of professional consultants, together with the new willingness of U.S. investors to place money internationally, allowed State Department officials to take a much more cautious, less activist, role in Western Hemisphere loans than they had assumed from 1919 to 1922. Under the General Loan Policy of 1922 bankers still had to submit foreign loan contracts in advance for State Department approval, but the department increasingly issued a formalized "no objection" response without the scrutiny or intricate involvement that had characterized the immediate post-World War I period. The deterioration in the quality of Latin American bonds after mid-decade thus corresponded to the decline in State Department oversight. Although in the early 1920s critics charged that the State Department was too heavily involved in passing on "private" lending, during the defaults of the 1930s Congress and the bondholding public assailed the department as having been too little involved in judging the soundness of loans.[39]

Finally, the Kemmerer commissions helped establish the new profession of foreign financial advising. Scholars who have studied the general process of professionalization stress that, to achieve its status, a profession must create a "market," design a "product" produced from consistent standards, establish a claim to "cognitive exclusiveness," assert claims to "scientific" validity, and develop some credentialing process. By all of these criteria, international financial advising became a "profession" under the influence of the Kemmerer commissions; Kemmerer and his coworkers did not go into foreign lands as colonial agents or as bankers' employees (even though the historical record clearly shows that government and bankers both supported and assisted them), but as "men of science" (a term Kemmerer often used to identify himself and his colleagues). The depoliticization and professionalization of financial advising, of course, paralleled a similar process in many areas of American life.[40]

Professionalization related structurally to other trends: the spread of anticolonial ideologies that challenged the right of some nations to assume control over others; the growth of American investment banking and mass marketing brokerage houses; the growth of specialized bureaucracies within the national state and the associated enlargement of foreign policy concerns to include economic and financial matters; and the rapid expansion of U.S. economic influence, as New York replaced London as the world's primary credit center. Professionalization of economic advising emerged as a logical structural component of such transformations. It was the ultimate corporativist marketplace replacement for colonial relationships.

Impact

This essay has focused on the changing forms and the overall structure of financial advising relationships. Professionalized advising proved more compatible with a marketplace mentality than did a paternalism based upon status. Only a few general observations can be offered here about the broad impact of advising—an important related topic. Foreign advisers—whether colonial agents or "independent" professionals—left ambiguous legacies. The consequences of their programs may seem "good" or "bad," depending upon one's vantage point within the domestic and world economic systems.

All the advisory structures—colonialism, treaty, "colonialism by contract," and professional consulting—yielded similar recommendations. Nearly all advisers sought to introduce gold-exchange currency reform managed by a central bank and to eliminate indirect taxation and boost receipts by instituting new sales, income, and real estate taxes. They also tried to increase government revenues by revising tariffs and rooting graft out of customshouses. In addition, advisers attempted to attract large U.S. loans to reorganize and refund the outstanding public debt, eliminating British bondholders. The loan programs were often tied to public works projects (contracted with U.S. firms) to build transportation infrastructure. Finally, American advisers usually recommended centralizing and streamlining budgetary processes by creating better auditing systems and a comptroller's office, or some equivalent. Their program generally paralleled the economic changes going on in the United States during this period and for the same reasons. The goal was to organize a flexible, yet rationalized, financial structure to make business possible on an ever-wider scale, with reduced risk.

Advisers believed, usually correctly, that such changes would bring potential benefits to host countries: lower interest rates on foreign loans, modern methods of accounting, greater efficiency in tax collection, formation of a national banking structure that facilitated exchange transactions, and valuable direct links to international bankers, traders, and direct investors. Such "benefits" had long-term consequences, for the domestic political economies of host countries and for their relationship to the global order.

The ultimate impact of advisers and of the increased international borrowing that they facilitated has been well summarized by Paul Drake, who has done the most thorough, multiarchival research on the Kemmerer commissions. Financial advisers, he concludes, helped bring "monetary stabilization [gold-exchange standard] . . . and the growth of domestic urban capitalism, the central state, and dependence on foreign trade and capital, ever more emanating from the United States." Advisers assumed that such integration into, and dependence upon, the international trading and financial system would ultimately bring political, economic, and social stability. The legacy of this peripheral capitalism, however, has been much more ambiguous, as scholarship on dependency has shown.[41]

The various forms of supervision had other important results. In some cases, for example, the presence of North American advisers provided the illusion of investment security, rather than its substance. Ironically, their presence may have contributed to the egregious overborrowing that made the international financial structure of the 1920s increasingly unsound. When Kemmerer came back from Bolivia in 1927, for example, he said, in private, that the country was dangerously overextended and recommended no further extension of credit. Yet the mere fact that he had visited Bolivia, and supposedly worked his economic magic there, boosted Bolivian bond prices and provided the basis for another large loan the country could ill afford.[42] Banks in the 1920s were not carrying the loans they made on their own books but brokering them to the general public: the illusion of security (provided, say, by a U.S. supervisor or commission) could be more important than any productive reality when highlighted to potential buyers in a prospectus.[43]

The conspicuous presence of a foreign adviser with control over revenue collection and, perhaps, with power over expenditures contributed to a nationalistic backlash. During the 1920s in Latin America coalitions of urban labor, industrial, and military groups saw U.S. loans and advisers as means to erode the power of traditional agriculture-based elites and to boost their own power bases while modernizing their countries. In the early 1930s, when declining exports, contracting capital markets, and bloated foreign indebtedness made servicing debts impossible, other nationalistic voices began to blame North American advisers and bankers for the trouble. They found domestic political support for massive default. Even in the absence of formal imperial structures, in debtor countries U.S. advisers came to be identified with colonialist dependency. North Americans may have seen their advice as apolitical, professional, and objective science. But in the 1930s, many Latin Americans believed that they had been victimized and assailed the U.S. supervisors, bankers, and government along with the domestic politicians who had promoted, and often personally benefited from, public indebtedness.Whether external dependence was embodied in colonial political arrangements or in marketplace contracts with bankers or consultants, the backlash of nationalism and charges against Yankee imperialism grew. The more subtle forms of structural dependence were less apparent to North Americans because responsibility and accountability had been removed from the political process, but they were apparent within dependent countries whose citizens felt themselves, one way or another, expected to follow the recommendations of foreigners on vital economic issues.

No simple formulation captures the legacy of financial advisers. Whether colonial agents or professional consultants, financial advisers worked with groups in host countries who saw their presence as enriching and modernizing. The advisers were attacked by those who resented or stood to lose from such foreign intrusion. If there was positive change in some sectors, in others structural dependency proved an affliction. To conclude that U.S. hegemony was beneficial or exploitative is impossible without detailed answers to questions such as "when" and "for whom." This essay, then, has sought less to join debate over the impact of colonialism or over dependency than to illuminate a broad process of structural change in the process and organization of hegemonic dominance flowing from the United States.

From 1898 to 1929, U.S. policymakers displayed ingenuity in adapting to the growing opposition—both in the United States and in Latin America—to visible imposition of financial controls. Throughout, however, they pursued a consistent goal: North Americans, through whatever form seemed most appropriate, should order the financial affairs of "backward" states and bring them into "modern," more globally integrated, economic structures. They never doubted that they had a paternalistic duty, especially toward other nations in the Western Hemisphere. Domestically and internationally, however, colonialism and political dependence were under increasing attack. The dialectic between a colonialist mentality and new notions of egalitarianism among states produced increasingly sophisticated structures that legitimized dependency relationships by moving them outside the supposed realm of politics and into the realms of law and professional expertise. Congressional and public involvement shrank as financial groups, working closely with the executive branch, set the material and ideological frameworks of international relationships. Loan contracts and professional consultant arrangements tended to preserve paternalism and hierarchy, but within processes that were styled as objective, scientific, apolitical, and mutually beneficial.

The reforms pursued by most types of advisers were similar, and most of the people who pursued careers in the new profession of financial advising held several types of appointments and had close professional links with one another. Kemmerer's own career, for example, displayed the transition from colonial administrator to professional consultant supported by bankers and governments. America's version of a colonial service, in the 1920s, comprised a growing cadre of private consultants who looked largely to Kemmerer as their intellectual mentor. Their efforts were enforced not by U.S. troops and law, but by an international order in which poor nations' desires to attract foreign capital could create situations somewhat analogous to debt peonage or to the "freedom of choice" in a company town.

Financial advising relationships in the Western Hemisphere in the early twentieth century can be viewed as a series of experiments in how emerging forms and trends—anticolonialism, corporativism, bureaucratization, economic expansionism, and professionalization—would fit together. Within the great transformation of the world economy at the turn of the century, there was a little-recognized historical connection that extended from highly "public" colonialism, to "private" contract law, to "private" professional relationships. The basic conception of an international system of hierarchically ordered states did not change during the early twentieth century, but the manner in which hegemonic relationships were constructed, conceptualized, and legitimated—in terms of apolitical marketplace contracts instead of colonial status—reflected an important paradigm shift between 1898 and 1930.

Notes

1. Merle Curti and Kendall Birr, *Prelude to Point Four: American Technical Missions Overseas, 1838–1938* (1954; reprint, Westport, 1978), is the only attempt at an overall history of American foreign advising.

2. For data on loans, see Cleona Lewis, *America's Stake in International Investments* (Washington, 1938), 605, 632–53; Max Winkler, *Investments of United States Capital in Latin America* (Boston, 1928); Robert W. Dunn, *American Foreign Investments* (New York, 1926); John Madden, Marcus Nadler, and Harry C. Suavin,

America's Experience as a Creditor Nation (New York, 1937), 50–104, 204–18; and, especially, –.51 file for each country, Decimal File, Records of the Department of State, RG 59 (National Archives). On American lending and its connection to foreign policy in Latin America, see Herbert Feis, *The Diplomacy of the Dollar: First Era, 1919–1932* (Baltimore, 1950); Hogan, *Informal Entente*, 80–82, 100–101; Joseph Tulchin, *The Aftermath of War: World War I and U.S. Policy toward Latin America* (New York, 1971), 155–205; Carl Parrini, *Heir to Empire: United States Economic Diplomacy, 1916–1923* (Pittsburgh, 1969); Joan Hoff Wilson, *American Business and Foreign Policy* (Lexington, Ky., 1971), 104, 105, 113, 118, 120, 168, 171.

3. J. H. Hollander, "The Finances of Porto Rico," *Political Science Quarterly*, 16 (Dec. 1901), 553–81; Shirley Jenkins, *American Economic Policy toward the Philippines* (Palo Alto, 1954), 111–13; Peter W. Stanley, *A Nation in the Making: The Philippines and the United States, 1899–1921* (Cambridge, Mass., 1974), 93, 119–22, 142–43, 232–48.

4. Livingston, *Origins of the Federal Reserve System*, examines the domestic agenda (gold standard and centralized banking) of these economists and their business allies. For fuller sketches of these men, see *ibid.*, 37–39, 53, 61, 76–78, 114–15, 135–37, 147–48, 198–200; and Emily S. Rosenberg, "Foundations of United States International Financial Power: Gold Standard Diplomacy, 1900–1905," *Business History Review*, 59 (Summer 1985), 169–202. On Charles Conant, see also David Healy, *United States Expansionism: The Imperialist Urge in the 1890s* (Madison, 1970), 194–209.

5. On the commission and the rise of the profession of foreign financial advising, see Rosenberg, "Foundations of United States International Financial Power," 169–202.

6. The best study of the development of investment banking is Vincent Carosso, *Investment Banking in America: A History* (Cambridge, Mass., 1970), see esp. 56–100. Alfred D. Chandler, Jr., *The Visible Hand: The Managerial Revolution in American Business* (Cambridge, Mass., 1977), esp. 155, 183–87; and Karl Erich Born, *International Banking in the 19th and 20th Centuries*, trans. Volker R. Berghahn (New York, 1983), esp. 92–99, also provide essential background.

7. Dana G. Munro, *Intervention and Dollar Diplomacy in the Caribbean, 1900–1921* (Princeton, 1964), 90–125; Cyrus Adler, *Jacob H. Schiff, His Life and Letters* (2 vols., New York, 1928), I, 208–11; Jacob Hollander, "The Readjustment of San Domingo's Finances," *Quarterly Journal of Economics*, 21 (May 1906), 405–26; *Foreign Relations of the United States, 1907* (Washington, 1910), 306–25.

8. Assistant Secretary of State to Alvey A. Adee, Jan. 13, 1911, 815.51/207, Records of the Department of State. Walter V. Scholes and Marie V. Scholes, *The Foreign Policies of the Taft Administration* (Columbia, 1970), provides an overview. For details on the receivership plans for Nicaragua, Honduras, Guatemala, and Liberia, see Munro, *Intervention and Dollar Diplomacy*, 90–125, 192–203, 239–45; Emily S. Rosenberg, "The Invisible Protectorate: The United States, Liberia, and the Evolution of Neocolonialism, 1909–40," *Diplomatic History*, 9 (Summer 1985), 191–214; and *Foreign Relations of the United States, 1912* (Washington, 1919), 506–11, 549–95, 1071–1132, 667–700. A fuller record is contained in the –.51 Decimal File for each country for the years 1911–1912, Records of the Department of State.

Bankers' interest in loans that had State Department support was evident in 1910, when officials of Speyer and Company charged the State Department with

favoritism in its selection of J. P. Morgan as the banker for the Honduras loan/
receivership plan and vented their anger directly to President Taft. The Secretary of
State then formally assured all bankers that in the future all loan proposals would be
treated impartially. See internal memos from March–Nov. 1910, 815.51/96, 97, 98,
151, 222, and Feb.–May 1911, 817.51/104, 128, *ibid.*

9. Munro, *Intervention and Dollar Diplomacy*, 90–125, 192–203, 239–45.

10. William Kammen, *A Search for Stability: United States Diplomacy toward
Nicaragua* (Notre Dame, 1968); and Hans Schmidt, *The United States Occupation
of Haiti, 1915–1934* (New Brunswick, 1971), are the best general histories of
American involvement. For the texts of treaties and related documents, see
Arthur C. Millspaugh, *Haiti under American Control, 1915–1920* (Boston, 1931),
211–15; and Isaac J. Cox, *Nicaragua and the United States, 1909–1927* (Boston,
1931), 827–40.

11. A formal position designated "Financial Adviser" and filled by an American began in 1919 in Panama, and a similar one in 1920 in Cuba. William Jennings
Price to Frank Polk, Feb. 6, 1919, *Foreign Relations of the United States, 1919* (2
vols., Washington, 1934), II, 688; Norman Davis to Boaz Long, Dec. 10, 1920,
Foreign Relations of the United States, 1920 (3 vols., Washington, 1935–1936), II,
49.

12. For a short description of the advisory power in each country, see Chester
Lloyd Jones, "Loan Controls in the Caribbean," *Hispanic American Historical
Review*, 14 (May 1934), 141–62. This extension of power was often accompanied
by brutal military occupation; see Richard D. Challener, *Admirals, Generals, and
American Foreign Policy, 1898–1914* (Princeton, 1973), 288–315, 332–44; and
Lester D. Langley, *The Banana Wars: An Inner History of American Empire,
1900–43* (Lexington, Ky., 1983). For an interesting discussion of the historical
evolution of the meaning of the term *imperialism*, see Norman Etherington, *Theories
of Imperialism: War, Conquest and Capital* (Totowa, 1984). We have relied on
Etherington's definitions of and discussions between the terms *imperialism* and
structural dependency, ibid., 278.

13. The classic formulation may be found in Sir Henry Maine, *Ancient Law:
Its Connection with the Early History of Society, and Its Relation to Modern Ideas*
(New York, 1888), 164–65.

14. Morton J. Horwitz, "The History of the Public/Private Distinction,"
University of Pennsylvania Law Review, 130 (June 1982), 1423–28.

15. Robert Gordon, "Legal Thought and Legal Practice in the Age of American Enterprise, 1870–1920," in *Professions and Professional Ideologies in America*,
ed. Gerald L. Geinson (Chapel Hill, 1983), 70–110, esp. 110. See also Clare
Dalton, "Deconstructing Contract Doctrine," *Yale Law Journal*, 94 (April 1985),
997–1114. For an example of how the "facts" and doctrines of early twentieth-
century American law helped to mask power politics in Central America, see
John T. Noonan, Jr., *Persons and Masks of the Law* (New York, 1976), 65–110.

The traditional liberal argument holds that contracts by definition involve
consent on both sides and must therefore be mutually advantageous. Yet marketplace
"choice" is not so simple. What conditions impinge to create what range of choices
available to whom? How meaningful is the term *freedom* when power is grossly
unequal? For thoughtful explorations of the problems of "choice" and "consent,"
which we would extend to the realm of international affairs, see Robin West,
"Authority, Autonomy, and Choice: The Role of Consent in the Moral and Political

Visions of Franz Kafka and Richard Posner," *Harvard Law Review*, 99 (Dec. 1985), 384–428; and Robin West, "Submission, Choice, and Ethics: A Rejoinder to Judge Posner," *Harvard Law Review*, 99 (May 1986), 1449–56.

16. For the texts of the 1911 loan and the subsequent Bryan-Chamorro Treaty (1914) and Financial Plan of 1917, see Cox, *Nicaragua and the United States*, 819, 827, 841. See also Harold N. Denny, *Dollars for Bullets* (New York, 1929), 9–11, 143–70.

17. On loans for China, see Scholes and Scholes, *Foreign Policies of the Taft Administration*, 196–246; and Jerry Israel, *Progressivism and the Open Door: America and China, 1905–1921* (Pittsburgh, 1971), esp. 55–56, 97–99, 153–54. On Mexico, see Robert F. Smith, "The Formation and Development of the International Bankers Committee on Mexico," *Journal of Economic History*, 23 (Dec. 1963), 574–86; on Liberia, see Rosenberg, "Invisible Protectorate," 191–214.

18. Boaz Long to Secretary of State Robert Lansing, Feb. 16, 1918, 711.13/55, Records of the Department of State.

19. Dana Munro to Sumner Welles, Feb. 28, 1922, 711.13/59, *ibid.* See the –.51 Decimal File for every country in Central America and northern South America. Only the southern countries of South America—Argentina, Brazil, Chile, Paraguay, and Uruguay—were not considered candidates for a loan/advisory arrangement.

20. On Kemmerer's views and activities, see Edwin W. Kemmerer, *Modern Currency Reforms* (New York, 1916); Edwin W. Kemmerer, "Economic Advisory Work for Governments," *American Economic Review*, 17 (March 1927), 1–12; Robert N. Seidel, "American Reformers Abroad: The Kemmerer Missions in South America, 1923–1931," *Journal of Economic History*, 32 (June 1972), 520–45; Bruce Dalgaard, "E. W. Kemmerer: The Origins and Impact of the 'Money Doctor's' Monetary Economics," in *Variations in Business and Economic History: Essays in Honor of Donald L. Kemmerer*, ed. Bruce Dalgaard and Richard Vedder (Greenwich, Conn., 1982), 31–44. His voluminous papers are invaluable. Edwin W. Kemmerer Papers (Seeley G. Mudd Library, Princeton University).

21. *Foreign Relations of the United States, 1919*, II, 283.

For a detailed account of Kemmerer and Guatemala, see Donald L. Kemmerer and Bruce R. Dalgaard, "Inflation, Intrigue and Monetary Reform in Guatemala, 1919–1926," *Historian*, 46 (Nov. 1983), 21–38. The State Department's heavy involvement in urging and even helping formulate the loan contract is illustrated especially in documents during May 1922, 814.51/371N94, Records of the Department of State.

22. Arthur N. Young, "Memo on the State of Financial Reforms in Honduras," May 13, 1921, 815.51/428, Records of the Department of State; Young, "Financial Reform in Honduras," Aug. 1921, 815.51/442, *ibid.*

23. Memo from the Office of the Economic Advisor, July 21, 1922, 815.51/494, *ibid.*; Young to Fred W. Dearing, Feb. 6, 1922, 815.51/495, *ibid.*

24. Minister of Foreign Affairs Juan Francisco Paredes to Secretary of State Charles Evans Hughes, Oct. 20, 1921, 816.51/176, *ibid.*

25. Hughes to Paredes, Feb. 28, 1922, 816.51/176, *ibid.* "El Salvador Bonds," file 3, box 33, Lester H. Woolsey Papers (Manuscript Division, Library of Congress), shows the extent to which Woolsey personally profited from the insider information he received as Minor Keith's lawyer and intermediary with the State Department. Knowing of the State Department's exchange of notes, before it became public, and understanding that the agreement would facilitate a new loan refunding old British

bonds at high rates, Woolsey bought up old bonds at low prices and exchanged them after the loan went through. Keith profited in like manner. See Munro to Francis White, Dec. 13, 1922, 816.51/237, Records of the Department of State.

26. See internal memos, Nov. 1922–Jan. 1923, 816.51/225, 237, 239, 243, 247, 255, 259, Records of the Department of State. See esp. Munro to White, Dec. 13, 1922, 816.51/237, *ibid.*; and memo of conversation between Hughes and Woolsey, Dec. 21, 1922, 816.51/259, *ibid.*

27. Regarding the prospectus and F. J. Lisman and Company's advertising, see State Department memos and correspondence with Lester Woolsey and Lisman during 1923, esp. Assistant Secretary of State Leland Harrison to Lisman, Oct. 23, 1923, 816.51/311, *ibid.*, and various other memos in 816.51/254, 258, 261, 301, 309, and 311, *ibid.* Many documents in 816.51/318–41 contain inquiries and complaints about the State Department's position. See, for example, the *Nation* managing editor to Hughes, Oct. 18, 1923, 816.51/318, *ibid.*; and Munro to White, Sept. 18, 1923, 816.51/309, *ibid.*

28. Memo from Solicitor Richard W. Flournoy, Jr., March 31, 1923, 824.51/261, *ibid.*; Memo of Foreign Trade Advisor Young, May 26, 1922, 824.51/129, *ibid.*

29. Memo from Solicitor, June 9, 1922, 824.51/199, *ibid.* See internal memos during June 1922, 824.51/199, *ibid.*; and Memo from Solicitor, March 31, 1923, 824.51/261, *ibid.*

30. Chargé W. Roswell Barker to Secretary of State Hughes, April 1, 1925, 824.51/307, *ibid.* For a highly critical contemporary account of this loan, including its text, see Margaret Marsh, *The Bankers in Bolivia* (New York, 1928), 94–121, 156–57. Other classic contemporary critical studies of such involvements are Scott Nearing and Joseph Freeman, *Dollar Diplomacy: A Study in American Imperialism* (New York, 1925); and Samuel Guy Inman, "Imperialistic America," *Atlantic Monthly*, 134 (July 1924), 107–16.

31. Leguía's remarks are reported in Minister William E. Gonzales to Secretary Hughes, June 7, 1921, 823.51/179, Records of the Department of State; and Gonzales to Hughes, May 16, 1921, 823.51/180, *ibid.*

32. Hughes to Gonzales, Sept. 7, 1921, 823.51/185, *ibid.*; J. R. Swan (of Guaranty Trust) to Undersecretary of State Henry Fletcher, Sept. 22, 1921, 823.51/194, *ibid.*; William Wilson Cumberland to Hughes, Oct. 31, 1921, 823.51/196, *ibid.* James C. Carey, *Peru and the United States, 1900–1962* (Notre Dame, 1964), 67–73.

33. Chargé F. A. Sterling to Secretary Hughes, Oct. 26, 1922, 832.51/276, Records of the Department of State; Cumberland to Assistant Secretary of State Leland Harrison, Nov. 7, 1922, 823.51/287, *ibid.*

34. For detailed treatments of the operation and effect of these missions, see, Kemmerer, "Economic Advisory Work for Governments"; Seidel, "American Reformers Abroad"; and Dalgaard, "E. W. Kemmerer."

35. Paul Drake, "The Origins of United States Economic Supremacy in South America: Colombia's Dance of the Millions, 1932–33" (manuscript in Drake's possession, University of California at San Diego).

36. Kemmerer, "Economic Advisory Work for Governments," 1–12, describes his method of operation. This and subsequent discussion of Kemmerer are also based on a thorough reading of the extensive Kemmerer Papers.

37. From 1924 to 1929 Kemmerer received three thousand dollars per year from Dillon and Read. Kemmerer to Robert O. Hayward (of Dillon and Read),

Oct. 13, 1923, Letters: April 1–June 10, 1925, Kemmerer Papers; Kemmerer to Hayward, Nov. 7, 1923, Letters: July 1924 to April 1925, *ibid.*; Hayward to Kemmerer, Jan. 3, 1924, Feb. 24, 1925, *ibid.*; Hayward to Kemmerer, Nov. 27, 1925, Chile, 1926: Letters, *ibid.*; Kemmerer to Dean Mathey (of Dillon and Read), Nov. 9, 1929, China: Correspondence, *ibid.* Kemmerer stipulated to the bankers that his obligation to them would terminate whenever he was in the employ of a foreign government and for sixty days thereafter. Kemmerer to Hayward, Nov. 7, 1923, Letters: July 1924 to April 1925, *ibid.* But he did often consult with the bankers before, after, and sometimes during his various missions. See his correspondence with Hayward and Mathey (both personal friends) during this period filed under "H" and "M" respectively in each letter box. And see, for example, Edwin W. Kemmerer Diary, Oct. 27, 1927, Nov. 17, 1927 (regarding Ecuador), April 5, 1928, Sept. 11, 1928 (Bolivia), Kemmerer Papers.

38. State Department files and Kemmerer's diaries indicate that the department supported his missions and that Kemmerer often met with department officials, especially with his close friends Arthur Young and Dana Munro. See, for example, Kemmerer Diary, Dec. 13, 1926 (meeting with Munro); Oct. 10, 1924 (conference and ball game with Young).

39. The –.51 files, Records of the Department of State, for any of the countries discussed above show the deterioration. See also Ilse Mintz, *Deterioration in the Quality of Foreign Bonds Issued in the United States, 1920–1930* (New York, 1951); and Max Winkler, *Foreign Bonds: An Autopsy* (Philadelphia, 1933), esp. 47–81. U.S. Congress, Senate, Committee on Finance, *Sale of Foreign Bonds or Securities in the United States*, 72 Cong., 1 sess. (Washington, 1931–1932), reflects attacks on the department's lax supervision of bonds.

40. See Larson, *Rise of Professionalism*, 14–15. On the professionalization of the foreign service, see especially Robert Schulzinger, *The Making of the Diplomatic Mind: The Training, Outlook, and Style of United States Foreign Service Officers, 1908–1931* (Middletown, Conn., 1975); and Richard H. Werking, *The Master Architect: Building the United States Foreign Service, 1890–1913* (Lexington, Ky., 1977).

41. Paul Drake, "Eclipse of the Chilean 'Papeleros,' 1925–32" (in Drake's possession), 1, 6.

There is an immense literature on dependency and its consequences. Classic formulations are Fernando Henrique Cardoso and Enzo Faletto, *Dependency and Development in Latin America* (Berkeley, 1979); Andre Gunder Frank, *Capitalism and Underdevelopment in Latin America* (New York, 1969); and Celso Furtado, *Economic Development of Latin America* (Cambridge, Eng., 1977). These works have been accompanied by two decades of discussion, debate, and refinement. See, for a sampling of views, Heraldo Muñoz, ed., *From Dependency to Development* (Boulder, 1981).

42. Committee on Finance, *Sale of Foreign Bonds*, 724–30, 2110–12. Compare Kemmerer's recommendation regarding Bolivia's credit potential in "Report on Public Credit," Bolivia, box 66: Public Credit, Kemmerer Papers; and Dillon and Read's loan prospectus, *ibid.*

43. Winkler, *Foreign Bonds*, 54–133, details the misleading tactics used by banks to sell foreign bonds in the late 1920s.

II

Privatization and Kemmerer

As armed colonialism became increasingly unpopular both at home and abroad, U.S. administrations wanted to reduce the economic and political costs of direct intervention and imperialism. Therefore, the U.S. and Latin American governments came to prefer financial intervention by private experts. Professor Edwin W. Kemmerer of Princeton University set the mold for these consultants.

Historian Robert N. Seidel provides a pithy summary of Kemmerer's missions to South America. Stressing the delicate interconnections among public and private, domestic and foreign actors, interests, and policies, Seidel argues that both the Kemmerer missions and general U.S. foreign policy in the 1920s were outgrowths of the Progressive Era and its beliefs in science, experts, technology, and reform. Seidel explains the involvement of money doctors in procuring not only outside loans but also the recognition of foreign governments. Once again, economic advisers could not escape the political entanglements surrounding their work.

In contrast with Seidel's emphasis on political history, Barry Eichengreen, an economist, focuses on the economic contents and consequences of Kemmerer's recommendations. He notes striking similarities and differences with the IMF, arguing that both the Kemmerer missions and the IMF, by sending "market signals" to investors, significantly increased foreign lending to the host countries.

Combining political and economic approaches, Albert O. Hirschman offers a classic account of "reformmongering" by international advisers. Although he emphasizes the Kemmerer mission in the 1920s, he shows that the history of privately contracted money doctors in Chile went back to the 1850s and continued to the 1950s, and he unveils remarkable continuities in their operations over that century. Even when foreign money doctors were absent, their formulas continued to be applied by their zealous local apostles, who became "more royalist than the king." By observing that such imported policy prescriptions encountered increasing resistance and resentment in the 1950s, Hirschman's analysis provides a bridge to the next section, which examines the International Monetary Fund.

5 Robert N. Seidel ◆ American Reformers Abroad: The Kemmerer Missions in South America, 1923–1931

To be an expert was to assume a position of special significance in public life during and following the Progressive Era in America. To be trained in scientific principles of medicine, sociology, public administration, or economics was to be prepared to develop the opportunities and promises of American life and to reform those institutions and ideas that hindered progress. Some attention has been drawn to the limited use by government of professional academic economists starting in the early years of the twentieth century.[1] But the work of American economists as advisers has generally been neglected, especially in relation to the study of American foreign relations.[2] Focusing upon the work of Edwin W. Kemmerer in the five Andean countries of South America between 1923 and 1931, this article is an attempt to indicate the possibilities for fruitful research into various dimensions of foreign economic advising.

A study of this nature may illustrate some characteristics of American economic foreign policy during the 1920s. First, it can show how domestic and foreign interests utilized a Progressive spirit of reform and a belief in the efficacy of disinterested public service. Certainly the effectiveness of reforms was compromised by the base political and economic considerations that many Progressives and experts abhorred. Second, this study can illustrate the formal and informal connections between public and private, domestic and foreign, interests. Financial experts were generally employed privately by the foreign governments. However, the work of the experts was often a factor in public policy, as in carrying out the Thomson-Urrutia Treaty between Colombia and the United States. It was also involved in questions of American recognition of de facto but unconstitutional regimes such as in the case of Ecuador in 1927 and in the determination by the United States that it had "no objection" to certain private American loans to foreigners. Similarly, the extension of major American loans to Latin American governments was at times dependent upon the institution of reforms recommended or supervised by experts. Third, financial advisers (especially the Kemmerer missions) were a necessary part of a two-fold economic purpose: the stabilization of national currencies, banking systems, and economies, and the international extension of North American institutions, trade, and finance. Although politics and economics cannot be neatly separated, this

From the *Journal of Economic History* 32, no. 1 (March 1972): 520–45. Reprinted by permission of Cambridge University Press.

paper emphasizes the political aspects of the financial advisory missions. The detailed economic policies that Kemmerer advanced and the results of these policies must necessarily be discussed in a separate essay.

I

Edwin Walter Kemmerer, who was to earn a reputation as an "international money doctor," began his eventful career in a post outside the United States. Having received a Ph.D. in 1903 from Cornell University, Kemmerer served as financial adviser to the United States Philippine Commission (1903) and as chief of the division of currency of the treasury of the Philippine Islands (1904–1906). He had been a student of Jeremiah W. Jenks, who had helped reform the currencies of Mexico, China, and the Philippines, and who had recommended Kemmerer for duty in the Philippines.[3] Later Kemmerer acted as financial adviser to the governments of Mexico (1917) and Guatemala (1919, 1924) and headed financial commissions to Colombia (1923, 1930), Chile (1925), Poland (1926), Ecuador (1926–27), Bolivia (1927), China (1929), and Peru (1931). He had been a principal member of the well-known Kemmerer-Vissering Gold Inquiry Commission to the Union of South Africa (1924–25), was an expert on currency and banking to the Dawes Commission (1925), and was cochairman of a commission to make an economic survey of Turkey (1934). An authority on the U.S. Federal Reserve System, he had prepared one of the significant studies for use by the National Monetary Commission (1910–11). He consistently advocated and defended the establishment of an American central bank, holding views similar to those of the bank's major promotors, such as Paul M. Warburg. His book, *The ABC of the Federal Reserve System*, was revised and reprinted numerous times.[4] Throughout his career, Kemmerer maintained an academic position, holding a major post in economics and finance at Princeton University from 1912.

Kemmerer's *Modern Currency Reforms* contains several themes that help identify the economist as being in tune with the Progressive reformism of his time. In explaining the adoption of gold exchange standards in India, Puerto Rico, the Philippines, the Straits Settlements, and Mexico, the author displayed his familiarity with and concern for properly conducted major reforms of currency. Kemmerer understood the necessity of making these reforms compatible not only with domestic conditions but also with world prices, the supply of gold, and exchange rates. He hoped that his book would "throw some light on fundamental principles" and, foreshadowing his later efforts, thus be of value to countries of Asia and Latin America "which are expected soon to undertake thoroughgoing reforms of their currency systems." Kemmerer's reformist sympathies stand out in his criticism of the introduction of U.S. currency into Puerto Rico. Kemmerer was convinced that the rate and manner of making the exchange of old for new currency in the country hurt debtors and favored large merchants and bankers. This he felt unfortunate and disadvantageous, for "the debtors were the more productive classes."[5] Kemmerer had shown similar concern for the status of workers when, in 1915, he had endorsed minimum wage legislation in New York on the basis that imperfect competition made it impossible for some groups to obtain a fair wage or to have sufficient bargaining power.[6]

Kemmerer was a devout practitioner of the gold standard and its variants. He maintained, even through the 1930s, his conviction that the discipline of gold was essential to proper regulation of currency and monetary policy.[7] An international gold standard was the subject of Kemmerer's address before the Pan-American Scientific Congress, which met in Washington during December, 1915 to January, 1916. In his talk, the economist outlined a "purely tentative plan" for a "Pan-American monetary unit." He argued that historical precedents urged its acceptance; that it would promote international trade, finance, friendship, travel, and flows of information; and that the "present . . . is an exceptionally opportune time for Pan-American action" on "monetary unity" since "economic obstacles to the adoption are much weaker" than they ever had been.[8] Kemmerer, despairing of a monetary unit that would include European currencies, proposed that all Western Hemisphere currencies, including that of Canada, be reestablished on the basis of the U.S. gold dollar.[9]

For its time, this was not an unreasonable proposal, since the necessary adjustments would not have been severe. Within a few years, however, the situation would be changed entirely. By 1920 all Latin America was off the gold standard, currencies were often inconvertible, and the exchange values of most currencies had fallen. In 1921, Chile's currency was barely 60 percent of its prewar parity exchange value in terms of dollars, the world's most stable currency. The values of the currencies of other countries in similar terms were: Colombia, about 80 percent; Bolivia, 60 percent; and Peru, 75 percent. Chile, plagued by persistent inflation, had been following inflationary policies that included rather indiscriminate issuing of currency and government borrowing. This borrowing was not carried on to cover budget deficits but to loan money to dominant agricultural interests. The promise of monetary reform in 1920, symbolized by the rise to power of Arturo Alessandri, was not fulfilled until 1925, when a Kemmerer mission was invited to Chile.[10] Ecuador, meanwhile, had engaged in a costly official support of the foreign exchange rate, since unofficially its currency could be obtained at a 20 percent discount in the street and then sold to the government at a profit. In short, what the Latin American countries needed most was a remedy to financial and economic instability that would be appropriate to the needs of each country. Hemispheric monetary unity would have to await the restoration of the gold standard and the institution of central banking and governmental reforms that could enforce monetary responsibility and stable currencies.

Professor Kemmerer emphasized the connection between trade, foreign investment, and the world economy. In an article on "The Theory of Foreign Investments," Kemmerer noted the "internationally political" aspects of foreign investment, implicitly criticizing instances where a government "uses private investments . . . as an excuse for political usurpation." Then, having dealt with the monetary and social differences between foreign and domestic investment and the way in which capital reaches the foreign field, he concluded: "Trade follows the investment, and the flow of investment capital together with the return flow of investment profits are substantial items in the foreign trade of an economically new country."[11]

Because of his thorough understanding of the intimate relationship between foreign investment and international trade, and his established expertise in currency and banking reform, Kemmerer's services would soon be much in demand. His acceptance of an invitation to provide financial counsel would be sufficient to improve prospects for a country's economic future and would seem tantamount to financial and economic reform itself. By 1926, Kemmerer's reputation was firmly established. The *New York Times* stated the case for the American economic consulting doctor in a statement that implied benevolence and disinterested intelligence to be the strong points of experts. The need for foreign advisers, the newspaper noted editorially, was due to:

> constant occurrence of a seemingly hopeless deadlock in plans of domestic legislators, sometimes due to political antagonisms, often to jealousy of special interests, always to mutual distrust. It seems to be the thought that this difficulty might be mitigated through recourse to specialists, with no banking or governmental affiliations, whose recommendations would be based purely on economic study and experience. . . . [The] systematic recourse of other depreciated-money States to the best international advice is one sign of promise for the world's emergence from the fiscal chaos in which the war plunged it. It proves at least that all nations are now recognizing the necessity of speedy return to the gold standard and international stability.[12]

While incorrect in implying that the specialists had "no banking or government affiliations," the *New York Times* had accurately identified an important aspect of the international context of the 1920s, a context that is crucial for a study of financial advisers for foreign governments. Two conferences, one at Brussels in 1920 and the other at Genoa in 1922, recommended measures to restore economic and financial stability to the world. They prescribed responsible government finance, balanced budgets, the freeing of central banks of issue from political controls, control of inflation, and a common standard of value based on a reestablished gold standard. The conference at Genoa resolved that cooperating central banks supervise the return to gold and that central banks be set up where they did not exist.[13] Both Kemmerer and Frank Tamagna, a current student of Latin American central banking, identified these conferences as a source of impetus for the institution of central banks in Latin America. Kemmerer's work in each of the South American countries he advised included the establishment of a central bank of issue and rediscount, with a currency based on the gold-exchange standard.[14]

But the significance of American financial advisers in American foreign relations is emphasized by three additional factors. First, there was the presistent American tendency to seek areas for economic and commercial expansion. A second idea, prevalent at the time, tied visions of a liberal world economy to international peace and understanding as well as to prosperity and the efficient use of resources. The third factor is perhaps the most important in understanding specifically the Kemmerer missions to South America. This was the altered position of the United States in relation to the countries of Europe, and especially England. The United States had become a major international creditor by the end of the war. America's status was enhanced by the fact that the costs of war and reconstruction inhibited the development of European investment and commerce in the rest of the world. A good example of this is the five-country area visited by Kemmerer in South America, where the majority of foreign interests were British and American. In 1913 British investments in this region were $531.5 million; American investments in the same area were $72 million. By 1929, British investments had increased by 13.6 percent while American investments had increased by 1241 percent, to exceed the British figure by over $360 million. This reversal was almost as startling as a similar one in Venezuela, where explorations for oil stimulated fantastic increases in both British and United States investments.[15] The position of the United States was perhaps best summarized by the influential financier Paul M. Warburg in a report to the president in 1921:

> My own belief is that capital in the old world will find so vast a field in work of reconstruction and colonization in "darkest Europe" that it will not be able to devote itself as liberally to the development of the countries of this hemisphere as it did in the past. The three Americas will, therefore, be drawn together in a commercial and financial union of growing strength and intimacy.[16]

The work of the Kemmerer missions is a good example of the participation of American financial experts in what Warburg termed a growing "commercial and financial union." Kemmerer's first advisory experience in

South America was in Colombia. Colombian leaders had wanted for some time to return to the gold standard and to stimulate foreign—and particularly North American—investments. An outstanding political issue between Colombia and the United States, arising out of the separation of Panama from the former country, was settled finally by the Thomson-Urrutia Treaty of 1921–22. This pact provided a $25 million indemnity for Colombia. President Pedro Nel Ospina's favorable attitude toward an American economic presence in his country, combined with U.S. desire to exploit Colombian oil resources, resulted in a Colombian request to the State Department for financial advisory aid.[17]

State Department economic advisor Arthur N. Young considered Colombia's request to be "of more than usual importance" because of the funds that country was about to receive. Colombia needed a reform of its customs collection system and a national bank. Young felt it necessary to develop "an economically sound program" for spending the $25 million. He selected Kemmerer for the job, from among such other notables as Norman H. Davis, Sumner Welles, and William P. G. Harding, because of the economist's special qualifications, which included his knowledge of Spanish and his recent tour of Argentina, Uruguay, Chile, and Brazil to study financial conditions.[18] Washington's official attitude was summed up in an admonition to the United States minister in Bogotá to "bear in mind . . . that the mission is an expert mission engaged by the Colombian Government, and that it is in no sense connected with the Government of the United States . . . [which] can assume no responsibility with respect to the specific activities and recommendations of the mission."[19] Meanwhile, Kemmerer was making preliminary inquiries in New York regarding the disposition of the first U.S. payment to Colombia of $5 million under the terms of the Thomson-Urrutia Treaty.[20]

A Colombian Bank of Issue had been created in 1922, but more stringent reforms were needed so long as Colombia remained off the gold standard. With the first U.S. payment of $5 million under the Thomson-Urrutia Treaty, this bank was reestablished as the Banco de la República in 1923, along the lines of a plan drawn up by Professor Kemmerer. Budgetary laws and controls were instituted, and modern supervision and administration of banks and of customs and duties were established or improved considerably as a result also of the recommendations of the Kemmerer mission.[21]

The Kemmerer mission aroused serious opposition in Colombia, and it was only through the firm Conservative leadership of President Pedro Nel Ospina that the reforms could be effected.[22] Some opposition came from banking interests. Banco Lopez, Colombia's "Gibraltar," was on the verge of failure in the midst of the preparations to write the reforms into law. Short of funds to meet current demands upon it, the bank was unable to obtain an emergency loan either in New York or London. This was a suspicious development, for it had been reported publicly that the Kemmerer group had been working for sometime to improve the country's finances, and this knowledge might have calmed bankers' doubts about the Colombian bank's security. Perhaps the Colombian government was applying pressure upon a vulnerable bank as a means of convincing the banking community to accept change in the form of centralized control of banking and currency. All turned out well, however, for the Central Bank was quickly set up, making Kemmerer and his small group heroes. Banco Lopez, after a four-day bank holiday, was able to satisfy its creditors and avoid a panic.[23] Other Colombian opposition was incensed at the amount of American influence in the country. Some people feared that Colombia would be reduced to a protectorate of the United States when accountant Thomas Russell Lill, a member of the Kemmerer mission, remained under contract with the Colombian government as "technical advisor to the government."[24] But Lill and Mr. R. Homan, who became technical adviser to the office of the Colombian comptroller through Lill's efforts, were less successful than Kemmerer. They continually objected to interference in their work from Bogotá. By mid-1925, Lill, disgruntled and feeling himself "ill-used" by Colombian authorities, returned to the United States.[25]

Foreign experts continued to aid Colombia. Swiss and German citizens helped reform the customs and the Colombian banking system. *The Economist* of London even noted somewhat condescendingly "that native [Colombian] financiers and administrators have been found capable of continuing and amplifying much of the good work that has been initiated" by the "American financial mission, headed by Mr. Walter Kemmerer."[26] More Americans came to Colombia also. In 1929 the minister of finance, Dr. Francisco de Perez, hired Adrian M. Landman and John Phillip Wernette, who helped prepare a bill to create a bureau of the budget. This measure supplemented the budget law of 1923 that had been drawn up by the Kemmerer mission.[27]

Colombia's central bank was sufficiently empowered to keep the nation on the gold standard and to avoid a banking crisis until the fall of 1931, when the effects of the depression were evident in every Latin American country. But Kemmerer's help was needed again in 1930.[28] Large government deficits and a desire to obtain additional financing in the United States necessitated reforms after the crash of 1929. In fact, the flotation of loans amounting to $20 million in 1930 was predicated upon control of government deficits and changes in the administration of the customs and railroads. Although the political situation in Colombia was somewhat uncertain, the government took Kemmerer's advice and secured the passage of laws that modified the standards for legal reserves of gold and for the redemption of notes by the Banco de la República.[29] It also instituted a new principle for taxing profits, limited the public debt, and gave supreme power over the preparation and supervision of the budget (including rules for determining taxes) to the minister of finance.[30]

Kemmerer's attitude about these reforms was that the revision of the statute governing the Central Bank should take precedence over the means of obtaining that revision. According to U.S. Minister Jefferson Caffery, Kemmerer "went so far as to suggest that [President] Olaya use 'arbitrary action' to force the bill through Congress; [he] said that in his opinion, the project was so important that arbitrary measures would be justified."[31] Kemmerer's second mission to Colombia, like the first, provided the confidence that made possible successful completion of American loans to the Colombian government.[32] In the earlier case, however, due to more optimistic investing prospects and the greater availability of capital in the United States, the initial loans were followed by numerous others to the government, municipalities, and departments, mainly for public works projects.[33]

A significant aspect of Kemmerer's visit to Colombia in 1930 involved a tax imposed on bananas exported from the country. In September, the local manager of the United Fruit Company, which had a virtual monopoly over the Colombian banana trade, inquired regarding the possibility that the Kemmerer group would propose a tax on bananas. Kemmerer told Minister Caffery that he had not considered it, but that Caffery should "thank the Fruit Company for the suggestion; we shall look into it at once, for we are looking for new means of taxation." When it became clear that the economist was seriously considering a tax of two cents on each bunch of bananas exported from Colombia, Caffery warned him of "the inadvisability" of such an action. Kemmerer insisted that the tax was necessary. The fruit company, equally insistent, declared that it would accept a tax of one and one-half cents only "under certain conditions," such as a ten-year contract under the terms of which Colombia could not alter the tax.

Kemmerer was affronted by this counterproposal. It was "undignified for the Colombian Government to bind itself in a matter of national taxation of this character, . . . the tax should be imposed unconditionally." Perhaps, he said, the proceeds of the tax might be used to maintain a tropical research laboratory for the advancement of agriculture in Colombia. Moreover, he wanted some assurance that the fruit company would not make its producers foot the bill by being paid less for their fruit. But Kemmerer's seemingly noble intentions were insufficient to protect the integrity of the Colombian government, for President [Enrique] Olaya [Herrera] soon approved a provision in the tax law that allowed a twenty-year contract with the United Fruit Company. As Caffery reported to Washington, "This is what is desired by the Fruit Company."[34] Caffery had acted in a way that was clearly partisan to the fruit company, but the Colombian government itself did not seem reluctant to extend most-favored-company privileges. The law levying the two-cent tax was passed in February, 1931, and provided for twenty years' stability of the tax. When President Olaya felt it necessary, in December, 1931, to raise the tax to three cents, a further concession to the United Fruit Company guaranteed that the export tax would be suspended should any other national, municipal, or departmental tax be levied upon the company in Colombia.[35]

Kemmerer continued an important if unofficial involvement in Colombian finances. Very shortly after Colombia's abandonment of the gold-exchange standard on September 25, 1931, Secretary of State Henry L. Stimson asserted that the United States could not offer "any sort of promise of a *quid pro quo* in the nature of financial assistance" to Colombia, meaning "that not only can this Government not exert pressure on private banks but also that its relationship to the Federal Reserve system precludes it from exerting any pressure upon this independent institution." As for action that might help Colombia in her financial emergency, Stimson wrote Caffery that "Professor Kemmerer has strongly argued the Colombian case to [the] bankers," in the hope that the latter would understand Colombia's inability to service as usual its debt and the necessity of a smaller and balanced federal budget.[36] The seriousness of the depression punctuated American relations with Latin America. Colombia and most other countries were finally forced to default on their foreign indebtedness and to resort to domestic resources and initiatives to begin economic recovery. With the advent of a Democratic administration in Washington, Kemmerer's role as a financial expert in Latin America ended, although this did not terminate the work of financial experts. Possibly Kemmerer's strong position against the devaluation of the dollar placed him outside the pale of experts acceptable to the New Deal administrators.

I I

A useful contrast to the Colombian case is that of Chile. Chile differed from the other countries of the west coast of South America in several respects. A historical background of relative political stability and efficient use of resources and finances helped make possible Chile's more sophisticated development of economic and financial institutions. Plans for a central bank had existed since the 1880s, although they had not come to fruition. Moreover, Chile's gold reserves were sufficient to maintain a stable foreign exchange rate from 1921 through 1923 in spite of a failure to avoid inflation and to conform to the gold standard. As in the rest of Latin America, however, World War I and the postwar period brought to the fore the vulnerability of Chile's export-oriented economy and severely aggravated domestic social and economic conditions.

Financial changes in Chile were closely connected to domestic politics. Conservative rulers of the country largely resisted efforts of middle classes to carry out social reform and the demands of agricultural and mining laborers for economic concessions. Finally in 1920 the election of Arturo Alessandri to the presidency signified a recognition that Chile's leaders must share power with the masses and correct their disdainful attitude toward reform. Alessandri's reformism as well as his efforts to obtain American financial advisers were frustrated for several years by the restraining influence of Congressional conservatives. In 1923, the president requested the assistance of Princeton-trained economist William Wilson Cumberland, who was currently employed by the Peruvian government. American ambassador William Miller Collier opposed the proposal, feeling that it would raise bitter opposition in Chile, and Cumberland did not accept the invitation.[37]

By late 1924 Chilean authorities were taking steps to obtain the services of a Kemmerer commission of financial experts, with the tacit approval of the State Department.[38] A military junta had replaced Alessandri earlier that year. A countercoup by another army group recalled Alessandri in March, 1925, for what was to be a term of only six months. During this period, Kemmerer's group occupied itself in Santiago writing seventeen proposals for legislative action. According to Ambassador Collier, the army, anxious also for institutional reform, "notified the Government that every measure recommended by the Kemmerer mission must be accepted without amendment."[39] Kemmerer himself was "much annoyed" at changes which the Chilean government made in his projects and even considered "quitting," according to the ambassador, who may have exaggerated a disturbing yet temporary difficulty posed for the American experts by Chilean political developments. But Collier, who had taken no overt action "implying that the United States government had any connection with [the Kemmerer mission]," advised the American economist "that it would be most regrettable to take any step that would indicate a failure to work in harmony with the [Chilean] Government." Collier's view was that successful completion of the experts' contracts would be a "great service to Chile and [would] strengthen our commercial and political relations."[40] Although Alessandri was forced to resign on October 1, 1925, the work of the commission of experts continued and some of its more important proposals were written into law.[41] Chile opened a Central Bank and reestablished its currency on the gold-exchange standard.[42]

Kemmerer returned to Chile for a few weeks in July, 1927. Financial and administrative reforms, including a new tariff law, seem to have flowed in some measure from the expert's visits.[43] Two notable facts stand out concerning these reforms. First, as the *New York Times* noted, the semidictatorial rule of Colonel Carlos Ibañez was necessary to institute reforms. Second, it was impossible to accomplish nonpolitical (which meant to the experts more scientific and sound) control of the central bank. What occurred was the result of a compromise between powerful forces, and the government merely conceded that it would share power over the bank with commercial bankers and some major private borrowers.[44]

The role of American experts in Chile was perhaps as significant as in Colombia. But the characteristics of the connections differed. While American investors placed $187 million in Chilean public institutions between June, 1925, and August, 1929 (compared with $53 million in the 1919–1925 period),[45] further research will be necessary to indicate specific relationships between the experts and American lenders. The linkages are clearer in the Colombian case. The American government maintained a respectful distance with regard to Chile, indicating a more mature state of international relations. A third point that deserves emphasis in all the examples outlined herein is the fact that the use of American specialists was a medium of conducting American-style reform, to the point that it became common to consider South American central banks to be models of the Federal Reserve System. This last was not the case, for Kemmerer banks in South America were central, not regional, and in general bolstered the trend toward strong governments and the economic and political primacy of capital cities.

Other Kemmerer missions to South America more nearly resemble the Colombian case. Still, the involvement of American experts in Ecuador, Bolivia, and Peru throws light on phases of U.S. relations with Latin America that are not emphasized by the missions to Colombia and Chile.

Kemmerer was not the first American economist to be employed by the three central Andean countries in the 1920s. Ecuadorian leaders desired a stabilization of the foreign exchange rate for their currency and increased foreign investment. The foreign manager of the country's leading railway, the Guayaquil and Quito, and the American minister in Quito hoped to persuade Ecuador's President José Luis Tamayo to accept an American adviser.[46] The State Department helped Ecuador secure the services of John S. Hord, who made a four-year contract as financial adviser to the Ecuadorian government. Hord was thought to have worked "well and industriously" but was unable to succeed in bringing about substantial reform. Toward the end of his contract period he was relegated to matters of "minor consideration." Personally, concluded American minister G. A. Bading, Hord "made no great impression upon the Ecuadorian public."[47]

"Mr. Hord unfortunately lacked the personality which would impress the Latin Americans, so notwithstanding his unquestioned ability, he did not succeed in accomplishing during the four years of his stay in Ecuador anything of note."[48]

A Permanent Fiscal Commission preceded the Kemmerer mission to Bolivia by three years. The commission's job, which specifically included supervision of banks, national fiscal accounting, and tax collection for a period of twenty-five years, was primarily to insure satisfactory execution of a loan contract for $25 million between Bolivia and the Equitable Trust Company of New York. The commission had been expected also to make a financial survey and recommendations for the improvement of Bolivia's financial system. But it had not satisfied Bolivian expectations and the government actively sought the services of Professor Kemmerer in 1925. Bolivian officials finally induced him to come to the country in 1927.[49]

William Wilson Cumberland, already mentioned as the object of a Chilean search for an expert economist in 1923, was Kemmerer's predecessor in Peru. From 1921, Cumberland's supervision of customs and his position as financial adviser gave him considerable authority over Peruvian finance and some influence over dictator Augusto B. Leguía. During Cumberland's stay in Peru the government established a Reserve Bank (ostensibly patterned after the United States Federal Reserve System), of which the economist was made manager.[50] The expert's experience in Peru prompted an observation of the difficulty of applying economic principles under the restraint of political interference—an observation that not only revealed some of his own frustration but also corresponded with views expressed four years later by the *New York Times*.[51]

> Finances and politics in a Latin American republic [Cumberland wrote to Assistant Secretary of State Leland Harrison] seem to be synonymous, and political management of finance is bound to be disastrous. In other words, the only possible solution of Peru's financial problem is some type of non-political control. This can only be instituted by means of a loan and a loan contract which will prevent executive irresponsibility in expenditure.[52]

State Department policies regarding recognition of revolutionary regimes and approval for American foreign loans were in part challenged by and dependent upon successful completion of reforms by the Kemmerer missions to Ecuador and Bolivia in the period from October 1926 to June 1927.[53] Ecuador's government in 1926–27 was controlled by President Isidro Ayora, a dictator who was not constitutionally elected president until 1928. Because of Ecuador's shaky financial situation and the unconstitutionality of its government, Kemmerer became involved in two matters that had until that time not occupied him.[54] He personally tried (although unsuccessfully) to negotiate a loan for Ecuador from Dillon, Read and Company. This issue raised serious questions concerning U.S. recognition of the regime. The economist urged that the United States grant recognition before the convening of Ecuador's Congress. He also wanted approval of the American loan to the Ecuadorian government before the latter fulfilled its long overdue commitments to bondholders of the important Guayaquil and Quito Railway. Kemmerer's position was contrary to current State Department policy, but the expert saw a need for temporary authoritarian rule in Ecuador.[55] He argued that: "it would not be wise to reestablish constitutionality until such a time as would enable the provisional Government to fully reorganize its various departments and by enforcing the decrees covering the recommendations of the commission firmly establish the new order of procedure regardless of opposition that might develop."[56] It was a simple matter that "with a duly elected Congress" it would be impossible to reorganize the government and also settle with the bondholders.[57]

The Kemmerer mission was able with some difficulty to obtain the establishment of a central bank and the issuance of a new currency, based on the gold-exchange standard. To carry out some other reforms and to supervise customs, banks, and railroads, five American experts were retained by the Ecuadorian government.[58] While Kemmerer was unable to reserve State Department recognition policy, Ecuador was able to rearrange its financing. It made payments to satisfy completely the English bondholders of the Guayaquil and Quito Railway, made a token payment on its similar debt to U.S. citizens (a debt that was reportedly in arrears since July 1913), and announced the election of a new National Assembly. On August 14, 1928, the United States granted de jure recognition to Ecuador.[59]

American bankers and investors had a particularly strong interest in Bolivian national finances by the time Kemmerer's group went to La Paz in 1927. By mid-1927 over 90 percent of Bolivia's external debt was held by Americans. On a per-capita basis, this would make Bolivia's debt similar to that of Peru and Colombia, but the former was based on much smaller current and potential trade and investment than in almost all other South American countries. The experts made proposals for fourteen laws and some of the Americans were employed by Bolivia to supervise railroads, revision of tariffs, government expenditures, and the institution of the reforms.[60] But Bolivian action on the reforms was predicated upon American financial resources and pressure. A Dillon, Read loan of 1927 "strengthened [Bolivian] President [Siles] with all classes" and helped him obtain passage of the reform measures.[61] Just as important was the fact that both State Department approval and the granting of a large new loan to Bolivia by Dillon, Read depended on the completion of the reforms. As Robert O. Haywood, of Dillon, Read, wrote Secretary of State Frank C.

Kellogg, "our discussions with the Bolivian Government have been based on the primary condition that before the loan is made, the Government shall adopt in full the entire Kemmerer program."[62] Again experts were a vital key in U.S. relations with another country, with public and private, economic and political influence being brought to bear upon the foreign state to overcome opposition to reforms written by the experts. J. Whitla Stinson, of the State Department's Division of Latin-American Affairs, believed that ironclad agreements would be the most effective means of insuring the use in Latin America of scientific reforms:

> As my survey of the organic banking and fiscal laws of Latin America proceeds, the desirability of incorporating in our treaties the more important and fundamental principles upon which these reforms turn seems more and more desirable and I think realizable. It is a matter at least which calls for serious consideration and would lend much greater security to American investments in Latin America than they now possess.[63]

The North American emphasis upon written law is evident in the statements of Cumberland, Kemmerer, and Stinson. There was clearly some confusion over what means—loans contracts, domestic decrees and legislation, or international treaties—would be most effective in bringing about reform. But then, Americans were willing to experiment pragmatically to secure what they considered sound economic relationships while holding firm their faith in scientific principles and law.

American diplomats were apprehensive concerning revolutionary possibilities in Latin America toward the end of 1930. U.S. officials in Lima thought a new loan and the advice of Professor Kemmerer would give Peruvian dictator Leguía's regime, which was threatened by domestic grievances and the effects of international depression, a "new lease on life." American bankers, Counselor Ferdinand Lothrop Mayer wrote Secretary of State Stimson, "would be most apt to follow Dr. Kemmerer's findings." While Mayer opposed U.S. interference in Peruvian politics, he believed that the "continuance of Mr. Leguía as President . . . would be desirable as regards our financial, political and commercial interests."[64]

Kemmerer's 1930 consultation with the Colombian government delayed the arrival of his commission of experts in Peru until early in 1931.[65] By this time, another dictator, Colonel Luis Sánchez Cerro, had replaced Leguía via a military revolt. Its efforts complicated by economic depression, Peru's inability to service foreign debt, and the reactionary nature of the regime and Peru's ruling classes, Kemmerer's group nevertheless succeeded in writing a long series of reports. In spite of his antipathy to Peru's leadership and his dislike of inflationary policies, Kemmerer "admitted [to American ambassador Fred Morris Dearing] that if the Government were faced with a question of self-preservation, it would be warranted in resorting to inflation as an alternative to annihilation," using as an analogy the necessity of most countries during World War I to do likewise. Still, Kemmerer warned, Peru "would have to take some strenuous measures."[66] Following the Kemmerer mission's advice, Peru placed its currency on a qualified gold standard, which temporarily stabilized the foreign exchange rate, and a reform was made in the Central Reserve Bank, with which American economist William Wilson Cumberland had been associated in the early 1920s.[67] Following a practice that was now common, Kemmerer left a member of his group, Walter Van Deusen, in Peru as adviser to the reorganized Federal Reserve Bank.[68]

III

This study, it is hoped, should provide a basis for continuing research. The role of American advisers in other countries, from the occupation of Cuba, Puerto Rico, and the Philippine Islands in 1898 to the present, should be the subject of careful scrutiny. Only then will there be described thoroughly the notable continuity in personnel and purpose, administration and types of reforms advanced that characterized public employment of missions of financial experts. Similarly, to trace the historical relationships of the advisory missions to the foreign governments and to the State Department would point out changing attitudes toward and uses made of professional economic specialists.

These missions were sent from the United States first to areas of actual American political and military control. They went next to countries where American economic interests were rapidly increasing. Third, and this was true especially in the 1920s, groups of experts went out to areas of the world where concerted American and British energies were being expended to stabilize economies and currencies. The Kemmerer missions to South America fall into the latter two categories, although the precise relationship to a coordinated effort—if this existed—must be spelled out. There was continuity in the recommendations made by the Kemmerer missions. Kemmerer requested and was sent the Philippine monetary, fiscal, and banking laws when he was in Colombia in 1923. Later, his proposals for reform in Colombia were forwarded to Haiti.[69] The package of reforms proposed by the Kemmerer missions included similar items in all five countries: projects for central banks and a new monetary law, plans for the supervision of banks and the governmental budget, and schemes to improve the collection of taxes, make the tariff system more efficient, and oversee railroad administration.

The striking continuity of personnel in the Kemmerer missions can be attributed to personal relationships, competence, and experience. For example, Edward F. Feely, who became American minister to Bolivia in 1930, served on the Kemmerer missions to Ecuador, Bolivia, and China. Others were actively involved in Latin American economic affairs as individuals and through service for the U.S. government. William F. Roddy, member of the Kemmerer mission to Peru in 1931, was adviser of customs in Ecuador, 1927, director general of customs in Ecuador, 1927–1930, and adviser of customs in Colombia, 1931. Stokeley W. Morgan also combined the public and private, domestic and foreign roles. He was general secretary of the Kemmerer mission to Peru in 1931 and had held other posts in Latin America. He had been secretary of the American embassy in La Paz (1920–1922), Bogotá (1922), and Panama (1924); chargé d'affaires to Tegucigalpa, Honduras; counselor of the embassy in Mexico City, 1929, and, after 1929, a member of the foreign department of Lehman Brothers of New York, investment bankers. Such continuity suggests the potential for research into the coordination of and cooperation between Americans who were vital links in U.S. economic relations with the countries of Latin America.

The economic implications of the work of the Kemmerer missions—and of the other American experts and advisers—deserve separate and careful consideration. Two sets of questions are subsumed under this category. One set can be answered almost entirely by the use of conventional economic data and statistical techniques. What were the economic consequences of the institutional changes wrought by the experts and the Latin American governments? Can these consequences be measured in terms of changes in the level of efficient administration, banking, or taxation? Can they be related to changes in the level of productivity, domestic and foreign investment, and international trade? Were the effects, in sum, a contribution to the welfare of the Latin American states and/or the United States? One of the answers is partially clear. This is that U.S. investments in the five Andean countries increased more rapidly between World War I and the Great Depression than in any area in Latin America with the exception of Cuba and Venezuela. The rate of increase in these five states was more rapid than that in any other generalized area (as Europe or Asia) except for Oceania. American investments in the area became vastly predominant over those of Britons during the same period. Financial missions were not necessarily causal in prompting such a spurt in American investment. Other factors were operative, such as the economic preoccupation of European countries with reconstruction and the large amounts of American capital that were available for investment abroad. Nevertheless specific loans were predicated on the completion of reforms. At the very least it can be concluded that financial experts played a significant role in the increase of U.S. investments in South America.

The second group of questions involves the appropriateness of similar institutional and legal changes in environments that differ culturally. Here the questions, although obvious, require careful definition and investigation. There was a divergence between theory and the assumptions demanded by theory on one hand, and the reality of Latin American political economy on the other. American experts commonly recognized this divergence; but it should also be asked whether their Latin American hosts perceived this state of affairs, and, if so, whether the perceptions held of this divergence were similar or different on the part of the two groups. If this divergence was commonly recognized by experts, then it should also be asked whether the divergences were similar or different on the part of Americans and their Latin American hosts. At a more profound level, it is necessary to see Latin American society in a lengthy process of unstable transition since the period of independence. Especially in countries like Peru, Bolivia, and Ecuador, there has not been clearly formulated a sound societal basis for economic (not to mention political) relations between widely separated sectors of the country. The most serious question is whether the attempt by experts to aid in institutional economic reform did make more difficult the integration and development of national economies. This question is based on the assumption that national development, whatever its characteristics and values, must be founded finally upon the real human, material, and intellectual conditions of the environment.

Finally, and perhaps most striking, is the paradox faced by American economists. They believed their profession a scientific one and wished to keep it separate from the debasing institution of politics. Yet they found their best considered projects either frustrated by political and economic conflict or effected precisely where the political power of the government was actually the greatest and most autocratic.[70] Kemmerer and his aides wrote proposals for monetary and fiscal reform that would make possible the freedom of economic institutions from pernicious political considerations. But in order to effect a minimum portion of the changes Kemmerer desired, he often had no choice but to work through strongmen or dictators whose power was sufficient to overcome political opposition. Even then there was no assurance that the mere passage of a new law would ensure that its provisions would be carried out. It was the Chilean military, for example, that insisted on complete acceptance of the reforms, but the constitutional apparatus still prevented their complete success.

Edwin W. Kemmerer did not support dictatorship. But he realized that authoritarian action was sometimes necessary to carry through his projects. The expert who had in 1916 opposed the "political usurpation" that was implied by American dollar diplomacy had been obliged to accept domestic usurpations of power in order to effect what he considered to be progressive and scientific reform.

Notes

1. Joseph Dorfman, *The Economic Mind in American Civilization*, III (New York: Viking Press, 1949), 351; Robert H. Wiebe, *The Search for Order, 1877–1920* (New York: Hill and Wang, 1967), p. 174.

2. Merle Curti and Kendall Birr, *Prelude to Point Four. American Technical Missions Overseas* (Madison: University of Wisconsin Press, 1954), ch. viii, is a notable exception to this general neglect. This chapter is a suitable introduction to the subject, although the connection between the financial advisers and the private and public foreign economic policies of the United States is not made clear. The emphasis of Curti and Birr is upon elucidating precedents for American technical assistance abroad, with major focus on the utility of the missions and with little analysis of their benefits and long-term results. See *ibid.*, ch. x.

The Kemmerer missions are mentioned superficially in Dorfman, *The Economic Mind*, IV (New York: Viking Press, 1959), 308–12; Wilfred Hardy Calcott, *The Western Hemisphere. Its Influence on United States Policies to the End of World War II* (Austin: University of Texas Press, 1968), p. 228. They are not mentioned in Samuel Flagg Bemis, *The Latin-American Policy of the United States* (New York: Harcourt, Brace and Co., 1943); William Appleman Williams, "Latin America: Laboratory of American Foreign Policy in the Nineteen-twenties," *Inter-American Economic Affairs*, XI (Autumn, 1957), 3–30; Robert Freeman Smith, "American Foreign Relations, 1920–1942," *Towards a New Past: Dissenting Essays in American History*, ed. Barton J. Bernstein (New York: Pantheon Books, 1968), pp. 232–62; and J. Lloyd Mecham, *A Survey of United States-Latin American Relations* (Boston: Houghton Mifflin Co., 1965). Kemmerer's papers are located at the Princeton University Library. Family restrictions upon this large and potentially valuable collection have made it impossible for the author to study them at this time.

3. Dorfman, *The Economic Mind*, IV, p. 308n.

4. Paul M. Warburg, *The Federal Reserve System*, I (New York: Macmillan, 1930), 112–13; Edwin Walter Kemmerer, "American Banks in Times of Crisis Under the National Banking System," Academy of Political Science, *Proceedings*, I (Jan. 1911), 233–53; Kemmerer, *The ABC of the Federal Reserve System* (Princeton, New Jersey: Princeton University Press, 1918), and many other editions.

5. Kemmerer, *Modern Currency Reforms: A History and Discussion of Recent Currency Reforms in India, Porto Rico, Philippine Islands, Straits Settlements, and Mexico* (New York: Macmillan, 1916), pp. viii, 207, 227.

6. Dorfman, *The Economic Mind*, III, p. 352.

7. See, for example, Kemmerer, "Gold and the Gold Standard," American Philosophical Society, *Proceedings*, LXXI, 3 (1932), 85–104; Stephen V. O. Clarke, *Central Bank Cooperation, 1924–31* (New York: Federal Reserve Bank of New York, 1967), p. 61.

8. Kemmerer, "A Proposal for Pan-American Monetary Unity," *Political Science Quarterly*, XXXI (Mar. 1916), 66–80.

9. These ideas of Kemmerer's should be contrasted with very similar ideas of Paul M. Warburg; see, e.g., Warburg's address before the International High Commission at Buenos Aires, May 3, 1916, Warburg, *Federal Reserve System*, II, p. 384.

10. Tom E. Davis, "Eight Decades of Inflation in Chile, 1879–1959: A Political Interpretation," *Journal of Political Economy*, LXXI (Aug. 1963), 389–90; Frank W. Fetter, *Monetary Inflation in Chile* (Princeton: Princeton University Press, 1931), ch. ix and *passim*. See also Guillermo Subercaseaux, *Monetary and Banking Policy of Chile*, ed. David Kinley (Oxford: Clarendon Press, 1922), 175–85.

11. Kemmerer, "The Theory of Foreign Investments," The American Academy of Political and Social Science, *Annals*, LXVIII (Nov. 1916), 1–9.

12. The *New York Times*, October 10, 1926, II, 8.

13. Dean E. Traynor, *International Monetary and Financial Conferences in the Interwar Period* (Washington, D.C.: Catholic University of America Press, 1949), ch. ii, iii.

14. Frank Tamagna, *Central Banking in Latin America* (Mexico: Centro de Estudios Monetarios Latinoamericanos, 1965), 39; Kemmerer, *Gold and the Gold Standard* (New York: McGraw-Hill, 1944), 109–10, 164–66; Traynor, *International . . . Conferences*, pp. 73–84.

15. Based on Frederic M. Halsey, *Investments in Latin America and the British West Indies*, United States Department of Commerce, Bureau of Foreign and Domestic Commerce, Special Agents Series, No. 169 (Washington, D.C.: G.P.O., 1918), p. 20; Paul R. Olson and C. Addison Hickman, *Pan American Economics* (New York: J. Wiley and Sons, 1943), pp. 416, 417, 419, 420; Max Winkler, *Investments of United States Capital in Latin America* (Boston: World Peace Foundation Pamphlets, 1929), pp. 275, 278, 280, 283.

16. Quoted in J. F. Normano, *The Struggle for South America: Economy and Ideology* (London: George Allen and Unwin Ltd., 1931), p. 253 n. 36.

17. The *New York Times*, June 2, 1922, p. 23.

18. Assistant Secretary of State Leland Harrison to Francis White, September 30, 1922, National Archives, General Records of the Department of State (Record Group 59) [hereafter cited as NA], 821.51A/2; Young to White, October 2, 1922, NA, 821.51A/3; Young to Harrison, November 7, 1922, NA, 821.51A/4.

Arthur N. Young studied economics at Princeton and took his Ph.D. work under Professor Kemmerer. He had been brought to Mexico in 1917 after the latter had been invited to assist in the work of Henry Bruère in Mexico. See Curti and Birr, *Prelude to Point Four . . .* , pp. 160–61. Kemmerer's work in Brazil is elaborated in the National Archives, Records of the Bureau of Foreign and Domestic Commerce (Record Group 151), "Foreign Exchange, Brazil," Jones to Ackerman, February 9, 1923; Ackerman to Schurz, February 13, 1923; and Schurz to Jones, April 24, 1923.

19. Harrison to United States Minister in Colombia, Samuel H. Piles, February 13, 1923, United States Department of State, *Foreign Relations of the United States*, I (Washington, D.C.: G.P.O., 1923), [hereafter cited as FR], 831–33.

20. Under Secretary of the Treasury S. P. Gilbert to Secretary of State Charles E. Hughes, January 3, 1923, NA, 821.51A/21. These inquiries were being made one month before Kemmerer and his four aides signed contracts with the Colombian government. The inquiries were directed to placement of the $5 million in the United States Treasury certificates of indebtedness through the Federal

Reserve Bank of New York. The members of the Kemmerer mission to Colombia in 1923 were, in addition to Professor Kemmerer, Howard M. Jefferson of the New York Federal Reserve Bank; Fred R. Fairchild (Yale Ph.D., 1904), professor of economics at Yale University; Thomas Russell Lill, accountant of Searle, Nicholson, Oakey & Lill of New York; and Frederic Bliss Luquiens, secretary of the group, of the Spanish Department of Yale University.

21. "Notable Achievement of a Notable Commission," Pan-American Union, *Bulletin*, LVIII (Feb. 1924), 164–66; David Joslin, *A Century of Banking in Latin America* (London: Oxford University Press, 1963), p. 241; E. Taylor Parks, *Colombia and the United States, 1765–1934* (Durham: Duke University Press, 1935), p. 472; International Bank for Reconstruction and Development, *The Basis of a Development Program for Colombia* (Washington, D.C.: International Bank for Reconstruction and Development, 1950), pp. 267, 567; Abel Cruz Santos, *Finanzas Publicas* (Bogotá: Lerner Ediciones, 1968), p. 205.

22. Piles (Bogotá) to Hughes, June 25, 1923, NA, 821.51/242; Maurice L. Stafford (Baranquilla) to Hughes, July 26, 1923, NA, 821.516/53; Harry Bernstein, *Venezuela and Colombia* (Englewood Cliffs, New Jersey: Prentice-Hall, 1964), p. 122.

23. "This run [on Banco Lopez] is supposed to have been ultimately caused by an official of the Government telegraph office refusing to accept a bill issued by this bank." Piles to Hughes, July 21, 1923, NA, 821.516/55; same to same, July 30, 1923, NA, 821.516/58; The reports to the *New York Times* gave the event a mysterious tone. Banco Lopez's request came late in the day at New York, the situation was confused, and the bankers asserted they had insufficient knowledge of the situation in Colombia. The Lazard Brothers in London granted a loan but afterward withdrew it when they heard New York had refused a similar request. The *New York Times*, July 20, 1923, p. 23; *ibid.*, July 28, 1923, p. 13.

24. Piles to Hughes, June 25, 1923, NA, 821.51/242; same to same, August 20, 1923, NA, 821.51/246; same to same, October 17, 1923, NA, 821.51A/28. The significance of the kind of expert work a man like Lill could do in South America was not underestimated by the Bureau of Foreign and Domestic Commerce, which, having determined the value of Lill's services in Colombia, tried unsuccessfully to place him in similar positions in Argentina, Chile, and Peru. NA, Record Group 151, "Finance and Investment, Argentina," R. F. O'Toole to Lew Clark, July 28, 1924; NA, Record Group 151, "Chile," O'Toole to Ralph H. Ackerman, July 28, 1924; and NA, Record Group 151, "Peru," W. N. Pearce to Julius Klein, September 4, 1924.

25. Patterson (Bogotá) to Hughes, May 6, 1926, NA, 821.00/599; same to same, May 17, 1926, NA, 821.51A/39.

26. *The Economist*, CIV (March 26, 1927), p. 635.

27. Caffery (Bogotá) to Secretary of State Stimson, April 20, 1929, NA, 821.51A/44; same to same, June 24, 1929, NA, 821.51A/45.

28. The 1930 Kemmerer mission to Colombia included Kemmerer; Joseph T. Byrne, expert in budget and accounting; Walter E. Langerquist, public credit; W. W. Renwick, customs; Kossuth M. Williamson, taxation; William E. Dunn, secretary of the group; J. Louis Schaefer, assistant secretary.

29. The Liberals came to power in the election of 1930 after virtually uninterrupted Conservative domination of Colombian politics since 1880. The new president, Enrique Olaya Herrera (former Colombian representative at Washington) took office on August 7, 1930 in one of the few peaceful transfers of power in Latin

America in the depression year of 1930. Conservative control of Congress continued, however, and this remained a check upon Liberal rule and complicated the passage of legislation.

30. Cruz Santos, *Finanzas Publicas*, pp. 228–29, 344, 382.

31. Caffery to Stimson, December 27, 1930, NA, 821.516/112.

32. Parks, *Colombia and the United States . . .* , p. 474.

33. Ralph A. Young, *Handbook on American Underwriting of Foreign Securities*, United States Department of Commerce, Trade Promotion Series, No. 104 (Washington, D.C.: G.P.O., 1930), pp. 100, 106, 115, 124, 132.

34. Caffery to Stimson, September 5, 1930, NA, 821.51A/49; same to same, September 12, 1930, NA, 821.51A/53; same to same, September 24, 1930, NA, 821.51A/55; same to same, December 22, 1930, NA, 821.51A Kemmerer Commission/25.

35. Charles David Kepner and Jay Henry Soothill, *The Banana Empire. A Case Study in Economic Imperialism* (New York: Vanguard Press, 1935), pp. 212–13, 291–94. The tax was not excessive, since bananas generally brought over $2.00 for a nine-hand bunch in northern wholesale markets throughout the 1920s.

36. Stimson to Caffery, October 6, 1931, FR, 1931, II, pp. 39–40.

37. Collier to Hughes, May 15, 1923, NA, 825.51A/orig. Cumberland was inclined to accept the invitation. He had an important position in Peru, but had expressed his disappointment in not being able sufficiently to institute sound economic measures removed from political control. He was finally convinced to remain in Lima on the grounds that his leaving Peru would reflect on United States prestige there. This is an interesting point, since Cumberland, like Kemmerer, was explicitly a private employee of the Peruvian government. Poindexter (Lima) to Hughes, May 16, 1923, NA, 825.516/27; same to same, July 3, 1923, NA, 825.516/31.

38. A. N. Young, Memorandum, October 13, 1924, NA, 825.51A/2. The following were the members of the Kemmerer mission to Chile: Kemmerer, expert on central banking and the gold standard; Joseph T. Byrne, of the New York firm, Byrne, Lindberg & Byrne, public accountants, accounting and fiscal control; Harley L. Lutz, of Stanford University, taxation; H. M. Jefferson, of the New York Federal Reserve Bank, banking organization and fiscal control; William W. Renwick, fiscal representative of the trustees of the American loan to San Salvador, customs; G. Van Zandt, Professor of Engineering, consulting engineer for rail transportation; Henry H. West, South American representative of the National Credit office in Buenos Aires, who had been secretary of the American Financial Commission to Peru, 1923; and Frank W. Fetter, secretary to Kemmerer. Renwick became Fiscal Representative of the Republic of El Salvador in December 1925.

39. Collier to Kellogg, August 22, 1925, NA, 825.00/423.

40. Collier to Kellogg, September 14, 1925, NA, 825.00/444; same to same, August 11, 1925, NA, 825.51A/10.

41. The *New York Times*, June 12, 1925, p. 27; *ibid.*, November 3, 1925, p. 40; Kemmerer, "Work of the American Financial Commission in Chile," American Bankers Association, *Journal*, XVIII (Dec. 1925), 411–12, 460. The laws passed were the Monetary Law, Central Bank Law, General Banking Law, Budget Law, and Railroad Administration Law.

42. Kemmerer, "Chile Returns to the Gold Standard," the *Journal of Political Economy*, XXXIV (June 1926), 265–73.

43. Engert (Santiago) to Kellogg, June 23, 1927, NA, 825.00/525; Cottrell (La Paz) to Kellogg, June 29, 1927, NA, 824.51A/9; *The Economist*, CVI (Mar. 17, 1928), 529; *ibid.*, CVII (Oct. 13, 1928), 644–45.

44. The *New York Times*, August 14, 1927, II, p. 12; Tom E. Davis, "Eight Decades . . . ," p. 390.

45. R. A. Young, *Handbook on American Underwriting* . . . , pp. 81, 86, 99, 106, 115, 124, 132.

46. G. A. Bading (Quito) to Hughes, December 28, 1922, NA, 822.51/377.

47. Memo of conversation with Dr. Elizalde, Minister of Ecuador, with William Phillips, Under Secretary of State, June 9, 1923, NA, 822.51A/3; Bading to Hughes, June 30, 1924, NA, 822.00/551; R. M. deLambert (Quito) to Kellogg, July 28, 1925, NA, 822.51A/21; Bading to Kellogg, March 6, 1926, NA, 822.51A/26; Winkler, *Investments of United States Capital* . . . , p. 132; Reuben A. Lewis, Jr., "Drafting the Brains Behind the Dollar," American Bankers Association, *Journal*, XVI (May 1924), 702.

48. Bading to Kellogg, February 15, 1927, NA, 822.51A/42.

49. *The Economist*, XCIV (Jan. 7, 1922), 6; Margaret A. Marsh, *The Bankers in Bolivia* (New York: Vanguard Press, 1928), p. 101; Lewis, "Drafting the Brains . . . ," p. 702; Cottrell (La Paz) to Kellogg, June 3, 1925, NA, 824.51/313.

50. Kemmerer actually had had an invitation to advise financial reorganization in Peru in early 1920. The significance of this is not yet explained. Secretary of State Robert Lansing, replying to Kemmerer's inquiry as to whether the State Department would "look with favor on such a mission," stated the Department's approval. Kemmerer to Lansing, January 23, 1920, NA, 823.51A; Lansing to Kemmerer, January 26, 1920, *ibid*. The relationship of the State Department to Cumberland is spelled out in Hughes to American Embassy (Lima), September 7, 1921, NA, 823.51/185; Sumner Welles to Federico Alfonso Peset, August 31, 1921, *ibid.*; Gonzales (Lima) to Hughes, September 20, 1922, NA, 823.51/190; F. A. Sterling (Lima) to Hughes, October 24, 1922, NA, 823.51/276. Cumberland was a foreign trade adviser for the Department of State at the time he decided to go to Peru. After leaving Peru in 1924, he served as financial adviser and general receiver of the Republic of Haiti (1924–1927) and as financial expert for the State Department in Nicaragua (1927–1928). He became a partner of Wellington and Company, members of the New York Stock Exchange. An investigation of Cumberland might be rewarding. For some indication of his role in Leguía's Peru, see James C. Carey, *Peru and the United States, 1900–1962* (Notre Dame: University of Notre Dame Press, 1964), pp. 18–19, 71–3; Lewis, "Drafting the Brains," p. 702; and, to see the similarity between Cumberland and Kemmerer in terms of attitudes, see Cumberland, "Our Economic Policy Toward Latin America," The American Academy of Political and Social Science, *Annals*, CL (July, 1930), 167–78. For some of the financial changes in Peru during Cumberland's stay see G. Butler Sherwell, "The Federal Reserve System in Peru," American Bankers Association, *Journal*, XV (June 1923), 801–5; "Federal Reserve Act of Peru," *Federal Reserve Bulletin*, VIII (May, 1922), 515–22; Oscar V. Salomon, "The New State Bank of Peru," Pan-American Union, *Bulletin*, LV (Sept. 1922), 262–65; *The Economist*, XCVII (Dec. 29, 1923), 1147.

51. The *New York Times*, Oct. 10, 1926, II, p. 8.

52. Cumberland to Assistant Secretary of State Leland Harrison, November 7, 1922, NA, 823.51/287.

53. The Kemmerer mission to Ecuador had the following members: Kemmerer, expert in central banking and currency; J. T. Byrne, accounting and fiscal control; E. F. Feely; F. W. Fetter; H. M. Jefferson, banking; Oliver C. Lockhart, public finances; B. B. Milner; Robert H. Vorfeld, customs administration. James H. Edwards, William F. Roddy, Earl B. Schwulst, and Harry de la Vergne Tompkins, together with Milner, were employed by the Ecuadorian government to administer the Kemmerer reforms. The Kemmerer mission to Bolivia was composed of Kemmerer, Byrne, Feely, Fetter, Edward L. Glenn (railroads), Jefferson, Lockhart, Vorfeld. Glenn remained in Bolivia. Feely, who joined Kemmerer's mission to China, later served the United States as Minister to Bolivia, 1930–1933.

54. The political significance for Ecuador of the institution of central banking and fiscal administration in the capital city of Quito was to ensure the success of the Revolution of July, 1925, the hegemony of the leadership of the Sierra over the country, and the defeat of the coastal "plutocracy," which was represented by the Commercial and Agricultural Bank of Guayaquil.

55. Bading (Quito) to Kellogg, January 30, 1928, NA, 822.51/451; same to same, February 2, 1928, NA, 822.51/449; same to same, March 19, 1928, NA, 822.51/456; same to same, March 29, 1928, NA, 822.51/465.

56. Bading to Kellogg, February 11, 1927, NA, 822.51A/41.

57. Memo of conversation, Kemmerer and Willoughby, Division of Latin-American Affairs, October 11, 1927, NA, 822.51A/57; memo of conversation, Kemmerer and Morgan, Division of Latin-American Affairs, December 29, 1927, NA, 822.51A/59.

58. Harry T. Collings, "Currency Reform in South America," *Current History*, XXVI (June, 1927), 475–76; "The Sucre: New Monetary Unit for Ecuador," Pan-American Union, *Bulletin*, LXI (Aug., 1927), 787–90; "Currency and Banking Reform in Ecuador," *Federal Reserve Bulletin*, XIII (July, 1927), 483–84.

59. The *New York Times*, June 20, 1928, p. 8; June 24, 1928, II, p. 11; July 11, 1928, p. 22; August 16, 1928, p. 2.

60. Marsh, *The Bankers in Bolivia*, p. 90; R. A. Young, *Handbook on American Underwriting* . . . , p. 158; Cottrell to Kellogg, June 29, 1927, NA, 824.51A/9; Memorandum of conversation, A. N. Young and Joseph T. Byrne, May 23, 1928, NA, 824.51A/23; David E. Kaufman to Kellogg, August 14, 1928, NA, 824.00 General Conditions/5.

61. Cottrell to Kellogg, December 19, 1927, NA, 824.00/450. J. F. McGurk, Second Secretary of the United States Legation at La Paz, wrote that Bolivian President Siles "is to all intent and purpose a dictator at the present time. He has stifled all opposition. . . ." McGurk to Kellogg, February 16, 1928, NA, 824.00/456. The implications were that Siles manipulated funds politically in order to secure the passage of the legislation. See also Herbert S. Klein, *Parties and Political Change in Bolivia, 1880–1952* (New York: Oxford University Press, 1969), pp. 103–5.

62. Hayward to Kellogg, June 13, 1928, NA, 824.51 D581/7. It should be noted that the Departments of Commerce and State differed with regard to approving the Dillon, Read loan to Bolivia. Nathan F. Brown, Acting Secretary of Commerce, wrote Secretary of State Kellogg that Commerce had some objections on economic grounds, but conceded that if State had overriding political reasons to accede to the loan, Commerce would go along. Brown to Kellogg, July 26, 1928, NA, 824.51 D 581/25. Dillon, Read had already extended a loan to Bolivia, the gross amount of which was $14 million, in February 1927. The $23 million loan, completed in September 1928, actually netted Bolivia only $18,880,000. U.S.

Senate, Committee on Finance, 72d Congress, 1st Session, *Sale of Foreign Bonds or Securities in the United States* (Washington, D.C., G.P.O., 1931–1932), Part 2, p. 505; R. A. Young, *Handbook on American Underwriting* . . . , pp. 124, 158.

63. Stinson to Dana G. Munro, May 3, 1929, NA, 824.51/512.

64. Mayer to Stimson, Confidential, July 18, 1930, NA, 823.00/584.

65. The members of the Kemmerer mission to Peru and their responsibilities were as follows: Kemmerer, currency and banking; Paul M. Atkins, public credit; Joseph T. Byrne, budget and accounting; William F. Roddy, customs; Walter Van Deusen, banking; John Philip Wernette, taxation; Stokeley W. Morgan, general secretary; and Lindsley Dodd, assistant secretary.

66. Dearing (Lima) to Stimson, March 4, 1931, NA 823.00 Revolutions/164; same to same, April 1, 1931, NA, 823.51/634.

67. Reserve Bank of Peru, Commission of Financial Advisors on Finances of National Government of Peru, Edwin Walter Kemmerer, President, *Projects of Laws* . . . *together with Reports in Support Thereof* (Lima, April 17, 1931), (Princeton: Princeton University Press, 1931); "Stabilization of the Currency in Peru," Pan-American Union, *Bulletin*, LXV (Nov. 1931), 1155–72; Kemmerer, *Money* (New York, 1935), pp. 162–64; U.S. Senate . . . , *Sale of Foreign Bonds* . . . , Part 4, p. 2122. The report of J. & W. Seligman & Company to the Johnson Committee (last citation above) indicates a continuous flow of American personnel to Peru to "study" financial problems, presumably due to concern over American investments.

68. Dearing to Stimson, July 30, 1931, NA, 823.51/720.

69. Piles to Hughes, March 23, 1923, NA, 821.51A/25; Leland Harrison to Brigadier General John H. Russell, American High Commissioner, Port au Prince, February 4, 1924, NA, 821.51A/33.

70. Kemmerer, "Economic Advisory Work for Governments," the *American Economic Review*, XVII (Mar. 1927), 8, and the *New York Times*, May 27, 1926, p. 10.

6 Barry Eichengreen ◆ House Calls of the Money Doctor: The Kemmerer Missions to Latin America, 1917–1931

> Once upon a time foreign money doctors roamed Latin America prescribing fixed exchange rates and passive gold exchange standard monetary rules. Bankers followed in their footsteps, from the halls of Montezuma to the shores of Daiquiri.
>
> Díaz-Alejandro (1982, p. 5)

Between 1917 and 1930 Professor Edwin Walter Kemmerer of Princeton University served as economic adviser or headed financial missions to seven Latin American countries. After diagnosing the financial condition of his patient (sometimes only under cover of night and with the protection of firearms), Dr. Kemmerer prescribed the standard remedies and engaged in the physician's favorite recreation: a round of golf with his colleagues. If the patient swallowed his medicine and responded to treatment, he was favored with bedside visits from long lost friends such as Dillon, Read.

Dr. Kemmerer's house calls were not limited to Latin America. Shortly after receiving his Ph.D. in 1903, he served as financial adviser to the U.S. Philippines commission and as chief of the division of currency of the treasury of the Philippine Islands. He headed financial commissions to South Africa in 1924–25, Poland in 1926, and China in 1929, served as a consultant to the Dawes Commission in 1925, and cochaired an economic survey of Turkey in 1934. Nor did Latin American governments rely exclusively on the most eminent of the money doctors: Kemmerer shared the practice with William Wilson Cumberland, a Princeton Ph.D.; Arthur Young, a research associate at the University of California and economic adviser to the U.S. State Department; Arthur's brother John Parke Young, prize pupil of Kemmerer's and student of Central American monetary affairs; and a number of other figures. Some countries such as Brazil preferred British practitioners like Otto Niemeyer or even Swiss and German specialists over American experts. But American money doctors dominated the practice through most of Latin America, and Kemmerer's name soon became synonymous with American financial missions to the region.

It is not hard to understand why Kemmerer involved himself in this practice. Not only was consulting for foreign governments heady stuff, it was lucrative as well. But why should Latin American governments solicit

From *Debt, Stabilization, and Development: Essays in Memory of Carlos Díaz-Alejandro*, ed. Guillermo Calvo et al. (Oxford, England, 1989), 57–77. Reprinted by permission of Blackwell Publishers.

the advice of foreign financial experts in general and North Americans in particular? Insofar as the financial reforms of this era entailed certain common steps—establishing a central bank, regulating the financial sector, reforming the fiscal system, and securing access to foreign capital—foreign experts could offer familiarity and even hands-on experience with previous plans. Their assessment of the economic situation was, for better or worse, detached from domestic political considerations.[1] As for why American experts were preferred, Kemmerer himself offered three reasons. The first was a presumption that the United States was not looking for political aggrandizement. But with the expansion of U.S. activities in Panama, Cuba, the Dominican Republic, Haiti, and Nicaragua, this notion came under increased scrutiny during the 1920s and better explained missions of American experts to China, Persia, Poland, South Africa, and Turkey than it did their employment in the Western Hemisphere.[2]

Kemmerer's second explanation was the rapid expansion and prosperity of the American economy. From a predominantly agricultural nation, seemingly an Argentina of North America, buffeted as recently as 1893 by Latin American-style convertibility crises, the United States had transformed itself into the world's leading industrial power and the only large country with finances sufficiently sound to maintain its gold-standard parity through the tumultuous post-First World War era. Until the Great Depression disabused them of any such notion, observers attributed this prosperity and financial stability to the reforms of central and commercial banking entailed in the Federal Reserve Act of 1914. Who better, therefore, than American financial experts to advise on the establishment of federal reserve systems for Chile or Colombia?[3]

Kemmerer's third explanation for the preference for U.S. advisers was the desire to attract American capital. The employment of American financial experts facilitated government bond flotations on the New York market and encouraged U.S. direct foreign investment. According to Kemmerer,

> a country that appoints American financial advisers and follows their advice in reorganizing its finances, along what American investors consider to be the most successful modern lines, increases its chances of appealing to the American investor and of obtaining from him capital on favorable terms.[4]

In their relationship to the international capital market, the Kemmerer missions bear a resemblance to IMF [International Monetary Fund] conditionality. In recent years commercial banks, when considering whether to extend loans, have been swayed by—indeed, often set as a precondition—the successful conclusion of negotiations with the IMF resulting in access to Fund resources in the upper credit tranches. In the 1920s, arranging the visit of a Kemmerer commission and implementing its recommendations seemed to exert a similarly reassuring influence over capital markets and to have a catalytic impact on foreign lending. In each case the visit by foreign financial experts served as a market signal. Acceptance of the provisions of an IMF stabilization plan or a Kemmerer report signaled to the market the government's acknowledgment of the desirability of policies consistent with the priorities of the lenders. Credible promises to balance the budget, stabilize the exchange rate, eliminate subsidies, and encourage wage moderation, all of which were recommendations of Kemmerer and IMF missions alike, while short of guarantees and not enforceable by lenders, still reveal information about the preferences of the government and thereby influence bankers' assessments of credit and country risk.

Admittedly, the analogy between IMF and Kemmerer missions is imperfect. The two differed in motives, circumstances, and provisions. IMF missions are typically initiated in response to an inflationary crisis entailing rapid exchange-rate depreciation and monetization of government budget deficits. In contrast, the Kemmerer missions of the 1920s were not a response to financial crisis. Although exchange rates were oscillating and many government budgets were in deficit, inflation remained at single-digit levels and no spiral of rapid depreciation was underway. Yet from the viewpoint of foreign investors, if not domestic officials, there was some danger that the situation might lapse into crisis. In the final decades of the nineteenth century, many of the countries of Latin America had experienced persistent inflation and exchange-rate depreciation, culminating in debt default. Only at the turn of the century had they taken tentative steps toward joining the gold standard—the single arrangement, in the view of the markets, capable of eliminating financial instability. But with the gold standard's worldwide suspension during the First World War, inflation had been rekindled and exchange rates unpegged. Without exchange-rate stabilization in the form of a gold standard peg, market participants feared that the situation might soon deteriorate to the point where it resembled late nineteenth-century conditions.

Moreover, the motives for inviting missions of foreign financial experts were not entirely the same in the 1920s as in the 1980s. In addition to its impact on international capital markets, Latin American governments desired the advice of foreign financial experts out of an interest in institutional reform. In many countries, efforts at domestic financial reform initiated some twenty-five years earlier had been hampered by the absence of a central bank to manage the gold standard and a regulatory apparatus to control the domestic banking system. In others, antiquated domestic tax systems and profligate bureaucracies fed the expansionary bias of fiscal policy, threatening to undermine any attempt to sustain the gold standard peg. The Kemmerer missions, and the reforms with which they were associated, represented the culmination of a long-standing Latin American interest in fiscal and financial reform. In a sense, the Kemmerer missions were a combination of the World Bank missions of the 1960s, concerned with institutional reform, and IMF missions of the 1980s, concerned primarily with stabilization and external borrowing.

Finally, Kemmerer and IMF missions differed in a critical provision. A notable feature of IMF stabilization programs, not shared by Kemmerer missions, is that countries now receive additional liquidity from a multilateral source outside the commercial banking system, funds which can be used for debt service or for investment projects likely to generate export receipts.[5]

Despite these differences, the analogy between Kemmerer and IMF missions raises a number of questions. One concerns the importance of the signaling function of a foreign mission compared to any catalytic impact on foreign lending of the injection of IMF liquidity. Another concerns the comparative advantage of purely private agents and supranational organizations in providing market signals. The Kemmerer commissions were, after all, nothing more than groups of foreign academics hired as consultants by Latin American governments, in part because of the reassuring influence of their seal of approval on potential foreign lenders. Purely private agents also figure in the market-signaling process today. Large money center banks, which engage in significant external lending, have devised practices broadly similar to the conditionality also practiced by supranational organizations and the Kemmerer commissions in the 1920s. Smaller banks often do not have sufficient information to make credit and country risk judgments and rely on the conditionality and lending decisions—in other words, on signals—transmitted by their larger, externally oriented counterparts.[6] In the 1920s, the thousands of small savers who purchased foreign bonds, and indeed some of the banks and issue houses that endorsed the prospectuses, found themselves in a similar situation and relied on the progress of a Kemmerer mission when assessing a country's creditworthiness. To put both questions baldly, if it is primarily signals that matter and if private agents can provide them, why not dispense with the IMF?

The Structure of Kemmerer Reforms

Although their precise details might differ, the central recommendations of the Kemmerer missions remained remarkably constant over time. Each commission submitted a series of memoranda centering on three recommendations: currency stabilization through restoration or establishment of the gold standard; legislation restricting the right of note issue to a central bank and regulating the activities of others in much the same manner that member banks were regulated by the U.S. Federal Reserve System; and reform of the tax structure and fiscal system so as to increase revenues and enhance economic efficiency.[7]

Kemmerer's advocacy of the gold standard stemmed not just from his belief that governments could not be entrusted with financial discretion, although he spoke repeatedly of the inability of government authorities to resist the temptation of inflationary finance, quoting proverbs to the effect that "We have gold because we cannot trust Governments."[8] He emphasized, in addition, the positive externalities of international money: its tendency to promote international trade, international finance, international migration, and international flows of information.[9] He viewed monetary instability as a source of uncertainty which everywhere depressed business activity but nowhere so much as in the international sphere, paraphrasing Napoleon to the effect that what the world most needs is "a common law, a common measure, and a common currency."[10] Failing monetary union, participation in the gold standard was the next best thing, "the gold standard . . . [being] the only standard which offers an early hope of becoming an international standard."[11]

The second set of recommendations concerned reform of the banking structure. The right of note issue and responsibility for managing the gold standard were to be entrusted to a central bank. Other banks should be regulated to insure that through reckless credit expansion they did not undermine the gold standard's stability. Kemmerer was involved in the establishment of the Banco de la Reserva del Peru in 1922, the Banco de la República in Colombia in 1923, the Banco Central de Chile in 1925, the Banco Central del Ecuador in 1927, and the Banco Central de Bolivia in 1929.[12] In Chile, the recommendations of the experts were embodied in the Monetary Law of 1925. By eliminating all restrictions on the import and export of gold and opening the mint to its free coinage, Chile was placed on the gold standard. The central bank was granted a fifty-year monopoly of note issue, and government agencies were prohibited from issuing "such money or documents that may circulate as money during the period of the Bank's concession."[13] In Ecuador, twenty-four new laws propounded by the commission provided the basis for reform. A new central bank, modeled on the U.S. Federal Reserve, was to serve as fiscal agent of the government, made the sole depository of public funds, granted a fifty-year monopoly of note issue, and obliged to peg the gold sucre to twenty U.S. cents.[14] Limiting the right of note issue to the central bank, going onto the gold standard, and precluding the monetization of budget deficits were seen as necessary to insure effective control of note circulation and maintenance of monetary stability.

The third strand of the typical Kemmerer report concerned budgetary reform. In Kemmerer's view, only a balanced budget was consistent with the maintenance of a fixed gold standard peg. He typically recommended adoption of a new budget law, entailing "modern and scientific" procedures for the imposition, collection, and disbursement of taxes and the accumulation of a reserve of surplus funds. To coordinate budgetary control, responsibility for the public finances was to be centralized in a single ministry. Special subsidies granted to railways, highways, and commercial enterprises were to be eliminated as expensive, inefficient, and regressive. The organic budget law might include statutory limitations on the ability of the authorities to finance one year's expenditures out of the next year's revenues, accounting procedures to permit the consistent estimation of total revenues and outlays, and Gramm-Rudman-like powers for the minister of finance to apportion revenues to ministries as they accrued and "order a reduction in the financial program of the Government if such reduction is deemed necessary for the financial stability of the Government."[15]

It is easy to see why the standard Kemmerer commission recommendations appealed to foreign investors. Going onto the gold standard and establishing an independent central bank precluded the financial excesses that the capital markets associated with a managed currency. Insuring that government expenditures, inclusive of interest payments, did not consistently outrun receipts protected a nation's debt-servicing capacity. Reforming the mechanisms through which funds were dispensed reduced the danger that borrowed funds would be dissipated by graft or squandered in nonproductive investment.

Anticipating the government's desire to turn to the international capital market, most Kemmerer commissions submitted a plan for the public credit. The shallowness of domestic capital markets and foreign ignorance of domestic firms, particularly in smaller countries, dictated that capital be both foreign and "be obtained in large part through government loans."[16] While the beneficent effects of foreign capital were never questioned, governments were instructed to exercise care that the rate of return on investments financed with foreign funds exceeded their interest cost. Borrowing to finance current expenditure was justifiable only under extraordinary circumstances such as war or national disaster. Ordinarily, borrowing should be resorted to, the commissioners recommended, only for permanent public improvements. In most Latin American countries, this meant public works such as railways, toll roads, and irrigation projects.

The commissioners were at pains to distinguish public works which would pay their way from those which would not. Borrowing for non-self-supporting public works such as schools, public buildings, and toll-free roads was justifiable only insofar as the public was able and willing to bear the taxation needed to service the loan.[17] Typically, the experts proceeded on the assumption that the contribution of general revenues would be minimal. For example, in 1927 the Kemmerer commission to Bolivia was requested to pass on the advisability of a proposal to construct a railroad from Cochabamba to Santa Cruz.[18] The commissioners first noted that the government had available little more than $6 million to fund a project whose estimated cost was between $21 million and $37 million. They then cited the opinion of "high engineering authority" that the line could not be expected to pay its running expenses and fixed charges for many years following completion. After observing that 75 percent of national revenue was already pledged to guarantee existing debt and that 37 percent of the estimated national government budget was devoted to interest and amortization, they questioned whether the government could succeed in securing a commitment from a reputable banking house, and argued that even if it proved possible to obtain foreign money, doing so would be unwise because of the heavy burden of existing debt and the non-self-financing character of the investment project. These criteria sound strikingly modern but for the absence of a distinction between private and social returns.[19]

The experts recommended that the political authorities create a central agency empowered to determine the character and priority of public works and to oversee their completion. Insuring that funds were devoted to those projects with the highest rates of return and that borrowing only proceeded to the point where returns equaled the interest cost required that the national government control the issue of funded debt by departments and municipalities; projects of law to this effect were submitted. The negative externalities experienced by many national and departmental governments due to overborrowing by the few were duly noted by the experts.[20]

Other recommendations mainly concerned strategies to minimize the cost of foreign borrowing. Countries were urged to plan carefully the distribution of maturities and amortization payments to avoid driving the price of bonds down when issued and up when repurchased for amortization. Diversification was also deemed desirable to minimize the risk that refunding activities would be concentrated at moments when the loan market was disturbed. Governments were instructed to insist on prepayment rights to permit them to capitalize on unanticipated declines in interest rates. Sinking fund provisions, which required amortized bonds, instead of being canceled, to be held by the bankers until maturity of the entire issue, were viewed as undesirable because of the additional expense of the commission involved and the danger that sequestered bonds might find their way back into the market. Governments were warned against provisions in some loan contracts binding the borrowing country to use loan proceeds for purchases of supplies from the country providing the funds or from specific concerns. The commissioners noted that such provisions proliferated in periods when the New York and London markets were disinclined to lend at favorable interest rates. Rather than representing a way to circumvent the capital market's hesitation, these provisions often entailed substantial hidden charges which the lenders might recoup many times over.[21]

Finally, borrowing nations were urged to establish strong connections with a reputable banking house. The commissioners noted that certain Latin American countries, like Colombia in 1923, had shopped around, using an offer from one banking house as a lever to obtain better terms from another. In the long run, they argued, this was inefficacious. Through a long-term relationship, a banking house can acquire a reputation as a source of information on economic conditions in the borrowing country. Since ignorance was seen as one of the principal impediments to borrowing, cultivation of what the commissioners described as a strong center of propaganda would rebound favorably on the borrowing country. A banking house which anticipated additional financing, they argued further, had an interest in maintaining an orderly market in the securities of the indebted country, which would lead it to intervene in support of that country's bonds if the market was disturbed by nearby revolution or default. Finally, a strong connection with a leading banking house was seen as useful in times of emergency. A temporary budget deficit could be tided over by short-term external borrowing only if the government possessed a firm connection with a foreign banker willing to incur the risks and expenses of such a loan in anticipation of future commissions.[22]

For countries in default, regaining access to the international capital market required adjustment of the existing debt and resumption of service. Ecuadorian debt service, at the time of the Kemmerer commission's visit, was up-to-date on only one of four issues recognized by the national government, and interest on the First Mortgage bonds, which accounted for 95 percent of the total foreign debt, was fourteen years in arrears. These interest arrears amounted to nearly two thirds of the total principal outstanding.[23] In its negotiations with the Corporation of Foreign Bondholders, the Kemmerer commission suggested that Ecuador press for a substantial reduction of the obligation. Most of the paper was held by speculators who had purchased it for 20 to 30 percent of par and who would reap generous returns were the bonds redeemed at 35. Ecuador might obtain more favorable terms, he noted, if it paid cash rather than issued refunding bonds. While careful to note that the specific terms of the settlement were outside the province of the financial commission, the experts nonetheless suggested general lines that negotiations might follow. In the Ecuadorian case, the principal and interest arrears would cost the country $7 million if paid off at 35; Kemmerer envisaged a loan of $9 million, leaving $2 million for other productive uses.[24]

A problem faced by new Latin American regimes attempting to gain access to the U.S. capital market was lack of diplomatic recognition. The State Department received letters from bondholders urging them not to recognize the new Ecuadorian regime until an acceptable debt settlement had been reached.[25] But as Kemmerer pointed out, this created a "Catch 22" situation: Ecuador was unable to settle with the bondholders until it contracted a foreign loan, but it could not float a loan in New York before securing recognition. Thus, Kemmerer urged upon the State Department the more farsighted policy of according recognition.

Kemmerer Missions and U.S. Lending

To analyze the capital market response to the Kemmerer missions, I employ data on the value of U.S. foreign lending through 1929 assembled by [Cleona] Lewis (1938). Lewis's tabulations have two advantages: first, she attempted to include all foreign securities purchased in the United States, not just publicly issued bonds and shares but also those privately taken; second, she sought to exclude any portion sold in foreign markets and securities of American-controlled enterprises. For each country and year, the total face value of issues is provided separately for short- and long-term debt and for national and provincial government, municipal and corporate issues.

The first test of the hypothesis that Kemmerer missions initiated a rise in U.S. lending is to compute the *t*-statistic for the difference in mean levels of lending between the two years immediately preceding and immediately following each mission. The power of the tests is not high, since Lewis's period encompasses only five Kemmerer missions: Colombia in 1923, Guatemala in 1924, Chile in 1925, Poland in 1926, and Bolivia in 1927 (see Table 4.1). The *t*-statistic is 1.40 for long-term national loans and 1.74 for long-term municipal loans, with a critical 90 percent value of 1.40 (one-tail test). In contrast, the *t*-statistics of 0.45 for short-term national loans, 1.00 for short-term municipal loans, and 0.15 for long-term corporate loans indicate insignificant increases in lending. (No short-term corporate loans to these countries are reported.) When the three years preceding and following each Kemmerer mission are compared, Bolivia must be dropped for lack of data for 1930, but the *t*-statistic for long-term national loans rises to 1.55 and for long-term municipal loans to 1.87, compared to a critical value of 1.44. Again, there is no evidence that either short-term loans or loans to nongovernmental entities were affected significantly by the Kemmerer missions.

Table 4.1 Aggregate Face Value of Foreign Dollar Loans Issued to Countries Hosting Kemmerer Missions (Millions of U.S. Dollars)

Year	Colombia (1923)	Guatemala (1924)	Chile (1925)	Poland (1926)	Bolivia (1927)
1921	—	—	44.0	—	9.3
1922	6.8	—	18.0	—	25.0
1923	—	—	—	—	—
1924	9.0	—	18.3	5.0	5.1
1925	4.0	—	55.2	44.4	—
1926	43.5	—	75.2	2.8	—
1927	68.4	—	22.5	47.0	12.3
1928	71.4	0.6	79.9	17.0	19.7
1929	1.8	—	42.4	—	—
1930	0.5	—	21.4	—	—

Source: Lewis (1938)

One approach to increasing the power of the test is to pool the five types of loans. The *t*-statistics are 1.46 for two-year periods and 1.47 for three-year periods, both compared to a critical value of 1.30; these are little different from those reported above. Another approach assumes that the impact of Kemmerer missions is the same across categories of borrowers but recognizes that average levels of lending to each category differed. Lending can be regressed on dummy variables for type of borrower and for periods after Kemmerer's visits. Results appear in the first two columns of Table 4.2. For three-year periods, the coefficient capturing the effects of Kemmerer's visits is statistically significant at the 95 percent level (one-tail test); for two-year periods it approaches significance at that level.

Since the previous paragraph suggests that the impact of Kemmerer missions on long-term national and municipal borrowing differed from their impact on short-term borrowing and borrowing by corporations, the dummy variables for long-term national or long-term municipal loans were interacted with the Kemmerer mission dummy. These results appear in the final two columns of Table 4.2. Only long-term loans to national governments appear to have been significantly affected by the Kemmerer missions. The coefficient on such loans interacted with periods succeeding a Kemmerer mission significantly exceeds zero at the 99 percent level when three-year periods are compared, and approaches significance at that level for two-year periods.

Table 4.2 U.S. Lending and Kemmerer Missions (Dependent Variable Is Value of Lending over Two- or Three-Year Period in Millions of U.S. Dollars)

Variable	Two Year	Three Year	Two Year	Three Year
Constant	-2454.5	-4414.0	-728.4	-910.5
	(0.64)	(0.65)	(0.19)	(0.13)
Long-term	17179.0	26995.0	8031.6	11814.0
national	(3.46)	(3.24)	(1.31)	(1.18)
Short-term	1785.1	2231.4	1785.1	2231.4
national	(0.36)	(0.25)	(0.38)	(0.27)
Long-term	3404.4	4005.5	3671.2	4589.0
municipal	(0.65)	(0.45)	(0.60)	(0.43)
Short-term	1400.0	1750.0	1400.0	1750.0
municipal	(0.28)	(0.20)	(0.29)	(0.21)
Period following	5129.0	9078.0	1656.7	2070.9
mission	(1.63)	(1.68)	(0.43)	(0.31)
Period following			18295.0	30363.0
mission* long-term			(2.36)	(2.44)
national				
Period following			-933.5	-1166.9
mission* long-term			(0.12)	(0.09)
municipal				
R^2	0.30	0.32	0.43	0.45
n	50	42	50	42

t-statistics in parentheses.

Source: See text

Since the recommendations of the experts pertained principally to central government financial and fiscal affairs, it is plausible that loans to national governments were affected mainly. Moreover, since some reforms affected state and local public finance and brought under centralized control borrowing by other levels of government (this was not uniformly the case), it is plausible that the results should suggest some, albeit weaker, influence over lending to municipalities. The impact of reform of public finance on lending to corporations, a relationship emphasized by those who believed that financial stability was critical for commercial and industrial prosperity, is not evident in the data.

It can be objected that these effects are properly attributable to the fact of stabilization and going onto the gold standard rather than to the intervention of financial experts. If so, then the same rise of lending between the periods immediately preceding and following stabilization should be observed in other countries. Evidence for twenty-two other countries to which the United States lent during the 1920s does not bear out this connection, however. Again, the two- and three-year periods preceding and following stabilization, chosen as the year in which that country returned to the gold standard de facto, may be compared. In every case the *t*-statistic for the difference in means is considerably smaller than the comparable *t*-statistic for countries with Kemmerer missions. In no case is the difference in means statistically significant at the 90 percent level.

The results of this section confirm that gold standard stabilizations which took place in conjunction with Kemmerer missions were unusually conducive to foreign lending. To understand how and why this was so, it is necessary to examine individual country experiences.

The Success of Kemmerer Reforms

Whether judged according to Kemmerer's priorities, which attached special importance to maintaining price stability, restoring the gold standard, and balancing the government budget, or according to the favorable reaction of the international capital market as reflected in the enthusiasm with which it responded to subsequent attempts to float a loan, the Kemmerer missions of the mid to late 1920s were more successful than those which came before or after. The explanation cannot lie in any improvement in procedures and recommendations since, as already noted, those procedures and recommendations changed little over time. Rather, the explanation must lie in the circumstances. Hence the contrast between the earlier and later missions sheds light on the circumstances under which Kemmerer-style conditionality is most likely to have a catalytic effect on international loan negotiations. That contrast suggests that changes in the domestic political and international economic environments, including the extent of political stability, trends in primary commodity prices, and conditions in the New York capital market, together account for the catalytic effect of the Kemmerer missions of the later 1920s.

The role of these three determinants of the outcome of the Kemmerer missions is illustrated by the contrasting cases of Mexico and Chile. The overarching importance of political stability is evident in the Mexican case. For most of the second decade of the twentieth century, Mexico had been racked by revolutionary and counterrevolutionary campaigns culminating in civil war. Service on the $600 million external debt was suspended in early 1914, and by 1915 political, economic, and fiscal institutions were nearing collapse. Following adoption of the Queretaro Constitution in 1917 and the restoration of some stability, Kemmerer was approached to organize a financial mission to the country. He and his associates recommended that the authorities balance the budget, stabilize the currency, and implement a program of fiscal reform designed to enhance the efficiency of tax collection and increase the progressivity of its incidence.[26]

No sooner had the commission begun to formulate these proposals than attempts to execute the land reform provisions suggested by the new constitution and to limit the power of the Church began to "unsettle confidence, reduce productivity, and make for unrest, with results involving both decreases in revenues and increases in expenditures."[27] Article 27 of the new constitution, which declared all subsoil resources the patrimony of the nation and raised the specter of nationalization of the petroleum industry, placed a cap on foreign investment. With the resurgence of unrest, railway lines were severed, agricultural output declined, and mining centers were overrun by bandits. The major banks were forced to close their doors and the nation was rendered dependent for money balances on the circulation of gold and silver coin and U.S. dollars.[28] Political turmoil, in conjunction with newly progressive taxation, provided a double inducement for capital flight which defeated attempts to place the budget on a stable footing.

These disruptions rendered irrelevant Kemmerer's recommendation that Mexico adopt the gold standard immediately upon achieving a minimum specie backing of 40 percent of note circulation, by ruling out any attempt to acquire the needed gold and threatening a run on reserves if the authorities were so reckless as to institute convertibility.[29] While provision for a central bank was incorporated into the new constitution, that bank was only established in 1925. Thus, the Mexican authorities had no opportunity to demonstrate either their commitment to, or the efficacy of, Kemmerer's newly designed financial arrangements. While the budget avoided collapse, it did not move into balance in the manner the commission recommended. The semblance of balance it retained was due to the tendency of the First World War and the postwar boom to stimulate oil revenues and inflate the prices of other mineral products. With the collapse of commodity prices after 1921 and the heavy expenditures incurred in suppressing the Huerta revolt of 1923–24, fiscal conditions disintegrated.

Not surprisingly, the capital market's response was not up to Kemmerer commission standards. The Mexican authorities sought to capitalize on Kemmerer's visit and on the commodity-price boom of 1920–21 by securing U.S. loans for use in stabilizing the currency, establishing the central bank, and financing reconstruction and development projects. But the Department of State, in collaboration with the International Committee of Bankers on

Mexico, embargoed loans to the new government.[30] Not only did the State Department discourage lending directly, but it withheld diplomatic recognition, effectively blockading access to the New York market. The officials and the bankers were united by the former's interest in securing Mexico's signature on a treaty which would nullify the provisions of Article 27 and the latter's desire to see debt service resumed.

After convoluted negotiations and continued State Department pressure, in 1922, President Alvaro Obregón announced Mexico's intention to resume payment on the external debt, subject only to agreement with the bankers on the size and schedule of payments and the disposition of back interest. Initially, discussions proceeded on the assumption that Mexico was not seeking new money. Just when the two parties seemed to have an agreement in hand, however, a loan to finance the establishment of the central bank was proposed by the minister of finance. This the American bankers refused. Mexico went ahead with the agreement nonetheless, recognizing an external debt of more than $500 million and interest arrearages of $280 million. However, the outbreak of the Huerta Rebellion made it impossible to transfer interest on schedule, and in June 1924, Obregón suspended the agreement with the bankers. As late as 1928, a committee of American financial experts reminded the bankers that "internal dissensions and strained international relations have repeatedly shaken confidence in such a way as to cause exports of capital and discourage investment in Mexico."[31]

Thus, the Mexican experience indicates that favorable commodity prices like those which prevailed in 1920–21 were, at best, a necessary condition for the successful implementation of the Kemmerer commission recommendations. Fiscal reform, however well conceived, was likely to be ineffective if it was not accompanied by domestic political stability, in whose absence the capital market was unwilling to respond.

In contrast to the Mexican experience, Kemmerer's 1925 mission to Chile epitomized the work of the successful financial commission. Nearly four decades of inflation provided the backdrop to Kemmerer's visit.[32] In Chile, the pressure for monetization had traditionally emanated, not from government budget deficits, but from loans by the agricultural mortgage banks to the landed interests. When inflation accelerated, wages lagged behind prices, savings were eroded, and commerce was disrupted, while the mortgage burden of the large landowners was lightened.[33] In response to this situation, the mercantile middle class, miners, and agricultural laborers all presssed for economic and social reform.

The election of Arturo Alessandri in 1920 reflected these pressures, and Alessandri's new regime was successful in stabilizing the exchange rate and in nearly bringing inflation to a halt. His attempts to reform the public finances and obtain a mission of American financial experts were frustrated, however, by continued Congressional dominance of the landed interests. The deadlock led to Alessandri's replacement by a military junta in 1924, his recall to power following a countercoup in 1925, and then his replacement by Colonel Carlos Ibañez and a semidictatorial regime before the end of the same year. There was then some resurgence of inflation. But however disturbing this political turmoil, it never involved the violence and disorder experienced in Mexico; if anything it strengthened the hand of those pressing for monetary reform. The 1924 revolution freed the government from the dominance of the landed interests, and until the adoption of a new constitution, the president was empowered to pass decree laws with only the approval of his cabinet. These powers greatly expedited the process of financial reform. The military group backing the new regime unanimously supported monetary stabilization, pressured the government to implement a program, and turned out en masse to greet Kemmerer on his midnight arrival in Santiago.

External stability, the second necessary condition, was also present in the Chilean case. In the mid-1920s conditions in world markets for nitrates and copper were relatively favorable, stimulating export earnings. These earnings remained respectable even though real wages had reversed most of the erosion previously caused by inflation. There was no structural deficit in the public sector accounts contributing to a trade deficit. The exchange rate had remained relatively stable for four years and even moved upwards in anticipation of the visit of financial experts. The government's reserve position was strong: its gold reserves and nitrate pledges would have been sufficient to retire all the paper money in circulation.

Optimism in international capital markets regarding the developing world, a third condition favoring the success of Kemmerer-style reforms, was also present in the Chilean case. American bondholders invested $187 million in Chilean public institutions between June 1925 and August 1929, more than three times the 1919–1925 total. It might be argued that the creditors' willingness to underwrite Chilean loans merely reflected the favorable political and economic developments described above. But in addition, the timing of Chile's stabilization was fortuitous: coming in 1925 it coincided with a boom in foreign lending by New York and London, which surely improved the terms and increased the availability of the loans that the Chileans secured. These loans permitted the monetary orthodoxy of the gold standard to coexist with loose domestic credit conditions and a highly expansionary program of public works.

Unlike those in Mexico, the authorities in Chile had an early opportunity to demonstrate the efficacy of, and their commitment to, these new arrangements. In the summer of 1926, the breakdown of Tacna-Arica negotiations with Peru created a war scare and a run on the central bank. In ten days the bank furnished $5 million in foreign exchange in a successful defence of the gold standard. Later, when the onset of the Great Depression forced other Latin American countries to depreciate their currencies in 1929, Chile remained on the gold standard through Britain's departure in September 1931.

While the roles of political stability, commodity prices, and capital-market conditions are somewhat less transparent in the Colombian case, the negotiations surrounding the Kemmerer missions to Bogotá in 1923 and 1930 shed special light on bank conditionality in the 1920s and on the role of American financial experts. As in other Latin American countries, labor, and the mercantile and industrial middle classes, challenged entrenched Conservative-Church leadership in the 1920s. The Colombian regime accommodated these pressures by passing legislation empowering the government to intervene in capital-labor disputes, to regulate health and safety, and to construct houses for the working class. But the post-First World War administration of Pedro Nel Ospina inherited a budgetary problem attributable, in part, to generous subsidies paid to the Church and Society of Jesus, and an inconvertible currency resulting from paper money issued during the European war.[34] Once Colombia's dispute with the United States over the separation of Panama was finally settled by the Thomson-Urrutia Treaty of 1921–22, Ospina turned to the United States for financial assistance. The 1923 Kemmerer mission offered the usual formula: establishment of a central bank, regulation of branch banking, reorganization of the customs system, adherence to the gold standard, maintenance of a balanced budget, and securing an arrangement with an exclusive fiscal agent.

The commission's recommendations were implemented with some difficulty only over the objections of domestic bankers who opposed regulation, government employees who opposed fiscal austerity, residents of outlying regions who opposed economic centralization, coffee growers who preferred the creation of an agricultural mortgage bank capable of providing liberal credit, and those who feared the undue influence of the United States. The capital market's response remained subdued until it became apparent that the new institutional arrangements would take.

As in Chile, an early demonstration of the efficacy of the new institutions, and of the authorities' commitment to them, proved critical. Not long after their adoption, the failure of one of the nation's largest importing and merchandising houses undermined the solvency of a major bank. As panic spread, the government declared a two-day bank holiday and took the opportunity to import bank notes by airplane. Through their free provision, the crisis was surmounted. Following this demonstration, Colombia's search for a fiscal agent initiated a competitive scramble between London and New

York. The government had previously borrowed in Europe, and Lazards stood ready to act as its exclusive agent. Britain's presence had been reinforced by establishment of a Bogotá office of the London and River Plate Bank in 1920, and of branch offices in subsequent years.[35] But Thomas Russell Lill, a member of the Kemmerer commission who remained under contract to Colombia as technical adviser to the government, used his influence to encourage the selection of an American banking firm. Recognizing the existence of a "unique financial opening . . . [an] entering wedge," the State Department's legation in Bogotá urged officials in Washington to arrange a cooperative offer from the principal American competitors, Blair and Morgan.[36]

Only $9 million of Colombian government bonds were floated in New York in 1924, and $8 million in 1925. But their value rose to $34 million in 1926, $67 million in 1927, and $79 million in the first half of 1928.[37] About this time observers grew alarmed over the nature and volume of Colombian borrowing. In 1928, the U.S. Commerce Department warned that Colombian credit may have been endangered.[38] In 1929, Jefferson Caffery of the American legation in Bogotá advised Washington that information provided by the municipality of Bogotá exaggerated the progress of public works, contained unduly optimistic revenue estimates, and was "highly misleading and obviously designed for bond market propaganda."[39] But it is unclear what role these fears, as opposed to the 1928 boom on Wall Street and concomitant decline in U.S. foreign lending, or the 1929 slump in coffee prices and deterioration in the government's budgetary position, played in the drop in American lending to Colombia after the first semester of 1928.

Another influence over American lending to Colombia was the dispute over oil concessions. At the end of 1927 and beginning of 1928, Colombia imposed new controls on the U.S.-dominated oil industry, requiring firms to obtain drilling permits and pay a doubled tax on production on private lands. Members of the British legation suggested that New York issue houses, with the encouragement of the State and Commerce departments, were refusing loans to Colombia and driving down the market prices of bonds to extract concessions on the oil question.[40]

The natural way to remedy the situation was to arrange a mission of foreign experts. First, a petroleum commission was appointed to prepare new legislation clarifying the position of foreign companies, but with the approach of the 1930 presidential election, the Colombian Congress adjourned before it could be adopted. The election brought to power the Liberal Enrique Olaya Herrera, formerly the Colombian representative at Washington, who was well respected in the United States and had campaigned on the promise to offer Kemmerer a return engagement. Following conferences at the Federal Reserve Bank of New York, he announced his intention to obtain a foreign loan and arranged a second Kemmerer mission. This time, however, Kemmerer recommended against foreign borrowing. While he suggested that defending the gold standard, reducing expenditures, and reforming the administration of the customs and railroads might do much to reassure foreign bankers, Kemmerer suggested that recession in Latin America and the depressed state of the New York market made it "extremely difficult to sell a large enough issue to fund the present deficit."[41] Instead, the government was urged to sell bonds domestically.

The market's response to the 1930 Kemmerer mission sheds light on which deterrents to foreign lending were binding. Contrary to Kemmerer's expectations, in 1930 Colombia successfully obtained $20 million in credit in New York, although Kemmerer's skepticism of Colombia's general ability to borrow in the Depression was subsequently proven correct. A syndicate headed by National City Bank advanced $3 million and turned over the residual in installments ending in June 1931. Obviously, recovery from the Depression was not a precondition for obtaining foreign money. The progress of petroleum legislation may have been more important, since Olaya's support for it was well known. Nonetheless, 60 percent of the proceeds of the dollar loan was transferred to Colombia before any legislation was drafted, much less before it was signed by the president in March 1931.

The principal determinant of Colombian creditworthiness was the conditionality practiced by the American banks in conjunction with Kemmerer's activities. In some respects, the National City Bank conditionality and the Kemmerer conditionality were complementary. National City required, as a condition of the loan, that Colombia balance its budget but for that portion which would be financed by an internal loan of six million pesos, and that it revise its financial and customs systems. The government's invitation to Kemmerer signaled its willingness to do so and its possession of a plan of action. "Kemmerer's reforms substituted for more direct banker supervision of government . . . [and] appeared 'scientifically' sound and less insulting to national pride."[42] But in other respects the two forms of conditionality did not complement one another. National City wished Colombia to adopt, in addition to other measures, a debt-ceiling law. Kemmerer objected to any such clause in the loan contract on the grounds that it was not enforceable if a future legislature wished to repeal it and that it would threaten the central bank's ability to lend freely in time of crisis. While favoring an exclusive arrangement with a fiscal agent, Kemmerer chided the bankers for their last-minute efforts to impose such conditions on Colombia in its time of need.[43]

By the end of 1930, Kemmerer's task was complete, whereas the bankers had yet to turn over the final installments of the loan. Before making the third payment in March 1931, the bankers demanded and secured the debt ceiling which limited interest and amortization to 30 percent of government revenues.[44] They attempted to withhold the final payment on the grounds that the government budget deficit exceeded agreed limits. Olaya responded that the bankers' objections were mere technicalities. Unlike Kemmerer, the Colombian president retained some leverage: he conferred with the American minister, who called the State Department, which encouraged National City Bank to turn over the remaining tranche.[45]

Conclusion

The resemblance of the Kemmerer missions of the 1920s to IMF conditionality as practiced in recent years has been noted previously, both by Latin American historians and by critics of the current international financial arrangements. Three questions are raised by the extent of the parallels. First, under what conditions is outside intervention needed to signal creditworthiness to the international capital market? Second, must the signal be provided by an international agency, or can the essential functions be carried out by the indebted government in conjunction with banks and experts from the private sector? Third, are there conditions under which the international capital markets fail to respond to signals of a country's fiscal and monetary orthodoxy, however convincing, creating an efficiency rationale for a transnational agency which can inject financial resources from a reserve outside the capital markets?

The Kemmerer missions shed light on the manner in which this market-signaling process works. In the 1920s, creditworthiness meant that the government had taken steps to balance its budget, create an autonomous central bank, limit money and credit creation to levels consistent with maintenance of the gold standard, and allocate borrowed funds to projects yielding, at least, the market rate of return. Together these measures increased the likelihood that the nation would retain the capacity to service its debt. An invitation to Kemmerer signaled the authorities' willingness to contemplate these measures. Successful completion of his mission indicated that the government possessed a plan of action, and legislation implementing its recommendations signaled that it was taking concrete steps toward implementation.

But if the Kemmerer commissions, despite their purely private status, were highly efficient providers of market signals, signals alone proved adequate only under favorable conditions. They worked well in the mid- to late 1920s, where working is defined as helping a country secure access to the international capital market, only because the industrialized countries were growing rapidly, export markets were buoyant, and financial centers were favorably inclined toward lending to developing regions. When these conditions disappeared, the response of the capital markets was disappointing; once trade collapsed and the fashion for foreign lending passed, Kemmerer's intervention was sufficient to restore access to foreign funds. The implication is that IMF conditionality—which differs by virtue of the Fund's own financial resources and by the leverage it can bring to bear on other lenders—is crucial precisely when access to external funds is most valuable.

Notes

For permission to cite materials from the Kemmerer papers, I thank the Princeton University Library. For permission to cite materials in the Public Record Office, I thank the controller of HM Stationery Office. Gustavo Franco, Jeffrey Williamson, and especially José O'Campo provided helpful comments.

1. As the Colombian president told his Congress in 1923, reforms were more likely to be implemented if recommended by foreigners "whose prestige would not be haggled away as would happen with our own professionals in a backward environment like ours, in which nothing and no one escape the objections and pettiness of politics." Cited in Drake (1979, p. 22).

2. Angell (1933, p. 4–41).

3. Kemmerer himself was a leading expert on the operation of the Federal Reserve System; see Kemmerer (1918a).

4. Kemmerer (1927, p. 4).

5. In this the Kemmerer missions contrast with the League of Nations' European stabilization loans in the early 1920s. For details, see Nurkse (1946).

6. Friedman (1984, pp. 109–10).

7. Prototypical is the 1926–27 Ecuadorian mission described below and, in more detail, by Pérez (1928).

8. Kemmerer (1944, p. 181).

9. Ibid. (ch. VII). See also Seidel (1972, p. 523).

10. Kemmerer (1916, p. 66).

11. Ibid. (1934, p. 13).

12. Ibid. (1926, p. 271).

13. Collins (1929, p. 476).

14. Pérez (1928, p. 82).

15. "Report in support of a project of an organic budget law," Kemmerer Papers, Princeton University (hereafter EWK), Box 432 (Colombia, 1930).

16. "Report on public credit" (submitted to the president of the republic and the minister of finance, on 15 March 1927, by the Commission of Financial Advisers), EWK, Box 216 (Ecuador, 1927), p. 1.

17. A clear statement of these rules appears in "Republic of Bolivia: report on public credit" (as submitted to the president of the republic and the minister of finance, on 2 July 1927 by the Commission of Financial Advisers), EWK, Box 66 (Bolivia, 1927).

18. "To His Excellency the President of the Republic of Bolivia" (La Paz, 24 June 1927), EWK, Box 137 (Bolivia, 1927). Other cost estimates are cited in the skeptical discussion of this project by Marsh (1928, pp. 83–86).

19. The absence of this distinction is notable in a 1930 Colombian report, in which the 2.1 percent rate of return before depreciation and interest charges on government investments in national railways is contrasted with the 12 percent cost of borrowed funds, without any mention of indirect benefits to the nation or to the government budget. "A plan of public credit," EWK, Box 122 (Colombia, 1930), section IX, p. 5. But this distinction was alluded to in a 1923 memorandum to Colombian officials. "Report on public credit," EWK, Box 95 (Colombia, 1923).

20. "A plan of public credit," EWK, Box 122 (Colombia, 1930), section III.

21. "Republic of Bolivia: report on public credit" (as submitted to the president and the minister of finance on 2 July 1927 by the Commission of Financial Advisers), EWK, Box 66 (Bolivia, 1927), pp. 20–21.

22. "Report on public credit," EWK, Box 95 (Colombia, 1923), p. 3; "Report on public credit" (submitted to the president of the republic and the minister of finance, on 15 March 1927 by the Commission of Financial Advisers), EWK, Box 216 (Ecuador, 1927), pp. 30–34; "Republic of Bolivia: report on public credit" (as submitted to the president of the republic and the minister of finance, on 2 July 1927 by the Commission of Financial Advisers), Box 66 (Bolivia, 1927), pp. 23–27.

23. "Report on public credit" (submitted to the president of the republic and the minister of finance, on 15 March 1927, by the Commission of Financial Advisers), EWK, Box 216 (Ecuador, 1927), p. 12.

24. "The financial situation in Ecuador" (conversation with E. W. Kemmerer), Department of State, Division of Latin American Affairs, 29 December 1927, National Archives M 1924 822.57a/59, p. 1.

25. Ibid., pp. 1–2.

26. Kemmerer's invitation was an outgrowth of consultations between representatives of the Mexican and American governments designed to paper over strains caused by the recently promulgated export tax on minerals and the impact of domestic unrest on the operations of foreign enterprises. Other members of the mission included Arthur Young and H. A. Chandler of Columbia University. The tax reform plan was sufficiently well received to provide the basis of the Mexican revenue system for a period of decades. Curti and Birr (1954, pp. 160–61).

27. "Report on the fiscal and economic condition of Mexico," prepared for the International Committee of Bankers on Mexico, Thomas W. Lamont, chairman, by Joseph Edmund Sterrett and Joseph Stancliffe Davis, New York, 25 May 1928, EWK, Box 107 (Mexico, 1928), p. 4.

28. Kemmerer (1918b, pp. 261–2).

29. The commission's monetary proposals are described in Kemmerer (1918b).

30. On the origins of the International Bankers Committee, see Smith (1963). Further information on the Mexican episode may be found in Kane (1973).

31. "Report on the fiscal and economic condition of Mexico," prepared for the International Committee of Bankers on Mexico, Thomas W. Lamont, chairman, by Joseph Edmund Sterrett and Joseph Stancliffe Davis, New York, 25 May 1928, EWK, Box 107 (Mexico, 1928), p. 28.

32. For discussion, see Fetter (1931) or Davis (1963).

33. Kemmerer (1926, pp. 269–70).

34. Bernstein (1964, pp. 120–21).

35. Joslin (1963, pp. 239–41).

36. "To the Honorable Secretary of State, Washington, from Samuel H. Piles, Legation of the United States of America, Bogotá, Colombia," No. 337, 12 January 1924, National Archives M 1294 821.51/251, pp. 2–3.

37. For these and related statistics, see Young (1930).

38. Rippy (1931, pp. 166–73); Parks (1935, p. 473).

39. "To the Honorable Secretary of State, Washington, from Jefferson Caffery, Legation of the United States of America, Bogotá, Colombia," No. 665, 31 October 1929, National Archives, M 1294 821.51a, p. 2. See also letter No. 669, dated 4 November from the same file.

40. On Commerce Department actions, see Bureau of Foreign and Domestic Commerce, Special Circular No. 305, reprinted in U.S. Senate (1931–32), pp. 730–38. On British interpretations, see "To the Right Honourable Arthur Henderson, Esq. M.P., Department of Overseas Trade from the British Legation Bogotá," British Public Record Office 371/13478, 19 November 1929.

41. "A plan of public credit," EWK, Box 122 (Colombia, 1930), section 6.

42. Drake (1979, p. 53).

43. Kemmerer Diary (transcript), EWK, 1930–175 (24 June 1930), 1930–262 (19 September 1930).

44. *New York Times*, 5 January 1931.

45. *New York Times*, 13 January 1932.

References

Angell, James W. (1933), *Financial Foreign Policy of the United States*, New York: Council on Foreign Relations.

Bernstein, Harry (1964), *Venezuela and Colombia*, Englewood Cliffs, New Jersey: Prentice-Hall.

Collins, Harry T. (1927), "Currency reforms in South America," *Current History*, pp. 475–77.

Curti, Merle, and Birr, Kendall (1954), *Prelude to Point Four: American Technical Missions Overseas, 1838–1938*, Madison: University of Wisconsin Press.

Davis, Tom E. (1963), "Eight decades of inflation in Chile, 1879–1959: a political interpretation," *Journal of Political Economy*, LXXI, 389–97.

Díaz-Alejandro, Carlos (1983), "Stories of the 1930s for the 1980s," in Pedro Aspe Armella, Rudiger Dornbusch, and Maurice Obstfeld (eds.), *Financial Policies and the World Capital Market: The Problem of Latin American Countries*, Chicago: University of Chicago Press, pp. 5–35.

Drake, Paul W. (1979), "The Origins of United States Economic Supremacy in South America: Colombia's Dance of the Millions, 1923–33," Woodrow Wilson Center Latin American Program Working Paper no. 40.

Fetter, Frank W. (1931), *Monetary Inflation in Chile*, Princeton: Princeton University Press.

Friedman, Irving S. (1984), "Private bank conditionality: comparisons with the IMF and the World Bank," in John Williamson (ed.), *IMF Conditionality*, Cambridge: MIT Press, pp. 109–24.

Joslin, David (1963), *A Century of Banking in Latin America*, London: Oxford University Press.

Kane, N. Stephen (1973), "Bankers and diplomats: the diplomacy of the dollar in Mexico, 1921–24," *Business History Review*, XLVII, 335–52.

Kemmerer, E. W. (1916), "A proposal for Pan-American monetary unity," *Political Science Quarterly*, XXXI, 66–80.

——— (1918a), *The ABC of the Federal Reserve System*, Princeton: Princeton University Press.

——— (1918b), "Money and prices: discussion," *American Economic Review*, VIII, 259–64.

——— (1926), "Chile returns to the gold standard," *Journal of Political Economy*, XXXIV, 265–73.

——— (1927), "Economic advisory work for governments," *American Economic Review*, XVII, 1–12.

——— (1934), *Kemmerer on Money*, Chicago: John C. Winston Company.

——— (1944), *Gold and the Gold Standard*, New York: McGraw-Hill.

Lewis, Cleona (1938), *America's Stake in International Investments*, Washington, DC: The Brookings Institution.

Marsh, Margaret Alexander (1928), *The Bankers in Bolivia*, New York: Vanguard Press.

Nurkse, Ragnar (1946), *The Course and Control of Inflation*, Geneva: League of Nations.

Parks, E. Taylor (1935), *Colombia and the United States, 1765–1934*, Durham, North Carolina: Duke University Press.

Pérez, Jorge Luis (1928), "Ecuador and its economic rehabilitation: financial reforms of the Kemmerer Commission," *Pan Pacific Progress*, p. 82.

Rippy, J. Fred (1931), *The Capitalists in Colombia*, New York: Vanguard Press.

Seidel, Robert N. (1972), "American reformers abroad: The Kemmerer Missions in South America, 1923–1931," *Journal of Economic History*, XXXII, 520–45.

Smith, Robert Freeman (1963), "The formation and development of the International Bankers Committee on Mexico," *Journal of Economic History*, XXIII, 574–86.

Young, Ralph (1930), *Handbook of American Underwriting of Foreign Securities*, United States Department of Commerce, Trade Promotion Series, No. 104, Washington, DC, USGPO.

7 Albert O. Hirschman ◆ Inflation in Chile

The early phase of the Chilean inflation has given rise to a widely accepted explanatory doctrine, complete with remote and immediate causes. Among the former, the nefarious influence of a French economist who spent some years in Chile as financial adviser around 1860 ranks high. . . .

The needs of the growing economy for means of payment and the distrust of governmental economic activities or regulation combined in 1860 to produce a banking law which established the principle of free, almost wildcat, banking. Private banks of issue were permitted to operate subject only to the provision that the right of such banks to issue notes would be limited to 150 percent of their capital. The legislation "fixed no minimum capital requirement, no limitation on the nature or maturity of loans, no reserve requirement against either deposits or notes, and no provisions of any kind for supervision or inspection by the government."[1]

This "extremely liberal and loose" law[2] has a double significance for our story: a good deal of the responsibility for the 1878 suspension of convertibility of bank notes into specie has been attributed to this law *and* it was drafted by the French economist Jean Gustave Courcelle-Seneuil, who had been contracted to come to Chile as professor of economics and adviser to the minister of finance in 1855 and stayed on in this capacity until 1863. The figure and role of this early "foreign expert" are of considerable interest.

A fervent partisan of free trade and laissez-faire, Courcelle-Seneuil was able to translate his ideas into reality by drafting a series of basic laws in the fields of money, banking, tariffs, and financial administration. Furthermore, as the University of Chile's first professor of economics, he instilled apostolic zeal in his students. Chilean writers and historians have traced to his influence a shift from a pragmatic to a doctrinaire economic policy: "Laissez-faire was substituted for the political instinct which [up to then] had oriented the march of the Republic."[3]

One of Chile's foremost historians, Francisco Encina, makes the suggestive point that Courcelle-Seneuil himself was quite well aware of the need to temper theoretical principles with realistic considerations but that his Chilean disciples, several of whom were to reach positions of great

From Albert O. Hirschman, *Journeys toward Progress: Studies of Economic Policy-Making in Latin America* (Westport, CT: Greenwood Publishing Group, 1965), 163–207.

influence, were far more royalist than the king and lost all sense of reality and of national interest in their desire to remain faithful to the "postulates of classical political economy."[4]

The greatest misdeed attributed to these disciples, notably Zorobabel Rodríguez and Marcial González, by their later critics was the surrender of the nitrate mines of Tarapacá to private foreign interests after Chile's victory over Peru and Bolivia in 1882 in the War of the Pacific. The outline of this story is quickly told. Peru had established government ownership and an export monopoly over the mines a few years before the outbreak of the war and had compensated private producers through twenty-year interest-bearing certificates. The Chilean government, advised by a committee dominated by Courcelle-Seneuil's disciples, decided after the war to return the mines to private ownership, that is, to the certificate holders, and to limit interference to the levying of a specific tax on nitrate exports. The certificates had greatly depreciated during the war and were bought up in Chile and Peru by such speculators as J. T. North, subsequently "King of the Nitrates," and after the Chilean decision were resold at huge profits largely on the London and Continental financial markets. Thus, from the point of view of later nationalist writers, Chile was deprived—through its own fault—of the fruits of victory because of the nefarious influence of a doctrine which held that the greatest of all evils is state management of business enterprises.[5]

Poor Courcelle-Seneuil! His one-man technical assistance mission could hardly have been more successful, according to ordinary standards of performance. His advice was punctiliously followed, the laws he drafted were passed, his bust stands in the University of Chile, and his influence as a teacher and publicist came to be widely felt. But just because of that, virtually every serious ill subsequently experienced by the Chilean economy, from inflation to monoexportation, has been traced to him. Monographs and even editorials are still being written today to debunk his doctrines and to show that foreign experts are unable to comprehend and give due weight to Chilean "reality" and national interests.[6]

The unkind way in which history has dealt with the well-intentioned Courcelle-Seneuil is nowhere so evident as in connection with his 1860 Banking Law. This law has generally been considered to carry much of the responsibility for the abandonment of convertibility in 1878. There were, of course, many other perhaps more basic forces at work, such as the adverse balance of payments resulting from the falling prices of copper, silver, and wheat in the seventies and increased governmental borrowings from the banks. But unsound banking, the fact that, in view of the highly permissive 1860 law, "the banks were doing business on a very small margin of safety,"[7] has been widely accepted as an important reason for the suspension of specie payments.

On the other hand, it was precisely to prevent such an outcome that establishment of an official bank of issue had been ruled out! The message introducing the 1860 bill said in fact:

> Several times the establishment of a bank by the state has been proposed; but on each occasion the government has rejected the proposal on the ground that it was extremely dangerous since it placed at the disposal of the Executive the means of exerting a powerful influence upon commerce. Not least to be feared are the possible dangers of paper currency fatal, eventually, to the political freedom and industrial prosperity of any country.[8]

Thus the 1860 Banking Law is the ancestor of that whole class of anti-inflationary measures which in the end conspire to bring about more inflation. It may seem surprising that Courcelle-Seneuil, coming from a country that had long had a bank equipped with the exclusive right of note issue, should not have insisted upon transplanting that institution to Chilean soil. But Courcelle-Seneuil was an ardent partisan of "free banking" and was strongly opposed to the monopoly of the Bank of France.[9] Here, then, is a characteristic foible of the foreign adviser: usually he is accused of wanting to do over the country he advises in the image of his own; but in reality he often aims far higher and attempts to endow it with those ideal institutions which he has been unable to persuade his own countrymen to adopt. . . .[10]

Chile's . . . return to the gold standard . . . is generally credited to the Kemmerer mission. From the point of view of short-run effectiveness and implementation this is probably one of the most spectacularly successful technical assistance efforts in history. The mission arrived early in June 1925, and the three principal bills it drafted were enacted by decree-laws from August to October of the same year. They were:

1) A monetary law that established the gold exchange standard and fixed the parity of the peso at six d., which was close to the average quotation of the preceding three years.

2) A law that established a central bank in Chile for the first time. The composition of its board of directors gave more scope to the representation of private, credit-using interests than had been the case in the Chilean drafts of similar legislation. The principal instruments of monetary control of the bank were to be the discount rate and, it was hoped, open-market operations.

3) Finally, a general banking law that did away with the permissiveness of Courcelle-Seneuil; the law "placed upon the commercial banks restrictions in line with the best banking practice, and provided for the appointment of a Superintendent of Banks, with

power and duties similar to those of a superintendent of banks in an American state."[11]

It all reads like a fairy tale: the metallic standard which had been in a deep, almost uninterrupted slumber for half a century was brought back to life by the magic touch of Professor Kemmerer, renowned money doctor, in what was perhaps the crowning achievement of his remarkable career.

Actually it is not too difficult to account for the accomplishment: President Arturo Alessandri, who had resigned in September 1924 largely because of his recurring difficulties with Parliament, returned triumphantly in February 1925 backed by a military junta and armed with full powers to enact a series of fundamental reforms. Among these reforms, monetary stabilization ranked high, for renewed inflation and the resultant discontent of the army had in part been responsible for the military takeover of 1924. Fetter describes this situation faithfully, if somewhat ingenuously:

> Although [*sic*] the political situation at the time was abnormal, it was favorable for the prompt acceptance . . . of the Commission's recommendations. The Constitution had been suspended and Congress was dissolved. . . . All legislation was in the form of "decree-laws" which required for their promulgation only the approval of the Cabinet and the President.[12]

Clearly, the political situation was favorable for the mission precisely *because* it was abnormal, because the democratic processes were in abeyance. Moreover, the mission, whose general doctrinal convictions were well known from Kemmerer's previous work, had strong advance backing for what it was going to advise. Upon arrival at the Santiago railroad station the North American professor was received by five or six civilians, officials of the finance ministry, and about three hundred officers in military uniform and formation! This was clamorous notice that the reforms he would propose would be "backed by the sword."[13]

Under these circumstances, the question arises as to why it was at all necessary to call in foreign experts. With the president all-powerful, why could he not decree the monetary reform that he deemed best? The answer here seems to be that since 1913, when a monetary and banking commission appointed by the government had issued its report, so many reform proposals had been endlessly and fruitlessly discussed that . . . "public opinion had reached a stage of confusion amid so much economic literature."[14] Fetter paints exactly the same picture:

> The sentiment of the country seemed to be overwhelmingly in favor of monetary reform, but the stronger the sentiment for reform became, the more diversified were the proposals and the more distant seemed its realization.[15]

Examination of the many proposals that were put forward with ever-increasing frequency in the period 1913–1925 makes it clear that the final Kemmerer bills did not contain any substantial innovations with respect to the crucial topics of restoration of the gold standard and establishment of the Central Bank. The conclusion is therefore inescapable that the mission served principally as an umpire, or perhaps even as a random device: in other words, it was the means for choosing one out of a number of competing proposals.[16]

This conception of the role of the mission naturally does not cast it in a very creative role. Nevertheless, it seems to be the only one that fits the facts of the case, and it is conceivable that the role it played was of critical importance in the decision-making process. Actually the idea of a foreign mission had arisen in 1923, in a period when Alessandri's administration was being paralyzed through senatorial opposition and when many monetary reform proposals were being debated.[17] The hope then must have been to bring in "impartial" outside experts whose authority would break the parliamentary deadlock. But even after parliamentary controls were removed there may well have remained some need for the outside experts' nudge since the protracted discussion of monetary and banking issues may have communicated uncertainty and vacillation to the executive branch itself.[18]

While it is frequently the role of parental authority to decide quite arbitrarily certain questions which the squabbling children are unable to settle among themselves, the exercise of this kind of parental authority is humiliating for the children. In the same way the need to resort to a foreign mission must have been rather galling to Chileans who had expended considerable intellectual travail and ingenuity over a long period on the attempt to bring order to their monetary and banking system. This resentment was still apparent twenty-five years later in Alessandri's reminiscences about this period in which he emphatically denied that Kemmerer had brought to Chile either the idea of establishing a central bank or the particular norms according to which it was to function.[19] Yet, on the whole, there was little *immediate* ill feeling toward the Kemmerer mission, in striking contrast to the treatment accorded the Klein-Saks mission which arrived on the scene thirty years later. What hostility there may have been was probably suppressed by the expectation that a reform bearing Kemmerer's name would provide Chile with access to the New York financial market which was then opening up widely.[20]

In one respect, the return to gold of 1925 represented a definite advance over that of 1895: in line with a number of stabilizations of the twenties, no attempt was made to increase the value of the currency before stabilization and thus deflation was avoided.[21] In addition, Chileans thought that they had improved decisively on the pure gold standard and its lack of "elasticity" by adopting that new invention of the twenties, the gold exchange standard, which allowed the Central Bank to redeem its notes in sterling or dollar drafts rather than in gold.[22] However, in a return visit in 1927, Kemmerer disabused his Chilean friends of any notions that the monetary system to which they had subscribed was lacking in discipline. When asked what kind of monetary policy should be followed in a crisis, he declared: "I do not hesitate to affirm and to reiterate that the Public Authorities must face all the consequences of the crisis before abandoning the gold standard."[23]

This last bit of advice was to be frequently and sarcastically recalled in Chile for it was followed with disastrous consequences. Proud of regaining its monetary stability, Chile was understandably reluctant to return to the slippery path of inconvertible paper money, and when the Great Depression came it fought a bitter and exhausting rearguard action to ward off the inevitable.

The extraordinarily violent decline in Chilean exports during the depression—their gold value fell by 88 percent from 1929 to 1932—is usually advanced as the sole and sufficient reason for the peculiar difficulties Chile experienced during the depression and its aftermath. But the misguided stubbornness in defending the gold standard—the Central Bank's discount rate was pushed up to 9 percent in the midst of falling prices—must share some of the blame. In contrast to such countries as Brazil, Argentina, Uruguay, and Mexico, which pragmatically opted for or stumbled upon "reflationary" techniques, Chile followed the famous "rules of the game" strictly until mid-1931. At that time the violent economic contraction, coupled with the government's total lack of any meaningful response to it, gave the opponents of General Carlos Ibáñez's thinly veiled military dictatorship their chance. Public protests, spearheaded by striking university students, led to bloody disorders and forced General Ibáñez (who had already been the power behind the throne during the second Alessandri regime of 1925) to flee the country. Fifteen months of political chaos marked by various coups and countercoups, including the proclamation of a short-lived "Socialist Republic," were to follow. Yet the futile attempt to defend the parity of the peso was continued until March 1932, six months after the devaluation of the pound!

> In 1930 and 1931, amidst widespread currency depreciation in South America, Chile, thanks to an ample gold reserve and the willingness of the authorities of the Central Bank to use this reserve for redemption purposes, has stayed on the gold standard.[24]

Completing his monograph in mid-1931, Fetter wrote this passage "not without a note of triumph," as was pointed out by a later commentator who, wiser by the depression decade, added: "The character of this defense of the gold standard and its costs, however, gives ample cause for reflection concerning the appropriateness of such a defense for a country in the position of Chile."[25] The judgment of Chilean observers was naturally far less restrained. In "those tragic moments of 1931," so writes one of them, "when any delay in decreeing inconvertibility could only aggravate the situation and lead to the pointless drain of our metal reserves, we remained true to the gold standard. . . . We have made it a habit in the conduct of monetary policy to sacrifice reality to theory. . . . Once more our leaders revealed . . . their complete lack of financial intuition."[26]

And the principal surviving *papelero* was, of course, particularly acid:

> Mr. Kemmerer had bequeathed to the directors of the Central Bank his unshakable faith in the interest rate device . . . and they were so devoted to [his] teachings . . . that they drowned the country in a crisis . . . without avail Congress requested the ministers to take measures which would permit the country to get out from the situation ineptly created by the real economic policy-makers who were hiding out behind the walls of the Central Bank.[27]

In sum, while Chile's second return to gold avoided some of the more spectacular mistakes committed in 1895–1898, the experience again left a most bitter taste. It displayed once more that propensity, noted by Encina in his comments on the influence of Courcelle-Seneuil and his disciples, to take imported doctrines more seriously and to apply them more rigidly and dogmatically in a foreign country than in their country of origin. . . .

In mid-1955, some of the leaders of the Opposition parties sensed that the deadlock between President Carlos Ibáñez and Congress must be broken if inflation was to be brought under some sort of control. An opportunity for achieving collaboration arose in August when the ministry of economy and, soon after, the finance portfolio were handed to Oscar Herrera, who, as education minister, had established good relations with deputy Enrique Serrano, a skillful congressional leader of the Conservative party. Herrera, an "Ibañista" of modest middle-class background, was a man of considerable energy and decision. He was convinced that, to push through an anti-inflationary program, the government needed the political support of some of the parties which had been voting with the Opposition since 1953. To accomplish this, however, was no easy task: No party could hope to gain in popularity by associating itself openly with an administration that was increasingly discredited. Ibáñez, in turn, still thought of himself as a sort of revolutionary nationalist and was not eager for support from "reactionaries" against the left wing.

However, the switching operation was considerably facilitated from September 1955 on by the arrival on the scene of a new foreign advisory mission put together by the Washington consulting firm Klein & Saks. This firm had been contracted by the Ibáñez government in July on the urging and through the intermediary of Agustín Edwards, publisher of *El Mercurio*, Santiago's respected, highly conservative daily newspaper. It is easy to understand the appeal which the idea of bringing in some deus ex machina in the person of an illuminated and somewhat authoritarian expert must have had in the chaotic situation that had developed by mid-1955. At that time, in fact, various alternative missions, by the International Bank, by a group of "California professors," and by Pierre Mendès-France, were also canvassed. The choice finally fell upon the Klein-Saks firm, in part on grounds of availability and on the basis of its previous record as advisers to the Peruvian government, but mainly because of its reputed good connections with the Republican administration and its financial agencies in Washington (Mr. Klein had been a member of the Hoover administration). The fact that Mendès-France was under active consideration simultaneously with Klein-Saks shows, however, that the government was anxious for any kind of advice, from whatever end of the ideological spectrum. The decision to contract Klein-Saks led to immediate protest, not only, predictably, from the extreme left but also from such thoughtful observers of the scene as Aníbal Pinto, the editor of *Panorama Económico*. In an article entitled "Mission without Mission," he claimed that the mission did not at all fill the need for "impartial experts" stressed by *El Mercurio* since the laissez-faire, orthodox bias of Klein-Saks was well known from its Peruvian record, and, secondly, that in any case Chile's problems were not technical but political and historical.[28] (At that time, Pinto could not have foreseen something which he fully realized later on, namely, that the mission's principal accomplishment was to be, as will be shown, not at all a technical but a political one.)

Headed by Prescott Carter, a retired vice president of the National City Bank with considerable experience in Spain and Latin America, the five-man mission arrived in Santiago in September 1955. It had originally been contracted for six months and, like the United Nations and International Monetary Fund missions of 1950, had been expected to survey the scene and write a "comprehensive" report with recommendations. But several factors conspired to substantially alter its course: One was precisely the failure of the earlier comprehensive reports to have a noticeable effect on policymaking; another was the background of the members of the mission who were monetary practitioners rather than theorists (two of its principal members had been associated with the Federal Reserve Bank of New York); but the most important reason was that the mission was drawn, immediately upon arrival, into the decisive anti-inflationary battle which shaped up toward the end of 1955.

In this battle the usefulness of the mission had various unorthodox but highly significant aspects. In the first place, its arrival produced an atmosphere of expectancy which gave the new finance minister a welcome respite, permitting him to lay his plans and to build his new alliances carefully. Once again, the most urgent question was whether, in January 1956, wages and salaries would be permitted to go up by the full extent of the rise in the cost of living during 1955, in which case they would be almost doubled. Clearly, any hope of fighting inflation successfully would be doomed were this to happen, as it would automatically under the existing legislation. Hence the minister repeated the attempt that had failed the year before and back in 1949–50: to get legislation passed that would end the automatic readjustment and would limit wage and salary increases to a portion of the rise in the cost of living. Instead of 60 percent he proposed a 50 percent readjustment, softening this blow by an increase in family allowances . . . by a somewhat theoretical price stop, and by the long-overdue establishment of a minimum wage alongside the minimum salary.[29]

Secondly, the presence of the mission acted as a binding agent for the newly emerging coalition of Ibañistas, Conservatives, and Liberals that was put together by the joint efforts of deputy Serrano and the finance minister. While Serrano organized a number of private, almost conspiratorial get-togethers of the finance minister, the principal parliamentary leaders of the new coalition, and some mission members, both the Ibáñez forces and the two traditional right-wing parties wanted above all to avoid a public embrace.[30] With the mission freely issuing its recommendations, both parties could and did claim that they were merely following the advice of *El Mercurio's* famous "impartial experts." In this fashion the new coalition could maintain an extremely loose structure: the new supporters of Ibáñez never entered the Cabinet and talked more to the mission than to their Ibañista allies whom they found distasteful.

This interpretation of the events is quite consistent with the excellent retrospective analysis given by Aníbal Pinto in *Panorama Económico* in the following terms:

> Oscar Herrera understood the need to create a political platform for the action of the government or, more exactly, for the development of this action in the crucial area of the fight against inflation. . . . For these purposes Herrera found the perfect ally: the Conservative Party which was won over by some leading parliamentarians of recognized ability and perspicacity. In the traditional political game it would have been natural for this alliance to be reflected . . . by the participation of that party in the Government. But here as elsewhere both promoters of the enterprise proceeded with singular skill. Both understood that this step would weaken rather than strengthen the enterprise. . . .
>
> But for the broader support other allies were needed, such as the Liberal Party and the business associations. . . . At this juncture the Klein-Saks

mission began to play its role. Its job was essentially to function as the shepherd of the suspicious, the lukewarm, and the recalcitrant. Its North American origin guaranteed the orthodoxy of its advice and raised expectations of support from the United States. This was without any doubt the cardinal contribution of the Klein-Saks mission—paradoxically not in the technical, but in the political arena.[31]

The greatest triumph of this singular combination of forces—the mission, Finance Minister Oscar Herrera, and the new parliamentary majority— came when the bill limiting wage and salary readjustments to 50 percent of the 1955 rise in the cost of living was voted on in Congress. It was approved in the Chamber with a comfortable margin on December 22, but in the Senate the voting on January 5, 1956, twice resulted in a tie which was broken only after members of the Klein-Saks mission were able to convince ailing Senator Cruz Coke, a prominent member of the Conservative party, to make an appearance and cast a favorable vote. A further hurdle was the general strike called in protest for January 9; it fizzled badly, however, not only because of repressive measures ordered by the government but also on account of "strike fatigue." Thus the stabilization program was launched. Along with the wage and salary regulations, new and tighter restrictions on bank credit were issued, and in March the foreign-exchange system was simplified. This resulted in financial assistance from the International Monetary Fund and from U.S. official and private agencies in the amount of $75 million. The program and the mission thus scored an important initial success.

Some further observations should be made, however, about the contribution of the Klein-Saks mission. For one thing, it is clear that the purely *technical* contribution of its "impartial experts" was minimal. A virtual consensus had emerged among Chilean technicians about the measures needed to stem the inflationary tide. Almost all the technical measures applied or proposed in 1956 had been suggested in the Central Bank memorandum of July 1955, and the proposal to decelerate the rise in money incomes by adjusting wages and salaries for only a portion of the rise in the cost of living had been put forward by Jorge Prat a year earlier. Since 1953 the Central Bank had been experimenting with its new powers to restrict credit, and the exchange rate reform had been anticipated in large part by Felipe Herrera in 1953 but had been rendered ineffectual by the continued inflation since then. The only new device suggested by the mission in conjunction with the exchange reform was the provision for advance deposits on imports which required importers to deposit a stated percentage of their intended purchase with the monetary authorities some time in advance of the actual obligation to settle with the foreign supplier. This device, however, was at that time coming into widespread use as an alternative to quantitative restrictions of imports: Ecuador, for example, had been experimenting with it rather successfully since 1953.[32]

In its technical aspects, then, the Klein-Saks mission resembled less the 1950 United Nations and Fund missions, which introduced newfangled proposals or an as yet unfamiliar type of monetary analysis, than the Kemmerer mission, which, as we have noted, also drew on existing plans and ideas. Despite their lack of innovation both missions had a considerable impact. But there the parallel ends. For the Kemmerer mission came to Chile when President Alessandri was holding virtually absolute powers while the Klein-Saks mission arrived when President Ibáñez had lost all of the prestige of his electoral victory, and a power vacuum had been created by his prolonged rift with Congress, his resulting inability to define any consistent line of policy, and his decision to abide by the constitutional rules. The situation required the exertion of some authority, and the Klein-Saks mission had no compunction about assuming a role inherited by default of the usual carriers of authority. If the statement "Sovereign is he who decides the emergency situation" be true, then the Klein-Saks mission, in cementing the new political coalition, took on the attribute of sovereignty as well for a short period in 1955–56.[33]

This anomalous situation was vaguely sensed and deeply resented. Indeed, some of the widespread criticisms of the mission become intelligible only in the light of this reaction.[34] For example, the mission was attacked for giving piecemeal advice as each problem arose instead of proposing a "general, integrated plan." But when the mission arrived in Chile there was neither the time nor the need for still another comprehensive report on inflation; to have any success at all it had to go into battle on the various issues of wage, credit, and foreign-exchange policy as each came to, or could be brought to, a head in the real world. It is not easy then to see why the mission should have been so vehemently criticized for acting in this way *unless* the criticism is understood as surprise and resentment at the mission's not having resigned itself to the somewhat frustrating task of writing a comprehensive report for the enlightenment of the real decision makers. Instead, by its memoranda on specific questions, its lobbying in Congress, and its general manner of operating, it, in effect, usurped the role of policymaker.[35] In so doing the Klein-Saks mission followed in the footsteps of that highly successful adviser-operator, Professor Kemmerer, who summarized his experience as follows:

> The expression "Commission's Report" . . . is misleading. With three exceptions none of the commissions with which I have been associated has presented any general report. It has been found more effective to submit specific

memoranda on specific subjects. These memoranda do not take the form of the usual government report, but rather of definite projects of law drafted in a form ready to be enacted by the legislature or definite administrative orders ready to be issued by the executive authority.[36]

Notes

1. Frank W. Fetter, *Monetary Inflation in Chile*, Princeton University Press, Princeton, 1931, p. 8. The responsibility of the 1860 Banking Law for the crisis of 1878 had been affirmed by Agustín Ross as early as 1886 in his pamphlet *Los bancos de Chile y la lei que los rije*. For similar later opinions see Guillermo Subercaseaux, *Monetary and Banking Policy of Chile*, The Clarendon Press, Oxford, 1922, pp. 73–75, and Julio Heise González, "La Constitutión de 1925 y las nuevas tendencias politico-sociales," *Anales de la Universidad de Chile*, Santiago, 1950, pp. 145–46 and 177.

2. Fetter, *Inflation*, p. 8.

3. Leonardo Fuentealba Hernández, *Courcelle-Seneuil en Chile*, Prensas de la Universidad de Chile, Santiago, 1946. This monograph gives a detailed account of the activities of Courcelle-Seneuil in Chile.

4. Francisco A. Encina, *Nuestra inferioridad económica*, Imprenta Universitaria, Santiago, 1912, pp. 309–16, and *Historia de Chile*, Edit. Nascimento, Santiago, 1951, Vol. 18, p. 285. Subercaseaux, Chilean economist and first president of the Central Bank created in 1925, ends his disquisition on Courcelle-Seneuil's theories and influence as follows: "Our most intelligent and illustrious statesmen have come until recently under the disturbing influence of these theories; they kept away from the realistic and inductive study of our economic problems, convinced as they were of the soundness of their principles." Guillermo Subercaseaux, *El sistema monetario y la organización bancaria de Chile*, Imprenta Universo, Santiago, 1920, pp. 126–27.

That Courcelle-Seneuil himself was, as Encina intimates, fully aware of the danger of transplanting foreign ideologies to a soil to which they were not suited, appears from the following suggestive passage:

"This revolution [against the Spanish colonial regime], born as it was from the French ideas of the Eighteenth Century, has introduced into the political system of Latin America a theoretical equality completely alien to its actual social structure. . . . To introduce democratic government and universal suffrage into societies previously dominated by a landowning aristocracy, necessarily resulted in a succession of military dictatorships, the frequent rise to power of savage tyrants owing to the support of an even more savage population, the utter lack of any regular administration and of security for either people's lives or their property. The evil was to reach its climax when, as a result of misplaced admiration for the prosperity of the United States of North America, the central power was dismantled and the people were abandoned to a multitude of local tyrannies, in the name of Liberty." J. G. Courcelle-Seneuil, *Traité théorique et pratique d'économie politique*, Guillaumin et Cᴵᵉ, Paris, 1858, Vol. 2, pp. 544–45.

5. This is essentially the version given by Encina, *Historia*, Vol. 18, Chapter 53, and retold by Aníbal Pinto Santa Cruz in *Chile, un caso de desarrollo frustrado*, Edit. Universitaria, Santiago, 1959, pp. 52 ff. Naturally, the Chilean historians are too thoughtful to attribute this denationalization of the nitrate mines to the influence

of Courcelle-Seneuil alone. For one thing, they point out that the inept and corrupt administration of the mines under the Peruvian monopoly had done its utmost to impress the Chilean government with the correctness of the master's teachings. Second, an important role appears to have been played by the desire of the Chilean elites not only to maintain their good credit rating abroad but to demonstrate to the world, and to the British in particular, that they were "different" and infinitely more civilized than the rest of Latin America.

6. See the editorial "Back to Courcelle-Seneuil?" in *Panorama Económico* of August 30, 1957 (No. 174) and "Subordination of Chilean Economic Thought" in *Panorama Económico* of March 1960 (No. 212). Courcelle-Seneuil has been accused of so many crimes that his rehabilitation is becoming a tempting task. It had come to be widely believed, for example, that the opening of coastwise traffic to foreign shipping legalized in 1864 through an ordinance drafted by Courcelle-Seneuil was responsible for a subsequent decline of Chile's merchant marine. This thesis has now been refuted in detail by the painstaking research of Claudio Véliz in his *Historia de la marina mercante de Chile*, Edic. de la Universidad de Chile, Santiago, 1961, Chapter 4.

7. Fetter, *Inflation*, p. 25. See also p. 164.

8. Subercaseaux, *Monetary and Banking Policy of Chile*, p. 73.

9. As he argued at length in his *La Banque Libre*, Paris, Guillaumin, 1867.

10. Some eighty years after Courcelle-Seneuil's mission to Chile, Federal Reserve experts equipped several Latin American central banks which they had helped to organize with highly sophisticated tools of monetary control that they had failed to secure from the U.S. Congress for the Federal Reserve System.

11. Fetter, *Inflation*, p. 178.

12. Ibid., p. 171.

13. Ricardo Donoso, *Alessandri*, Fondo de Cultura Económica, Mexico, 1954, Vol. 1, p. 409. Cf. also Fetter, *Inflation*, p. 171.

14. In a farewell article for Kemmerer in *La Nación* of October 6, 1925.

15. Fetter, *Inflation*, p. 163.

16. Naturally the foreign mission will come forward with a version somewhat different from any of the existing ones. But this does not change the situation. Suppose that at a certain time five variants of a reform proposal exist; it is then quite easy to imagine additional variants formed through a process of permutation and slight modification of the various components of the basic proposal. The mission will then pick one of these conceivable variants rather than any of the existing ones.

17. Fetter, *Inflation*, p. 170, and Arturo Alessandri Palma, "Las cuestiones económicas, el régimen parlamentario y la cuestión social en Chile desde 1891 hasta 1925," *Atenea*, April 1950, p. 148.

18. A Chilean economist later remarked that the use of foreign experts to draft important legislation is congenial to dictatorial regimes which are anxious not to have their projects known and discussed by the public prior to promulgation as full-fledged laws (Enrique L. Marshall, "Régimen monetario actual de Chile y sus antecedentes históricos," *Revista de la Facultad de Economía*, Vol. 14, 1945, p. 98). While this is an excellent point, it does not seem to cover the Chilean situation of 1925 very well, in view of Alessandri's earlier call for Kemmerer's services.

19. Alessandri, "Las cuestiones económicas," pp. 148–50. Note also the following comment: "The project elaborated by the 1912 Commission which was

about to become law and its subsequent drafts make it quite clear that Chile counted with an adequate number of persons qualified to advise the Government on the task that it had set out to do." (Marshall, "Régimen monetario de Chile," p. 95.)

20. Kemmerer listed this expectation as one reason for the popularity of American-led financial missions in the twenties. "Economic Advisory Work for Governments," *American Economic Review*, March 1927, pp. 1–12.

21. There also were some conspicuous exceptions, for example, the pound sterling and the Italian lira, which repeated the Chilean mistake of 1895.

22. "To avoid the danger that a situation might arise in the future similar to that which in 1898 obliged us to take up again with paper currency, the law . . . establishes the . . . so-called gold exchange standard." Subercaseaux in *La Nación*, October 6, 1925.

23. E. W. Kemmerer, interview published in *La Nación*, July 31, 1927, reprinted in *Funcionamiento de nuestra legislación bancaria y monetaria*, Balcells & Co., Santiago, 1927, p. 39.

24. Fetter, *Inflation*, p. 182.

25. William Adams Brown, Jr., *The International Gold Standard Reinterpreted, 1914–1934*, National Bureau of Economic Research, New York, 1940, Vol. 2, p. 909.

26. Marshall, "Régimen monetario de Chile," pp. 99–100.

27. Enrique Zañartu Prieto, *Hambre, miseria e ignorancia*, Ercilla, Santiago, 1938, p. 98.

28. *Panorama Económico*, No. 126, July 15, 1955.

29. Law No. 12,006.

30. Note the following comments of Ibáñez, reported by his biographer: "The two traditional parties [Liberals and Conservatives] which supported the economic plans [of the Klein-Saks mission] were ostentatious about their political independence. When elections drew near, their leaders repeated that they had nothing in common with the Government and that the support of certain economic reforms was not incompatible with being in the opposition." Luis Correa Prieto, *El Presidente Ibáñez*, Orbe, Santiago, 1962, p. 182.

31. *Panorama Económico*, No. 145, May 25, 1956, pp. 231–32.

32. See Jorge Marshall, "Advance Deposits on Imports," *International Monetary Fund Staff Papers*, April 1958, pp. 239–57.

33. Quoted from Carl Schmitt by Franz Neumann in "Approaches to the Study of Political Power," *Political Science Quarterly*, June 1950, p. 178, reprinted in Neumann, *The Democratic and the Authoritarian State*, The Free Press, Chicago, 1957.

34. A cartoon in *Topaze* of November 11, 1955, shows Prescott Carter of the Klein-Saks mission watching with great alarm a storm-tossed launch marked "Chile" from which a carefree and relaxing Ibáñez calls out: "What does it matter to you if the boat founders? Is it yours by any chance?"

35. The mission's report is a collection of memoranda, mostly addressed to the minister of finance: *El programa de estabilización de la economía chilena y el trabajo de la Misión Klein & Saks*, Edit. Universitaria, Santiago, 1958. It is preceded by a "comprehensive report" (pp. 1–38) which, however, was written in retrospect, toward the end of the mission's stay in 1958.

36. "Advisory Work for Governments," *American Economic Review*, March 1927, p. 7.

III

Institutionalization and the International Monetary Fund

Following World War II the Great Powers assigned money doctoring mainly to a new public multilateral agency, the International Monetary Fund. They designed the IMF to be an apolitical source of policy recommendations and lines of credit. The Fund became a hot center of controversy in Latin America, however, particularly when labor and leftists denounced its recessionary stabilization programs, which reduced the income of workers.

Miles Kahler, a political scientist, argues that the IMF, like most economic advisers, has not been able to avoid playing a political as well as technocratic role. Its four main political roles have been: 1) serving as an honest broker with outside policy advice; 2) fostering policy choices and coherence within the government; 3) assisting in coalition formation to sustain policies; and 4) providing a lightning rod for attacks on policies. The IMF missions function as intermediaries, who must sell their programs in both the host country and in Washington. As Kahler indicates, "transnational alliances" can be crucial to their success. Also important for implementation are the Fund's resident representatives, who are comparable to the North American monitors that Kemmerer used to leave in his wake.

Selection 9, written by economist Roberto Frenkel and political scientist Guillermo O'Donnell (both of whom are Argentines), illustrates criticisms of the IMF in Latin America during the 1960s and 1970s. Their discussion also illuminates the financial buildup in the 1970s to the debt crisis of the 1980s. They provide an excellent analysis of how the Fund works, how its medicine varies little from country to country, how its diagnosis often dovetails with the preexisting interests and beliefs of local elites and technocrats, how its policies relate to loan issues, and how its programs have differential consequences among social sectors in the host country. In particular, Frenkel and O'Donnell are concerned with the IMF's role in bureaucratic authoritarian regimes in South America.

Another political scientist, Karen L. Remmer, discusses the differential impact and effectiveness of IMF proposals for authoritarian or democratic regimes. Contrary to conventional wisdom, dictatorships may not have any advantage over democracies in carrying out stabilization measures, she shows. Most conducive to policy innovations are changes in regime types. Remmer also underscores how difficult it is for any government actually to put into practice IMF programs. She reminds readers not to exaggerate the influence of foreign advisers on either economics or politics; their recommendations must be refracted through domestic actors and institutions.

8 Miles Kahler ◆ External Actors and Adjustment: The Role of the IMF

Since their creation, the International Monetary Fund (IMF) and its sister guardian of the Bretton Woods order, the World Bank, have had a divided view of politics and their involvement in the political life of members. From the outset, two views—roughly the British and the American—competed for control of the Fund's activities. While the British, led by John Maynard Keynes, argued for relatively automatic access to Fund resources and a large role for the organization's technocratic staff, the Americans pushed for closer political control by national governments and for what came to be known as conditionality. At the Savannah Conference the American viewpoint seemed to triumph, prompting Keynes to issue his much-quoted warning:

> I hope that Mr. Kelchner has not made any mistake and that there is no malicious fairy, no Carabosse, which he has overlooked to ask to the party. For if so the curses which that bad fairy will pronounce will, I feel sure, run as follows:—"You two brats will grow up politicians; your every thought and act shall have an *arrière-pensée*, everything you determine shall not be for its own sake or on its merits but because of something else." [1]

Ironically, the Keynesian vision of the Fund remained strong; the Americans won at best half the battle. Although conditionality was eventually enshrined in the practice of Fund lending to member states, the technocratic ideal endorsed by Keynes became the official ideology of the organization. Expertise, and especially economic expertise, was a major, if not the major, offering of the IMF to its members, apart from its financial resources. That reliance on technical expertise also became the principal shield of the Fund staff from interference by member states. "Politics" was banished from the Fund more thoroughly than even Keynes, master academic and bureaucratic politician, could have hoped.

At least this was the case officially. Despite the continued resolute opposition of the Fund staff to any "politicization" of the organization, the Fund management and staff have ventured into new realms of policy intervention during the last decade that make official disclaimers that the Fund can ignore political developments increasingly threadbare. Even in official statements of Fund policy and programs, politics is acknowledged as an important element in the success or failure of Fund programs. In a review of recent adjustment programs, the managing director of the Fund placed political determinants at the head of a list of "ingredients of successful economic management":

> *Political commitment and support* for a program is an indispensable element of successful adjustment. This means not only that the authorities believe in what they are doing and are determined to implement the program but also that the rationale of the program is effectively communicated to the public at large so that the measures—the immediate impact of which is often hard to bear—are well understood and supported.[2]

A study of adjustment programs in Africa by the director of the Fund's African department has noted that slippage in the implementation of Fund programs was due in part to "an inability to mobilize sufficient political support for the requisite adjustment measures."[3] Yet while the importance of political elements in adjustment is increasingly acknowleged, organizational concern with the risks of too-explicit dabbling in the political remains high. The conflict between organizational ideology and practice is demonstrated in a recent statement by C. David Finch, director of the Exchange and Trade Relations Department of the Fund. On the one hand, Finch vigorously defends what he calls the "principle of political neutrality," the notion that the Fund must confine itself to the task of offering advice and financial resources for adjustment narrowly defined; on the other hand, Finch makes clear that the political dimension of adjustment is critical:

> In the making of these decisions, there is an unavoidable and complex interplay of politics and economics. It would serve no purpose to insist that the purely economic considerations must dominate, simply because an ideal solution is of no interest if political power tò implement and achieve it does not exist. On the other hand, the prevalence of political weakness cannot be accepted as a justification for failure to take the necessary economic actions.[4]

In short, despite the perceived value of its emphasis on a narrow definition of adjustment and providing only the economic expertise required for an effective adjustment program, the Fund has been tugged, in large measure by the evolution of its programs, toward a recognition of the importance of politics in the adjustment process.

Although the analysis which follows is concerned principally with the IMF, the World Bank faces similar dilemmas and similar resistance to incorporating political analysis explicitly in its work.[5] The World Bank experiences its conflicts over political involvement in a slightly different form, however: its deeper involvement in structural adjustment (public enterprises, trade regimes, and the like) makes the political sensitivity of its work greater; the IMF can still rely on the greater distance that macro-economic management provides from the pull and push of economic interests. But the fact that the Fund is involved in "high economics" means that the risk of nationalist reaction around its intervention is decidedly greater, at least in some regions of the developing world. . . .

The IMF can encourage adjustment not only in the provision of Fund resources but also in the process of surveillance under Article IV of the Articles of Agreement. Article IV consultations (usually annual) give the Fund staff an opportunity to scrutinize the exchange-rate policies of member states, and, to the degree that broader economic policies affect the "orderly underlying conditions that are necessary for financial and economic stability" (Article IV, Section 1), those economic policies as well. For the major industrial countries, which committed themselves to a deepening of Fund surveillance at the Versailles Summit in 1982, and for other countries that are not using high-conditionality Fund resources, Article IV consultations are the principal means by which the IMF can influence economic policy. (No industrial country has turned to the Fund for balance of payments support in the 1980s.) Although Fund comments on economic policies can be used as ammunition in the bureaucratic maneuvering within governments, Article IV consultations are, for the most part, less significant means of influence than programs governing the use of Fund resources. Intellectual suasion is at the core of the consultation process, without the leverage that financial resources provide. For this reason, although the Article IV process bears a faint resemblance to the politics surrounding Fund programs, principal attention is devoted to the negotiation and monitoring of high-conditionality (that is, posing significant policy commitments) Fund programs, in which Fund influence may be greater and the political situation is certainly more hazardous.

The "Ideal" Adjustment Environment

It is worth sketching an "ideal" political setting for adjustment to suggest the elements in the situation that the Fund can and cannot influence. Such a promising picture would include:

- An influential and competent technocratic cadre within the key economic ministries (usually the Ministry of Finance and the Central Bank)
- A united political leadership that supports those technocrats and accepts, at least in broad outlines, the diagnosis of the Fund staff
- Experience in conducting successful adjustment programs
- A long-time horizon (one that is not likely to be affected by the electoral cycle or by change of regime)
- Governmental willingness to invest the political capital necessary to ensure at least the acquiescence of the population in the adjustment program

- Willingness of other external actors to coordinate their actions with the Fund, particularly those that could provide alternative means of finance
- Adequate means for implementing a program—particularly revenue, budgetary and monetary instruments—are in place

Such a list makes clear the tight policy constraints under which the Fund operates. In effect, given its policy preferences and expertise, the ideal political environment for the Fund is the "Keynesian" state (Keynesian in terms of structure, not necessarily policies) staffed by disinterested civil servants and distanced politicians with limited active state involvement in production or employment. The picture of economic policymaking in such a state is technical, not political; the data and the personnel are good, and the aims of policy are agreed.[6] Of course, most of the newest members of the Fund, and those in which the Fund is likeliest to have programs in the 1980s, have states that bear only the faintest resemblance to this ideal. And in such less-than-ideal political settings, few political parameters are likely to respond to Fund influence—and even fewer in the short term. Before examining the limited means by which the Fund can shape the political environment for adjustment, however, the channels and points of contact for exerting that influence must be examined.

Avenues of Influence

The best-known means of Fund influence are the periodic missions of the Fund staff to member countries, either for Article IV consultations or for negotiating and monitoring the use of Fund resources. Fund missions are usually headed by a senior staff member from the relevant area department and include other, more junior members from that department; a representative of the Exchange and Trade Relations Department; occasionally a member from the Fiscal Affairs or the Treasurer's Department; and, more rarely, a member from the Central Banking Department.

The organization of the "missionaries" is largely in the hands of the mission chief, and there is considerable variation from mission chief to mission chief and across departments. Usually the mission chief handles the most delicate negotiations with the ranking ministers of the country in question, although many fairly junior team members are able to pose questions and participate in the negotiating process. Negotiations in particularly difficult cases may continue for weeks; the site of discussions may move to Washington, and other, more senior Fund staff may become involved.

Fund missions and contacts between Fund staff in Washington and their interlocutors in member countries are one clear means by which the Fund can shape the environment in the course of bargaining. The roles that the Fund can play are described in more detail below, but it is important to note that the bargaining undertaken by a Fund mission takes place on two fronts. First, there are many incentives for a mission chief to negotiate a program that proves successful. But several staff members have commented that the "toughest negotiations" take place between the mission chief, his or her director, and the other departments after the mission returns with its trophy. Programs must be approved by the Exchange and Trade Relations and the Treasurer's departments, which are the organizational "skeptics" that ensure consistency across programs and maintenance of Fund guidelines. Thus, just as the ministers and civil servants in a given country must first "sell" the program to their political superiors, the mission chief and his or her department must then "sell" the program to the Fund management and the Executive Board.

Resident Representatives

In addition to the periodic visits of Fund missions, countries in which a program is under way (and some without programs) often have a resident representative of the Fund. The role of the resident representative follows different patterns according to the relations of the host country with the Fund. Usually a promising young staff member, the "res rep" serves in the best of circumstances as a source of technical advice for the government and as an "outside opinion" on economic policy. In certain cases, the presence of a res rep has also been valued as further evidence of an IMF seal of approval for private creditors. In cases in which a country program is underway, the role of the res rep may involve more friction with the host government, since one of his tasks is to serve as a watchdog and monitor for the program.

The Fund may consider the posting of a res rep as an essential part of a program, and his or her presence, in contrast to technical assistance from the Fund, can be required. The resident representative is always included in the work of a Fund mission in the country and, after the mission chief, is often most deeply involved in the mission. In addition, he or she is an important source of information for the Fund on the program and economic conditions in the country. In general, the res rep reinforces the influence that the Fund staff can exert only episodically through the visits of missions.

Technical Assistance

One role of the International Monetary Fund that is crucial to its influence in the longer term is its technical assistance. Directed through the Fiscal Affairs and the Central Banking departments, technical assistance is "consumer-oriented": it is kept separate from Fund conditionality and dependent upon requests from member countries. (Of course, missions and area departments can strongly urge technical assistance upon governments.) The incentive for these departments are somewhat different in that they are oriented less toward programs and more toward use by member governments. Fiscal Affairs experiences some conflict, since members of the department are involved in program negotiation and monitoring as well as technical assistance.

Although both departments make use of outside experts, Fiscal Affairs is more staff-centered than the Central Banking Department. The placement of the experts in member governments is also somewhat different. Those from Fiscal Affairs remain closely attached to the Fund, whereas those recruited by the Central Banking Department become part of the host country's organization during their contract, reporting monthly on the progress of their work and receiving visits by members of the Department staff.[7] In both cases, the permanent staff of the departments is also involved in technical assistance, although seldom on a long-term basis.

Executive Board

Keynes feared that a resident executive board would impose politicized constraints on the technical experts who made up the staff of the Fund. He neglected the possibility that the Executive Board could serve as an additional channel for conveying the "Fund view" to member countries. The Executive Board is also unusual in that all members—save the G-5, China, and Saudi Arabia—represent a constituency of countries that are often quite diverse. In some instances, it seems, the executive director does serve to put forward the interests of his constituency members during negotiations with the staff. In other cases, the executive director and his staff stay well away, although they will certainly offer advice if requested and may intervene if the negotiations reach an impasse. These observations are based on a limited number of cases. In general, however, this channel of influence seems less important than direct contact between the management and staff of the Fund and national governments.

Fund Influence and the Politics of Adjustment

The IMF can use its channels of influence to shape, in a limited way, the political environment in which adjustment takes place. The Fund may play at least four roles, two of which are relatively passive and two that are more active and controversial. Each of these roles—each of these efforts to exercise influence—poses dilemmas for the organization.

The most familiar role, and that with which the Fund is most comfortable, is as an *outside source of economic advice* directed toward a set of adjustment measures that will be least damaging to the interests of other members of the Fund. Even in its role as the honest and expert broker, however, the Fund confronts difficult choices in how far it should go in offering advice and assistance, particularly in program design. In some cases the analytic capabilities of a government may be so weak that the temptation is for the Fund to write the program, which then becomes a "Fund program" rather than a program of the government that is supported by the Fund. Such a program is likely to inspire less political commitment on the part of the government and enjoy higher chances of failure.

The second role, that of *forcing policy coherence* within the government, is also a passive one. In requests for data and in the process of the IMF's negotiation itself, governments are forced to produce out of the confusion of day-to-day politics a set of economic policies that reflects their priorities. This role, particularly its data-gathering aspect, is not well publicized, but the statistics collected are often critical to the development of policy within the government itself.

Each of these passive roles has distinct limitations, however. Whatever the advice offered by the Fund (even when combined with the carrot of Fund resources), whatever the coherence that simply dealing with the Fund can impose, the political prerequisites for an adjustment program as outlined earlier are simply not present. Even the economic portrait painted by the Fund may be rejected by the government; an unwillingness to admit economic crisis is characteristic of many governments, particularly if there are few internal partisans of the Fund's diagnosis. Rather than the ideal political situation described above, the Fund more often confronts a divided government and a population that is hardly convinced of the need for an adjustment program. The time allotted for change is short—usually until the next election—and often past experience with the Fund is not recalled with fondness.

The Fund staff often faces a government that is divided into three factions. First, the technocratic stabilizers—who for the most part are found in the ministry of finance and the central bank—are the natural allies of the Fund.[8] One should not assume that *all* technocrats are allies, however; they may disagree with the Fund prescriptions, or their bureaucratic position in a spending or investing ministry may cause them to oppose the Fund. Nevertheless, greater opposition can be expected from those ideologically opposed to Fund prescriptions. Composing the second group, these are often ministers or political figures who have little part in the Fund negotiations and are rarely seen by the Fund staff but who may carry great weight in the final political deliberations surrounding a program. If the country in question has a political system in which organized parties play an important role, they are often attached to a particular party.

When resistance from this group is strong, the Fund must concentrate its attention on the third and most important faction, which is comprised of those who could be labeled the politicians. These politicians have two concerns that might lead them into opposition to the Fund and its technocratic allies: the impact of adjustment on the state itself (an important source of patronage and their personal power); and the differential effects of a program on groups within the population, particularly those groups key to their governing coalition. In many cases, the Fund must deal with these fears in order to swing the political leadership into alliance with the technocrats.

This decomposition of the political setting for Fund influence points to two more active roles that the IMF may undertake in an adjustment program. One step beyond presenting economic advice and forcing policy coherence is to *assist in coalition formation*. The possibilities for the Fund should not be overestimated, however. Although the IMF may help in transforming a latent governmental coalition into an active one, if some of the constituents of that coalition are not already in existence, the Fund staff cannot create them out of whole cloth. Some staff members and mission chiefs are more cautious than others on this score, but as one staff member involved in a number of programs put it, "If you want the program to succeed, then you must work for it."

Transforming a latent coalition for adjustment could mean circumventing an obstructionist central bank governor, or it could mean briefing and involving ministers and civil servants outside the ministry of finance or the central bank who will be crucial to the success of the program (even if the minister of finance is later upset that the briefing has taken place). It may often mean respecting the budgetary "sacred cows" that permit the politicians to support tentatively an adjustment program. Chief among these politically sensitive items are food subsidies and military spending. But, finally, in negotiating a successful program and keeping it on track, the staff and the mission chief in particular must be prepared to undertake an endless campaign of persuasion. As one mission chief for a successful African program explained, "You do a lot of talking and write a lot of short memos." In order to allay fears of repercussions from the program and to begin the next round of persuasion for further adjustment steps, the Fund's staff may frequently visit cabinet ministers and even the president.

Such an active role poses yet another dilemma. How involved should the Fund staff become in "selling" an adjustment program, within the government and outside it? In the Article IV consultation process, the Fund staff often ranges widely in its discussions with nongovernmental groups, though there are departmental variations. In the European Department, for example, consultations do not extend beyond government ministries.

In the course of negotiations on the use of Fund resources, the circle of those involved is much smaller in all departments. Staff often actively involve ministries that are necessary to the implementation of the program. Outside the government, they usually will see anyone the government requests them to see. Jamaica was a breakthrough in the movement of the Fund beyond purely governmental contacts to meetings with nongovernmental groups as requested by Jamaican leaders.[9] Outside the government, the Fund seems to respect carefully the gatekeeping role of the national authorities. One staff member did assert, however, that he would insist on seeing nongovernmental groups—such as union leaders—whose support was essential to the success of a program.

Before turning to the final role of the Fund in the adjustment process, mention should be made of the role of the Fund's technical assistance programs in coalition formation over the longer term. The technocrats within the economic ministries are the natural interlocutors and allies of the Fund staff during negotiations; technical assistance programs ensure that the transnational alliances that are critical for the success of Fund programs can be sustained. A second and perhaps even more important role of technical assistance lies in shoring up the implementation of Fund programs. The Fund staff may succeed in designing a program that proves acceptable to even a recalcitrant government, but implementation can only be monitored inadequately if expertise within the national government is lacking.

The last role of the Fund, and perhaps its most dramatic (and lamented), is that of the *lightning rod*. One final means by which a reluctant political leadership can be swung behind an adjustment program is by offering the IMF as a scapegoat. Graffiti in the streets of Rio de Janeiro and Buenos Aires and mobs in the streets of Khartoum testify to the remarkable success of an international organization with barely one thousand professional staff members in this role.

Notes

1. Cited in Richard N. Gardner, *Sterling-Dollar Diplomacy in Current Perspective* (New York: Columbia University Press, 1980), 266.

2. Remarks by J. de Larosière, Managing Director of the International Monetary Fund, before the Centre d'études financières, Brussels, Belgium, February 6, 1984 (IMF Press release), 9.

3. Justin B. Zulu and Saleh M. Nsouli, "Adjustment Programs in Africa," *Finance and Development* 21, 1 (March 1984), 7.

4. C. David Finch, "Adjustment Policies and Conditionality," in John Williamson, ed., *IMF Conditionality* (Washington, D.C.: Institute for International Economics, 1983), 79.

5. On the resistance to political analysis, see William Ascher, "New Development Approaches and the Adaptability of International Agencies: The Case of the World Bank," *International Organization* 37, 3 (Summer 1983), 431.

6. Cf. Robert Skidelsky: "Keynesian politics assume two things: that governments have enough autonomy to be able to act rationally; and that there is enough of a market for market manipulation to work." (In Colin Crouch, ed., *State and Economy in Contemporary Capitalism* (New York: St. Martin's Press, 1979), 67.

7. The recruitment pool for the two programs is also somewhat different. Central banking draws upon active staff from major central banks; fiscal affairs has obtained most of its "panel experts" from recently retired civil servants.

8. "Moreover, as is well known, in a not inconsiderable number of cases ministries of finance and central banks welcomed the support given by IMF missions to retrenchment policies that these financial authorities were having difficulty in persuading other sectors of the government to accept." Sidney Dell, "Stabilization: The Political Economy of Overkill," in Williamson, *IMF Conditionality*, 39.

9. Jennifer Sharpley, "Jamaica, 1972–1980," in Tony Killick, ed., *The IMF and Stabilisation: Developing Country Experiences* (London: Heinemann Educational Books, 1984).

9 Roberto Frenkel and Guillermo O'Donnell ◆ The "Stabilization Programs" of the International Monetary Fund and Their Internal Impacts

This study is the product of our broad interest in the interactions between politics and economics during the periods that precede and follow the establishment of what we have called the "bureaucratic-authoritarian" states (from here on, BA) in contemporary Latin America.[1] In this work we address ourselves to one of the topics within that particular set of problems: the standby agreements established with the International Monetary Fund [IMF] shortly after the coups d'état that abruptly terminated processes experienced by numerous sectors (including, very prominently, the internal ruling classes and their foreign supporters) as deep political and economic crises. Argentina, Chile, and Uruguay are particularly appropriate examples of this phenomenon.

Therefore it is necessary to start by summarizing what we understand to be the purpose of the orientation and intervention of the IMF. We will then proceed to show how its intervention, regardless of the prevailing political arrangements, has an effect that hardly accords with its orientation. These effects are also very different from the effects that similar policies tend to produce in more homogeneous productive structures. This will allow us to see how state policies designed to implement agreements with the IMF generate effects that are highly slanted toward the benefit of a small group of economic participants—basically toward the sectors involved in the production of primary products and in finance capital.

At that point we will discuss some of the specific results of the shaking of the productive structure and the sociopolitical system of domination that the implantation of the BA state seeks to "solve," as well as the results of the subsequent efforts to reestablish a particular order in society. The policies agreed upon with the IMF converge with these processes. These policies are the new state's main instrument for undertaking one of the great tasks arising out of its preceding crisis: the achievement of a no less peculiar "normalization" of the economy. It is in the context of this dynamic overlapping of politics and economics that we will take up again some of the questions that will emerge in the next two sections; they are related to the

From *Capitalism and the State in U.S.-Latin American Relations*, ed. Richard R. Fagen (Stanford, 1979), 171–203. Reprinted with the permission of the publishers, Stanford University Press. © 1979 by the Board of Trustees of the Leland Stanford Junior University.

reasons behind the adoption and continuation of certain policies, as well as to the influence that the agreements with the IMF might have on these policies. . . .

How the IMF Works

The IMF formally established its "tranches policy" in the mid-1950s in response to the new problems involved in financing peripheral economies. This policy rules that hard currency requests are to be handled according to their ratio to the quota contributed to the IMF by the member country in question.[2] Applications within the gold tranche (leaving the IMF with no more than 100 percent of the applying country's currency) are approved almost automatically; within the first tranche (between 100 and 125 percent of the quota), applications are usually handled with a "liberal" attitude; beyond that limit, applications need a "substantial justification" to be approved. The precise meaning of this phrase was established in 1958; applications beyond the first tranche would receive favorable treatment if the funds were to be used for "supporting an effective program for establishing or keeping the stability of the currency of the member country at a realistic exchange rate."[3]

This tying of currency withdrawals to the presentation and approval of stabilization programs came to be the main activity of the IMF, especially through the standby agreements, the importance of which increased substantially over the years. A large number of credits has now been approved. There is no reference to the standby agreements in the founding documents of the IMF, since they were not conceived of until later. Technically, the implication is that the member country may purchase hard currency up to a fixed limit during a given period, without having to rediscuss its general situation and policies. Originally, this was envisioned as a line of credit that would be open for a certain period of time, during which the country could withdraw funds with no limitations other than those set by the general rules of the IMF. Later, however, it developed into the main instrument for making the availability of IMF resources conditional on the internal adoption of certain policies, once the application has exceeded the first tranche. Approval of the standby agreement requires the signing of a "letter of intention," in which the member country, after discussing the subject with IMF representatives, sets forth its policies and agrees to implement them. The standby agreement is a resolution by the IMF setting forth the terms under which the member country can purchase hard currency; it includes certain goals the economy must reach and the policy procedures to be used, as well as the criteria to be observed in order for the IMF not to suspend withdrawal rights. The letter of intention includes indicators of the economy's behavior and of economic policy; the limits established by these indicators cannot be exceeded for the duration of the agreement. Violation of these clauses may lead to the suspension of the agreement; in this regard there are generally clauses establishing the need to consult the IMF before certain policy decisions are made, as well as renegotiation clauses in case one of the objectives is not met.

By virtue of these standby agreements, the IMF has tended to become an autonomous and interventionist institution in its relations with economically less powerful countries. The standby-agreement clauses have been under constant revision to "protect the resources of the Fund from undue use."[4] Legally, access to resources can be interrupted on the basis of the IMF's contractual right to decide unilaterally that nonattainment of certain goals of the program may mean improper use of its funds. However, the IMF's role as the "technical secretariat" of the central economy's finance capital is even more important in increasing the institution's leverage. The IMF's decision to enter into a standby agreement with a member country is considered by other international financial sources a sign of approval for the stabilization program set forth in the letter of intention. The consultation and evaluation clauses in the agreement allow the IMF to exercise a permanent auditing function, so to speak, over the national economy of the country that is party to it, a task of great interest not only to the IMF itself but also to finance capital. The unwritten rules of international finance have led both private and public financiers to wait for a decision by the IMF regarding a standby credit before negotiating their own agreements, which often involve access to considerably higher amounts of hard currency than those provided by the standby credit itself. In relation to the country in need of external funds, transnational finance capital thus acts as a giant monopolist, imposing conditions that are made explicit by the IMF. It would be difficult to find any better indication of the convergence between the interests of finance capital regarding the evolution of the debtor country on the one hand, and the policy and evaluation criteria of the IMF on the other. We will return to this point after examining these criteria.

The criteria and quantitative goals that have to be met by the recipient country's economic policy, according to the standby agreement, constitute a program based on the IMF's principles of how the problems of external disequilibrium and inflation should be approached. These phenomena are approached in many peripheral countries with programs that—although not identical—are based on a common body of ideas, which constitute what we might call the "outlook" of the IMF. This outlook includes not only a diagnosis of the situation but also standards that specify the most desirable state of the economy in any given country and the conduct of international economic relations. These notions are expressed in the form of seemingly unquestionable "technical" criteria, expressions of an apparently axiomatic economic rationality. The IMF thus attributes universality and objectivity to a particular view of the functioning of the world economy and of what ought to be the "best" situation of the national economies.

Focusing our attention on the behavior of the IMF in various Latin American countries, especially in Argentina and Chile during the last two decades, we will now attempt to make a synthesis of this outlook. The IMF considers external disequilibrium and inflation to be problems generated by "distortions" in the economic-development process. As countries try to expand public services and accelerate economic growth, they often generate a tendency to overspend, thus creating considerable pressure on the balance of payments and on prices. Excessive expansion of credit to finance consumption or private investment is often responsible for this pressure, but more commonly it is considered a result of large government deficits financed through bank credits. Excessive public spending is caused by subsidies to producers or consumers (for example, in the form of an inflated public payroll), operational deficits of public enterprises (determined largely by their pricing policy), and excessive public investment. Inflation and balance-of-payments deficits are manifestations of disequilibria caused by an excess of demand in relation to available supply. This demand is attributed to excessive money supply, in turn generated basically by the government deficit and by pumping too much credit into the economy. On the other hand, the existence of these disequilibria in various markets implies a distortion of the price system—both internally and in relation to international prices. This distortion is caused by state-imposed obstacles that do not allow the free working of the price system in those markets. In the IMF's view, distorting state actions stand in the way of an automatic correction of these disequilibria. Excessive demand for available resources derives largely from the claims of various social sectors to increase their share of a limited national income. Bad economic leadership or political incompetence is responsible for supporting relatively distorted prices, partly as a response to the pressures of these social sectors.

The IMF's outlook can be summarized in the following propositions: there is a price system operating in commodities, wages, exchange rates, and interest rates. This price system equilibrates markets and provides stability to the economy. If inflation and external-payments difficulties arise, it is because of a distortion of the price system through excessive money supply as well as because of obstacles to the free play of market forces. This ideal equilibrium system is optimal, in the sense that it makes full use of resources and provides the best indicators for their allocation. The more it reflects the international price system, the better it will guide investment and production according to the advantages of the country in international trade. This outlook provides the basis for stabilization programs whose substance is relatively simple: the idea is to lead markets and prices to their points of equilibrium, thus allowing a broad action of market forces and eliminating excessive money supply. As far as balance-of-payments difficulties are concerned, the main objective is to adjust disparities among internal and international prices. This generally implies a significant devaluation.[5]

To eliminate excessive money supply, the IMF establishes programs that include general limits to its expansion as well as more specific limits to the expansion of private and public credit and government financing. In the latter case, control clauses may include specific numeric references to the government deficit and to limits to public spending as well as to public saving goals. In general, the financial objectives of the public sector demand a strong increase in the price of goods and services produced by it.

The exchange measures and financial policies that form the basis of the program are often complemented by direct action on prices and salaries. In this respect, stabilization programs show a remarkable asymmetry in the way they treat commodities and labor markets. Whenever price controls and regulations are in force, the program tends to demand their elimination; conversely, when the IMF considers that the government has sufficient power to establish ceilings on salary increases, they are imposed by the program. This incongruence goes considerably beyond the criteria based on the theoretical outlook and implies a socially biased pragmatism whose political significance is demonstrated most clearly under authoritarian regimes.

We cannot undertake an exhaustive analysis of this outlook here, but we must refer to two lines of criticism. They have emerged largely from the debate brought about by the repeated experiences of dependent countries with these programs. The first refers to the presumed optimality, in terms of general welfare and economic-development criteria, of the objectives of the stabilization policies—objectives that the program sets for itself, assuming that its measures would effectively lead the economy to a stable position.

The origins of the criticism of the IMF's outlook in this regard can be traced back to the first postwar writings on development and international trade in Latin America.[6] Since then it has repeatedly been argued that the trade- and capital-accumulation patterns resulting from an unregulated international market tend to favor a persistent deterioration in the relative position of the peripheral economies. More recently, economists have emphasized the basic inequality existing between the center and the periphery in matters of international trade.[7] Initially, the notions that inspired the IMF clearly reflected the purpose of rebuilding the type of world order in existence before 1929. In that kind of international order, however, the peripheral economies' role was reduced to that of producers of raw materials and consumers of manufactured products. The persistence of these notions—and the consequent perpetuation of the old division of labor they assume—has obvious normative implications. They indicate that the IMF embodies the specific financial and commercial interests of the centers of world capitalism, which join forces in partial but decisive manner in the IMF to impose certain economic guidelines on the peripheral countries.

The substance of these guidelines becomes apparent once we take up the second criticism of the IMF's outlook. It deals with the theory that is used to explain inflation and balance-of-payments deficits and provides the basis for the stabilization program's policies. Starting with the work of the "structuralists," Latin American economists have long been concerned with refuting the IMF's arguments on this matter.[8] There is no need to go into the whole debate here; suffice it to say that this body of work made it possible to start building a theory of inflation and foreign trade that would allow for the structural specificities of the Latin American economies. In marked contrast with these efforts, the IMF's outlook is abstract and ahistorical; its diagnosis and policies are considered valid and are in fact recommended under almost any circumstances, regardless of time and place. Its notions are part of the neoclassical and monetarist perspective that became very influential in academia from the 1950s onward. These intellectual currents "guarantee" the scientific accuracy of the IMF's outlook, which thus seems to enjoy a monopoly on technical rigor. However, this is no longer a mere academic issue; the IMF's perspective has become the official doctrine of several Latin American governments, and it has long been the official language of most international financing institutions. This perspective thus performs an important function: it provides a logical, elegant, simple basis for stabilization policies whose social impact has been profound and painful. It is from this notion of the IMF's outlook as an ideological support system for certain policies that we can move toward examining the stabilization program's impacts and the type of international interests that seem to be embodied in the IMF.

Both the rapid growth and the absolute levels reached in the 1970s by the medium- and long-term foreign debt of the peripheral countries have raised worrisome questions in the world's financial centers. Foreign debt has risen from thirty-six billion dollars in 1967 to approximately two hundred billion by the end of 1976. Even more important than its accelerated growth is the fact that during this period multilateral financial institutions and the governments of the central countries were largely replaced by international private banks as main lending sources. Using World Bank figures, one study has concluded that out of 200 billion dollars owed by peripheral countries by late 1976, 120 billion (60 percent) was owed to private financial sources.[9] It seems logical that the zeal of these financial centers has been exacerbated by these developments; the balance-of-payments problems of some peripheral countries are so severe that not only the position of their creditors but also the stability of the international financial system as a whole may be endangered. Under these conditions, international creditors are bound to promote strongly the types of economic policies that, by improving the balance-of-payments positions of these countries, allow them to pay their debts. The Latin American experience in this regard shows that the stabilization programs of the IMF perform this function rather well, although at a high internal cost in terms of economic growth and income distribution.

The increasing influence of the IMF and its notions is thus not totally unrelated to the processes through which the international financial system has been going lately. In sum, the IMF's outlook and its growing influence correspond to the new and important role private finance capital has come to play in the peripheral economies. Increasing demands on the peripheral economies, generated by the spectacular growth of foreign debt, have led to stabilization programs geared fundamentally toward guaranteeing the external financial solvency of the debtor countries. The IMF, officiating as the "technical secretariat" of transnational finance capital, provides not only the programs but also the logical foundation to make them coherent, plus the type of "auditing" services needed to ensure that the debtor country will comply with the agreement. . . .

Impacts of the Stabilization Programs

The objective of this section is to illustrate the recessive and redistributive impacts of the stabilization programs oriented by the IMF's outlook. With that purpose in mind we will examine some aspects of the recent Argentine experience. Our purpose, nonetheless, is to point out the marked incongruence between the effects the program was supposed to have achieved and those it has in fact achieved, on the one hand, and the remarkable distortion of the distribution of benefits and losses, on the other. Accordingly, we will look especially closely at those aspects of economic policy directly related to the assumptions and objectives of the stabilization plans. . . .

Devaluation brings about an increase in agricultural prices and a lowering of real wages. This leads to a recession in the internal-market sector. The recessive impact of a drop in effective consumer demand is not offset by a sufficiently strong expansion of export activities; as a consequence, the gross national product falls. Imports are reduced, and the amount of goods available for export increases. Devaluation alleviates the balance-of-payments situation largely through its recessive effects and its impact on the income and consumption of wage earners. The magnitude of the recession depends on the size of the devaluation and on the evolution of prices in the internal-market sector. On the other hand, the reduction in public spending and tightening of credit that goes along with these changes in relative prices intensifies the effects of the recession. The larger the reduction in effective demand induced by the devaluation—and backed up by fiscal and monetary policy—the larger the recessive impact of the stabilization program. Another important effect of the program is regressive income redistribution. Wage earners are confronted with a drastic reduction of their income, whereas the income of those in the export sectors, especially the rents of the Pampa Húmeda (wet pampa) landowners, is increased substantially.

The stabilization program we are concerned with began in March 1976 as the official economic policy of the new military authorities. [10] At that time the economy was clearly undergoing a crisis: there were serious difficulties in meeting foreign payments, and, since mid-1975, the inflation rate had accelerated, reaching peaks of 30 percent a month. This was largely the result of a frustrated attempt by the previous government to enact a somewhat similar stabilization program but in a situation where the trade unions had strong bargaining power to defend wage levels. Accordingly, there was an intense struggle for the appropriation of income, in which the state found itself arbitrating an increasing number of recurrent conflicts. Nonetheless, during the first quarter of 1976 the devaluations of the Peronista government increased the ratio between the value of foreign exchange and wages by more than 70 percent, [11] whereas real wages fell during the same period by 22 percent. This meant that some of the main elements of the stabilization program were being implemented when the new government started to develop its policy. In this regard, the most significant elements of the new stabilization program—besides the increase in the exchange rate—can be seen to be the virtual elimination of price controls in the internal market and the freezing of nominal wages. . . .

A summary of the main effects of the stabilization program . . . can thus only conclude that of all its explicit short-term objectives the only one that has been achieved is a definite easing in the international payments situation. Inflation goes on unabated at a high and fluctuating level; the "freedom-of-prices" policy, apparently imposed as a counterinflationary measure, has merely meant that the state has lost its capacity to regulate and control. Something similar has happened in capital markets, where, with the participation of foreign finance capital, heavy speculation takes place; this has resulted in an unstable financial situation that reduces the options available to the state in this regard. [12] There has been a drop in productive investment, and the conditions created by the program do not seem to have attracted direct investment by transnational enterprises. Long-term confidence on the part of the local bourgeoisie and transnational investors has not been restored. Present internal-market tendencies and inflation make it unlikely that confidence will be restored in the near future. The country is thus faced with a strong recession, a drastic reduction in real wages, and a regressive redistribution of income that is unique in Argentine history. [13]

It is by no means easy to identify the beneficiaries of this economic policy in the industrial sector. [14] Even though, as in all recessionary processes, there has been an expansion of some groups to the detriment of others, the contraction of the internal market has affected industrial activity to such a degree that, in some sectors, one would have to go back ten years to find production levels similar to the ones of 1978. The direct beneficiaries of this economic policy should be those in the traditional export sectors that are identified by the program as the axis on which the economy will be rebuilt. However, inflation and the more recent exchange policy have reduced considerably the benefits they originally received from the program. The most direct beneficiaries are unquestionably those sectors related to financial speculation, an activity that has attracted a significant part of business profits.

If it is difficult to find direct beneficiaries of the stabilization program among internal social participants, this is not the case once we move to the international scene. The critical balance-of-payments situation was quickly solved by the program; this made it possible for the country to pay 1.1 billion dollars as foreign-debt service during 1976 and 1977. [15] In this respect, the success story of the Argentine stabilization program can be best told by international creditors. Not only have they been paid punctually, but they have also been offered, as a warranty, a foreign currency-reserve stock equal to a fifteen-month import bill. [16] International creditors could hardly be happier regarding the success of the IMF's recommendations.

Politics and Economics

Robert Campos, Otávio Bulhoes, Jorge Cauas, Guillermo Vegh Villegas, Adalbert Krieger Vasena, and José Martínez de Hoz—champions of the stabilization programs undertaken by the Latin American BA states—all have one thing in common. Before becoming cabinet ministers they all belonged to the group that, in their own countries, had extensive personal relations with private and public international financial circles. In fact, they were all part of the local "chapter" of those circles. This was one of the reasons they were appointed to their positions in the first place. The abrupt implantation of BA states, starting with the Brazilian coup of 1964, was an effort to put an end to a situation perceived by many as a deep political and economic crisis. A high inflation rate and an acute balance-of-payments crisis were some of its elements.[17] To overcome this situation it seemed imperative to reach an agreement with the "international financial community"—starting with the IMF—on a set of policies that would make available the resources needed to alleviate the crisis. Nobody could do a better job in going north with the programs, it was thought, than these cabinet ministers. They already enjoyed considerable prestige in such circles, and they were convinced, too, that the objectives and policy measures embodied in the programs were the expressions of an economic rationality without which it would be impossible to rescue these countries from their respective crises. We will elaborate further on this topic, but it is important to emphasize at the outset that we are dealing with an issue involving complex causality. It is simplistic to believe that "somebody" imposed these programs from abroad. But it is also simplistic (or diplomatic) to assert that a given government "freely" elected a certain program that was "later" approved by the IMF. What we are really facing is a convergence of determinations, or better still, a case of overdetermination. Even without the need for the IMF's blessings, the stabilization program of these cabinet ministers would have been similar to the one they agreed on with the IMF. But even if the respective economic teams did not believe that these policies would succeed, the need to formulate a program to satisfy the IMF and the international financial community would also have determined a policy package similar to the one actually approved. This convergence is one of the issues we are interested in exploring here.

It would be superfluous to again go into the various analytical points we have made in other studies quoted above. We shall limit ourselves, then, to setting out a few crucial aspects of the establishment of the BA state, which is generally founded as a fearful response to what many consider a deep economic crisis. Politically, society seems to be characterized by great disorder; the state shows a decreasing capacity to guarantee the current system of domination; the possibility that society might collapse is seen as very real. Thus threatened, the bourgeoisie rallies around its basic interest— the ability to reproduce itself as a class. This provides the support for the coup undertaken by the armed forces, in turn permeated by the doctrine of national security, which acts as a reinforcing factor. The middle sectors, incensed by disorder and the "insolence" of formerly passive sectors of society and by the economic uncertainty they are going through, also throw their support behind the coup.

This predetermines the two great tasks that the emerging government sets for itself. The first is to reintroduce order, which involves dismantling any threatening popular political activities, eliminating their political self-expression, and putting trade unions under strict control. This, with the suspension of all institutions of political democracy, results in the political exclusion of the popular sectors and their allies. The second great task is to "normalize" the economy; that is, to stabilize some crucial variables, and, supposedly, in the long term to again begin economic growth on the basis of a more efficient and healthy productive structure. There are, however, serious obstacles in the path of these objectives.

First, the political and economic uncertainties of the previous period have led almost everyone—including the bourgeoisie—to speculative behavior that in turn deepens the crisis. This has resulted in a lack of investment, the flight of capital, and a dislocation of the capital accumulation circuit. Second, especially in the cases of Chile (1973) and Argentina (1976), the situation has expressed itself in an extremely high and fluctuating rate of inflation. The growth rate of the economy as a whole, however, has slowed down, and the balance-of-payments situation has reached a point where the country might be unable to meet its foreign obligations.

It is in this context that the stabilization programs insert themselves. Their objective is to redress the economic situation, approaching first the problem that is both the most urgent and the easiest to handle—the balance-of-payments situation. To overcome its foreign-payments problem the country needs three things: new credit lines; a comprehensive renegotiation of its foreign debt, since the burden of the debt has been made even more unbearable by the previous crisis; and a consequent easing of conditions for other commercial and financial international transactions.[18] As long as one of the immediate manifestations of the crisis is in the balance-of-payments situation, and its alleviation requires some sort of solution in that sphere, the problem "naturally" comes under the IMF's jurisdiction. Policies that are required to obtain the IMF's and the international financial community's support then emerge.

The restoration of international confidence in the country becomes a crucial task for the new governments and their internal supporters. This is by no means easy. The image of a previous situation that generated deep pessimism about the future has to be overcome. This was an evaluation not only of a certain government, but also of a country that had the explosive potential to reach such a situation. Nevertheless, in spite of the efforts to restore order, the renewal of trust in the future of the economy also demands a guarantee that order will be maintained at least for the period of time considered sufficient by potential investors. The political exclusion of the popular sectors and their allies is the main component of that guarantee. But this implies also that the popular sectors—especially the working class and the public employees—lose the capacity to participate in determining their income. This leads to additional measures to put the trade unions under control; the right to strike is eliminated, and wage levels are set by the government in a manner that leads to a severe, regressive redistribution of income. As a consequence, the popular sectors are also excluded economically. Again, there is an understanding that these controls (an aspect of the class dimension of the imposed order) will continue for the time span set by those who are evaluating the new economic situation. After all, the history of these countries has shown recurrent attempts to impose strong governments, and, with or without them, to enact stabilization programs that were aborted because of political activism and the ability of the popular sector and its allies to formulate economic demands. For that reason, to be able to obtain trust and confidence neither a new strong government, nor a "correct" economic program, nor prestigious cabinet ministers are enough. All these are necessary but not sufficient conditions; the important point is to convince the international financial community that "this time" these arrangements will last.[19]

Paradoxically, the very deepness of the previous crisis lends credence to such an assertion. The deeper the crisis, the greater the effort and cost needed to impose order; accordingly, it seems more and more probable that to return to the demagogic past is out of the question. But this is not enough. The top positions in the state are held by members of the armed forces. Yet, institutionally this is the segment of the state and the social group that is, in principle, least compatible with the stabilization policies to be undertaken and with their executors. Is it possible to make the socialization of the armed forces (reinforced by national-security doctrines centered on the potentialities of the nation) compatible with the basic approach and consequences of a policy that in so many ways implies precisely the opposite? The internationalization of the productive structure, the predominance of "efficiency" criteria over those of national origin and control, and the dismantling of a significant portion of industry (precisely that sector under unquestionable national control) are only some of the consequences of the stabilization programs. They appear to be, prima facie, deeply opposed to the very heart of the belief system the armed forces are supposed to have. This puzzle cannot be solved by analyzing the discourse of those involved, and this is not the place to attempt to do so. Suffice it to say that for the period dealt with in this study (the adoption and initial implementation of the stabilization programs), there is one factor providing a common bond between the members of the armed forces and the economic "technicians"— a belief that the deepness of the previous crisis demands unhesitating, drastic action. The armed forces view the nation as a sick body needing surgery, even terrible surgery, to be saved. The technicians view the situation as the ideal occasion to use another sort of scalpel, namely, their belief in an economy saved from "demagogic temptations" through the suppression of "politics" and the elimination of the pressures that for many years prevented them from putting their policies into practice in the "right manner" (that is, using drastic measures that last as long as necessary to obtain the desired effects). Since both groups tend to see a similar "illness," they can communicate on the similarities of the hard tasks—order and normalization— that both are taking up with their respective tools.

The second important problem of these policies is that they not only punish many by excluding them, but that they also bring severe hardship to many supporters of the coup. Only a small group in those sectors that back the establishment of a BA state benefits from these programs. The need to cut the government deficit leads to a drastic drop in income among public employees as well as to numerous dismissals that highlight the uncertainty of even those meager salaries. The recession, credit and cash shortages, and the increased concentration on the productive structure tend to harm a broad spectrum of people, from small merchants (lumping together, in its typical fate, most of the petty bourgeoisie that had been so active against disorder) to a significant portion of the industrial and commercial bourgeoisie. And we are not referring here merely to a drop in income or to an increase in the number of bankruptcies; the basic problem arises from the lack of protection of various bourgeois factions from the actions both of oligopolistic sectors and of the more internationalized segments of the bourgeoisie itself. Many enterprises find that they cannot any longer rely on the state—which may have been demagogic but was also nationalist and protective—and that this change has occurred precisely at the moment when, owing to the recession, their economic space is shrinking.[20]

The question, then, becomes more complex than simply one of guaranteeing the continuity of these policies against the opposition of the excluded. Continuity has to be preserved despite the grumblings of those who were part of the coalition backing the BA state. Some of these bourgeois sectors are difficult to repress, and they can hardly be accused of having supported the previous, threatening process. In addition, the middle sectors and the local bourgeoisie can voice an argument that is bound to be much more amenable to the armed forces' outlook than the rationale of the technicians. How is it possible to think about the potentialities of the nation if the long-term result of these policies is a productive structure dismantled for cold "efficiency" reasons, with an extremely meager local bourgeoisie and with a state apparatus that has also been dismantled (at least in terms of the technicians' statements)? How can these objectives be reconciled with a process favoring the export sector and finance capital to the detriment of productive activities of an industrial and commercial nature? And a strong argument for those worried about subversive activities—how will such an economic arrangement provide employment to the masses, who presumably will not remain silent indefinitely? . . .

In sum our argument is the following: (1) the adoption and implementation of policies that are considered reasonable by the IMF and the international financial community is a necessary condition for alleviating the balance-of-payments situation once the BA state has been implanted; (2) the deeper the preceding crisis, the more urgent that alleviation is bound to be, and the more strict and orthodox the design and implementation of policy measures have to be to "merit" international support; (3) a speculative economy is thus recreated, not only excluding the popular sectors but also suffocating the internal productive structure; although (4) the consequent improvement in the ability to meet foreign obligations is perfectly congruent with the interests of transnational finance capital.

Notes

1. See especially Guillermo O'Donnell, "Reflexiones sobre las tendencias generales de cambio en el estado burocratico-autoritario," Document CEDES/G.E. CLACSO no. 1, Buenos Aires, 1976.

2. Emphasizing the short-term nature of the credits, a number of changes in the rates to be charged were approved in late 1951; in the same resolution the duration of the credits was reduced. The so-called Rooth Plan was approved shortly afterward; it included a number of rules foreshadowing the future standby agreements. Among other things, it established that the normal repurchasing period would be three years (with five as the maximum) and changed the "tranches policy," making a distinction between applications within the gold tranche and the rest. See J. Keith Horsefield and Gertrud Lovasy, "Evolution of the Fund's Policy on Drawings," in *The International Monetary Fund 1945–1965* (Washington, D.C., 1966), vol. 2, chapter 18.

3. IMF Annual Report 1959, in Horsefield and Lovasy, "Evolution of the Fund's Policy," p. 404.

4. Joseph Gold, "Use of the Fund's Resources," in *The IMF 1945–1965*, vol. 2, chapter 23, p. 534.

5. If it is considered that the devaluation needed for these purposes is too high, the IMF allows for the possibility of "gradualist" policies to raise the exchange rate in several stages. In case of very high inflation, the exchange policy includes regular adjustments of the exchange rate, according to the evolution of internal prices. In this case, the stabilization program is aimed at a gradual lessening of the inflation rate; however, as long as inflation goes on, successive devaluations are needed to achieve a change in relative prices. In these cases, control clauses include specific references to the relationship that has to exist between the evolution of the exchange rate and certain price indicators, in addition to the budgetary and balance-of-payments controls that are usually included.

6. See Raul Prebisch, *The Economic Development of Latin America and Its Problems* (New York, 1950).

7. See Arghiri Emmanuel, *L'échange inégal* (Paris, 1969), and Samir Amin, *L'accumulation à l'échelle mondiale* (Paris, 1971).

8. Juan F. Noyola, "El Desarrollo Económico y la Inflación en México y otros Países Latinoamericanos," *Investigacion Economica*, vol. 16, no. 1, 1956; Osvaldo Sunkel, "La Inflacion Chilena: Un Enfoque Heterodoxo," *Trimestre Economico*, vol. 25, no. 4, 1958; and Julio G. Olivera, "La Inflación Estructural y el Estructuralismo Latinoamericano," in *Inflación y Estructura Económica* (Buenos Aires, 1967).

9. Miguel S. Wionczek, "La Deuda Externa de los Países de Menor Desarrollo y los Euromercados: Un Pasado Impresionante, un Futuro Incierto," *Comercio Exterior*, vol. 27, no. 11, 1977.

10. The new authorities were faced with urgent external-payments problems. They immediately obtained 300 million dollars in 6-month maturity loans from commercial banks; creditors also allowed them to roll over to the fourth quarter an additional 350 million dollars owed by the public sector in the second quarter of 1976. The economic program was presented for the first time to international financiers at the annual meeting of governors of the Inter-American Development Bank at the beginning of May. On May 27, delegations from the IMF and the World Bank arrived in Buenos Aires. The Argentine Government applied for a number of long-term credits to the World Bank, and the latter released a public report highly favorable to the program. By mid-June, Minister of Economics Martínez de Hoz traveled to the United States, where he made all the necessary arrangements with the IMF to obtain the first tranche immediately and two-thirds of the second tranche by April of 1977, depending on the Argentine government's presentation of a program for the first half of 1977. On August 6 the agreement with the IMF was signed, and 180 million dollars were drawn, which correspond to 160 million in Special Drawing Rights. Simultaneously, a standby agreement with international private banks had been sought. A consortium of U.S., European, and Japanese banks, headed by Chase Manhattan, extended a line of credit for slightly over a billion dollars, with a four-year maturity rate and at an interest rate 1 7/8 higher than LIBOR. Dealings with the IMF culminated in April 1977, when it approved the economic program for the first half of 1977 and made the 100-million-dollar balance of the agreement available to the Argentine Government. See *Boletín Semanal del Ministerio de Economía*, various numbers, 1976 and 1977, and *Mercado*, various numbers, 1976.

11. During the first quarter of 1976 the exchange rate for traditional export products went up by 137.6 percent.

12. During the last quarter of 1977 and the first of 1978, there was an inflow of over one billion dollars of private finance capital into the country. Data from the Central Bank, Republic of Argentina.

13. The total amount of foreign direct investment during 1977 was only 52 million dollars. Data from the Central Bank, Republic of Argentina.

14. This evaluation refers to enterprises considered sectorial activities and encompasses only the short term. There is no doubt that industrial entrepreneurs have made immense profits through commercial and financial speculation in this period. On the other hand, it is not our purpose to refer here to the long-term accumulation strategy that might be implicit in the short-term measures of the stabilization program. In this regard, our evaluation in this paper is limited to the framework of the objectives that have been explicitly acknowledged by the authorities. A good sample of these objectives can be found in the memorandum

that provides the technical foundation for the agreement with the IMF for the first half of 1977: *Boletín Semanal del Ministerio de Economía*, no. 179, May 2, 1977.

15. Data from the Central Bank, Republic of Argentina.

16. As of March 31, 1978. Considering the level of reserves as of December 31, 1977, and 1977 imports, Argentina ranked first in a world ranking of external liquidity coefficients (reserves/annual imports). The Argentine coefficient duplicates that of the country occupying second place in the ranking. Data from IMF, *International Financial Statistics*, March, 1977.

17. On the Brazilian BA state, see Guillermo O'Donnell, "Reflexiones sobre las tendencias generales," and "Tensiones en el Estado Burocrático—Autoritario y la Cuestión de la Democracia," CEDES/GE. CLACSO no. 11, Buenos Aires, 1978.

18. Undoubtedly helped by the hostility toward the internal situation showed by governments and private creditors.

19. The previous bureaucratic-authoritarian experiment in Argentina (1966–70) shows this very clearly. After the success of its relatively unorthodox stabilization program (in turn related to a significantly less serious preceding crisis), the great social upheavals of 1969 led to a rapid evaporation of confidence and an aggravated resurgence of the crisis the 1966 coup had apparently eliminated.

20. For an initial approach to these topics, see Guillermo O'Donnell, "Notas para el estudio de la burguesía industrial local en sus relaciones con el capital internacional y el aparato estatal," CEDES no. 12, Buenos Aires, 1978, and Instituto Latinoamericano de Estudios Transnacionales (ILET).

10 Karen L. Remmer ◆ The Politics of Economic Stabilization: IMF Standby Programs in Latin America, 1954–1984

During the late 1970s authoritarian rule in Latin America began to give way to processes of political liberalization and democratization. The debt crisis of the early 1980s accelerated this trend. Under the weight of crippling external financial obligations, the region slid into its worst recession since the 1930s. Widespread unemployment, plummeting living standards, acute shortages of foreign exchange, declining investment, and severe inflation all magnified the vulnerabilities and contradictions of authoritarianism. By 1985 elected governments had displaced military regimes in Argentina, Bolivia, Brazil, Ecuador, Honduras, Peru, and Uruguay. Among those countries with some prior democratic experience, only Chile resisted the continentwide shift away from authoritarian rule.

For participants and outside observers alike, the key question raised by these developments was the viability of liberal democracy under conditions of economic austerity. Circumstances that favor regime emergence are not necessarily conducive to regime consolidation, and in the case of Latin America it became immediately apparent that the economic crisis undermining authoritarianism also reduced prospects for the consolidation of democratic institutions. As a variety of analysts have suggested, economic growth creates conditions conducive to political compromise, but when the economic pie is shrinking conflict and opposition tend to mount.[1] The problem confronting Latin American democracies during the 1980s, however, has not been simply that of survival in the face of economic decline. To retain access to international financial markets, governments throughout the region have been forced to adopt politically painful stabilization measures involving currency devaluations, wage and credit restrictions, and strict fiscal controls. Most observers have questioned the willingness and capacity of democratic leaders to implement such measures, despite the obvious costs of failure and the absence of viable policy alternatives. According to conventional wisdom, stabilization policies pose such unacceptably high political risks for democratic governments in Latin America that authoritarianism is virtually a prerequisite for successful adjustment.[2]

The purpose of this study is to reexamine this conventional wisdom regarding the politics of economic stabilization. Does the historical record

From *Comparative Politics* 19 (October 1986): 1–24. Reprinted by permission of the author and *Comparative Politics*.

sustain the view that Latin American democracies are singularly ill-equipped to manage programs designed to correct serious and persistent balance-of-payments deficits? Do conventional stabilization policies carry higher political risks for democratic governments than for authoritarian ones? How have the trade-offs between coercion and consent affected the relative capacity of military and democratic governments to impose stabilization measures? Under what conditions, if any, has democratic rule produced successful stabilization, and authoritarianism resulted in failure? The answers to such questions are not only central to theoretical debates over the relationships among regime, public policy, and economics in Latin America; they are of real practical significance to democratic regimes struggling with the problems of economic stabilization.

Theoretical Perspectives

The proposition that authoritarianism is a necessary albeit insufficient condition for successful stabilization is buttressed by several highly plausible lines of argument. Most begin with the assumption that stabilization policies are inherently unpopular because they tend to cut into popular-sector living standards. Particularly in Latin America, where extensive past experience with stabilization has left a legacy of cynicism and distrust, simply announcing that an agreement has been reached with the International Monetary Fund (IMF)—the international agency charged with helping member nations to carry out stabilization programs—may provoke political protest. To make matters worse, stabilization programs also alienate comparatively privileged political support groups. Local entrepreneurs, for example, are likely to react strongly to restrictions on credit as well as to measures designed to produce a more efficient allocation of resources. For governments dependent on consent rather than coercion, stabilization consequently poses a major dilemma. As Joan M. Nelson has emphasized, "the only alternative to planned and guided adjustment is chaotic adjustment, entailing higher costs in terms of controls, scarcities, inflation, unemployment, and atrophied output and growth."[3] Yet voters are unlikely to evaluate the costs and benefits of stabilization programs against some counterfactual alternative. Democratic leaders thus face strong pressures to postpone corrective action as long as possible or to abandon programs once their costs become palpable, particularly since any resulting economic hardship can plausibly be blamed on exogenous forces rather than on government actions.[4] It can be argued that under authoritarian rule the political calculus pushes policymakers in a rather different direction. The benefits of postponing corrective action are likely to appear less significant to regimes whose survival does not depend on popular approval, while the long-term dangers of inaction are likely to loom much larger.

A related line of argument stresses the greater capacity of popular sector groups to disrupt or thwart the implementation of stabilization policies under democratic rule. Democracies not only offer more channels of protest and influence on policymaking to subordinate groups than do authoritarian regimes; they also create more favorable conditions for the development of strong and independent popular sector organizations capable of resisting efforts to curtail private consumption. Policies designed to curb inflationary wage increases, for example, are obviously more likely to founder where workers enjoy the freedom to organize and strike than where trade unions are controlled or suppressed. As Robert R. Kaufman has argued with specific reference to the three large Latin American nations, "the ability to sustain stabilization initiatives . . . has varied inversely with the capacity of [popular-sector] forces and their leaders to escape the orbit of state supervision and control."[5]

The argument linking effective management of economic stabilization with authoritarianism may be related as well to characteristics of the policymaking process. The recent history of countries such as Chile suggests that technocrats are likely to enjoy considerable autonomy under authoritarian rule, whereas in liberal democracies control over government expenditures and other key aspects of stabilization programs may be left in the hands of persons lacking the convictions and technical competence necessary for program success. The concentration of political authority characteristic of authoritarianism would also appear to permit greater coherence in program implementation. Democratic rule fragments decision-making authority among branches of government and relatively independent loci of political power, allowing opponents of stabilization to interfere with program design and implementation.

Last, but not least important, the belief that a "firm hand" is necessary for successful economic adjustment places democracies at a distinct disadvantage. Such a belief reduces incentives for individual trade unions or business firms to respond to the appeals of democratic leaders for sacrifice, and the logic of collective action makes the incentives for program cooperation minimal even in the best of circumstances.[6] The level of confidence in program success also influences capital flows and the willingness of external banks and financial agencies to extend the additional credits necessary to overcome temporary economic dislocations. In short, the greater the skepticism about the possibility of program success, the greater the probability of failure.

Against these supposed advantages of authoritarianism in the management of austerity programs may be set the greater legitimacy and popular support typically enjoyed by democratic regimes, which increase the appeal of programs calling for short-term sacrifice on behalf of the nation as a whole. To the extent that policy information and feedback are vital to the success of stabilization programs, democracies may be seen to have other advantages as well, particularly as compared with authoritarian regimes that are not cohesive, technocratically oriented, or capable of overriding popular dissent and particularistic claims with coercion. At the very least, the advantages supposedly enjoyed by authoritarianism in managing stabilization programs would appear to be undercut by the greater support, legitimacy, and access to information available to democratic policymakers.

The chief question mark about the theoretical linkage between authoritarianism and stabilization, however, has less to do with the reputed strengths of institutional democracy than with the explanatory power of the regime variable. Virtually by definition the process of policy formation varies with regime type, but other influences on policy outputs and outcomes are so numerous and the phenomena embraced by broad regime categories such as "democracy" so diverse that there is reason to question whether regime per se actually has any significant impact on the political sustainability of stabilization programs. The willingness and ability of governments to implement stabilization policies may depend instead on other factors. The level of industrial development and structure of trade unionism, for example, clearly condition the capacity of popular sector groups to sabotage stabilization measures. Similarly, the degree of technocratic control over policy may reflect variations in educational infrastructure or bureaucratic traditions rather than regime type. Thus certain nations might experience successful adjustment under both democratic and authoritarian regimes while the histories of others are littered with records of failure. Failure at one point in time may also enhance the probability of subsequent failure. Carlos Díaz-Alejandro hypothesized that "the longer the history of failed stabilization plans, the smaller the chances of success (and/ or greater the costs of success of any new plan)."[7] Again the obvious implication is that the success of stabilization efforts varies with national setting, not regime.

The sociopolitical context in which stabilization is attempted may also be important for other reasons. Drastic regime change, in particular, appears to create exceptional space for the adoption of controversial programs.[8] Indeed, it is striking that the most widely cited examples of successful authoritarian stabilization in Latin America are those in which comparatively traumatic democratic breakdowns paved the way for the initiation of austerity policies. While such examples are often used to bolster arguments about the superiority of authoritarianism in addressing intractable economic problems, they also provide a basis for optimism about the viability of democratic stabilization following the breakdown of authoritarianism.

Nonpolitical factors also enter the picture and call into question the significance of regime differences in explaining variations in the sustainability of stabilization programs. Stabilization has been easier in some time periods than in others, due to such factors as the availability of external funding, the dynamism of world trade, and the rate of imported inflation. Numerous other influences on the success of stabilization efforts might be mentioned as well, including the severity of economic problems at the start of the program, policy errors, price fluctuations for major export commodities, natural catastrophes, import and export elasticities, and the speed with which resources can be shifted to the tradables sector.

In short, although the theoretical arguments linking authoritarianism and economic stabilization are highly plausible, there are also grounds for questioning the explanatory power of the regime variable. If the capacity to adjust is chiefly determined by factors that vary independently of the type of regime in control, then the conventional wisdom about the politics of economic stabilization is seriously misleading.

Previous Research

Doubts about the theoretical significance of regime type for the analysis of economic stabilization are reinforced by previous research, which supplies surprisingly little support for the proposition that authoritarianism is a necessary condition for stabilization. Studies of public policy formation in Latin America, in particular, have consistently failed to uncover any strong empirical relationship between political regime and policy outputs or economic performance.[9] Economic stabilization policies may represent an exception, as Jorge Dominguez has suggested, because policy content is less of an issue in stabilization than implementation, which presumably depends on such regime attributes as techniques of political control.[10] Nevertheless, the evidence linking authoritarianism and stabilization is slim and largely confined to studies of the three largest Latin American nations.

The most influential study of this type has been Thomas Skidmore's analysis of stabilization in Argentina, Brazil, and Mexico [ABM countries]. According to Skidmore's widely cited conclusions, the experience of the ABM countries during the 1950s and 1960s demonstrates that:

> (1) governments in competitive political systems find it *extremely* difficult to reduce inflation once it has exceeded 20 percent, and they have paid very high political costs for their efforts; (2) no such government has proved able to pursue a successful (as defined earlier) anti-inflation effort; (3) all of the cases of successful stabilization have been carried out by authoritarian (or one-

party) governments; and (4) even authoritarian governments must have a high degree of internal consensus to carry through a successful stabilization.[11]

Robert Kaufman's more recent study of stabilization in the ABM countries arrives at a similar conclusion. According to Kaufman, "authoritarian regimes in the ABM countries are, in fact, so far the only ones in which stabilization programs have actually restored some degree of price and exchange equilibrium and a resumption of economic expansion."[12]

The difficulty is that the experiences of the large Latin American nations provide a fragile basis for broader generalizations about the relationship between regime and economic stabilization. Not only are the ABM countries rather atypical of the continent as a whole in terms of economic structure and bargaining power vis-à-vis international creditors and lending agencies; over the past two decades they have enjoyed less than five years of democratic rule among them. The exceptional weakness of democratic impulses in the ABM nations clearly makes them inappropriate cases for assessing the relative strengths of democracy and authoritarianism in the management of stabilization programs and raises the possibility that the tension between democracy and stabilization in Latin America has been exaggerated.

Research on other world regions points in the same direction. Because it explicitly considers the linkage between regime and policy, Stephen Haggard's study of IMF Extended Fund Facility (EFF) programs during the 1975–1984 period is of particular interest. On the basis of an analysis of thirty cases (eight of them Latin American), Haggard not only dismisses any connection between stabilization programs and the collapse of democratic regimes, but he also argues:

> While it seems that stabilization and adjustment can't live with democracy, they don't fare well without it either. The social consensus possible under democratic, or at least inclusive regimes, may permit policy packages which in the short-run achieve some adjustment aims.[13]

According to Haggard, however, the political capacity to adjust depends less on regime than on the economic ideologies of governing elites, the existence of a cohesive group of economic technocrats, the importance of political clientelism, the nature of broader political competition affecting government time horizons, the failure of the previous government's economic policies, and the availability of non-IMF resources.[14] Hence, he concludes that "the existence of an authoritarian regime does not—in itself—guarantee the ability to adjust, and may in certain instances undermine it."[15] These conclusions are echoed in Joan M. Nelson's recent work. On the basis of an analysis of five non-Latin American nations, Nelson also emphasizes the wide variety of nonregime factors that condition the political sustainability of stabilization programs, including the prevalence of patron-client politics, the real and anticipated program impact, and the adequacy of mechanisms to control government spending.[16]

Previous research consequently leaves the relationship between authoritarianism and economic austerity very much open to question. The literature on stabilization in Latin America has consistently emphasized the significance of contrasts between authoritarian and democratic regimes. Comparative studies of public policy in Latin America, on the other hand, have consistently dismissed the explanatory importance of regime differences, as have comparative analyses of economic stabilization focusing on other world regions. The sole point of consensus among scholars is that politics affect economic stabilization. Even the IMF, which has traditionally ignored political risks in designing economic programs, concedes this point. An IMF staff review of agreements signed in the 1978–1980 period, for example, concluded that "political constraints" and/or "weak administrative systems" accounted for 60 percent of the breaches of credit ceilings, whereas exogenous shocks, both domestic and external, led to only 26 percent of the breaches.[17] Critics of the IMF might also cite inaccurate economic diagnoses and inappropriate policy targets to explain program failures, but for IMF supporters and detractors alike, the political sustainability of stabilization programs is a central issue.

IMF Programs in Latin America

To resolve some of the unanswered questions about the importance of authoritarianism to economic stabilization, this study provides both a cross-sectional and diachronic analysis of the implementation of IMF programs in Latin America during the 1954–1984 period. The analysis focuses specifically on Latin American countries that have attempted to implement at least one IMF standby arrangement under both democratic and authoritarian regime auspices. Thus, countries that have not enjoyed any period of liberal democratic rule since 1954, when the principles governing IMF standby arrangements were first formalized, are excluded from analysis (Mexico, Paraguay, Cuba, Panama, Nicaragua, El Salvador, Guatemala, and Haiti). Also excluded are three countries (Dominican Republic, Costa Rica, and Venezuela) that have signed IMF agreements under only one kind of regime. The resulting sample, which encompasses more than half of the total number of conditional lending agreements between the IMF and Latin America during the 1954–1984 period, consists of 114 standby arrangements signed by nine different countries.

Emphasis is placed on IMF standby arrangements for several reasons. Perhaps most important, such a focus facilitates the process of identifying a large number of stabilization programs in a variety of different countries over a thirty-year period. The resulting list of programs is not necessarily inclusive, inasmuch as larger countries and those with exceptional access to other sources of credit, such as Venezuela, often have found it unnecessary to resort to IMF lending. Non-IMF stabilization programs also proliferated during the 1970s, when the widespread availability of commercial loans transformed the IMF into a lender of last resort. Nevertheless, in the 1954–1984 period taken as a whole, a high proportion of Latin American stabilization programs have involved IMF standby agreements. The reason is not merely that access to IMF resources in the upper-credit tranches hinges upon the introduction of stabilization policies; countries facing persistent balance-of-payments disequilibria also seek the IMF "seal of approval" in order to expedite debt renegotiation, attract other outside funds, reduce currency speculation, and reverse capital flight.

Since IMF stabilization programs evince a number of key similarities, restricting analysis to standby arrangements also facilitates comparison by limiting the range of variance. The institutional role played by the IMF creates a major commonality among standby programs, one that encourages opponents of stabilization to accuse political authorities of "selling out" at the same time that it allows authorities to attempt to shift blame for austerity to the Fund. The politics of stabilization are likely to be rather different where an outside villain cannot be identified so readily. The institutional role played by the IMF also creates pressures and incentives for countries to adhere to their stabilization programs. Standby arrangements require countries to submit to IMF scrutiny of their economic situation and policies, and since 1956, when "phasing" was introduced, drawings under standby arrangements have depended on the maintenance of satisfactory performance as defined by a "letter of intent" establishing an agreement with the Fund.

Despite the evolution of IMF programs and operating procedures over time, basic similarities in IMF prescriptions and lending policies also create a basis for comparison across time periods and national units.[18] Until very recently, the time horizons of IMF standby programs have been short-term. The overwhelming majority of programs considered in this study, for example, involved only one-year commitments, although a high proportion were renewed. In contrast, other stabilization programs, particularly those initiated in connection with World Bank structural adjustment lending or the IMF's own Extended Fund Facility, have emphasized longer-term structural adjustment. The similarities among IMF stabilization programs are also marked inasmuch as standby agreements have typically emphasized demand management techniques of fiscal and monetary policy plus exchange-rate adjustments. It is precisely this orthodox approach and its attendant squeeze on popular-sector living standards that is at the root of arguments concerning the incompatibility of democracy and economic stabilization. Of course, the specific program targets that are incorporated into IMF conditional lending agreements vary from case to case, but countries typically resort to Fund lending in the upper-credit tranches to cope with a common set of problems—persistent balance-of-payments deficits associated with moderate to high inflation—and the economic diagnoses and medicines dispensed by the Fund also evince major commonalities. Indeed, critics frequently charge the IMF with adopting a "stereotyped approach" that ignores important economic contrasts among countries.[19]

The subsequent analysis makes no attempt to assess the wisdom of IMF lending policies or to provide a full explanation of their variable impact. It focuses instead on two explicitly political questions: (1) are stabilization programs politically riskier for democratic than for authoritarian regimes, and (2) are authoritarian regimes more successful at implementing stabilization programs than democratic regimes? It should be emphasized that for the purposes of this study "success" is defined strictly in terms of policy implementation and does not refer to economic outcomes such as inflation. Although the issue of policy outcomes has figured prominently in previous discussions of the politics of stabilization, it cannot be assumed that short-term stabilization policies have any impact at all on economic performance, much less a positive impact. Even the Fund's own analyses show only a moderate correlation between the implementation of IMF prescriptions and the achievement of desired economic results.[20] Moreover, economic models of stabilization remain so highly controversial that policy outcomes cannot be analyzed in any manner not open to serious theoretical and empirical challenge. For example, according to neostructuralist analysts, orthodox stabilization programs produce perverse results: instead of reducing inflation, such programs provoke it by raising interest rates.[21] Likewise, it is possible to construct models showing that monetary restraint reduces exports and increases imports.[22] Hence, lowered inflation rates and improvements in the trade balance might plausibly be construed as signs of program breakdown or "failure" rather than as indicators of "success." The farther one moves away from policy in the direction of outcomes and economic performance, the more tenuous the conclusions that may be drawn about the impact of regime.

Table 1 provides basic information about the cases analyzed in this study. The sample is divided relatively equally between programs initiated by democratic and authoritarian regimes, which in itself suggests that Latin American democracies do not go to unusual lengths to avoid economic stabilization. Indeed, if one considers the relative frequency of democratic rule in the nine countries, which was less than 50 percent for the 1954–1984 period as a whole, the data indicate that democratic regimes are even more likely to introduce stabilization policies than authoritarian ones. The same is true even if the question of time period is taken into account. The propensity to resort to IMF lending was greatest during the 1960s, when democratic rule was unusually prevalent in Latin America. Nevertheless, in every decade except the 1980s, which accounts for only nine of the total number of cases, the percentage of standbys initiated by democracies exceeds the frequency of democratic rule. Individual country data show similar trends, although Brazil, Ecuador, and Uruguay stand out as exceptions inasmuch as democratic sponsorship of standbys is a little low relative to years of democratic rule. In general, however, the cross-national differences emerging from Table 1 reflect variations in the extent of democratic experience. Hence, Brazil, which has signed most of its standby arrangements under military rule, has enjoyed far fewer years of democracy than Chile or Colombia, which have initiated a high proportion of their stabilization programs under democratic rule.

Table 1. IMF Standby Arrangements in Nine Latin American Countries, 1954–1984

	Democratic Regime Initiation	*Authoritarian Regime Initiation*	*Total*
Argentina	4	6	10
Bolivia	6	7	13
Brazil	2	8	10
Chile	10	3	13
Colombia	13	2	15
Ecuador	5	5	10
Honduras	8	5	13
Peru	11	6	17
Uruguay	6	7	13
	65	49	114

SOURCE: International Monetary Fund, *Annual Report*, 1954–1984.

Even if democratic regimes are not more reluctant to initiate standby programs, do they nonetheless fall victim to stabilization policies more frequently than their authoritarian counterparts? The evidence fails to support such a conclusion. As indicated by Table 2, regime change followed the initiation of 12.0 percent of the stabilization programs, but democratic regimes proved no more vulnerable than authoritarian ones. If anything, the data point in the opposite direction because the breakdown rates for authoritarian regimes are marginally higher. Moreover, with the single exception of Bolivia, every nation that has experienced democratic-regime collapse after signing a standby arrangement has also experienced authoritarian-regime collapse under similar circumstances. Even in the Bolivian case, the first phase of a transition from authoritarian to democratic rule occurred after a standby agreement had been reached with the IMF in early 1980, although the transition was not completed until 1982.

The overlap between authoritarian and democratic regime breakdown not only suggests that some countries are more vulnerable to political instability than others; it also points to the variable impact of stabilization policies, which can be implemented with far less economic dislocation—and presumably political risk—in some settings than in others. In the countries considered here, the highest rate of regime breakdown was registered in Argentina, where stabilization has proved notoriously costly and difficult. While Argentine exports respond slowly to incentives such as devaluation, stabilization policies tend to have unusually immediate and highly negative effects on food prices, real wages, and income. Such policies therefore provoke intense resistance from popular sector groups, which traditionally have been both well organized and politically assertive.

Table 2. Regime Survival Rates under IMF Standby Arrangements (in Percentages)

	Democratic Regimes	Authoritarian Regimes
Breakdown[a]	10.8 (7)	14.0 (7)
Survival	89.2 (58)	86.0 (42)
	100.0 (65)	100.0 (49)

[a]Includes all cases of transition from democracy to authoritarianism or authoritarianism to democracy under standby arrangements or during the twelve-month period following the initiation of such arrangements.

In general, however, the experience of the nine countries considered in this study suggests that political risks of stabilization have been overdrawn. During the 1954–1984 period, 46 percent of the regime changes in the nine countries occurred in conjunction with stabilization programs. Although this figure sounds high, it is surprisingly low considering that stabilization programs were in effect 44 percent of the time. To put it another way, the odds of regime collapse during years in which standby arrangements prevailed and years in which they did not were 1 out of 9.4 and 10.5, respectively, or not significantly different. Moreover, an analysis of the fourteen regime changes that occurred while standby programs were in effect indicates that stabilization policies often had little political impact and that even when such policies did contribute to regime breakdown, as in the Argentine coup of 1962, they were not the sole or even the major factor. A higher rate of regime change might have been anticipated simply on the grounds that the economic difficulties typically associated with standbys, such as inflation and shortages of foreign exchange, are in themselves politically destabilizing. At least in Latin America, regimes are either more resilient or standby arrangements less consequential than observers have assumed. In view of the propensity of Latin American nations to resort repeatedly to IMF credit, the latter explanation seems particularly plausible. Hence, it can be hypothesized that standby arrangements have not caused more regime instability because the risky cures recommended by the IMF simply have not been administered.

The Implementation of IMF Programs

To address the question of implementation, this study relies upon a common set of indicators of credit expansion and fiscal performance. It thereby attempts to remain as close as possible to the issue of policy (as opposed to policy outcomes) without totally reducing the question of implementation to one of "success" versus "failure." The majority of stabilization programs fall somewhere between these extremes inasmuch as governments typically administer some stabilization measures more energetically and effectively than others. Hence, policy implementation cannot be assessed adequately on the basis of such criteria as program suspension or cancellation. Even when some of the criteria specified in a letter of intent are not met and drawings of IMF credits are suspended, compliance may still be impressive with respect to other aspects of a stabilization program. Moreover, program breakdown, whether resulting from cancellation by borrowing countries or IMF suspension, establishes no objective basis for comparison. Not all IMF standby programs are equally demanding, stringent, or realistic, nor are all countries treated equally with respect to the flexibility of conditionality.[23] Variability in program content and flexibility also makes it difficult to evaluate policy implementation on the basis of IMF performance criteria or program-specific goals. In any case, information about the targets of specific programs usually remains confidential, making it necessary for non-IMF researchers to rely on other indicators of implementation.

Indicators of credit expansion and fiscal performance were selected to assess policy implementation in this study chiefly because credit ceilings and fiscal targets have been emphasized more heavily and consistently by the IMF itself than other performance criteria. This emphasis has been criticized, especially with respect to credit ceilings; nevertheless, as Tony Killick has shown, "ceilings on total domestic credit and on that part of it lent to the public sector are almost invariably components of Stand-by and EFF programmes and . . . in most cases observance of these ceilings is the most serious hurdle the government must surmount in order to retain access to the credit in question."[24] Fiscal performance targets have been the second most common criteria of implementation since the 1960s, reflecting the IMF's traditional emphasis on fiscal restraint. Indeed, Fund programs often begin with the assumption that rapid inflation and balance-of-payments deficits are rooted in government deficits. According to a sample of thirty countries receiving upper-tranche credits in the 1964–1979 period, IMF standby missions identified public sector management as an "acute" problem more frequently than any other except the balance of payments itself.[25] Consequently, during the 1969–1978 period, nearly 80 percent of standby programs included fiscal performance clauses, and many of those that did not nevertheless included statements by government authorities about their fiscal policy intentions.[26] Due to the confidentiality of IMF programs, it is impossible to know precisely what proportion of programs included fiscal targets in the pre-1969 period, but available information suggests that the emphasis on government-sector performance has not increased over time.[27] Certainly most other performance criteria have fluctuated much more widely in importance both over time and among cases. Devaluation, for example, traditionally has been considered a central component of IMF policy packages; yet in the 1969–1979 period less than a third of upper-tranche lending agreements involved exchange rate action.[28]

Fiscal policy also warrants emphasis because failure to adhere to public-sector performance targets constitutes the single most important reason for the breakdown of IMF programs.[29] Expenditure targets have created particular difficulty and, according to an IMF staff analysis, were achieved by only 43 percent of the standbys during the 1969–1978 period.[30] This rate of success is low relative to that for other targets, even domestic credit ceilings, which were attained by 55 percent of the IMF standby programs during the same period.[31] Moreover, public-sector performance is controlled more directly by the government than most other indicators of policy implementation. Hence, to the extent that regime differences do produce variations in the ability of governments to sustain stabilization efforts, those variations should be particularly evident in public-sector behavior.

Subsequent tables compare the relative success of democratic and authoritarian regimes in controlling fiscal deficits, real expenditures, and rates of credit expansion during three different sets of years. Tables 3 and 5 present data only for those years in which the IMF actually disbursed funds

Table 3. Performance during Years with Credits Disbursed under IMF Standby Arrangements[a] (in Percentages)

	Democratic Regimes	Authoritarian Regimes	Mixed Regimes	All Regimes
Government Deficit as % GDP[b]	2.16 (32)	3.41 (15)	3.20 (6)	2.63 (53)
% Change in Gov't Deficit as % GDP[c]	-12.65 (33)	-10.89 (16)	-7.17 (6)	-11.54 (55)
Growth of Real Government Expenditures[d]	5.03 (29)	4.31 (15)	-8.20 (6)	3.23 (50)
Growth of Domestic Credit	34.60 (38)	96.65 (18)	52.23 (6)	54.32 (62)
% Change in Rate of Growth of Domestic Credit[e]	34.96 (37)	-15.34 (18)	14.17 (6)	39.62 (61)

SOURCE: International Monetary Fund, *Monthly Financial Statistics*, 1954–1985; idem, *International Financial Statistics*, 1954–1985; United Nations, *Statistical Yearbook*, 1955–1969.

[a] Excluding data for Colombia, which only made drawings of IMF credits under democratic rule.

[b] Data missing for nine cases.

[c] Data missing for seven cases.

[d] Data missing for twelve cases. Differences among categories significant at .05 level.

[e] Data missing for one case.

under standby arrangements to the countries considered in this study. Table 4 describes the implementation of IMF programs during years in which standby agreements were at least nominally in effect for eleven months or more, regardless of whether or not IMF credits were actually utilized. Finally, a third case is considered in Table 6, which presents data for all years in which standby programs were at least nominally in effect for six months or more. It should be emphasized that in all cases the data represent averages of individual years rather than individual standby programs, a number of which lasted more than a single year. The tables

Table 4. Performance during All Calendar Years Fully Covered by IMF Standby Arrangements[a] (in Percentages)

	Democratic Regimes	*Authoritarian Regimes*	*Mixed Regimes*	*All Regimes*
Government Deficit as % GDP[b]	1.76 (37)	3.42 (16)	1.68 (10)	2.17 (63)
% Change in Gov't Deficit as % GDP[c]	1.09 (36)	77.62 (19)	63.64 (9)	32.61 (64)
Growth of Real Government Expenditures[d]	5.04 (21)	13.04 (18)	6.02 (9)	8.23 (48)
Growth of Domestic Credit[e]	21.43 (40)	70.65 (20)	17.34 (10)	34.91 (70)
% Change in Rate of Growth of Domestic Credit[f]	47.71 (39)	20.27 (20)	30.42 (10)	37.25 (69)

SOURCE: International Monetary Fund, *Monthly Financial Statistics*, 1954–1985; idem, *International Financial Statistics*, 1954–1985; United Nations, *Statistical Yearbook*, 1955–1969.

[a] Includes all calendar years during which IMF standby arrangements were at least nominally in effect for eleven months or more. Data exclude Uruguay and Brazil, which experienced full-year standby programs as defined for the purpose of this table under only one type of regime.

[b] Data missing for seven cases. Differences among categories significant at .001 level.

[c] Data missing for six cases.

[d] Data missing for twenty-two cases.

[e] Differences among categories significant at .05 level.

[f] Data missing for one case.

consequently compare average performance during years in which democratic regimes administered standby programs with performance during years of authoritarian or mixed regime administration. Included in the "mixed" category are all cases of regime change that resulted in a single regime ruling less than eleven months of the year.

Looking first at Tables 3 and 4, we find no support for the view that the political sustainability of standby programs is any greater under authoritarianism than democracy. Although caution is necessary in comparing data averaged across widely disparate cases and time periods, democratic regimes actually outperformed authoritarian ones in terms of seven of the ten comparisons shown in the two tables. Moreover, on the basis of the F test, the only statistically significant differences between democratic and authoritarian regimes are those pointing in the direction of superior democratic program implementation in Table 4.[32]

The results are similar if the data are approached simply in terms of the direction of change of the various indicators. As Table 5 indicates, democratic regimes consistently outperformed authoritarian ones during years in which the IMF disbursed credits under standby arrangements, although the differences are not significant. The results are virtually identical if the analysis is expanded to include all years in which standby arrangements were nominally in effect for at least six months, regardless of whether credits were cancelled, suspended, or never utilized. Such findings cannot be dismissed on the grounds that the magnitude of adjustment problems increased in the post-1973 period, when military rule was particularly prevalent. Deleting the post-1973 period from the analysis presented in Table 5 only widens the gap between democratic and authoritarian performance. The figure for democratic budget reductions in Table 5, for example, rises to 64.5 percent while the success rate for authoritarian regimes falls to 37.5 percent.

The data presented in Table 5 also underline the high rate of failure of IMF programs. During years in which IMF credits were actually utilized, governments succeeded in pushing individual performance indicators in the right direction only approximately 60 percent of the time. Simultaneous reductions in all three indicators were achieved only 34 percent of the time. The rates are even worse for years in which standby agreements were nominally in effect for at least six months. For example, during such years governments succeeded in lowering the fiscal deficit as a percentage of GDP less than 50 percent of the time. In light of previous research on the IMF, much of which emphasizes the high breakdown rate of standby arrangements, these figures are not altogether surprising; nevertheless, the data presented here do lend concrete support to the view that the average IMF program has had a limited impact in Latin America. If a high proportion of IMF standby arrangements have failed to reduce the fiscal deficit as a proportion of GDP or even to lower the rate of growth of real expenditures and domestic credit, there is little basis for thinking such arrangements have profoundly reduced domestic consumption, damaged local industry, or increased inequality either.

The weak impact of standby arrangements is further underlined if the analysis shifts from average performance data to implementation strictly on a "before" and "after" basis. For this purpose IMF programs that formed part of a continuing series of stabilization arrangements are ignored in favor of programs that actually initiated stabilization policies. Hence, the implementation of standby programs is evaluated by comparing the performance of key variables in the twelve months preceding and following program initiation, but solely in relation to years in which no prior standby arrangement was in effect with the IMF. Because such a high proportion of Latin American programs have formed part of a continuing series, this procedure sharply reduces the number of programs that can be considered, but it also provides more meaningful information about program impact.

Table 5. Success Rates during Years with Credits Disbursed under IMF Standby Arrangements[a] (in Percentages)

	Democratic Regimes	*Authoritarian Regimes*	*Mixed Regimes*	*All Regimes*
Reduced Gov't Deficit as % GDP[b]	62.5 (32)	46.7 (15)	83.3 (6)	60.4 (53)
Reduced Rate of Growth of Real Expenditures[c]	53.8 (26)	53.3 (15)	83.3 (6)	57.4 (47)
Reduced Rate of Growth of Domestic Credit	68.4 (37)	61.1 (18)	66.7 (6)	66.1 (62)
Reduced Two of Three Indicators	69.2 (26)	66.7 (6)	53.3 (15)	63.7 (47)
Reduced All Three Indicators	38.5 (26)	33.3 (6)	26.7 (15)	34.0 (47)

SOURCE: International Monetary Fund, *Monthly Financial Statistics*, 1954–1985; idem, *International Financial Statistics*, 1954–1985; United Nations, *Statistical Yearbook*, 1955–1969.

[a] Excluding data for Colombia, which only made drawings of IMF upper-tranche credits under democratic rule.

[b] Data missing for ten cases.

[c] Data missing for fifteen cases.

To assess the impact of standby arrangements on expenditures, deficits, and domestic credit, the data on program implementation were calculated as weighted averages, with the weights determined by the month of program initiation and the differences between the before and after samples evaluated on the basis of a nonparametric test for differences in frequency distributions.[33] The results of this analysis strongly reinforce the findings reported above. The twenty-four IMF programs falling within the sample that were implemented by authoritarian regimes had no statistically significant impact on indicators of expenditures, deficits, or domestic credit. The implementation record of democratic regimes was also weak, but the twenty democratic programs in the sample did effect a reduction in the rate of growth of real expenditures that was significant at the .05 level. Hence, again democratic and authoritarian regimes evince similar patterns of weak policy implementation, but democracies turn in a slightly better performance record.

Looking at the most and least successful cases in the before and after sample is also revealing. Nine of the forty-four programs considered produced major improvements in two of the three performance indicators. Seven of these nine (Argentina 1959 and 1967, Ecuador 1961 and 1969, Brazil 1965, Chile 1974, and Colombia 1957) were administered by new governments that had been in power less than one year, and five were liberal democracies. At the other extreme stand four cases (Brazil 1961, Bolivia 1973, Honduras 1968, and Argentina 1983) distinguished by virtue of their economic policy failures, three of which were authoritarian regimes that had been in power for a period of five or more years. Particularly abysmal are the performance records of military regimes in Bolivia and Honduras during the late 1960s and early 1970s. For example, after entering into an agreement with the IMF in January 1973, the Bolivian military allowed real expenditures to increase 18 percent in a single year. Hence, while newly established regimes often compile dismal records of economic stabilization, particularly because of their propensity to consolidate a basis of political support by increasing government spending, the evidence also suggests that regime change enhances the possibilities for effective stabilization, particularly under democratic auspices.

Other evidence of the linkage between regime change and effective stabilization also emerges from Tables 3 to 5 above, which show that better than average performance rates have characterized years of mixed regime administration. The numbers are small, however, and the findings open to more than one interpretation. Is effective stabilization a cause or a consequence of regime change? Do new regimes find it easier to administer stabilization programs, or are the relatively high success rates for years of regime change a product of vigorous program administration resulting in regime breakdown? The cases of unusually effective stabilization that emerge from the before and after sample point to the importance of regime change as a precondition for effective stabilization. Table 6, on the other hand, suggests that the relationship between regime change and stabilization is more complex. The data presented here show that, while program administration may be unusually vigorous in the year of regime breakdown itself,

Table 6. Success Rates of IMF Programs and Political Change[a]
(in Percentages)

	Reduced Gov't Deficit as % GDP	*Reduced Rate of Increase of Real Government Expenditures*	*Reduced Rate of Growth of Domestic Credit*
Years Preceding Regime Change	41.7 (12)[b]	66.7 (9)[c]	83.3 (12)[c]
Years Following Regime Change	62.5 (16)	46.7 (15)[b]	50.0 (16)
Democratic Program Administration	83.3 (6)	60.0 (5)[b]	50.0 (6)
Authoritarian Program Administration	50.0 (10)	40.0 (10)	50.0 (10)
Years Following Democratic Elections	50.0 (14)[d]	55.6 (9)[e]	64.3 (14)[d]
All Standby Years[f]	49.1 (116)	54.0 (87)	56.1 (123)

SOURCE: International Monetary Fund, *Monthly Financial Statistics*, 1954–1985; idem, *International Financial Statistics*, 1954–1985; United Nations, *Statistical Yearbook*, 1955–1969.

[a] Includes all years preceding and following regime change in which IMF standby arrangements covered a period of at least six months. Data calculated on the basis of performance during the full calendar year.

[b] Data missing for one case.

[c] Data missing for four cases.

[d] Data missing for three cases.

[e] Data missing for eight cases.

[f] All years IMF standby arrangements at least nominally in effect for six months or more. Data missing for eleven, and four cases in columns 1, 2, and 3, respectively.

success rates for years following regime change are somewhat mixed. The implementation of IMF standby programs also appears less than uniformly superior in years following democratic elections. New governments, whether resulting from regime change or elections, do not necessarily excel at economic stabilization. In terms of indicators of domestic credit and government expenditures, the average performance of new regimes, particularly authoritarian ones, even falls below par.[34] The success rates of regimes implementing IMF standby programs during years prior to regime breakdown, on the other hand, exceed average figures, except in the deficit category. Vigorous implementation of IMF programs consequently appears to enhance the risk of regime breakdown, although ineffective stabilization is not necessarily a recipe for political survival. The cases of regime change analyzed in Table 6 include instances of unsuccessful as well as successful implementation of standby programs, presumably because a deteriorating economic situation undermines political support and/or because underlying political weaknesses contribute both to implementation failures and to regime change. In this connection it may be noted that, in the nine countries considered by this study [Argentina, Bolivia, Brazil, Chile, Colombia, Ecuador, Honduras, Peru, and Uruguay], economic stabilization followed regime change more frequently than regime change followed efforts to achieve economic stabilization.

Looking at the data on a country-by-country basis provides additional confirmation of previous findings as well as further insights into the relationship between regime change and economic stabilization. As far as government expenditures are concerned, military regimes have outperformed their democratic counterparts in only two countries: Chile and Peru. Moreover, in most cases the gap between authoritarian and democratic performance has been considerable. The relative success of democracy and authoritarianism in implementing IMF programs has varied considerably from place to place. Again, however, Chile and Peru stand out by virtue of the effectiveness of authoritarianism in restricting the expansion of both government deficits and domestic credit. The cases falling at the other extreme include Argentina, Bolivia, Ecuador, and Uruguay, where democracies have outperformed authoritarian regimes in terms of all three indicators of implementation.

The country-by-country patterns consequently conform to broader trends. Few differences emerge between democratic and authoritarian implementation of stabilization programs, and those that do tend to point in the direction of greater democratic effectiveness. Marked evidence of superior authoritarian performance exists only in the cases of Chile and Peru. Moreover, both of these cases present weak exceptions in the sense

that the achievements of authoritarianism occurred in a context of exceptionally high levels of government expenditure and were confined to a brief
time period. In the Peruvian case, severe cutbacks in real expenditures in
1978 and 1979 produced negative figures although they left the ratio of
government spending to GDP at a figure of 23 percent. Similarly, in Chile
government spending had reached unprecedented levels during the Allende
period, and the contrasts between authoritarian and democratic performance reflect the deep budget cuts of 1974. The success of military regimes
in Chile and Peru in cutting the rate of expansion of domestic credit and
budget deficits as a percentage of GDP likewise represents developments in
a brief time period characterized by exceptional financial disequilibrium
rather than a long-term pattern. In both Chile and Peru the deficit had risen
to over 7 percent of GDP—a figure other countries considered in this study
have yet to approach, with the single exception of Bolivia in the early
1980s.

Yet if the deviant cases provide only weak counterevidence, they are
nevertheless revealing in terms of the issue of regime change. In Chile a
traumatic regime breakdown paved the way for unusually vigorous
implementation of IMF policy prescriptions under authoritarian auspices—
an experience that illustrates the political risks of deferring economic
stabilization as well as the link between regime change and successful
stabilization. The Peruvian case, on the other hand, underlines the political
costs of severe stabilization measures to an authoritarian regime. Against a
background of unsuccessful non-IMF stabilization, the austerity policies of
the 1976–1979 period mobilized opposition and intensified divisions within
the Peruvian military government, generating a profound political crisis that
culminated in a transition to democracy. The two cases are similar in that a
severe economic crisis placed authorities in a predicament in both countries
and thereby paved the way for regime change. The response of Chilean and
Peruvian authorities to that crisis, however, differed significantly, creating
very disparate incentives and opportunities for economic stabilization after
regime breakdown.

The Chilean and Peruvian cases consequently shed additional light
upon the complex relationship between regime change and economic
stabilization. They suggest that regime transitions result less from stabilization
policies than from economic crisis, but that the policy responses of authorities
to economic crisis are nonetheless important for understanding the outcome
of regime change processes. The type of political coalition emerging after
regime breakdown and the related willingness and capacity of new authorities
to implement orthodox stabilization policies are conditioned by the perceived successes and failures of their predecessors. At stake here is the

much neglected issue of political learning. The political sustainability of economic stabilization subsequent to regime change varies with the intensity of prior implementation efforts.

Conclusion

Is authoritarianism a necessary condition for economic stabilization? This analysis of IMF standby programs in Latin America over the past three decades suggests that the answer to this question is "No." Authoritarian regimes may inspire greater outside investor confidence or otherwise surpass their democratic counterparts in economic management, but they are no more likely to initiate stabilization programs or to survive their political reverberations. Authoritarian regimes do not excel at the implementation of orthodox stabilization programs, either. Whether the data are pooled, approached on a country-by-country basis, considered by time period, or analyzed in terms of the before and after performance of key indicators, the results are the same: the implementation of stabilization programs is no more rigorous under authoritarianism than democracy. Indeed, to the limited extent that regime differences are significant, the edge appears to be with democracies.

The findings of this study consequently provide no support for conventional wisdom about the politics of economic stabilization. Regime type is far less important than has been supposed. But perhaps even more to the point, the study casts doubt upon the widespread assumption that democracies are singularly inept at coping with economic crisis and managing austerity programs. The evidence presented here, although not conclusive, actually points to greater authoritarian ineffectiveness in the implementation of stabilization programs. Obviously democracies enjoy strengths that have been denigrated or overlooked, such as legitimacy and popular support; but perhaps more to the point, the rationality, efficiency, unity, expertise, political isolation, and coercive capability of authoritarian governments appear to have been grossly exaggerated. As measured by increases in budget deficits, expenditures, and domestic credit, the most egregiously unsuccessful IMF stabilization programs in Latin America over the past thirty years have been those managed by authoritarian—not democratic—regimes. Hence, while the conceptualization of regime differences that has prevailed in the literature on Latin America may conform to the claims of military rulers, who characteristically tout the strength, efficiency, impartiality, and effectiveness of authoritarianism, that conceptualization provides a distorted lens through which to view empirical reality.

This study also sheds additional light on a major theoretical paradox: research on Latin America has centered around the issue of regime change, yet most comparative evidence, including that presented here, emphasizes the limited importance of regime differences in explaining political outcomes. The appropriate conclusion is not that regime is irrelevant or important only in understanding strictly political variations over time or among cases. As this study indicates, regime change may make a significant difference even if regime type does not. Virtually every instance of unusually successful policy implementation identified in this study was a product of regime change. These data suggest that regime breakdowns occurring in conjunction with economic crisis create unusual space for the implementation of stabilization policies, particularly when regime collapse is attributed to policy inaction rather than to austerity measures. Hence, as in the case of Chile, authoritarian regimes may succeed where their democratic predecessors have failed. Likewise, regime change may enhance the willingness and capacity of democratic authorities to implement stabilization policies.

The dominant theme to emerge from this analysis of IMF programs is not that of success, however, but of failure. Unsuccessful implementation of IMF recipes has been the norm in Latin America, not the exception. A high proportion of standby programs have failed to push key indicators of government finance and domestic credit even in the right direction. Moreover, examining IMF standby programs on a before and after basis shows that changes in key indicators are more readily attributable to chance than to the operation of IMF stabilization programs. The obvious conclusion is that the economic, social, and political impact of IMF programs has been overstated. To describe the IMF as a "poverty broker," as does the title of a recent book, or to charge the Fund with undermining democracy in Latin America is to indulge in hyperbole.[35] The power of the IMF remains a useful myth for governments seeking a scapegoat to explain difficult economic conditions associated with severe balance-of-payments disequilibria, but the ability of the IMF to impose programs from the outside is distinctly limited. Indeed, the Fund perhaps can be more justly criticized for the ineffectiveness of its advice, which appears to be ignored more often than not and, perhaps, with good reason.

These findings create a basis for questioning the supposed incompatibility of liberal democracy and economic austerity in Latin America during the 1980s. The depth and breadth of the current crisis enhance the leverage of the IMF and create highly intractable economic problems for newly established democratic regimes, but the lessons of the past suggest that Latin American democracies nevertheless may weather the crisis of the 1980s. Particularly in countries such as Argentina, where democratic rule is a product of recent regime change, democratic authorities have been able to blame economic problems on their military predecessors, much as those predecessors attributed the need for austerity in the 1960s and 1970s to "populist" economic mismanagement. Moreover, as in the past, economic crisis and regime breakdown have discredited prior political formulas, opening up room for new authorities to maneuver in the face of economic necessity. Authoritarian regimes in Latin America, which as of 1985 were all more than a decade old, face a far greater challenge in the 1980s. Past experience suggests that the political risks of economic stabilization are likely to be even greater for such old regimes than for new democratic ones, and that their willingness and ability to sustain stabilization programs will also prove more limited. Under these conditions the attractions of conservative-authoritarian rule may continue to diminish.

Notes

1. For the application of this argument to Latin America in the 1980s see Richard E. Feinberg, "The Adjustment Imperative and U.S. Policy," in Richard E. Feinberg and Valeriana Kallab, eds., *Adjustment Crisis in the Third World* (New Brunswick: Transaction Books, 1984), p. 13.

2. See, for example, *LASA Forum*, 15 (Winter 1985), 1, in which the former president of Latin American Studies Association, Helen Safa, commented: "Southern Cone countries such as Argentina and hopefully Uruguay and Brazil, are now returning to civil democracy after years of military rule. . . . But they are faced with enormous debt problems, which seriously endanger the process of democratic transition. . . . Many Latin American scholars feel that the policies of the International Monetary Fund are hindering the democratic process in these countries, not only by forcing the new civilian governments to institute harsh unpopular measures regarding wages, inflation, and investment policies, but by seriously weakening the strength of labor unions. . . ." See also Rosemary Thorp and Laurence Whitehead, "Introduction," in Rosemary Thorp and Laurence Whitehead, eds., *Inflation and Stabilisation in Latin America* (New York: Holmes & Meier, 1979), pp. 11, 18; Robert R. Kaufman, "Democratic and Authoritarian Responses to the Debt Issue: Argentina, Brazil, and Mexico," *International Organization*, 39 (Summer 1985), 473–503; Barbara Stallings, "Peru and the U.S. Banks: Privatization of Financial Relations," in Richard R. Fagen, ed., *Capitalism and the State in U.S.-Latin American Relations* (Stanford: Stanford University Press, 1979), pp. 217–253; Roberto Frenkel and Guillermo O'Donnell, "The 'Stabilization Programs' of the International Monetary Fund and Their Internal Impacts," in ibid., pp. 171–216; Thomas E. Skidmore, "The Politics of Economic Stabilization in Postwar Latin America," in James M. Malloy, ed., *Authoritarianism and Corporatism in Latin America* (Pittsburgh: University of Pittsburgh Press, 1977), pp. 149–190; John Sheahan, "Market-oriented Economic Policies and Political Repression in Latin America," *Economic Development and Cultural Change*, 28 (January 1980), 267–291; Alejandro Foxley, *Latin American Experiments in Neoconservative Economics* (Berkeley: University of California Press, 1983); Christian Anglade and Carlos Fortin, eds., *The State and Capital Accumulation in Latin America*, vol. 1 (Pittsburgh: University of Pittsburgh Press, 1985), p. 8; Riordan Roett, "The Foreign Debt Crisis and the Process of Redemocratization in Latin America," in William N. Eskridge, Jr., ed., *A Dance along the Precipice: The Political and Economic*

Dimensions of the International Debt Problem (Lexington: Lexington Books, 1985), pp. 207–230.

3. Joan M. Nelson, "The Politics of Stabilization," in Feinberg and Kallab, eds., *Adjustment Crisis in the Third World*, pp. 99.

4. It may be noted that Joan M. Nelson applies this argument to all types of Third World governments (ibid., p. 103).

5. Kaufman, "Democratic and Authoritarian Responses," p. 478. See also Skidmore, "Politics of Economic Stabilization," p. 179.

6. Kaufman, "Democratic and Authoritarian Responses," p. 479; Mancur Olson, *The Rise and Decline of Nations: Economic Growth, Stagflation, and Social Rigidities* (New Haven: Yale University Press, 1982), p. 44.

7. Carlos Diaz-Alejandro, "Southern Cone Stabilization Plans," in William R. Cline and Sidney Weintraub, eds., *Economic Stabilization in Developing Countries* (Washington, DC: Brookings Institution, 1981), p. 120.

8. Ibid., p. 123.

9. For a summary and review of this literature see Karen L. Remmer, "Evaluating the Policy Impact of Military Regimes in Latin America," *Latin American Research Review*, 13 (1978), 39–54. More recent studies include William Ascher, *Scheming for the Poor: The Politics of Redistribution in Latin America* (Cambridge, MA: Harvard University Press, 1984); Robert Wesson, ed., *Politics, Policies, and Economic Development in Latin America* (Stanford: Hoover Institution, 1984); Steven W. Hughes and Kenneth J. Mijeski, *Politics and Public Policy in Latin America* (Boulder: Westview Press, 1984).

10. Jorge Dominguez, "Political Changes in Central and South America and the Caribbean," unpublished paper, Center for International Affairs, Harvard University, June 1984, p. 19.

11. Skidmore, "The Politics of Stabilization," p. 181.

12. Kaufman, "Democratic and Authoritarian Responses," p. 482.

13. Stephen Haggard, "The Politics of Stabilization: Lessons from the IMF's Extended Fund Facility," paper presented at the 1984 meeting of the American Political Science Association, Washington, DC, August 30–September 2, 1984, pp. 12, 47–48.

14. Ibid., pp. 8–9.

15. Ibid., p. 32.

16. Nelson, "The Politics of Stabilization."

17. As cited in Tony Killick, "The Impact of Fund Stabilisation Programmes," in Tony Killick, ed., *The Quest for Economic Stabilization: The IMF and the Third World* (New York: St. Martin's, 1984), p. 261. See also C. David Finch, "Adjustment Policies and Conditionality," in John Williamson, ed., *IMF Conditionality* (Washington, DC: Institute for International Economics, 1983), p. 79; Omotunde Johnson and Joanne Salop, "Distributional Aspects of Stabilization Programs in Developing Countries," *IMF Staff Papers*, 27 (March 1980), 23.

18. For an analysis of the evolution of IMF programs and practices over time see Sidney Dell, *On Being Grandmotherly: The Evolution of IMF Conditionality*, Princeton Essays in International Finance 144 (Princeton: Department of Economics, October 1981). See also E. M. Ainley, *The IMF: Past, Present and Future*, Bangor Occasional Papers in Economics 15 (Bangor: University of Wales Press, 1979); J. Keith Horsefield, ed., *The International Monetary Fund, 1945–1965: Twenty Years of International Monetary Cooperation*, 3 vols. (Washington, DC: International Monetary Fund, 1969); Margaret Garritsen de Vries, ed., *The*

International Monetary Fund, 1966–1971: The System under Stress, 2 vols. (Washington, DC: International Monetary Fund, 1976).

19. Sidney Dell, "Stabilization: The Political Economy of Overkill," in Williamson, ed., *IMF Conditionality*, pp. 17–45.

20. For a summary of this evidence see Killick, "The Impact of Fund Stabilisation Programmes."

21. Lance Taylor, "IS/LM in the Tropics: Diagrammatics of the New Structuralist Macro Critique," in Cline and Weintraub, eds., *Economic Stabilization in Developing Countries*, pp. 465–503; William R. Cline, "Economic Stabilization in Developing Countries: Theory and Stylized Facts," in Williamson, ed., *IMF Conditionality*, pp. 182–186.

22. Milton Charlton and Deborah Riner, "Political Dimensions of Economic Stabilization Programs in Latin America: A Rapporteurs' Report," Working Paper no. 50, Latin American Program, Woodrow Wilson International Center for Scholars, p. 3. In this connection it may be noted that much depends on whether emphasis is placed on short-run or long-run impact. See Rudiger Dornbusch, "Stabilization Policies in Developing Countries: What Have We Learned?" *World Development*, 10 (September 1982), 701–708.

23. Tony Killick, "IMF Stabilisation Programmes," in Killick, ed., *The Quest for Economic Stabilization*, pp. 183–226.

24. Ibid., p. 213.

25. Ibid., p. 224. See also Claudio M. Loser, "The Role of Economy-Wide Prices in the Adjustment Process," in Joaquin Muns, ed., *Adjustment, Conditionality, and International Financing* (Washington, DC: International Monetary Fund, 1984), p. 94.

26. W. A. Beveridge and Margaret R. Kelly, "Fiscal Content of Financial Programs Supported by Stand-By Arrangements in the Upper Credit Tranches, 1969–78," *IMF Staff Papers*, 27 (June 1980), 220.

27. Killick, "IMF Stabilisation Programmes," pp. 192, 224–226.

28. Ibid., p. 195.

29. Killick, "The Impact of Fund Stabilisation Programmes," pp. 252–253. See also Thomas Reichmann and Richard Stillson, "How Successful Are Programs Supported by Stand-By Arrangements?" *Finance and Development*, 14 (March 1977), 25.

30. Beveridge and Kelly, p. 227.

31. See Killick, "The Impact of Fund Stabilisation Programmes," pp. 252–255, for a summary of this evidence.

32. Differences among regime categories are statistically significant in terms of the indicator of government spending shown in Table 3; however, that significance is due to spending reductions that occurred under mixed regimes. The differences between authoritarian and democratic regime spending during years in which IMF credits were utilized are not statistically significant. The results are virtually identical if the data base is broadened to include all calendar years in which standby programs were at least nominally in effect for a period of six months or more. Out of a total of more than one hundred observations, the average performance of democratic regimes is again superior to that of authoritarian regimes, although the differences among categories are not statistically significant.

33. The specific test used was the Mann-Whitney test, which is considered a useful alternative to the parametric t-test when the test assumptions are not met. For a more detailed discussion of the procedures followed here, which are similar to

those used by other IMF researchers, see the methodological appendix of Killick, "The Impact of Fund Stabilisation Programmes," pp. 266–268.

34. It may be noted that a similar picture emerges from an analysis of data on the seventeen twelve-month IMF programs that followed regime changes in the nine countries. These data also show that on average program implementation by new regimes was not particularly vigorous and that the performance of new authoritarian regimes was distinctly worse than that of new democracies.

35. Martin Honeywell et al., *The Poverty Brokers: The IMF and Latin America* (London: Latin America Bureau, 1983).

IV

Import Substitution and
the New Academics

During the financial inflow and outflow of the 1970s and 1980s, Latin Americans searched for new expertise to cope with the debt crisis and the need for neoliberal restructuring. They diversified not only their trading and investing partners but also their economic advisers, thus reducing their dependence on any one source. They engaged consultants from universities, government institutions, numerous multilateral and bilateral agencies, and from Europe as well as the United States. Sometimes they substituted local advisers educated abroad for imported economists; other times they sidestepped international institutions by turning to independent foreign academic wizards reminiscent of Edwin Kemmerer in his heyday. But whether practicing import substitution or importation, they were mainly tapping the economic wisdom and prestige of U.S. universities.

The most famous case of importing U.S. economic models through Latin American students trained in the United States was that of the Chicago Boys in Chile, analyzed here by Patricio Silva. In some ways, these graduates of the University of Chicago were more staunch believers than their own teachers. Like other money doctors, they stressed their technocratic, scientific, objective purity above petty politics. Their opponents, however, assailed these economists for serving an authoritarian regime notorious for its destruction of democracy, its violations of human rights, and its mistreatment of the working class. Nevertheless, the technocratic modality of the Chicago Boys was also adopted by their domestic adversaries. As Silva shows, dissident intellectuals were able to criticize publicly the dictatorship of General Augusto Pinochet (1973–1990) because of their credentials as professional, academic economists schooled and certified overseas.

In the 1980s and 1990s, governments also borrowed luster from the economics profession in the world's wealthiest country by hiring professors from premier universities. The most remarkable was Harvard's Jeffrey

Sachs, who treated seemingly incurable patients from both Latin America and Eastern Europe, leading one journalist to dub him "Doctor Debt."

Robert E. Norton reveals that Sachs was an admirer of both John Maynard Keynes of England and Milton Friedman of Chicago. Unlike the Chicago Boys, however, Sachs insisted on advising only democratic governments. He usually recognized the political as well as the economic aspects of his work. Norton shows how Sachs transferred his expertise from a country on the periphery of the international capitalist system, Bolivia, to one on the periphery of the international socialist system, Poland—from a country where capitalism was disintegrating to one where it was suffering the pangs of birth.

In the twentieth century, Bolivia may have hosted more monetary medics than any other country in Latin America, and Sachs's participation in the country's neoliberal adventure is analyzed by political scientist Catherine M. Conaghan. She shows that the success of the program was mainly due to the backing of a domestic coalition that was committed to the plan before Sachs arrived. Like his predecessors, Sachs provided technical expertise, international legitimation, and a consoling bedside manner to keep the patient on the road to recovery. Although suggesting some generalizations about money doctors, Conaghan also cautions that their reforms must be understood within the historical context of particular cases.

In both countries, Sachs, like the Chicago Boys in Chile, recommended shock treatment to create functioning market economies. In his enthusiasm for his recommendations, he tried to help rally support among the citizens of the host country through speeches to politicians and the public. Because he advocated leniency on debt repayments, he served the interests of his clients more than those of their creditors. Finally, by fortifying and expanding the market system, Sachs, like other money doctors, helped hold world capitalism together.

11 Patricio Silva ◆ Technocrats and Politics in Chile: From the Chicago Boys to the CIEPLAN Monks

During the last twenty-five years Chilean society has experienced profound socioeconomic, political, and even cultural changes. From 1964
to 1970 there was a "revolution in liberty" under Eduardo Frei, from 1970 a
"Chilean road to socialism" under Salvador Allende, and from 1973 to 1989
a "silent revolution" under Augusto Pinochet.[1]

Most of the studies dealing with this period of Chilean political history
have correctly stressed the marked differences existing among the policies
applied by the governments of Frei, Allende, and Pinochet. However,
despite their different and even antagonistic ideological and political
orientations, a body of technocrats played an important role at the highest
level of policymaking in all these governments.[2]

Although a process of increasing technocratization of decision making
was clearly underway during the Frei and even the Allende governments, it
was officially ignored because of its negative, elitist implications. In a
climate of strong ideological polarization, the official discourse adopted a
populist character, stressing the alleged popular nature and orientation of
the power bloc.

Under the military government, however, there was a radical revaluation
of the technocrats' role in the formulation and application of governmental
policies. No longer neglected, the technocratization of decision making was
now presented as the only guarantee of "rational and coherent" policies. In
stressing the need to "technify" the entire society, the military government
intended to convince the population of the inability of "politics" (and,
hence, of democracy) to solve the problems of the country.

This article has two main objectives. First, to identify the main political
and economic factors which permitted the so-called Chicago Boys to play a
strategic role during the military government. This group of young neoliberal
technocrats became the designers and executors of the economic policy
applied during the Pinochet period. They also decisively contributed to the
formulation of the official ideological discourse.

Our second objective is to stress the fact that although the era of the
Chicago Boys is over, the "technocratization of politics" associated with
them has become a permanent new feature in Chilean politics.

From the *Journal of Latin American Studies* 23, no. 2 (May 1991): 385–410.
Reprinted by permission of Cambridge University Press.

Paradoxically, the opposition to authoritarian rule also adopted an increasingly technocratic character. Several private research institutes were established, from which experts in different fields of the social sciences and economics undertook critical studies of government policies and formulated alternative programs to be implemented after the restoration of democracy. This dissident technocracy played a key role in the creation of a broad opposition to the military government and in the achievement of the subsequent victory in the presidential elections of December 1989.

The new democratic government of Patricio Aylwin is also characterized by a marked technocratic orientation. Like the Chicago Boys during the military government, a new group of technocrats, the so-called CIEPLAN Monks, has emerged as the most powerful strategic group inside the democratic government.[3]

This article does not argue that the hegemonic role played by political parties and traditional *políticos* within the Chilean political system is coming to an end.[4] But it does claim that their position today is much less monopolistic and all-embracing than it was in the past and that technocrats have become very visible and legitimate actors within Chilean politics.

Technocracy and Decision Making

The process of the "technocratization" of decision making in Chile has been stimulated by the administrative and overall modernization experienced by the country during the last twenty-five years. The "globalist" character of the developmental goals pursued by the Chilean governments since 1964 did serve to strengthen the technocratic orientation of public administration in the context of a relatively complex society. The expansion of the state apparatus, the application of the land reform, the nationalization of the copper mines, and the administration of the expropriated enterprises in the period 1964–1973 set this process into motion. Together with this, the radical and ambitious neoliberal reforms implemented by the military government, together with the increasing complexity and urgency of macroeconomic problems (such as the foreign debt) during that period, have contributed to the strengthening of the position of highly qualified individuals at top levels within governmental circles.[5]

There are manifold reasons for the underestimation of the role played by technocrats in governmental decision making in most of the studies on Chilean political development since 1964.

To begin with, most of the Chilean scholars who have written about social and political issues during this period came themselves from technocratic ranks. They commanded high academic positions within state and private universities. These technocrats also participated in decision making at governmental level (as *técnicos*, advisers, etc.), and enjoyed considerable political power within the political parties (as intellectuals, ideologues, or even as members of the central committees).[6]

As a matter of fact, most scholars prefer to look at society "as a whole," rather than to look at themselves in the mirror. Just as most painters prefer a landscape to a self-portrait, intellectuals are almost instinctively reluctant to analyze their own role in social and political processes. This reluctance is partly an expression of what [Antonio] Gramsci called a "social utopia" by which intellectuals think of themselves as "independent," autonomous, endowed with a character of their own.[7] Hence, they prefer not to think that they might constitute a social actor comparable to other social actors such as the military, the entrepreneurs, the peasantry, etc. To recognize their political role in society would lead automatically to an acceptance of the existence of their own interests in both the institutional and the private spheres. It would also imply that they share (together with the other social actors) a portion of the responsibility for events occurring in civil society. As [Albert] Hirschman has categorically pointed out:

> When a series of disastrous events strikes the body politic, everyone's responsibility must be looked at, including that of the intellectuals. . . . They ought to be more fully aware of their responsibility, which is the greater because of the considerable authority they are apt to wield in their countries. Because of this authority, the process that in the realm of science and technology is known as the protracted sequence from invention to innovation often takes remarkably little time in Latin America with respect to economic, social and political ideas. With social thought turning so rapidly into attempted social engineering, a high incidence of failed experiments is the price that is often paid for the influence intellectuals wield.[8]

Another factor which has impeded the analysis of the role played by technocrats in national decision making has been the hyperideologization which characterized Chilean politics during the period 1964–1973. The Christian Democratic government stressed the notion of "popular participation" in its efforts to organize new social actors such as the urban marginals and the peasantry. While the implementation of the "revolution in liberty" led to an increasing participation of technocrats within the government, the attention of government officials was focused on the various socioeconomic problems they had to deal with and not on the technocratic nature of decision making.[9]

The rhetorical populism of official discourse became even more accentuated during the Popular Unity government. The authorities defined themselves as the people's government. The middle-class origin and the intellectual and technico-professional backgrounds of most of the leading figures (Carlos Altamirano, Luis Maira, Jaime Gazmuri, et al.) were not seen as a governmental asset but rather as a handicap to efforts to obtain the support required from the popular sectors and the organized mass movement. During the Allende years the term "technocrat" acquired an extremely negative connotation, used sometimes as an insult to accuse someone of total social insensibility and (revolutionary) incompetence. [10]

Since the military government, a major novelty has been the great public visibility and positive evaluation the technocrats have acquired. Before 1973, most of the people occupying leading governmental positions were also technocrats and intellectuals, but they carefully avoided emphasizing their professional-cultural backgrounds. In a period of strong political radicalization and *obrerismo*, the holding of a university degree revealed petit-bourgeois origins, making the holders seem less reliable to the revolutionary process. Before the military takeover technocrats cautiously kept their diplomas in their desks, while since the era of the Chicago Boys they have been hung proudly on the wall.

From the Academic Cloister Back to Civil Society: Waiting for a Chance

The origins of the Chicago Boys are directly related to the debate which took place in the late 1950s and 1960s between structuralists and monetarists on the causes (but especially on the possible solutions) of the developmental problems of Latin America. [11]

According to the structuralist approach, Latin American governments needed to play a very active role in promoting economic development by adopting a planned policy to generate import-substitution industrialization. This policy had to be accompanied by protectionism for domestic industry, such as high tariffs for the import of consumer goods, the manipulation of exchange rates, and the adoption of a series of fiscal measures intended to expand the internal market. To back this up, the structuralist recipe stressed the need for land reforms and the redistribution of income to stimulate consumer demand.

The United Nations Economic Commission for Latin America (ECLA), led by the Argentine economist Raúl Prebisch, was the most important bastion of structuralist thought in the region. [12] From its headquarters in Santiago de Chile, ECLA successfully propagated its theories on economic development throughout the continent, obtaining a clear intellectual hegemony in the early 1960s among economists and technocrats, many of whom occupied government positions.

The monetarists, on the contrary, considered state intervention one of the main sources of the existing problems. They stressed the need to adopt free-market policies in which private initiative should lead the process of development according to principles of economic profit, without any state interference.[13]

During the 1950s and 1960s in Latin America, monetarist views were sustained only by a small group of economists who had to operate within a highly adverse climate dominated by political sectors who favored social reformism. In the mid-1950s the department of economics of the University of Chicago initiated a strong counterattack against the spread of Keynesianism (and the ECLA approach, which was seen as its Latin American version) in the new field of development economics.

In 1955 Professor Theodore W. Shultz, president of the department of economics at the University of Chicago, visited the faculty of economics of the Universidad Católica de Chile at Santiago in order to sign an agreement for academic cooperation. Under this agreement a select group of Chilean students were offered the opportunity to pursue postgraduate courses in economics in Chicago.[14] Between 1955 and 1963 a total of thirty young economists from the Universidad Católica made use of the Chicago grants. Many of them later became well-known academicians, industrialists, executives of financial conglomerates, and, in particular, leading figures in the implementation after 1975 of the neoliberal model under the military government (see Table 1).

During their Chicago training most of these Chilean economists became unconditional disciples of Professor Milton Friedman.[15] They were convinced that the full introduction of a totally competitive free-market economy was the only solution to Chile's developmental problems. After their postgraduate studies at Chicago most of them went back to the department of economics of the Universidad Católica, where they disseminated monetarist prescriptions to a new generation of students.

In 1968 these neoliberal economists established their own think tank, the CESEC. This center drew up the economic program of the right-wing candidate Jorge Alessandri in the 1970 presidential elections. However, it was clear that the political climate in Chile at that time was not favorable to their radical neoliberal recipes. They proposed the liberalization of markets, the encouragement of private initiative, the diminution of the state by the reduction of bureaucracy and the sale of public enterprises, the opening of the economy to international competition, and the end of government discretionality in economic decisions.[16]

They did not have enough support, even among right-wing circles. As [Phil] O'Brien has pointed out, "the Chicago model was opposed by many of Alessandri's business supporters and had to be put into cold storage 'as it was a program difficult to implement within a democracy' as one leading

Table 1. Chicago Boys Who Occupied Key Positions during the Military Government

Name	Governmental Post
Sergio de Castro	Adviser to Ministry of Economic Affairs, Minister of Economic Affairs, Minister of Finance
Pablo Baraona	Adviser to Minister of Agriculture, President of Central Bank, Minister of Economic Affairs, Minister of Mining
Alvaro Bardón	CORFO official, President of Central Bank, Deputy Minister of Economic Affairs, President of Banco del Estado
Rolf Lüders	Bi-Minister of Economic Affairs and Finance
Sergio de la Cuadra	President of Central Bank, Minister of Finance
Carlos Cáceres*	President of Central Bank, Minister of Finance, Minister of Interior
Jorge Cauas*	Vice-president of Central Bank, Minister of Finance
Cristián Larroulet	Adviser to ODEPLAN, Chef de Cabinet at Ministry of Finance
Martín Costabal	Budget Director
Jorge Selume	Budget Director
Andrés Sanfuentes	Adviser to Central Bank, Adviser to Budget Agency
José Luis Zabala	Chief of Study Department, Central Bank
Juan Carlos Méndez	Budget Director
Alvaro Donoso	Minister Director of ODEPLAN
Alvaro Vial	Director of National Institute of Statistics (INE)
José Piñera	Minister of Labor, Minister of Mining
Felipe Lamarca	Director of Tax Agency (SII)
Hernán Büchi*	Banking Supervisor, Deputy Minister of Health, Minister Director of ODEPLAN, Minister of Finance
Alvaro Saich	Adviser to Central Bank
Juan Villarzú	Budget Director
Joaquín Lavín	Adviser to ODEPLAN
Ricardo Silva	Chief of National Account, Central Bank
Juan Andrés Fontaine	Chief of Study Department, Central Bank
Julio Dittborn	Deputy Director of ODEPLAN
María Teresa Infante	Adviser to ODEPLAN, Deputy Minister of Social Security, Minister of Labor
Miguel Kast	Minister Director of ODEPLAN, Minister of Labor, Vice-president of Central Bank

*These did not study in Chicago, but they are cataloged as Chicago Boys because of their total support for the Chicago approach and their active participation within the neoliberal economic team.

Source: Manuel Délano and Hugo Traslaviña, *La herencia de los Chicago boys* (Santiago, 1989), pp. 32–36.

businessman . . . put it. Nevertheless, the campaign was useful in winning important adherents to the Chicago plan among key businessmen."[17]

Following the Popular Unity victory in the 1970 presidential elections, the neoliberal technocrats continued their efforts to formulate a general economic program. They expected that sooner or later the Allende government would be overthrown by the army.[18] After the military takeover, however, the new authorities chose to apply more moderate economic policies. The first economic team appointed by General Pinochet was mainly constituted by uniformed men and civil technocrats associated with the National Party and the Christian Democrats. The Chicago Boys initially obtained only secondary positions as advisers in several ministries and state agencies. However, after a period of time they obtained control of the State Planning Agency, ODEPLAN, which became their operational base within the government. ODEPLAN was later used as a springboard to secure control of the rest of the state apparatus.

The relatively moderate economic policies adopted after the coup did not yield the expected results, while the international crisis (involving a strong increase in oil prices and a dramatic fall in Chilean export revenues) made the situation even worse. In this critical scenario, the harsh recipes proposed by the Chicago Boys began to gain a broader audience and some support among the military leaders. By the end of 1974, the Chicago Boys controlled most of the strategic centers of economic planning. In order to achieve full control of the formulation and implementation of economic policies, in March 1975 the neoliberal think tank Fundación de Estudios Económicos organized a seminar on economic policy, which received massive and orchestrated media coverage. The Chicago Boys invited well-known foreign economic experts (among them, their old teachers Milton Friedman and Arnold Harberger) who expressed their total support for the application of a severe austerity program to the Chilean economy, the so-called shock treatment.[19] A month later, the leader of the Chicago Boys, Sergio de Castro, was appointed as minister of economic affairs. Immediately afterwards he announced the application of the neoliberal prescription, marking the initiation of what later became known as the neoliberal revolution.

The Chicago Boys: The Organic Intellectuals of the Military Regime

The new neoliberal economic team presented the technocratization of decision making as a guarantee that the government would pursue a rational economic model. From that moment on, government decisions were to be inspired by "technical and scientific" principles and not by political and ideological postulates as in the past.[20]

In the blunt words of Pablo Baraona, the pattern of development introduced by the neoliberal technocracy aimed to construct a so-called technified society,

> meaning by this a society in which the most capable take the technical decisions they have been trained for. . . . Historically, in our country professional capacity has been overshadowed by political factors. The new democracy must be technified, so that the political system does not decide technical questions, but the technocracy has responsibility for utilizing logical procedures to solve problems and to offer alternative solutions.[21]

This technocratization of decision making was strengthened by the process of selective capitalist modernization which was put into motion by the neoliberals. This led to the acquisition of the middle and upper classes of very sophisticated patterns of consumption vis-à-vis the modernization of the banking system and the management of enterprises.[22] At the same time, the entrepreneurial sectors became more integrated into the world economy and its technological standards. Also, the service sector was modernized, but it remained accessible only to privileged social groups. The majority of the Chilean population, however, did not participate in the benefits of this process of modernization because of the inegalitarian nature of the economic model and the unwillingness of the economic team to implement redistributive policies.[23]

The Chicago Boys presented themselves as the bearers of an absolute knowledge of modern economic science, thereby dismissing the existence of economic alternatives. All possible criticism of the economic model was rejected by portraying it as the product either of ignorance or the covert promotion of particular interests.[24]

For many years the dismissal of criticism coming from individuals who were not qualified in economic science, together with the repression exercised by the military against traditional *políticos* and their organizations, left little room for opposition to the Pinochet government and its economic policy.

The increasing influence of the Chicago Boys within the government and among rightist political organizations and entrepreneurial circles was directly related to their ability to manage the crisis and to produce economic growth. The supporters of the military government also realized that the neoliberals could count on the support of the international financial system. As [Robert R.] Kaufman has pointed out, these technocrats

> were more than simply the principal architects of economic policy: they were the intellectual brokers between their governments and international capital, and symbols of the government's determination to rationalize its rule primarily in terms of economic objectives. . . . Cooperation with international business, a fuller integration into the world economy, and a strictly secular

willingness to adopt the prevailing tenets of international economic orthodoxy, all formed a . . . set of intellectual parameters within which the technocrats could then "pragmatically" pursue the requirements of stabilization and expansion.[25]

After a severe economic recession in the years 1975–76 (produced by the application of the shock treatment), there followed years of economic improvement. In 1978 the rate of inflation reached a very low level, the fiscal deficit disappeared, the balance of payments displayed a growing surplus, and the economy in general (especially the export sector) showed a vigorous dynamism. In the period 1978–1981 the Chilean economy continued to grow rapidly, and many economists in Chile and abroad began to talk about "the Chilean *wirtschaftswunder*." The strongest supporter of the neoliberal plans inside the military junta was General Pinochet himself. He was well aware of the fact that for the definitive consolidation of his personal rule he needed the continuous achievement of successes on the "economic front."

In a climate of total triumphalism, the Chicago Boys developed and implemented what they called "the seven modernizations" in order to establish the rules of neoliberalism in all spheres of society. These "modernizations" involved the introduction of new labor legislation; the transformation of the social security system; the municipalization of education; the privatization of health care; the internationalization of agriculture; the transformation of the judiciary; and the decentralization and regionalization of government administration.[26]

The Chicago Boys also played a key role in the attempt to institutionalize the dictatorship. Acting as true organic intellectuals, they elaborated a sophisticated discursive answer to the latent contradiction in the coexistence of economic liberalism and political authoritarianism.[27]

Supporting themselves on the theoretical framework elaborated by Friedrich von Hayek, they argued that the political system Chile had experienced in the past was a mere pseudodemocracy because only organized groups such as the political parties and the unions were able to push through their demands, to the detriment of the interests of the majority of the population.[28] The laws legislated by Parliament and the policies implemented by the government were, in their view, the result of unacceptable pressure from these organized groups. They stressed the need for a strong government which was able to impose a system of general and impartial rules upon the entire society, without permitting the pressure of sectoral interests. Only the supposedly impersonal and nonarbitrary laws of the market would permit the achievement of equality of opportunities for all citizens. They stated that the achievement of (total) economic liberty constituted a key precondition for the very existence of genuine political liberty. The corollary is that only under the supervision of an authoritarian government was the establishment of the basis for liberty (that is, the installation of a free-market economy) possible. The very existence of the military government was also presented as a temporary phenomenon which would become unnecessary after the full consolidation of the new economic system.[29] However, the Chicago Boys pointed out that the future democracy would be "authoritarian" (following again the constitutional recipe of von Hayek) in order to defend it from its enemies. This meant that in the plans for the future political system there was no room contemplated for leftist ideas.

A landmark in the attempt of the military-technocratic alliance to institutionalize the "new order" was the adoption in September 1980 of a new constitution. This was officially named the "Constitution of Liberty" in a clear act of acknowledgment of von Hayek's philosophical thought.[30]

The Heritage of a Technocratic Style

The supremacy of the Chicago Boys reached its highest point at the moment of the adoption of the 1980 Constitution, and almost nobody could imagine then that within a year the economic neoliberal model would be confronted with a severe crisis. One of the major weaknesses of this model was the fact that most of the economic development obtained during those years was financed by expensive short-term foreign loans, leading to a rapid increase in Chile's indebtedness. Underlying this was the policy of state withdrawal from economic life which produced a lack of official control over the way in which private conglomerates (the so-called *grupos económicos*) utilized those foreign resources, making financial speculation an easy and very profitable business.[31]

The collapse in March 1981 of a leading financial group resulted in a speculative wave which provoked, in its turn, a general panic among entre-preneurial circles. Many financial institutions (*financieras*) and enterprises went into bankruptcy, global production decreased dramatically, and underemployment jumped to critical levels. At the end of that year the global national product declined by 14 percent.

Despite the intensity of the crisis, the Chicago Boys continued to argue with a dogmatic confidence that the economic difficulties were only tempo-rary, and that "market mechanisms" would produce an "automatic adjust-ment" to restore economic equilibrium. However, the economic situation became even worse as a result of the international banks' decision to cut down the stream of loans to Chile. The confidence of the population in the government and its economic policies began rapidly to dissolve and in April 1982, Pinochet found himself forced to reshuffle his cabinet. Sergio de Castro lost his post as minister of finance and his position as leader of the economic team, and the Ministry of Economic Affairs was placed under the command of an army general. The dismissal of de Castro, however, represented only a cosmetic move aimed to deflect the increasing unpopularity of the government. He was replaced by Sergio de la Cuadra, another Chicago Boy who decided to continue the policies of his predecessor.

The economic crisis produced the rise of an active political opposition to the government, which now had to deal with a major political challenge coming from both the center and the left. The outlawed political parties began to operate almost openly, while the military government, showing clear signs of weakness, searched for some formula to tackle the new situation in the country. Pinochet appointed Sergio Onofre Jarpa as minister of the interior, and he initiated a "dialogue" with the opposition. This was intended to win time and to create divisions among its different political currents. Jarpa, a leading representative of the traditional right wing, had never sympathized with the "new right," symbolized by the Chicago Boys. He convinced Pinochet of the need to expel the remaining Chicago Boys from leading positions within the government. In his view, they had to be replaced by an economic team who could implement a more pragmatic policy to tackle the economic crisis. This led to a new cabinet reshuffle in April 1984 in which Pinochet appointed two of Jarpa's associates, Modesto Collados and Luis Escobar, as ministers of finance and economic affairs, respectively.

After the adoption of a series of unorthodox measures, the economy began to show clear signs of recovery. However, the expansionist nature of the new economic approach clashed with financial restrictions imposed by the IMF [International Monetary Fund] which exercised strong pressure on the Chilean government to readopt a stricter financial policy.

On the political level, the government recovered its control of the situation. The opposition recognized the limitations of staging "days of national protest" when these did not lead to the fall of the military government. The political momentum of mid-1983 gradually declined.

At that point, the military government estimated that the political situation was sufficiently safe to revert to a neoliberal economic position. Accordingly, in February 1985, Pinochet appointed Hernán Büchi as minister of finance. Despite the fact that he was not a Chicago Boy in the strict sense (in fact, he studied at Columbia University) he had collaborated with the neoliberals since 1975 and fulfilled several minor functions within the neoliberal economic team. He had the advantage of being relatively unknown to the general public, who were unaware of Büchi's close connection with the Chicago Boys.

Büchi continued to implement neoliberal reforms, and in a relatively short time he was able to restore the confidence of the international financial agencies in the Chilean economy. By the end of 1985 the last signs of the economic crisis had disappeared and the country's overall economic performance returned to very satisfactory levels. The strong recovery experienced by the Chilean economy ever since led to the increasing popularity of Minister Büchi.[32] Even economists from the opposition recognized Büchi's sophisticated technical ability as a manager of the economy. The prestige obtained by Büchi contributed to the restoration of the technocrats' popular image, which had become seriously damaged as a result of the economic crisis initiated in 1981.

In clear contrast to the other countries in the region, where ministers of finance have very short-lived careers and are often the most unpopular members of the government (owing to the bad shape of most Latin American economies), the nomination of Hernán Büchi in Chile as the government's candidate for the presidential elections of December 1989 did not surprise anyone.[33] During his campaign, he proudly stressed the alleged advantages of his technocratic approach toward developmental issues and repeatedly insisted he was not a *político*. Although he came in second to the opposition's candidate, Patricio Aylwin, he obtained, together with the other right-wing candidate, Francisco Javier Errázuriz, a respectable 42 percent of the vote (against 56 percent for Aylwin). Most political commentators agree that Büchi's major handicap was not his technocratic background but his connection with the Pinochet regime. Hence, he became indirectly linked to the human-rights abuses commited by the military government, which constituted a major issue during the elections.

Despite Büchi's electoral defeat, it is likely that most of the structural reforms introduced by the neoliberal technocracy in the period 1975–1990 will remain almost unaltered under the new democratic government. Even in the hypothetical case that the current authorities wish to do so, it is almost impossible to reverse the new pattern of capitalist development established by the Chicago Boys. But what it is more important to emphasize here is that within the democratic political forces this desire has been absent.[34]

After all, the Chicago Boys succeeded in their efforts to expand public support for their free-market ideas. Even among leftist circles, one can observe a growing acceptance of many economic postulates defended by the Chicago Boys under the military government such as (a) the need to relegate the state to a subsidiary role in economic matters; (b) a revaluation of the role played by both foreign investment and the local private sector in achieving economic development; (c) acknowledgment of the importance of using market mechanisms and efficiency criteria to allocate and to support certain economic activities; and (d) the need to keep public finances healthy and to consolidate macroeconomic stability.[35]

This radical shift in the traditional economic thinking of the left is, in my view, the result of three major factors. First, the Chilean left has already had the experience (during the Popular Unity government) of implementing a socialist-oriented economic policy which was clearly unsuccessful. With that experience in mind, there is almost no one in Chile today who would dare to recommend the application of such an approach to the current Chilean economy.[36] Second, despite the general criticism of the negative social aspects of the neoliberal model, many people within the left-wing political parties admit (openly and tacitly) that at present the Chilean economy functions well and that it is now in better shape than at any other point during the last twenty-five years. And third, the current process of political and economic transformation in Eastern Europe in which the system of centralized economy is being eliminated almost everywhere, has constituted the coup de grace for those who dogmatically and ideologically still insist on the advantages of such an economic system.

Most Chilean leftist sectors also accept today the idea that the achievement of economic growth and the maintenance of financial equilibrium constitute a precondition for improving the living standards of the less favored segments of the population. This implies a recognition of the importance of maintaining an efficient administration of the economy.

The Rise of a Technocratized Opposition

The increasing political role played by technocrats after 1973 is by no means a phenomenon confined exclusively to government circles. This trend can also be observed in opposition quarters, where an increasing technocratization of the formulation and implementation of strategy has taken place. Since 1973, a large number of (oppositional) research institutes and nongovernmental organizations (NGO) have been established, playing a key role in the struggle against the authoritarian regime.[37] In 1985, for instance, there existed around forty private research institutes in the social sciences employing 543 researchers (not including research assistants and grant holders), of whom 30 percent are holders of M.A. or Ph.D. degrees obtained abroad. Around 65 percent of these researchers work on a full-time basis. The impact on national academic "production" of these institutes is enormous. With the exception of economics, the majority of social science articles and books written by Chilean scholars and published in Chile and abroad have been produced by researchers associated with these private institutes. So, for example, in the period 1980–1984 a total of 101 books were published by the thirteen private research institutes which have a regular plan of publications.[38]

This process of professionalization of the political opposition is, in my view, the result of several interrelated social dynamics which came into operation after the breakdown of democracy in 1973. The first historical fact one must take into consideration is the severe persecution of intellectuals which took place directly after the coup. Many of them were imprisoned or killed by the military, while a larger group were dispersed all over the world as political exiles.[39] Many Chilean academics exiled abroad found a new life teaching, pursuing research, or following postgraduate courses in their new countries of residence. Others, with the support of local authorities and political organizations, created their own research centers dedicated to the analysis of Chilean reality.[40]

What is important to stress here is the fact that many political leaders (the professional *políticos*, who in Chile had lived from party resources) were often obliged by circumstances to become incorporated into academic circles. Although most of them were academically trained (mainly in law, sociology, or economics), they had not worked as academics before, or for only a very short time. In many cases, the new academic experiences influenced their political outlook or, at least, changed their "political style." They became more scholarly and technocratic and more involved with new theoretical debates taking place in the world. Many of these political figures learned for the very first time to work (and to achieve common goals) together with people who did not start from the same philosophical and political visions as they did. This was after years of having inhabited semi-ghettoes within the narrow margins of their own political organizations.[41]

Those politicians and intellectuals who were able to remain in Chile were expelled from the universities and the public institutions where they had worked. For the first time, Chilean intellectuals were radically cut off from their traditional source of income: the state. Their second source of subsistence, the political parties (who in turn also lived from state resources), was also attacked by the security forces. The repression of the intellectuals produced a marked dispersal with each individual fighting literally for his or her own life. After a couple of very repressive years, however, a difficult process of regrouping and reorganization started. Intellectuals from similar academic disciplines and with congenial political outlooks began to establish research institutes as a means of surviving (economically). They were mainly financed by Western European and North American organizations for international cooperation as a way of keeping alive an intelligentsia opposed to military totalitarianism.[42] Some of these institutes also received funds obtained from time to time by Chilean political parties in exile.

The academic status of these institutes and the scholarly content of their activities initially constituted their only "right of existence" within an extremely repressive environment. Any criticism of the military government had to be carefully formulated in academic terms and presented in an abstract manner. This led to the almost complete disappearance of the slogans and rhetoric which had characterized party politics before the coup.

In 1975 the Catholic church founded the Academia de Humanismo Cristiano (AHC) to ensure the legal status of several research centers (which became associated to it) and to protect them from direct state repression. In addition new research centers were created under the AHC umbrella to shelter persecuted academics and to monitor the policies applied by the military government in different fields (labor legislation, agrarian policy, education, human rights, etc.).

Many of the research institutes initially tolerated by the military had a Christian Democratic orientation and were basically specialized in macroeconomic and financial themes. From mid-1974 the Christian Democratic party (which initially had supported the coup and offered technical assistance to the military government) began to move into opposition. Those Christian Democratic academics who still taught at the universities were pressured by *gremialista* and neoliberal forces to abandon their posts. That was the case of the members of the Centro de Estudios y Planificación Nacional (CEPLAN), an institute associated with the faculty of economics of the Catholic University. This center was formed in 1970 as an alternative to the Chicago Boys as they began to acquire a dominant position within the university. In 1976 the academics associated with CEPLAN decided to break their links with the Catholic University and to establish themselves as a private institute under the new name of Corporación de Investigaciones Económicas para América Latina (CIEPLAN).

This research institute concentrated on monitoring the economic policy of the Chicago Boys. Paradoxically, the first open (tolerated) activities opposing the military government and the neoliberal technocracy came from this group of technocrats, experts in financial and macroeconomic matters. This team of highly qualified academics accepted the neoliberal challenge ("the theme of economic policy can only be treated by specialists") and began to elaborate very sophisticated technical studies in which they expressed their criticism of the economic policy of the military government. The scholarly tone utilized by many opposition research institutes in their criticism of neoliberalism made possible the dissemination of their ideas (although in a limited way) through the publication of working papers and the organization of academic symposia on specific matters. For many years this constituted the only authorized way of diffusing ideas other than the official ones.

After a couple of years, CIEPLAN became a true think tank of the Christian Democratic party. It expanded its activities from monitoring economic policies to the elaboration of proposals for an alternative socioeconomic model and for a new political system to be adopted after the expected departure of the military. The CIEPLAN Monks also began to occupy the few spaces left open to the independent press to expand their ideas and criticism to a broader public by publishing articles and comments in *Mensaje* (property of the Catholic church) and later in *Hoy*, the first authorized oppositional weekly (of Christian Democratic orientation).[43] During the last years of the military government Alejandro Foxley, director of CIEPLAN, became a well-known public figure who, behind his economic expertise, successfully ventured into the field of political science and in particular the study of political consensus.[44]

Democratic Transition and Technocratization in Chile

After the beginning of relative political liberalization in 1983, new mechanisms of cooperation and consultation were created between academics and intellectuals associated with the different research institutes. They were initiated by experts on a specific subject who held similar political views (mostly members of the same political party). Through the organization of regular meetings and workshops, these professional collectives (the so-called *equipos técnicos*) worked out a common diagnosis of the existing situation in a specific field and formulated proposals to be implemented after the expected restoration of democratic rule. Thus, a group of socialist-oriented economists worked together for many years in an attempt to formulate a new economic policy, which was later adopted by the Socialist party as its official economic program. The same was done by the other political parties and in other areas such as housing, social security, health care, defense, agriculture, education, foreign policy, etc. This technocratization of party policymaking was facilitated by the fact that, at that time, open consultation with the party rank and file through a congress was unthinkable for security reasons.

In 1984 the Christian Democrats, together with the moderate wing of the Socialist party and other minor center-left political organizations, formed the Alianza Democrática (AD), an opposition coalition which aimed to defeat the military regime by political means. According to the 1980 constitution, a national referendum was to be held before the end of 1988. The people had to choose between the prolongation of Pinochet's rule till 1997 (the *yes*-option) or the holding of free elections within a year after the referendum (the *no*-option).

The AD campaign for the no-option led to very productive cooperation among the different *equipos técnicos* of the political parties joined in this coalition. For the first time in modern Chilean politics, technocrats from the center and from the left worked together to formulate a common political program and to elaborate sectoral policies for a future democratic government. This exercise was especially fruitful for two reasons. First, it reduced if not eliminated the historical fears and prejudices existing between them. This was eased by the fact that they shared similar technical and professional approaches and in many cases had studied at the same academic centers both in Chile and abroad. This cooperation at the technocratic top strongly contributed to the initiation of the rapprochement among supporters of different parties at the bottom, who for many decades had inhabited separate and even antagonistic political subcultures. Second, the existence of these multiparty technical teams greatly facilitated the formulation of a coherent governmental program for the presidential elections held in December 1989 and the subsequent constitution of multiparty *equipos técnicos* to occupy positions in ministries and state agencies upon achieving electoral victory. In this way many technocrats from the different political parties who were appointed to official positions after the installation of the government of Patricio Aylwin in March 1990 had already worked together for more than seven years.

The new Chilean democratic government has a marked technocratic outlook. Most of the holders of top governmental positions are experts in the specific field to which they were appointed. The technocratic nature of the Aylwin government was stimulated by three major factors. First, due to the coalitional nature of the government, Aylwin needed some modus operandi for government appointments. He announced from the very beginning that he did not intend to distribute posts on the basis of party quotas. The distribution of functions according to party membership rather than the professional skills of the candidates constituted one of the most (self-) criticized features of the Allende government, and one which everyone (including the parties which participated in the Popular Unity coalition) now wanted to avoid. Accordingly, Aylwin stated that governmental posts would be awarded to "the most capable" in their specific technical field. In fact, the democratic government accepted the principle introduced by the neoliberal technocracy that technical and not political skills must be the main criterion of selection. This goes to show that the technocratic nature of decision making in the country has lost the taboo character it had within Chilean politics prior to the coup, becoming an accepted reality. Second, the phenomenon of exile contributed among other things to the overall academic upgrading of the dissident intelligentsia and the political class in general. Many of the figures who now hold government positions lived in exile where they obtained specialized academic training. In addition, those who remained in Chile during the Pinochet government gained access to postgraduate courses in developed countries as a result of the institutional links developed between many dissident research institutes and foreign university centers. So, for example, in 1983 there were 3,185 Chileans studying at foreign universities, one of the largest groups of Latin Americans studying abroad (in relation to total population).[45] This high degree of technocratization of governmental decision making has been made possible by the large number of individuals with a high level of specialized academic training among the leading figures of the political forces which make up the government. Finally, one of the major concerns of the Aylwin administration has been the maintenance of financial and economic stability in the country. The democratic government is well aware of the fact that it will be almost impossible to consolidate the democratic system in a climate of economic instability.

Owing to the very complex nature of the economic process, the technocratization of decision making and the relative importance of financial and economic expertise above other professional skills have been accentuated. Moreover, during recent years the Chilean political system has become strongly internationalized. External institutions such as the IMF and the World Bank are important actors which the Chilean government now has to take into account in the formulation and implementation of its social, economic, and financial policies.

The composition of the *equipo económico* of the new democratic government has three main features. First, almost all of the officials appointed to high-level positions have undertaken postgraduate studies abroad (see Table 2). Never before has a democratic government in Chile had so many highly specialized technocrats at ministerial level. Second, almost all of the high-ranking officials worked during the military regime in the oppositional private research institutes, such as CIEPLAN, AHC, ILADES, CED, CES, and CLEPI. The same trend can be observed in other ministries and state institutions. So, for example, members of FLACSO and PHE perform key roles at the Ministry of Education, as do PET researchers at ODEPLAN.[46] Last but not least, one can observe that the ex-members of CIEPLAN occupy many of the most strategic positions within the economic team.

The current finance minister, Alejandro Foxley, together with his CIEPLAN colleagues, has been able to assemble a cohesive team with a strong esprit de corps which shows many resemblances to the Chicago Boys.[47] From the very beginning, Foxley displayed a "relative autonomy" within the cabinet, demanding the right personally to choose his nearest collaborators in the *equipo económico*. He argued that this was the only way to achieve the needed coherence in the formulation and application of his financial policies. He also managed to influence the appointment of another CIEPLAN monk, René Cortázar, as labor minister. Cortázar plays a very strategic role in the search for consensus between workers and entrepreneurs

Table 2. Members of the Economic Team of the Aylwin Government: Foreign University Affiliation

Name	Position	University
Ministry of Finance		
Alejandro Foxley[a]	Finance Minister	University of Wisconsin
Pablo Piñera[a]	Deputy Finance Minister	Boston University
Andrés Velasco[a]	Chef de Cabinet	Columbia University
José Pablo Arellano[a]	Budget Director	Harvard University
Javier Etcheverry[a]	Tax Director	University of Michigan
Manuel Marfán[a]	Policy Coordinator	Yale University
Ministry of Economic Affairs		
Carlos Ominami	Minister of Economic Affairs	Université de Paris
Jorge Marshall	Deputy Minister of Economic Affairs	Harvard University
Alejandro Jadresic	Coordinator of Sectorial Policies	Harvard University
Juan Rusque	National Fisheries Service	University of Wales
Fernán Ibáñez	Secretary of Foreign Investments	MIT
Other institutions		
Andrés Sanfuentes	President of Banco de Estado	University of Chicago
Eduardo Aninat	Coordinator of Foreign Debt	Harvard University
Ernesto Tironi[a]	General Manager of CORFO	MIT
Hugo Lavados	Supervisor of Stock Markets	Boston University
Roberto Zahler	Adviser to Central Bank	University of Chicago
Ricardo Ffrench-Davis[a]	Director of Studies at Central Bank	University of Chicago
Alvaro Briones	Operation Manager of CORFO	U. Autónoma de México
Ernesto Edwards	Vice-president of Banco del Estado	Boston University
Alvaro García	Sub-director of ODEPLAN	University of California
Fernando Ordoñez	Sub-director of ODEPLAN	University of Edinburgh
Nicolás Flaño[a]	Director of Solidarity Fund	Yale University
Alex Guardia	Institute of Statistics (INE)	Université de Paris

[a] Formerly members of CIEPLAN.
Sources: El Mercurio, 11 April 1990, p. (B)1; *Southern Cone Report*, RS-90-03 (19 April 1990), p. 4.

over moderating socioeconomic demands in order to avoid labor unrest and the increase of social tensions, which could lead to economic instability. Foxley is already being seen within certain political circles as the "natural successor" to Patricio Aylwin at the next presidential elections.[48] His eventual nomination as the official presidential candidate would be another sign of the increasing technocratization of Chilean politics. If this happens, for the second time in a row a finance minister with a marked technocratic approach would reach a position that in the past was reserved only for all-round *políticos*.[49]

The CIEPLAN case shows the strategic role that a private research institute can play as a think tank, especially as a kind of "fitness center" and "waiting room" for a group of technocrats ready to take command of specific governmental tasks when the time is right.[50] In the past, when political abilities were more in demand than technical skills, in times of opposition the political class sought refuge in its own party structures. Since the military government, it seems that political-party headquarters have been replaced by private research institutes.

This new reality should also apply to the neoliberal technocratic elite who have had to leave their governmental positions. Indeed, Hernán Büchi and his closest associates established a new private research center, the Instituto Libertad y Desarrollo, only three weeks after the installation of the Aylwin government. As his executive director, Cristián Larroulet, has pointed out, "recent Chilean experience has shown that this kind of center—such as CIEPLAN—is very important in the production of ideas."[51] This institute has clearly adopted the "CIEPLAN-formula": it seeks to monitor government policies in fields such as education, justice, transport, economy, and investments. But at the same time, it intends to formulate alternatives which could be implemented by a future government.

Conclusion

In this article I have tried to show the increasing political role played by technocrats since the 1960s at the highest level of policymaking in Chile. Although already underway, this phenomenon was officially neglected by the democratic authorities before the coup d'état because its elitist connotations contradicted the allegedly popular orientations of the Frei and Allende governments. The military government, however, not only recognized the growing technocratization of decision making but also presented it as a guarantee of the adoption of sectoral policies which would be based not on political but on "technical and rational" considerations.

The Chicago Boys played a central role in this technocratization of decision making. With a strong esprit de corps, this group of young economists conducted a kind of revolution "from above," transforming the social, economic, political, and even cultural bases of Chilean society. Because they achieved an economic success, the neoliberal technocracy became legitimized among important sectors of the population. The alliance between the military and the civil technocracy represented for years a workable formula, permitting the military government to count on considerable political support from the population until the beginning of the 1980s.

In addition, the opposition to the military regime became increasingly technocratized. The dissident intelligentsia organized its opposition from a series of private research institutes which conducted academic studies on the nature of the authoritarian regime and on the results of its policies. For years, scholarly criticisms made by these experts were the only voices tolerated against the military dictatorship. Furthermore, during exile abroad many opposition political leaders became connected to the academic world, acquiring expertise in specific subjects.

The revival of political activities after the economic crisis of 1981 did not lead to a massification of politics but to the search for consensus at the top between different oppositional currents in order to establish a broad coalition against Pinochet. The political forces united by the opposition formulated common goals through the establishment of *equipos técnicos*, constituted by technocrats from different political parties, who were experts in specific fields such as education, health, economics, etc.

After the establishment of democratic rule in March 1990, the new authorities did not readopt populist policies and rhetoric as had been the case before the 1973 coup.[52] The technocratic character of decision making, which became firmly fortified during the military regime, has been maintained. For the appointment of most of the government's leading figures, special attention has been paid to technical skills. As has been shown, ministerial posts and other important positions in the state agencies are now occupied by highly specialized technocrats. The key role played by the technocrats of CIEPLAN in the new government also shows the increasing importance that research institutes have attained within Chilean politics, to the detriment of political parties, as reservoirs of an alternative technopolitical class. The Chicago Boys have also received the message, establishing a CIEPLAN-like think tank in order to monitor the performance of the Aylwin government and to wait for political change in the future for the deployment of their policies.

The struggle for political power between competing technocratic groups entrenched in their respective think tanks has become a new feature of Chilean politics. The strong populist and demagogic discourse used in the past by the political parties and the traditional *políticos* seems definitively to have been replaced by a technocratic approach in which the search for "rational" solutions for the social and economic problems of the country is stressed.

Notes

1. Leonard Gross, *The Last Best Hope: Eduardo Frei and Chilean Christian Democracy* (New York, 1967); Ann Zammit (ed.), *The Chilean Way to Socialism* (Austin, 1973); L. H. Oppenheim, "The Chilean Road to Socialism Revisited," *Latin American Research Review*, vol. 24, no. 1 (1989), pp. 155–83; Joaquín Lavin, *Chile: revolución silenciosa* (Santiago, 1987); Eugenio Tironi, *Los silencios de la revolución* (Santiago, 1988).

2. "Individuals with a high level of specialized academic training which serves as a principal criterion on the basis of which they are selected to occupy key decision making or advisory roles in large, complex organizations—both public and private." David Collier (ed.), *The New Authoritarianism in Latin America* (Princeton, 1979), p. 403. I include in this definition not only the traditional *técnicos* (economists, agronomists, financial experts, et al.) but also those social scientists (sociologists, political scientists, et al.) commonly cataloged as intellectuals.

3. As the members of the private research center CIEPLAN have been dubbed by the Brazilian sociologist and senator Fernando H. Cardoso. See "CIEPLAN monks take command in Chile," *Southern Cone Report*, RS-90-03 (19 April 1990), p. 4.

4. On the role of political parties in the Chilean democratic transition see Manuel Antonio Garretón, "Partidos políticos, transición y consolidación democrática," *Proposiciones*, no. 8 (January 1990), pp. 72–84.

5. See for instance Catherine Conaghan, who argues that the severe economic crises of the 1980s have favored technocratic decision making at the government level in Andean countries. Conaghan, *Capitalists, Technocrats, and Politicians: Economic Policy-Making and Democracy in the Central Andes*, Kellog Institute Working Paper, no. 109 (Notre Dame, IN, 1988).

6. Most of the political parties in Chile before the coup d'état were essentially elite parties in which intellectuals played a key role. This was certainly the case of the Christian Democratic party and the Socialist party. See James Petras, *Politics and Social Forces in Chilean Development* (Berkeley, 1970). See also Federico Gil, *The Political System of Chile* (Boston, 1966). Two universities, the Universidad de Chile and the Universidad Católica of Santiago, historically have constituted the main sources of recruitment of the intelligentsia who controlled the political parties. As Angel Flisfisch has pointed out, the expression "los de la Católica" versus "los de la Chile" clearly reflects the main front line dividing the Chilean intelligentsia. See Adolfo Aldunate et al., *Estudios sobre los sistemas de partidos en Chile* (Santiago, 1985), p. 159.

7. Antonio Gramsci, *Selections from the Prison Notebooks* (London, 1971), p. 8.

8. Albert O. Hirschman, "The turn to authoritarianism in Latin America and the search for its economic determinants," in Collier, *The New Authoritarianism*, pp. 86–87.

9. This was made possible by the rapid expansion of existing state institutions and by the foundation of new ones. This resulted in the creation of thousands of new jobs for young professionals, militants of the Christian Democratic party.

10. A clear example of the antitechnocratic bias which dominated Chilean politics at that time was the dismissal of the minister of agriculture, Jacques Chonchol. He was severely criticized by radical sectors (from within and outside the Popular Unity coalition) for slow implementation of the land reform. He was finally accused by his political opponents in the government of being a "technocrat," a label which provided his political "death sentence." Soon afterward he was replaced.

11. See Cristóbal Kay, *Latin American Theories of Development and Underdevelopment* (London and New York, 1989).

12. Prebisch later synthesized his criticism of the monetarist (neoliberal) school in his "Diálogo acerca de Friedman y Hayek, desde el punto de vista de la periferia," *Revista de la CEPAL*, no. 15 (December 1981), pp. 161–82.

13. See Eric Calcagno, *El pensamiento económico latinoamericano: estructuralistas, liberales y socialistas* (Madrid, 1989).

14. For a detailed study of the University of Chicago's activities in Chile, see Juan Gabriel Valdés, *La Escuela de Chicago: Operación Chile* (Buenos Aires, 1989).

15. Considered the most influential exponent of the Chicago School. His book *Capitalism and Freedom* (Chicago, 1962) became a leading handbook among his Chilean followers. Friedman was awarded the Nobel Prize for Economics in 1976.

16. Manuel Délano and Hugo Translaviña, *La herencia de los Chicago boys* (Santiago, 1989), pp. 23–27.

17. Phil O'Brien, "The New Leviathan: The Chicago Boys and the Chilean Regime 1973–1980," *IDS Bulletin*, vol. 13, no. 1 (December 1981), p. 39. See also Phil O'Brien and Jackie Roddick, *Chile, the Pinochet Decade: The Rise and Fall of the Chicago Boys* (London, 1983).

18. Marisol Vial, "Chicago boys: cómo llegaron al gobierno," *Que Pasa*, no. 548 (October 1981), p. 26. See also Arturo Fontaine, *La historia no contada de los economistas del presidente Pinochet* (Santiago, 1989).

19. Friedman's address to the seminar was simultaneously published and distributed in the form of a small book by the Fundación de Estudios Económicos. See *Milton Friedman en Chile: bases para un desarrollo económico* (Santiago, 1975).

20. Tomás Moulian and Pilar Vergara, "Estado, ideología y políticas económicas en Chile, 1973–1978," *Colección Estudios CIEPLAN*, no. 3 (June 1980). It must be said, however, that the leaders of the *gremialista* movement (an ultraconservative political current of Catholic origin) also played an important role concerning the political system promoted by the military regime (being the authors of the junta's *Declaración de Principios* of 1974 and the 1980 Constitution). *Gremialistas* such as Jaime Guzmán and Sergio Fernández were as much the architects of the new order as the Chicago Boy Sergio de Castro. The fact that neoliberals and *gremialistas* came from totally different intellectual backgrounds (and held opposing positions on many issues) was no impediment to their cooperation with the military regime, nor to their joint activities in the formation of the right-wing party Unión Democrática Independiente (UDI). As Vergara has clearly shown, the convergence achieved between the Chicago Boys and the *gremialistas* was primarily the result of the gradual "neoliberalization" of the latter. Pilar Vergara, *Auge y caída del neoliberalismo en Chile* (Santiago, 1985), pp. 168–75.

21. Dirección de Presupuesto (DIPRE), *Somos realmente independientes gracias al esfuerzo de todos los chilenos: documento de política económica* (Santiago, 1978), p. 305.

22. For instance, between 1975 and 1981 the number of cars in Chile doubled. By 1984, 42 percent of families in Santiago were paying back one or more consumer loans. Javier Martínez and Ernesto Tironi, *Las clases sociales en Chile: cambio y estratificación 1970–1980* (Santiago, 1985).

23. Patricio Meller, "Los Chicago boys y el modelo económico chileno, 1973–1983," *Apuntes CIEPLAN*, no. 43 (January 1984). See also Ernesto Tironi, *El modelo neoliberal chileno y su implantación* (Santiago, 1982).

24. Raúl Arias et al., "El monetarismo como ideología," *Economia de América Latina*, vol. 6, no. 1, p. 174.

25. Robert R. Kaufman, "Industrial change and authoritarian rule in Latin America," in Collier, *The New Authoritarianism*, pp. 189, 190.

26. Rodrigo Baño et al., *Las modernizaciones en Chile: un experimento neo-liberal* (Rome, 1982).

27. Defined by Gramsci as the thinking and organizing members of a particular fundamental social sector who have the task of directing the ideas and aspirations of the group to which they organically belong. Gramsci, *Prison Notebooks*, p. 3.

28. Professor von Hayek (Nobel Prize for Economics, 1974) taught in the Faculty of Philosophy at the University of Chicago. His book *The Road to Serfdom* (London, 1944) gave the Chicago Boys the required theoretical and doctrinal foundations to expand their neoliberal thought from economics to the social and political spheres. Professor von Hayek became intimately involved in the application of neoliberal precepts in Chilean society. He accepted the position of honorary president of the Centro de Estudios Públicos, established by the Chilean neoliberal intelligentsia in 1980. He also visited the country several times, expressing his total confidence in the policies implemented by his ex-pupils (see, for example, his interview in *El Mercurio*, 16 April 1981).

29. Vergara, *Auge y caida*, pp. 89–106.

30. Named after von Hayek's book, *Constitution of Liberty* (Chicago, 1960).

31. See Ricardo Ffrench-Davis, "El experimento monetarista en Chile: una síntesis crítica," Colección Estudios CIEPLAN, no. 9 (December 1981). See also Alejandro Foxley, *Latin American Experiments in Neoconservative Economics* (Berkeley, 1982).

32. See Darío Rojas, *El fenómeno Büchi* (Santiago, 1989).

33. See Barry Ames, *Political Survival: Politicians and Public Policy in Latin America* (Berkeley and Los Angeles, 1987).

34. Délano and Translaviña, *La herencia*, pp. 179–83.

35. "The democratic government neither envisages nor desires a return to a state-based pattern of development. On the contrary, the government will stimulate private initiative, interfering as little as possible with market decisions. . . . It is also necessary to stimulate foreign investments. Fortunately, the ideological polarization that existed in the past in Chile on this matter has been overcome." President Patricio Aylwin, in a speech to a seminar on foreign investment (*El Mercurio*, international edition, 17–23 May 1990, pp. 1–2). Minister of Economic Affairs Carlos Ominami (a member of the Socialist party) explained the economic philosophy of the new Chilean government in similar terms to a group of leading industrialists and investors in Tokyo (see *El Mercurio*, international edition, 31 May–6 June 1990, p. 4).

36. One must not minimize the impact of exile in East European countries on many Chilean left-wing political leaders. Their negative personal experiences of

the socialist economics finally convinced them that this was not the kind of economic system they wanted for Chile after the restoration of democracy.

37. For a list of private research centers in social sciences established in Chile after 1973 see María Teresa Lladser, *Centros Privados de Investigación en Ciencias Sociales en Chile* (Santiago, 1986). On the role played by the NGOs opposing the military regime see Taller de Cooperación al Desarrollo, *Una puerta que se abre: los Organismos no Gubernamentales en la Cooperación al Desarrollo* (Santiago, 1989).

38. José Joaquín Brunner, "Las ciencias sociales en Chile: el caso de la sociología," *Documento de Trabajo FLACSO*, no. 325 (December 1986), pp. 26–28.

39. See Diana Kay, *Chileans in Exile: Private Struggles, Public Lives* (London, 1987).

40. That is the case of centers such as ASER Chile (Paris), Casa Chile (Antwerp), Casa de Chile (Mexico), Centro de Estudios y Documentación Chile-America (Roma), Centro Salvador Allende (Mexico), CETRAL (Paris), CIPIE (Madrid), and the Institute for the New Chile (Rotterdam).

41. See Alan Angell and Susan Carstairs, "The Exile Question in Chilean Politics," *Third World Quarterly*, vol. 9, no. 1 (1987), pp. 148–67. The so-called *"proceso de renovación"* experienced by several Chilean left-wing political parties since the late 1970s (which led to a definitive break with Leninism and toward a revaluation of democracy) is also directly related to the exile question. The exile of many Chilean political leaders in Eastern European countries was rather traumatic. There they directly confronted the dark side of "real socialism." This is, for instance, the case of political figures such as Jorge Arrate (current leader of the Socialist party) who moved after difficult years in former East Germany to the Netherlands, from where he initiated a profound theoretical and programmatic discussion within the Chilean socialist movement. See his *El socialismo chileno: rescate y renovación* (Rotterdam, 1983), and *La fuerza democrática de la idea socialista* (Barcelona and Santiago, 1985). For an analysis of the significance of the socialist renovation for Chile's process of democratization see Manuel Antonio Garretón, *Reconstruir la Política: transición y consolidación democrática en Chile* (Santiago, 1987), pp. 243–92.

42. Thus, in an evaluation made by the Swedish Agency for Research Cooperation with Developing Countries (SAREC) it is stated "[We] succeeded in preserving research capacity under conditions of repression and political crisis. Support for private national centers has enabled people to continue research projects after military intervention in the universities. These centers also house researchers expelled from academic or government agencies because of political persecution." H. Spanding et al., *SAREC's Latin American Programme: An Evaluation* (Stockholm, 1985), p. 1

43. José Pablo Arellano et al., *Modelo económico chileno: trayectoria de una crítica* (Santiago, 1982). This is a selection of these articles published between 1977 and 1981. This book became very controversial at that time, because it showed that since 1977 the researchers at CIEPLAN had constantly been predicting the eventual collapse of the neoliberal economic model, which finally occurred in 1981.

44. Alejandro Foxley, *Para una democracia estable* (Santiago, 1986).

45. José Joaquín Brunner, *Recursos Humanos para la Investigación en América Latina* (Santiago, 1989), p. 115.

46. The democratic government has given ODEPLAN a ministerial status and changed its name to MIDEPLAN.

47. For instance, the CIEPLAN technocrats are sometimes referred to by the press as the "CIEPLAN Boys," to stress the similarities with their predecessors (see, for example, *El Mercurio*, 11 May 1990).

48. See, for instance, "Foxley, el hombre fuerte," *Hoy*, no. 664, 9–15 April 1990, pp. 3–5.

49. Despite their relative autonomy from the traditional party structures, one must still keep in mind that Chilean technocrats continue working *inside* political parties. Their current prominence has perhaps been strengthened by the fact that since March 1990 political parties are still defining their role after many years of inactivity. But even if in the near future (as a result of the normalization of party activity and competition) more traditional politicians come to the fore, I do not expect a restoration of their old pivotal position within the Chilean political system. They can perhaps find a redoubt in the parliament, but not in leading positions at ministerial levels, as was the case before September 1973.

50. It must be said that a similar process of technocratization of politics (although less extreme) can be seen in Argentina, Brazil, and Uruguay, where many technocrats who worked at private research institutes have occupied high positions at governmental levels after the reestablishment of democratic rule. See José Joaquín Brunner and Alicia Barrios, *Inquisición, mercado y filantropía: ciencias sociales y autoritarismo en Argentina, Brasil, Chile y Uruguay* (Santiago, 1987). In the Argentine case a group of prominent intellectuals has stated, "We do not recall in the history of our country any other government with a greater participation of public servants coming from the intellectual field, and not necessarily from political militants, than the government presided over by Raúl Alfonsín. . . . One of the most singular aspects of Alfonsín is his continuous attempts to attract technocrats and intellectuals into government and into the sphere of politics." Adolfo Canitrot, Marcelo Cavarozzi, Roberto Frenkel, and Oscar Landi, "Intelectuales y política en Argentina," *Debates*, no. 4, October-November 1985, pp. 4–8. Actually, the same can be said for the Mexican case since the government of de la Madrid, and especially during the current government of Carlos Salinas de Gortari. See Roderic Camp, *Mexico's Leaders: Their Education and Recruitment* (Tucson, 1980).

51. "Instituto Libertad y Desarrollo: para producir ideas," *El Mercurio*, 1 April 1990, p. 11.

52. "President Aylwin's government will preserve Chile's macro-economic stability and avoid the adoption of populist measures which has brought other nations in the region to a situation of hyper-inflation." Minister Alejandro Foxley in his "Estado de la hacienda pública" speech to the Parliament, Valparaíso, 25 October 1990.

12 Robert E. Norton ◆ Jeff Sachs—Doctor Debt

B rash, bright, sure-of-himself Jeffrey Sachs, thirty-five, has delivered economic sermons from Washington to La Paz to Budapest. His peers in academe consider him one of the very smartest economists of his generation, just on the basis of his theoretical writings. His position at the front lines of economic reform in the Third World and Eastern Europe puts him in a special category.

His unique talent is not only to size up quickly and accurately what it will take to fix a broken economy but also to persuade people to follow his advice. Says Paul Krugman, thirty-six, the wunderkind of the Massachusetts Institute of Technology's economics department: "What sets Jeff apart is that he is a first-rate theorist who is also a major political force. It's a pretty amazing combination."

In 1989 alone he visited Poland a dozen times as an adviser to Solidarity. He went to Bolivia five times to advise the president and also touched down to counsel officials in Argentina, Brazil, Ecuador, Mexico, Peru, Czechoslovakia, Hungary, and Yugoslavia, among others. His work in Poland is paid for by a foundation started by George Soros, the Wall Street wizard and a native Hungarian. The United Nations pays for many of his trips to Latin America. His arrival in Warsaw this year was a homecoming of sorts. Though he grew up in suburban Detroit, his family's roots are in Grodno, now in the Soviet Union and once part of Poland. His wife of ten years fled with her parents to the United States from Czechoslovakia in 1966, when she was twelve.

A trip to East Germany the summer before his freshman year at Harvard triggered his interest in economics. He spent a week with a high-school pen pal who harangued him on the virtues of socialism and the sins of capitalism. Sachs knew little about either, so he picked up an English translation of the works of Karl Marx. After puzzling over Marx's murky theories, he began reading other economists. By the time he showed up for classes, Sachs was hooked: "I started out trying to understand what makes for a good economic system, and I spent four years trying to find the right answers to my pen pal's questions."

Sachs took to Harvard, and Harvard to Sachs. His second economics course, as a sophomore, was in macroeconomics at the Ph.D. level, and he got the highest grade. He graduated third of 1,650 in 1976, having completed

From *Fortune* (January 29, 1990): 129–34. Reprinted by permission from *Fortune*, © 1990 Time Inc. All rights reserved.

all requirements as an undergraduate for a doctorate in economics, save a thesis. He also had an answer for his East German friend: Socialism was a dead end.

As a graduate student, Sachs was elected a junior member of Harvard's Society of Fellows, a super-elite group that includes economists Paul Samuelson and James Tobin, both Nobel laureates. In 1983, at twenty-nine, he was made a full, tenured professor.

Had that been the only story, Sachs today might be spending more time in Cambridge and less on airplanes. But while a freshman he discovered John Maynard Keynes as a role model. An academic who worked in the British Treasury at various crucial moments between 1915 and 1946, Keynes became the most influential economic thinker of the twentieth century. Says Sachs, reverently: "Keynes showed what it was to be both a theoretical economist and a man of practice, and how there is no clear distinction between economics and politics—something I believe very much."

Sachs began leavening his Harvard studies in mathematical economics with summer internships in Washington. He later came to appreciate an economist he had been taught to hate at Harvard: Milton Friedman. "His very clear message—his faith in markets, his constant insistence on proper monetary management—is far more accurate than fuzzy structuralist or pseudo-Keynesian arguments one hears a lot in the developing world," says Sachs.

In 1985 he got the chance to put his ideas into practice in Bolivia, invited by politically-active Bolivian Harvard graduates. Barren, desperately poor, and up to the Andes in debt, the country's chaotic economy was gripped by hyperinflation, defined as a rate of more than 50 percent per month. Through the sorcery of compounding, a 50 percent rate produces annual inflation of more than 10,000 percent. Bolivia's reached 24,000 percent.

His prescription was shock treatment that included immediate deep cuts in wages and state spending. The government adopted his ideas, and Sachs headed back to Harvard. A few months later the plan faltered and inflation began rising again. This time the government summoned him.

He persuaded the Bolivians to persevere. Says Dwight Perkins, director of Harvard's Institute for International Development, which also worked with the Bolivians: "He built a relationship with the senior leaders there. He impressed them as someone who really knew what he was talking about and that he had no separate agenda, that he was genuinely interested." The harsh cure worked: Inflation by 1987 fell below 15 percent per year and has stayed there.

Bolivia had suspended payments on its international debt, and Sachs advised the government not to resume. Four years later, Sachs bristles when he recalls Bolivia's situation: "Here was a country whose debts were 140 percent of GNP [gross national product], where the debt service would have been well over 100 percent of all government tax revenues, where real per capita GNP had fallen by 25 percent in the preceding years, where there was hyperinflation, and the International Monetary Fund [IMF] and the U.S. government marched down there and said, okay boys, you'd better start paying. This was stunning, ahistorical, financially nonsensical, and it got me rather upset." Eventually, most of Bolivia's debt was written off.

After Bolivia, Sachs's phone began ringing from unlikely places, ultimately from Warsaw. A succession of Communist governments had succeeded only in creating third-world living standards in the heart of industrialized Europe. They tried to borrow their way to prosperity in the 1970s, then squeezed the population to repay the loans in the 1980s. [In 1989] the economy finally spun out of control.

Facing mounting unrest, the Communists in early 1989 negotiated with Solidarity to devise reforms. One reason for the change of heart was that with Mikhail Gorbachev pursuing his own revolution, the Polish regime could no longer count on Soviet troops to keep it in power. After being legalized, Solidarity trounced the Communists in an election, and by August, Poland had a coalition government. The economic crisis, however, was deepening.

Sachs had rejected overtures from the Communists. He works only for democratic governments or ones that are moving in that direction. Once Solidarity was recognized, he packed his bags. While he is just one of many experts and economists helping to shape the new government's thinking, his role has been crucial. Early in the debate last summer he argued forcefully that Poland needed the same kind of shock therapy that had worked in Bolivia—not a smooth transition but an abrupt break with the failures of the past.

By speaking before parliament and to groups of workers and economists, appearing on television, and giving interviews to newspapers and magazines, Sachs galvanized public opinion. Says Jan Mujzel, sixty-six, an economist at the Polish Academy of Science and a gray eminence in Polish economics: "His main idea, that the reform can succeed only if it is implemented as quickly and decisively as possible, was well understood by Polish economists. But his persuasive articulation of this idea played a significant role in preparing the program. He's a talented man, and has a talent to influence the people."

Parliament rushed through the reform measures in December, and they went into effect with the new year. To balance the budget, the government eliminated most subsidies of consumer goods and services. The price of coal, Poland's chief fuel, jumped 600 percent for households; gasoline doubled to 98 cents a gallon. Subsidies to money-losing state businesses were cut too, a move that will shortly lead to widespread bankruptcies and unemployment.

The zloty, Poland's currency, was sharply devalued to bring the official rate in line with that of the black market, which presumably is close to the zloty's real value. As a result, prices of imports will rise. Wages are to be held below the inflation rate.

If all this works, inflation—after one last surge as the price increases bite—will drop to single digits within a few months. Then the second phase of reform should gain speed: a massive privatization of the state-owned enterprises, which account for more than 80 percent of industrial production.

Many Poles are worried that all these changes may be too sudden. Although Mujzel supports the government's goals, he says, "There is perhaps some limit, some border of endurance for the people, and if that line is crossed and the people massively protest, this unique chance to democratize the society and marketize the economy would be lost."

Sachs's main worry is that the Poles might ease up too soon. Speaking at a meeting of Polish economists in Warsaw, he said, "Governments try to muddle through, or they get scared, or they do halfway measures. I've seen in Latin America that the gradual way is doomed to fail. This is the moment to act, and I really pray that the government sees this and takes the chance."

Back home in Cambridge, Sachs explains his longer-term fears. "One could imagine that if the reforms get bogged down, and the process becomes paralyzed, that the country ends up getting stuck in a nether world that is a half-planned and half-market economy, where very strong particular interests act as blocking coalitions to real reform. That's been the situation in Argentina for a long time."

Sachs also advised the Poles to suspend most of their debt payments, and they negotiated temporary reductions with commercial banks. He tells anyone in Warsaw who will listen that Poland should make no payments at all, at least during the next four years. His reasoning: The Poles can't afford to repay the debt and have little moral obligation to do so since it was unwisely incurred by the hated Communist government.

He argues that three quarters of the debt is owed to Western governments, whose interests are better served by seeing Poland succeed than by collecting on the loans. Commercial bankers, who hold the balance, may grumble, he says, but in the end they will settle for far less than 100 percent on the dollar, just as they would in a commercial bankruptcy.

For Poland, such economic glasnost will be crucial over the next few years. Instead of paying out $1.5 billion a year in debt repayments, the Poles will be receiving more than that in aid and loans from the IMF, the World

Bank, and Western governments. The United States and fourteen other nations are extending a $1 billion loan to help the Poles stabilize the zloty. But Sachs thinks the West should do far more, including canceling most Polish debts and promising explicitly that Poland will be welcomed as a full partner in the European Community. "These are the kinds of things that give a society the capacity to continue," he says. "And instead of vision in the West, there's coyness and there's confusion."

13 Catherine M. Conaghan ◆ Reconsidering Jeffrey Sachs and the Bolivian Economic Experiment[1]

Bolivia's 1985 neoliberal experiment is one of the most remarkable stories of contemporary political economy. Not since the heyday of the Chicago Boys in Chile had Latin America witnessed such a radical shock treatment of short-term economic stabilization measures and long-term market-oriented reforms.[2] Rarely had economic policies produced such immediate and dramatic effects. Within ten days of President Víctor Paz Estenssoro's announcement of his New Economic Policy (NEP) in August 1985, Bolivia's hyperinflation came to a dead halt.

Bolivia's economic turnaround attracted great attention in the international community. Much of Bolivia's success was attributed to the advice rendered by the United States' newest money doctor, Jeffrey Sachs. An accomplished Harvard economist, Sachs served as an adviser to the Paz government during the initial application of the program. Riding on the success of Bolivia, Sachs went on to become a top international adviser; he figured prominently in the making of Poland's post-1989 economic reforms and headed a team of economists that advised Russian president Boris Yeltsin.

Press descriptions of Sachs's role generally have been effusive. He is routinely referred to as the wunderkind who was the "architect" of the NEP in Bolivia.[3] He is the "boyish" professor who "salvaged the inflation-wracked economy of Bolivia."[4] He "is a first-rate theorist who is also a major political force."[5] Perhaps the flashiest description came from the *Los Angeles Times*, which labeled Sachs "the Indiana Jones of economics."[6]

The interpretation of Bolivia's economic reforms as a function of the advice rendered by a brilliant young Harvard economist makes good copy and appeals to a variety of audiences. For economists, the Sachs-centered interpretation reinforces their predilection to believe that sober technical advice is the antidote for economic ills. For those with an ethnocentric tilt, there is something satisfying in the story of a first-world brain setting the natives straight (yet again). For yuppies and academic wanna-bes, Sachs is the world-traveling workaholic with an adoring family and a staggering professional vitae. What gets lost in the eulogies to Sachs, however, is the more complicated history of how the Bolivian experiment originated and the role that Bolivians themselves played in the process.[7] Neither Sachs's presence nor the tenor of his advice was particularly new—the history of Bolivia is filled with examples of foreign advisers pressing Bolivians to reform themselves and restructure their state. Moreover, Bolivia had a prior record of stabilization programs, many of which featured measures similar to those undertaken in the NEP. What was truly extraordinary about the 1985 program was that it found the backing of a new antistatist domestic coalition and that it was championed by political leaders willing to pursue the program zealously.

This essay focuses on the origins of the NEP and the political dynamics of its implementation. By clarifying Bolivia's historical record and placing Sachs's contributions in perspective, my goal is to draw attention to the peculiarities of the local and international environments that facilitated the pursuit of the NEP. Because Bolivia is cited often as an exemplary case of economic reform, it is important to take a closer look at exactly what the Bolivian experience tells us about the kind of conjuncture that facilitates neoliberal economic reform.

A Legacy of Professional Prescriptions

Sachs's arrival in La Paz was yet another installment in a long history of Bolivia's encounters with foreign economic advisers. Professor Edwin Kemmerer of Princeton proffered advice in 1927 that resulted in substantial fiscal and administrative reforms. Kemmerer's prescriptions in Bolivia were similar to those he promoted throughout the Andes in his missions from 1917 to 1930.[8] The next wave of foreign experts, the Bohan mission, came in 1942 as part of an effort by the U.S. government to promote economic development. Most of the mission's recommendations focused on the need to develop physical infrastructure and create an atmosphere conducive to foreign investment.[9] Along with expert advice, the U.S. government provided aid to underwrite some of the construction projects. In 1951 a United Nations technical mission studied the Bolivian economy and recommended the creation of a development bank and the installation of a permanent U.N. presence in Bolivia in its "Keenlyside Report."[10] Bolivia agreed to the idea of a permanent technical mission, and Carter Goodrich, a Columbia University professor of economics, was designated the first head. By the mid-1950s, the U.N. technical mission had over fifty experts posted at ministries and agencies of the Bolivian government.[11]

Much of the early advice to Bolivia urged the government to take a more systematic and activistic role in leading economic development. But Bolivia's 1952 revolution gave birth to a government that was far more ambitious and progressive than anything foreign advisers had prescribed. The revolution, born in a popular uprising uniting peasants and tin miners against the military government, swept Víctor Paz Estenssoro into the presidency. Paz led the populist party, the Movimiento Nacionalista

Revolucionario (MNR), and the public policies that followed reflected the multiclass character of the populist coalition. The government enacted universal suffrage and legalized peasant-land seizures through a comprehensive agrarian reform law in 1953. Bolivia's largest tin mines were nationalized and reorganized around a workers' management arrangement overseen by the new public-sector firm, the Corporación Minera de Bolivia (COMIBOL). Finally, the political power of trade unions was institutionalized through *cogobierno*, an arrangement that gave unions control over the ministeries of Mining, Peasant Affairs, Labor, and Public Works. [12]

Rather than breaking ties with the revolutionary government, the United States maintained relations with Bolivia, a stance that was advocated by Milton Eisenhower, head of a U.S. mission to Bolivia in 1953. Foreign aid became the lever by which the United States influenced domestic policy; it was offered hand-in-hand with economic advice. [13] As early as 1953, economic stabilization was on the MNR's agenda. Faced with rising inflation, the Paz government drafted a memorandum outlining a narrowly gauged stabilization program that it presented to Eisenhower. Enacted in May 1953, the stabilization package was a heterodox mix of currency devaluation, credit restrictions, and price controls. Arthur Karasz, a member of the U.N. technical mission, advised Paz on the measures.

As the economic deterioration continued, U.S. experts continued to address the problems of the Bolivian economy. A U.S. operations mission to Bolivia issued a comprehensive critique in 1956. Written by Cornelius Zondag, a former World Bank staffer, the report called for a fundamental "change in philosophy," arguing that Bolivia could resolve its economic crisis only by a firm commitment to free-market principles. Zondag's long list of defects in the Bolivian economy included deficit spending, price controls, high labor costs, and excessive regulation. Anticipating the "illness" metaphor that later would become the stock-in-trade of money doctors (including Sachs) in the 1970s and 1980s, Zondag argued that

> Bolivia's situation could well be compared with the case of a person who has cancer. He knows he faces that most dangerous and painful operation which monetary stabilization and a number of other measures will undoubtedly be. Yet he has no alternative. Continuing our medical analogy, we might also compare Bolivia's case with that of a neurotic who becomes more and more dependent as more help is being extended to him. As time goes by, the patient loses completely all confidence in himself until finally somebody shakes him out of his lethargy and makes him face the facts of life again. [14]

The U.S. government and the International Monetary Fund (IMF) were eager to oversee the "cure" of Bolivia's economic illnesses. Contracted by the International Cooperation Agency (a predecessor to USAID) to become Bolivia's new money doctor, George Jackson Eder came to the job with experience, having acted as an economic and legal consultant to the governments of Cuba (1930), Colombia (1931), Chile (1935–1937), and Argentina (1946–47).[15] He arrived in Bolivia in June 1956, just prior to presidential succession from Paz to Hernán Siles Zuazo. A monetarist, Eder described what he believed needed to be done to resolve Bolivia's inflationary problem:

> There were no doubts in my mind about the prime cause of the inflation— briefly, spending by the government and government enterprises in excess of their means, with deficits financed by the Central Bank through the issuance of additional paper currency. The obvious remedy for this situation was simple, but, of course, it meant the repudiation, at least tacitly, of virtually everything that the Revolutionary Government had won over the previous four years. Hence, my task was twofold: 1) to expose the fallacies propounded by the "structural" economists and neo-Keynesians, who for four years had misled the MNR government; and 2) to convince the new administration that stabilization would only be possible with an almost complete change in course from a controlled to a free-market economy. . . .[16]

In a series of meetings with President Paz, President-elect Siles, and key cabinet ministers, Eder argued effectively for the monetarist view of inflation. He also pushed for the immediate formation of a monetary stabilization council, endowed with emergency decree-making powers, to oversee government policy. Eder believed that concentrated executive power (and a marginalization of the legislature) was a "structural prerequisite" for successful stabilization.[17] He assumed the post of the executive director of the council and maneuvered to make sure that "structuralists" like Karasz were kept out.

Having laid a new intellectual and institutional foundation, Eder worked quickly to develop a comprehensive set of policy measures. His "Forty Points" discussion became the basis of the "Fifty-Step" stabilization plan that was subsequently enacted by the Siles government in December 1956. The plan prescribed a generous dose of economic orthodoxy that included: 1) a 40 percent reduction in government spending coupled with tariff and tax increases aimed at balancing the budget; 2) an elimination of deficits in public-sector enterprises; 3) cuts in consumer subsidies and the elimination of price controls; 4) an initial cost-of-living wage hike to cushion price hikes, to be followed by a wage freeze; and 5) a unification of exchange rates.

Eder's remarkably detailed account of the policymaking surrounding the stabilization plan provides a fascinating view of the multiplicity of roles he played in the process. He acted as an adviser to Bolivian officials in their negotiations with the U.S. government and the IMF, and he legitimated the Bolivian stabilization effort to the international community. Eder also saw himself as a morale-booster, convincing the Siles government to press on with the painful stabilization measures.[18] All of these functions—the provision of technical expertise, international legitimation, and "therapeutic" services—were later replicated by Sachs.

Implementation of the Eder Plan required a change in relations between trade unions and the MNR government. Using a variety of tactics, President Siles maneuvered to divide trade unions on stabilization and to split the peasant-worker coalition, all of which helped disorganize popular resistance to the package.

In 1956 the stabilization plan, along with a highly critical report by the U.S. engineering consultants, Ford, Bacon and Davis, put the idea of reforming COMIBOL squarely on the public agenda. After his reelection to the presidency in 1960, Víctor Paz Estenssoro pursued the idea of streamlining COMIBOL with the "Plan Triangular," a plan that originated in a technical mission sent by the German state firm Salzgitter Industriebau Gaselichaft, in 1960. Collaborating with the Germans were Canadian consultants from the Toronto firm C. C. Huston and Associates, under contract with the Inter-American Development Bank. Their studies laid the basis for a multimillion-dollar aid package to Bolivia that included grants from the United States and Germany for new investments in COMIBOL. As part of the deal, the Bolivian government agreed to revamp the firm with wage cuts and massive layoffs. After initial resistance to the cuts, the miners' union backed down in the fall of 1963 during a dramatic face-off with government forces at the Catavi XX mine.

The swan song of the Bolivian labor movement (in the words of James Malloy), Catavi signaled the final breakdown of the 1952 populist alliance and a permanent exclusion of mineworkers from successive ruling coalitions.[19] Bolivian tin miners were to bear the brunt of attempts to cure the economy of the pathologies ascribed to it by domestic and foreign observers. The subsequent military governments of General René Barrientos (1964–1969) and General Hugo Banzer (1971–1978) were characterized by wage compression and political repression.[20] The military governments, however, remained uninterested in proposals to liberalize the economy and check public-sector growth. Riding on an initial wave of export revenues and international credit, the Banzer administration presided over a huge expansion of the public sector.[21]

In 1977 another team of economists delivered its recommendations on how to reform the Bolivian economy. Led by Harvard economist Richard Musgrave and composed of experts from the United States, Canada, Israel, and Bolivia, the mission concluded its study with a broad range of recommendations that focused on achieving development through "internal and external balance"—that is, by matching domestic savings to investment and export revenues to import bills. Specific measures suggested by the mission included: 1) comprehensive tax reform aimed at reducing reliance on export taxes and increasing domestic and consumption-oriented taxes; 2) administrative and legal reforms designed to ensure central government control over the fiscal behavior of public enterprises and decentralized agencies; 3) elimination of the subsidy on the domestic consumption of petroleum; and 4) the adoption of a uniform tariff. All of these measures were to reappear as part of Paz's New Economic Policy, and several Bolivian government officials who collaborated on the Musgrave mission—David Blanco, Carlos Calvo, and Juan Cariaga—went on to play important roles in the genesis of the NEP.[22]

The Musgrave mission reiterated the notion, already articulated in the 1956 stabilization program, that a substantial overhaul of the public sector was critical to Bolivian economic development. This idea—that there was something fundamentally wrong with the Bolivian state—found especially fertile ground by the late 1970s inside Bolivia's business-interest groups and gained broader appeal as Bolivia staggered through a succession of political and economic crises from 1978 through 1985.

A New Antistatism

Clearly, ideas about revamping the public sector and moving the Bolivian economy toward a free-market model had been circulating among domestic elites and prescribed by U.S. economists for decades prior to the NEP of 1985. Yet, no policymaker in the MNR or military government could tolerate this U.S.-prescribed medicine for long. The 1956 stabilization effort waned as President Siles made "concessions to reality"—giving in to popular pressures for moderate price and wage increases. Siles's capitulations established a pattern that later would be replayed not only by himself but by other executives as well. Orthodox measures were initiated—in part to please the U.S. government and foreign creditors—but later abandoned. Neither MNR nor military policymakers were particularly interested in orthodox reforms because there was no social constituency for such a project. Both MNR politicians and the military used state spending and public-sector enterprises to maintain their political networks. Of the grand populist coalition formed by peasants, tin miners, and urban middle-class groups during the 1952 revolution, no one wanted to see the end of the employment-generating, free-spending state. The agrarian reform and the mine nationalizations of the revolution had stripped away the economic and political preeminence of what remained of Bolivia's traditional oligarchy. Thus, no class or group in Bolivian society was ready to oppose the state-centered development model authored in 1952.

By the mid-1970s, however, a new domestic business elite was taking shape and began to voice concerns about the size and role of the public sector. Ironically, these elites owed much of their own development to subsidies and protections provided by the activist state of which they became critics. Incentives enacted during the Barrientos government nurtured the development of new economic groups centered around "medium mining" ventures. In Santa Cruz, agrarian capitalists took advantage of the subsidized credits that in the 1960s and 1970s flowed generously from the central government. At the same time, a small circle of import-substituting industrialists in La Paz, Cochabamba, and Santa Cruz benefited from protectionist tariffs and the subsidies inherent in the multiple exchange-rate system. In short, the new bourgeoisie that developed in the wake of the revolution was, at least in part, the product of the "hothouse" environment created by the state.

Bolivia enjoyed an unprecedented economic boom during the first half of the 1970s. Average annual gross domestic product (GDP) growth in the period between the years 1971 and 1976 stood at 5.7 percent. The boom began with price increases for Bolivian exports in international commodities markets and was sustained by prevailing circumstances in international financial markets. Flush with Euro-currency, foreign bankers sought clients throughout Latin America, even in "credit-risk" countries such as Bolivia.[23] The military government led by General Hugo Banzer contracted substantial foreign loans to underwrite its policies of state spending and private-sector credit.

Business elites were relatively quiescent during the boom years of the Banzer government. But as boom turned to bust, leaders within the business community started to critically reassess the state-centered development model. The notion that the state was "dysfunctional" to economic development began to be voiced with some frequency by leaders within the Confederación de Empresarios Privados (CEPB), the leading association representing all business-interest groups. Among their specific concerns was the state's voracious consumption of resources and its capacity to preempt private-sector investment. In 1979 the CEPB issued a position paper entitled "Toward a New Economic Policy" (coining a phrase that later would be used by the Paz government).[24] Among its recommendations was a demand for the reorientation of the state "so that the state is fundamentally concerned with public services and infrastructure, leaving the rest of activities to the private sector." From that point on, the CEPB made frequent calls for "A New Economic Policy" that revolved around a minimalist state and free-market competition. In his 1981 institutional report, CEPB president Marcelo Pérez Monasterios reiterated business's growing antistatism, stating flatly that the inefficient, oversized, deficit-creating public sector was the "principal cause of the economic crisis affecting the country."[25]

The CEPB's antistatist campaign became more intense under the leadership of Fernando Illanes. Elected to the CEPB presidency in 1982, Illanes undertook a drive to professionalize the interest group. He installed computers and hired full-time staff members. Fernando Candia, an economist and graduate of Harvard's Kennedy School, directed a research project aimed at refining the CEPB's policy positions. In 1984 the CEPB published its recommendations for economic recovery, and the proposals that it outlined closely prefigured the measures enacted in 1985 as D. S. 21060.[26] In the document, the CEPB argued for a series of short-term emergency measures and basic structural reforms such as: 1) the elimination of the fiscal deficit and a freeze on public-sector growth and employment; 2) tight controls over monetary emissions; 3) strict regulations governing debt contracting by public enterprises; 4) tax reforms aimed at broadening the domestic tax base; 5) adoption of a unified exchange rate; 6) elimination of price controls, particularly on agricultural goods; and 7) a reform in labor laws to increase "flexibility" for employers.

The CEPB became a hotbed of neoliberal thinking. Along with Illanes, other business elites urged the "reinventing" of Bolivia as a free-market economy. Among the most notable advocates of this line was Gonzalo Sánchez de Lozada, whose business interests included his family-owned firm, COMSUR, one of the three leading firms in the "medium mining" sector.[27] Sánchez de Lozada urged his fellow businessmen to take an active role in politics. He served as an MNR deputy in the 1982 Congress and was elected to the Senate in 1985. Other leading businessmen assumed important positions within the center-right party, Acción Democrática Nacionalista (ADN), which was led by ex-dictator Hugo Banzer. Among the inner circle of businessmen and professionals close to Banzer were Carlos Calvo, David Blanco, Ronald Maclean, and Mario Mercado. (Calvo, Blanco, and Mercado had been involved in the 1977 Musgrave mission.) All were part of the ADN group that initiated contact with Sachs in 1985.

The CEPB played an important role in creating the conditions for a paradigm shift in Bolivian public policy, becoming a venue for circulating neoliberal ideas and translating them into specific policy recommendations. CEPB leaders transmitted those ideas to political parties through their personal involvement in politics. In addition, CEPB activities helped to create a consensus within the business community on the virtues of free-market economics. Many businessmen who had grown up under the old state-centered model were fearful of the changes proposed by neoliberals and had to be convinced of their feasibility. The CEPB proselytized its own membership, using newsletters, press releases, and meetings to argue for neoliberalism. At the invitation of the CEPB, Alvaro Alsogaray, an Argentine free-enterprise crusader, visited Bolivia in 1983 and fanned the flames of antistatism for a business audience. In the same spirit, the CEPB sponsored a "National Free Enterprise Meeting" in May 1983. Among the conclusions authored by its participants was a list of "beliefs" that asserted the importance of the private sector while lashing out at unproductive state bureaucracy and economic planning.[28]

The intellectual ferment and ideological mobilization within the business community helped stir the winds for the sea change in public philosophy that came with the NEP. Arguments that the time was ripe for change gained plausibility as chaos appeared to descend upon Bolivia during the beleaguered presidency of Hernán Siles Zuazo (1982–1985). By the time Sachs arrived in Bolivia in 1985, many Bolivian elites and a substantial portion of the public at large were ready to take a chance on neoliberal policies as a last ditch effort to reconstruct the devastated economy and disintegrating social order.

The Prelude: Hyperinflation and Hypermobilization

The CEPB's activation was one part of the broader "resurrection of civil society" that took place in Bolivia in conjunction with the transition to civilian rule.[29] With the exception of two interim governments led by Walter Guevara and Lydia Gueiler, respectively, Bolivia was subject to authoritarian military regimes throughout the 1970s. The nadir of this decade came during the government of General Luis García Meza (1980–81), an administration notorious for repression and its links to international drug trafficking. The installation of Hernán Siles Zuazo in the presidency in 1982 was the product of a broad societal consensus on the need to restore civilian leadership and constitutional rule. The CEPB, political parties, trade unions, civic organizations, and the Roman Catholic church were all protagonists in the campaign for a democratic regime.[30]

From the start, the Siles presidency was beset with an extraordinary range of political and economic problems, many of which were the legacy of years of military rule. As the first president in the newly constituted democracy, Siles believed that he had to allow for a thorough political decompression—that is, groups in civil society would have to be allowed to exercise their freedoms and express the frustrations and demands that had accumulated during a decade of authoritarianism. Political decompression, however, became part of an explosive mix as Bolivia's economic situation deteriorated. Siles assumed the presidency just as Mexico's moratorium on debt payments sent shock waves through the international financial community and shut down credit lines to the rest of Latin America. The debt crunch converged with a decline in international prices for Bolivia's mineral exports to produce a catastrophic financial crisis.

Siles's government was based on a heterogenous political coalition—the Unión Democrática y Popular (UDP). An electoral front, the UDP brought together Siles's own Movimiento Nacionalista Revolucionario-Izquierda (MNR-I, a splinter from the original MNR), the social democratic Movimiento de Izquierda Revolucionario (MIR), and the Partido Comunista de Bolivia (PCB). The diversity inside the coalition contributed to the difficulties in developing a coherent policy response to the growing economic crisis.

Siles's initial response came in a heterodox package of short-term stabilization measures enacted in November 1982. The package included: 1) exchange-rate devaluation; 2) a 200 percent increase in petroleum prices; 3) tariff increases; 4) price increases on basic foodstuffs; and 5) compensatory wage increases to cushion the effects of the price hikes. Successive packages came in November 1983, April 1984, November 1984, and February 1985.[31] None was successful in stemming the inflationary tide. Throughout the succession of packages, the Siles government was unable to reduce the fiscal deficit and continued to cover the debt by increasing monetary emissions.

This seniorage financing was a primary cause of the hyperinflation that began in April 1984 and continued until the NEP was decreed in August 1985. Monthly inflation during the seventeen-month period averaged 46 percent. In February 1985, Bolivia beat existing Latin American inflation rates by registering a one-month increase of 182 percent.[32] The IMF reported the yearly inflation rate for 1985 as 11,804 percent.

The labor movement, under the leadership of the Central Obrera Boliviana (COB), resisted the government's attempts to raise prices and keep wage increases below inflation rates, and the COB's salary militance was not without historical justification. Wage compression had been part of the policy package under years of military rule. Average real wages had declined by 17.2 percent in the decade 1971–1981, and by the end of 1982 the decline in income stood at 39 percent.[33] With a democratic government in place, the COB was free to defend labor against further impositions. As part of a significant increase in strike activity, it called nine general strikes to protest government economic policies. Furthermore, the number of industrial disputes skyrocketed—five hundred were registered in 1984 alone.[34]

Labor was one of many collective actors in Bolivian society that took to the streets to express their demands. Peasant organizations, regional civic committees, and interest groups joined in protests against the government. In an analysis of collective protest action, Roberto Laserna reported that an average of fifty-three "collective action events" (that is, strikes, building-occupations, roadblocks, etc.) were staged per month during the Siles government, totaling 1,799 events during 1982–1984. Of all such collective protests taking place in Bolivia from 1970 through 1984, 40 percent occurred during the Siles administration.[35]

Siles balked at using repressive tactics to quell the tide of public disorder; he believed that such a response was antithetical to democratic principles and that the preservation of the constitutional order was his foremost responsibility. In explaining his toleration of the wave of public disturbances, Siles remarked, "I don't care if I'm judged as indecisive or a bad administrator. What's important to me is having my hands clean of repression and that history recognizes the extent of my commitment that Bolivia continue being a land of free men."[36]

By 1984, both the political conjuncture and economic situation were extremely chaotic. Price-controlled products disappeared from store shelves, lines appeared wherever basic foodstuffs were sold, U.S. dollars replaced pesos as the preferred currency, and prices escalated wildly (sometimes changing hourly).

On the political side, the MIR withdrew from the government coalition in 1983 and joined in with the incessant criticism of the Siles government. Congress became a venue for continual attacks on the president, including talk of a "constitutional coup" to remove Siles and replace him with Jaime Paz, vice president of the dissident MIR. In the course of chronic cabinet shuffles, the Communist party assumed a higher profile inside the government. Along with the COB, the left rejected "monetarist measures" and pushed the notion that more aggressive state intervention was needed—in other words, a public takeover of commercial banking, strict price controls, and more public investment. In September 1984, COB put its revolutionary cards squarely on the table and declared its intention to push Bolivia toward socialism via "people's democracy."[37]

In short, President Siles found himself in a situation reminiscent of that faced by President Salvador Allende of Chile nearly ten years earlier. Like Allende, Siles headed a government blamed for an economic crisis caused by heterodox policies. At the same time, however, the heterodoxy fell fall short of the demands of labor and the left. Siles's failed efforts to accommodate labor and his unwillingness to use violence against popular organizations further alienated business elites. For everyone in Bolivian society, hyperinflation combined with the breakdown in public order to turn day-to-day living into an uncertain and stressful exercise.

As in Chile under Allende, the pervasive crisis created the political conditions which facilitated the neoliberal economic experiment that followed. Political forces on the right were able to present themselves as the only real alternative to the chaos associated with the "left." As Jeffrey Sachs later argued, the "inflation tax" was a phenomenon felt across social classes. The public wanted a government that would take decisive measures to provide relief from the chronic disruption of everyday life. The failure of heterodoxy helped reinforce the notion among political and economic elites that only a dramatic departure in economic management could restore investor confidence and lay the basis for a rapprochement with the international financial community. The crisis did not create a popular consensus on the neoliberalism per se, but it did create a reservoir of support for "change." As such, it engendered a certain degree of resignation on the part of the public to the ensuing economic experiment.

Cambridge, Washington, La Paz: Converging Ideas

Siles's decision to leave office early by pushing forward the elections to July 1985 dropped the question of how to resolve Bolivia's economic crisis into the laps of the opposition parties. The two leaders, the Movimiento Nacionalista Revolucionario-Histórico (MNR-H), led by Víctor Paz Estenssoro, and the Acción Democrática Nacionalista (ADN), headed by Hugo Banzer, refrained from explicit discussion of any prospective shock-treatment program.[38] For the purpose of the campaign, the two presidential candidates kept their economic platforms vague, preferring to frame the election as a retrospective judgment on the Siles government and, by extension, the left. The 1985 campaign was not used by political elites as a vehicle to engineer a popular consensus on neoliberalism. Instead, it became a crucible for solidifying the elite consensus on neoliberalism. Behind the scenes, businessmen, technocrats, and politicians came together to hammer out a specific agenda for the incoming government.

The process began among leaders inside ADN. With Banzer emerging as the early front-runner in the presidential race, the "shadow" economic team inside the ADN (members of which included Ronald Maclean, David Blanco, Carlos Calvo, and Mario Mercado) began discussions on a prospective economic program. Internal disagreements prompted Maclean to suggest a sort of intellectual retreat. Because of the group's connections to the Kennedy School, Harvard was chosen as the venue for a seminar on the Bolivian economy. Juan Cariaga, a Bolivian economist and political "independent," was invited to present his views.

Among the Harvard participants in the seminar was the economist Jeffrey Sachs. Already recognized for his work on European labor markets, Sachs had become a full professor at Harvard at the age of twenty-nine and had a long list of professional accomplishments.[39] As an IMF consultant in 1982, he was known in policy circles, and he was a member of the Brookings Institution as well as the Council on Foreign Relations.[40]

Sachs's commentaries about the links between inflation and tax systems prompted an invitation from David Blanco to "try out his ideas on Bolivia." En route back to their country, the Bolivians stopped in Washington to discuss their findings with World Bank officials and were greeted with enthusiasm.[41]

The Harvard-inspired ADN program was never made public. The ADN issued an invitation to Sachs and arranged for his first trip to Bolivia in July 1985, when he was supposed to supply the "finishing touches" to Banzer's secret program. In meetings with CEPB leaders, Sachs made the case for shock treatment by underscoring the need for a rapid and comprehensive application of orthodox stabilization measures. His position contrasted with theories of "heterodox shock," that were being put in practice elsewhere in Latin America at the time. While Sachs's ideas about stabilization were undoubtedly percolating through elite circles (by his own account he gave talks and "met a lot of people"), he never got the chance to author the stabilization program for Banzer.[42] The Bolivian constitution stipulates that a president must be elected by an absolute majority. In the absence of a majority vote for one candidate, the election is thrown into the Congress for resolution. Banzer won a slim plurality in the popular vote, but in the congressional horse-trading that ensued Víctor Paz Estenssoro emerged as Bolivia's new president.

Unlike the ADN, the MNR did not have a well-crafted plan for dealing with the economic crisis, nor did Paz have a cohesive economic team. Although a working group had formed under the direction of Guillermo Bedregal during the campaign, Bedregal, an experienced politician, was not an economist, nor was he inclined toward talk of orthodox stabilization.

Unhappy with the work of the in-house MNR group, just days after his August inauguration, President Paz created an emergency task force to formulate an economic plan. He turned to Gonzalo Sánchez de Lozada, the CEPB leader and MNR-H senator, to head the group. The rest of the team included Juan Cariaga (the "independent" economist and banker who had participated in the Harvard seminar), Fernando Romero (a political "independent" and influential leader in the CEPB), and Fernando Prado (an economist and former MIR partisan), and Bedregal and Roberto Gisbert, whom Paz had appointed minister of planning and minister of finance, respectively. They also consulted with the team on the political dimensions of implementation. By consciously designing the emergency team to be small, exclusive, and secretive, Paz wanted to minimize any interference by parties or pressure groups—particularly labor—in the formulation of the plan.

For seventeen days, the team labored furiously in the home of Sánchez de Lozada.[43] This frenetic work was influenced by a variety of sources: the team reviewed the measures of the 1956 Eder plan; Sánchez de Lozada and Romero were familiar with the technical studies and policy recommendations favored by the CEPB; and Cariaga, the economist who had attended the Harvard seminar, had knowledge of Sachs's recommendations.[44] Moreover, Sachs had reinforced arguments in favor of shock treatment in his July visit to La Paz. But perhaps even more critical to the deliberations was the position taken by President Paz. According to team members, Paz was completely disillusioned with the state-centered economic model that he had helped bring to life in 1952. In fact, Paz had never been a devotee of populist economic policies. Swept to power in 1952 through a mass insurrection, Paz had little choice but to sanction the structural reforms and public spending demanded by his revolutionary constituency. Other interludes in Paz's career, however, were marked by economic conservatism. Paz's tenure as an economics minister (1943–1946) during the government of General Gualberto Villaroel was notable for his devotion to expenditure cuts and currency stability. And, as already noted, Paz used his second presidential term to pursue the COMIBOL cuts in the Plan Triangular.

Paz visited the team frequently and exhorted them to author draconian measures, reassuring them of the political feasibility of such an approach. Sánchez de Lozada recalls Paz's admonitions.

> Paz used to quote Machiavelli: "Do bad things all at once and do good things little by little." So he kept saying, "If we don't do this now, we'll never do it. Do it! Do it!" He kept telling us that people were ready, that they were going to accept it. He'd come in and find us wishy-washy—and he'd be hard-line. He kept saying, "If you are going to do it, do it now. I can't operate twice. . . ."[45]

Paz's strong convictions on the need for rapid and drastic measures clearly steered the team away from any serious consideration of a gradualist approach. The unequivocal thrust of opinion, from Sachs to Paz, was in favor of shock treatment. But Paz's interest in the economic program went far beyond the immediate (and extremely pressing) question of how to cure hyperinflation. Paz saw the economic package as the cornerstone of an ambitious remaking of state-society relations in Bolivia.

Both Paz and Sánchez de Lozada believed that Bolivia's economic problems were rooted in the hypertrophied, inefficient, and corrupt state structures. This was not a new idea; as the earlier discussion in this essay shows, the idea of a failed state had been circulating since the critiques of George Jackson Eder and Cornelius Zondag in the 1950s, and the demonizing of the public sector had become standard fare in CEPB documents. What was notable about their point of view was the way in which they envisioned the connections between neoliberal economic reform and reconstituting the power of the state. In their view, the legitimacy and authority of the state could only be restored by downsizing the state and yielding allocative powers to the market. Neoliberal economic reforms would make the state leaner *and* meaner (that is, enhance the capacity of the state to intervene effectively across a more limited range of problems). At the same time, a reduction in the public sector and economic liberalization would substantially weaken the trade-union movement and further erode the political power of the left. Sánchez de Lozada characterized the NEP as "more than strictly an economic plan." It was a "political plan."[46]

Its scope broad, the plan included a series of fiscal correctives aimed at increasing government revenues and containing spending along with measures to deregulate the economy. Juan Antonio Morales described the program as stabilization cum liberalization. Key measures included in the plan were: 1) substantial price hikes on gasoline and petroleum products produced by state-owned enterprises; 2) removal of price controls on agricultural products; 3) elimination of consumer subsidies on foodstuffs and utilities; 4) a freeze on public-sector wages; 5) massive reductions in public-sector employment, especially in COMIBOL; 6) a unification in the exchange rate resulting in a de facto devaluation of 93 percent; 7) imposition of a uniform import tariff of 20 percent; 8) liberalization of labor laws to facilitate dismissals of workers; 9) tight regulations on budgets of public enterprises; and 10) tax reforms to broaden the tax base and increase efficiency of collection.[47]

Before enacting the plan, Paz sequestered his cabinet in a twenty-four-hour meeting, explaining the plan and bullying cabinet members into supporting it. On August 29, 1985, Paz decreed the New Economic Policy in a single executive decree: D. S. 21060.[48] In a radio and television address that followed, Paz characterized the program as a last resort. Calling on Bolivians to "work and sacrifice," Paz portrayed Bolivia's situation in the bleakest of terms. Conjuring up the medical metaphor, he said that the country was "dying," that the economy was "in a coma," and that "emergency treatment" was necessary.[49]

Sachs had no direct involvement in the formulation of the original NEP. He was not consulted at any point in the deliberations by the emergency team, nor was he called on during the initial months of its implementation. Yet, the plan was certainly in the spirit of the reforms he had discussed with business and party elites in Cambridge and La Paz. Sachs's initial foray into Bolivian policy circles did not so much change minds but rather provided further verification (and a Harvard imprimatur) of the conclusions that business leaders and the political right had already reached. Leaders in the CEPB had gone far in advancing antistatist ideas, even generating blueprints for a neoliberal program in their position papers. As the CEPB prepared the intellectual climate for a neoliberal experiment, poor economic management of the Siles government was discrediting heterodox policies. A master politician, President Paz recognized the opportunities opened up by hyperinflation; Bolivia had reached a critical juncture by 1985 and Paz was ready to pursue the neoliberal cure for the failed state.

Deals, Stalls, and Force

Given Bolivia's record of failed stabilization packages, Paz and his cabinet knew that even the best laid economic plans could easily be run off course. Paz moved swiftly in the weeks following the decree to ensure that no effective opposition could emerge to derail the economic program. He combined political deals, stalling tactics, and selective repression to eliminate popular organizations, parties, and the Bolivian Congress as obstacles to the implementation of the NEP.

Within hours of the enactment of D. S. 21060, the COB registered its opposition and began to mobilize against the measures. On September 9, the COB called for a general strike, setting off a wave of marches, roadblocks, building takeovers, and hunger strikes. The COB headquarters was surrounded by government forces, and, on September 19, Paz declared a state of siege. The government proceeded to arrest approximately two hundred COB leaders. Over one hundred were subsequently sent to internment camps in the remote provinces of Beni and Pando. They were detained without legal recourse until October 5, when the COB agreed to suspend the general strike and enter into a "dialogue" with the government.

The ensuing meetings between the COB and the cabinet were inconclusive, but they gave the government the time to begin implementation of the NEP and to strike a crucial political alliance in support of the NEP. On October 16, Paz Estenssoro signed an agreement with Hugo Banzer. The agreement, called the *pacto por la democracia* (pact for democracy), allied the MNR and the ADN and effectively guaranteed a docile Congress that would not attempt to block the NEP through either legislation or the interpellation and censure of cabinet ministers. The ADN pledged its support for the NEP in exchange for the MNR's promise of legislative cooperation on electoral reforms and a number of appointments in state enterprises.

The strategy and tactics used by Paz in the first several months of the NEP were repeated through the duration of the government. Episodic shows of force by the government and continual verbal threats of force by Interior Minister Fernando Barthelemy helped to contain popular protests. Throughout 1986, the press was filled with reports of arrests, injuries, and deaths that occurred in conjunction with strikes and protests against the NEP.[50] In

August 1986, Paz declared a second state of siege in response to the *Marcha por la vida* (March for Life). Led by five thousand miners from Oruro, the march was staged to protest the government's plan for massive reduction in the work force of COMIBOL. The protestors headed toward La Paz and were joined by university students, leftist leaders, peasants, and Catholic church representatives. Fearing an occupation of La Paz by the marchers, Paz ordered the army to encircle them in the outskirts of the city. Meanwhile, journalists and leftist leaders in La Paz were arrested. Cut off from food supplies and facing possible military action, the marchers retreated.[51]

This hard-line approach was supplemented with intermittent conciliatory gestures such as "dialogues" with the COB, but none of the meetings ever produced any substantial modification of the NEP. At the same time, Paz worked to keep the pact with the ADN in place. In 1988, an addendum to the pact was signed which pledged that the two parties would support the winner of the popular vote in the next presidential election.

Clearly, Paz's finely honed political skills and his willingness to use presidential power were pivotal in launching and maintaining the NEP. Unlike Siles, Paz Estenssoro had no qualms about using force to quell popular opposition. Moreover, he was firmly committed to the goals and philosophy underpinning the NEP, which to him was not simply a set of economic measures but a part of the historical project he had laid out for his last presidential term. Paz wanted to be remembered for turning Bolivia away from a failed economic model, and he labored to keep the political environment from undermining the NEP.

Sachs Redux, Team Revised

An external shock that threatened to undo the NEP became the catalyst for Sachs's return to Bolivia and his incorporation into Paz's economic team. In an unexpected downturn, prices for Bolivia's major export—tin—fell by 60 percent in the London Metal Exchange in late October 1985. Paz's economic ministers were unprepared for the crisis and responded by deviating from the tight fiscal and monetary discipline laid out in the NEP; they resorted to monetary emissions in order to issue the traditional Christmas bonuses of public-sector employees. At the same time, the state petroleum company was resisting the new governmental controls over its expenditures. Speculation against the peso was reignited by the decision to reduce the amounts of foreign exchange offered in the Central Bank auctions. The inflation that resurged in December and January threatened to erode both the domestic and international confidence that the September 1985 termination of hyperinflation had generated.

As uncertainty about the future of the NEP grew, the CEPB invited Sachs to Bolivia in November 1985 to prepare a memorandum for President Paz on how to proceed with the NEP. In order to monitor public spending, Sachs recommended the creation of a stabilization council consisting of the president and top ministers, much like that suggested by Eder in 1956. Sachs also underscored the need to move rapidly on tax reform. In addition to policy adjustments, he argued for a change in the personnel of the economic team. Because the driving personalities behind the program, Juan Cariaga and Gonzalo Sánchez de Lozada, did not take cabinet positions in August 1985, the two economic ministers charged with overseeing the program, Guillermo Bedregal and Roberto Gisbert, were not the chief intellectual architects of the NEP. Sachs argued that Sánchez de Lozada had to take over the management of the NEP in order to ensure a coherent application of the program.[52]

By early January 1986, the NEP was in imminent danger of collapse. The consumer price index rose 13.3 percent the week of January 6–12, and an 8.9 percent increase was registered the following week. Currency speculation resurged along with inflation; in the same two-week period, the price of the U.S. dollar in the free market increased by 23.9 and 14.6 percent, respectively.[53] With the economy spinning out of control once more, Paz recalibrated the cabinet by bringing in the NEP architects to manage the program. Sánchez de Lozada took over at the Ministry of Planning while Bedregal was bumped to the Foreign Ministry, and, in another shuffle, Cariaga replaced Gisbert as minister of finance. Even as the cabinet changes were taking place, Sachs was en route to La Paz, having signed on as an adviser to the Paz government.

The cabinet changes produced an economic team with an intense ideological and psychological commitment to the implementation of the NEP. Sánchez de Lozada, Cariaga, and Sachs were "true believers" in the principles underlying the program. As the original designers of D. S. 21060, both Sánchez de Lozada and Cariaga had high personal stakes in the success of the program. Moreover, both were "holistic" in their approach to the project. They were convinced that the program had to be applied in its entirety to be successful and were resistant to any suggestions that it be modified. Sánchez de Lozada's conception of the NEP as a political reform— the restoration of the authority of the state—added moral and historical imperatives to the technical arguments about why the NEP could not be modified.

After being sworn in on January 22, 1986, the team took immediate actions to reassert fiscal and monetary controls. A stabilization council was struck to oversee government spending, and new restrictions on expenditures by state enterprises went into effect. To stop monetary emissions, the government delayed pay to public-sector workers for more than a month. A temporary increase in the legal-reserve requirements for banks was raised to 100 percent, and, to ease speculation against the peso, Sachs recommended an increase in the amount of foreign exchange offered by the Central Bank in its auctions. In conjunction with the tight monetary policy, the move quelled speculation with no adverse effects on Bolivia's foreign reserves. By early February, inflation ceased and the exchange rate was stabilized.

The immediate effects of the measures established the competence of the new economic team and reestablished the credibility of the NEP. Moreover, Paz's recomposition of the team sent out a powerful message to domestic adversaries and the international community—the NEP was the government's top priority and would be pursued relentlessly. In the ongoing process of "signaling" seriousness at home and abroad, Sánchez de Lozada, Cariaga, and Sachs became symbols of a new sobriety and competence in Bolivian economic management.

Managing the NEP

Sachs remained intensely involved in the day-to-day decision making on the economy throughout the remainder of 1986. By his own account, he made at least twenty visits to Bolivia during the year. When he was not in La Paz, he had near nightly telephone conversations with Sánchez de Lozada. He took a special interest in the development of the tax reform program, which, passed by Congress in March 1986, included the imposition of a value-added tax and new wealth taxes.

Sachs, like his predecessor George Jackson Eder, became a target for personal criticisms by political opponents of the government. A dispute broke out in March 1986 about alleged comments and conduct by Sachs during a Harvard seminar in February; a story circulated that Sachs had mocked Bolivians and accused the Siles government of corruption. In an emotional letter to President Paz published in the newspaper *Hoy*, Sachs denied the charges. Stating that he had cried, not laughed, about the plight of the Bolivian economy, Sachs confirmed that he called the administration of the Central Bank corrupt and had characterized policy management of the Siles government as shameful. "The members of the Siles government do not have the right to judge me, nor much less the current government," Sachs wrote snappishly. "Their only right, in my opinion, is to apologize to the country for the disastrous lack of leadership capacity they demonstrated." In an angry response, nineteen former members of the Siles government published a letter demanding that Sachs clarify and verify his charges of corruption.[54] Although the controversy faded, Sachs's prominence in economic policymaking continued to be a sore spot among some Bolivian elites. In August 1986, Carlos Serrate Reich, an outspoken congressional opponent of the NEP and publisher of the *Hoy*, wrote to Finance Minister Cariaga and demanded to know the details of Sachs's employment, the utility of the advice he rendered, and why Bolivian professionals could not be trusted to provide the same caliber of advice.[55]

The sniping at Sachs was ignored by the Paz government, much as the criticism of the NEP itself was simply dismissed. Sachs engaged in some public discussions of the NEP in Bolivia; for example, he met with COB leaders in August 1986.[56] But for the most part Sachs preferred to maintain a low profile. As he later observed, "Much of my work is just sitting quietly in a back room analyzing data with members of the government."[57] The bulk of the public defense of the program fell to the economic ministers. In the style of the "dialogues" with the COB, the economic ministers met with aggrieved groups: industrialists and agricultural producers expressed their concerns about the effects of abrupt tariff liberalization; and regional civic groups, university students, and bureaucrats complained about budget cutbacks. Throughout the rounds of meetings, however, the position of the economic team remained intransigent. There was to be no substantial modification of the policies set out in the NEP.

The political star who ascended in the process of managing the NEP was Gonzalo Sánchez de Lozada. His peculiar background and personality made him perfect for the role that he cultivated as the "tough but honest" manager of the NEP. Sánchez de Lozada's upbringing in the United States was evident in his "gringo" Spanish, which was an endless source of public amusement. Known for his keen sense of humor and his no-nonsense manner, "Goni" was acknowledged as charming and intelligent by even the most ardent opponents of the NEP.[58] His disarming and innovative political style undercut portrayals of the team as a cabal of cold-blooded Chicago Boys, though the policies it pursued were every bit as hard-line as the original Chilean experiment.

Sachs credits Sánchez de Lozada with having the bravery and intelligence to proceed with the wrenching structural reforms in the package, the most dramatic of which was the streamlining of the state-owned mining firm, COMIBOL. Under the euphemism of "relocalization," from 1986 through 1988 twenty-three thousand workers were either dismissed, retired, or forced to quit their COMIBOL jobs. Cutbacks in other public-sector jobs were combined with layoffs in the private sector, which were caused by the economic recession and the liberalization of labor laws that made it easier for employers to fire workers. The net effect of the changes was a "deproletarianization" of the labor force.[59] Displaced workers faced open unemployment or were forced into the informal sector of the economy. Estimates are that between forty thousand to sixty thousand formal sector jobs disappeared by the late 1980s, with open unemployment estimated to be between 20 to 25 percent. The unregulated, untaxed informal economy is believed to employ 60 percent of the labor force.[60]

Although the immediate effects of the COMIBOL cutbacks were mitigated somewhat by lump-sum severance payments to "relocalized" workers, the human toll of the economic experiment was undeniable, and the economic team was concerned about the potentially explosive social conditions it was creating. Sánchez de Lozada and Sachs went to work on lobbying the international community to finance an emergency program that would provide temporary employment on public-works projects. The result was the Fondo Social de Emergencia. Founded in late 1986 and headed by businessman Fernando Romero, the fund received financing from the U.S. Agency for International Development (USAID), the World Bank, and the governments of Sweden, Canada, and the Netherlands, and, in 1987–88, generated one hundred thousand temporary jobs on community construction projects.[61]

The Fondo was not the only vehicle cushioning the impact of D. S. 21060. Bolivia's involvement in cocaine production and international drug trafficking also helped to offset some of the effects of the massive dislocations in the formal sector of the economy. Most experts agree that the cocaine trade created new opportunities for rural employment, absorbed displaced workers, and boosted incomes across social classes.[62] While the economic team was loath to acknowledge publicly the beneficial effects of drug trafficking on Bolivian stabilization, the drug trade must be taken into consideration in explaining why massive social convulsions did not materialize in response to the NEP.

The Debt Deviation

As his involvement in the genesis of the Fondo Social suggests, Sachs believed that international support for the Bolivian reforms was crucial. Perhaps Sachs's greatest contribution to sustaining the NEP came in his role as adviser in Bolivia's foreign-debt negotiations. In the course of his participation in the negotiations, Sachs emerged as an influential spokesman not just for Bolivia but for the cause of Third World debt reduction.

Sachs concurred with the Paz government's view that the NEP could not be sustained if Bolivia were forced to resume payments on its international debt of over four billion dollars. Payments on the debt had already been suspended by the Siles government in 1984, but the suspension came after two years during which Bolivia struggled to make payments even as external shocks rocked the economy. The result was that Bolivia transferred the equivalent of 6 percent of its GNP to foreign creditors during the period from 1982 to 1984.[63]

As the economic team pressed on with its austerity and economic restructuring program in the spring of 1986, the U.S. government and the IMF reverted to their usual demands that Bolivia commence repayments. Indeed, the IMF urged further currency devaluation to facilitate the reinitiation of payments to commercial banks.[64] Believing that public toleration for the NEP would break down completely if it became a vehicle of debt repayment, the Paz economic team resisted the orthodox prescription. Instead, Sachs and the economic team argued that both creditors and debtor nations like Bolivia could benefit from a program of systematic debt reduction.[65] In a significant departure from previous positions, both the IMF and the U.S. government acceded in mid-1986 to Bolivia's arguments that it could not be pressed to reinitiate payments without endangering the success of the NEP. The IMF disbursed standby credits of SDR 51.9 million to Bolivia in 1986 and in 1988 agreed to a loan from its Enhanced Structural Adjustment facility for SDR 136.05 million. The American policy reversal on the Bolivian debt coincided with U.S. efforts to gain Bolivian cooperation on the militarization of the war against drug trafficking. In July 1986, the Paz government went along with "Operation Blast Furnace," a joint action by U.S. and Bolivian troops to rout out drug operations in the countryside.

Bolivia's new relationship with the IMF opened the doors for the team to seek concessions from its private commercial creditors. Successful negotiations with the Paris Club concluded in 1987 and provided for rescheduling. In addition, arrangements were made for Bolivia to repurchase one half of its debt at eleven cents per dollar of face value. The money for the purchase was provided by foreign governments.

Sachs's presence in the debt negotiations lent intellectual clout to Bolivia's claim that it could not be expected to repay. His technical expertise as an economist and his considerable academic reputation gave credibility to a position that might not have been taken seriously by international lenders if it had been put forth by Bolivians alone. Sachs's arguments had a profound effect on the international community's view of the debt situation, helping to shift the terms of the debate from rescheduling to debt reduction. This change in the intellectual framework on debt became evident in March 1989 with the unveiling of the U.S. government's "Brady Plan." Breaking with the 1985 Baker Plan, which had advocated lengthening the time frame for repayment, the Brady Plan acknowledged the inability of debtor countries to repay.[66]

In Sachs's view, this new approach gave Bolivia the "time and the international support" to proceed with the stabilization program. Sachs's skillful advocacy of debt relief and financial aid for Bolivia provided the latitude that the Paz government needed to continue with the NEP.

Money Doctoring, Storytelling, and Economic Experiments

Whether the policies laid out in the NEP will be sustained by successive governments and whether those policies will produce economic growth in the long run remain unanswered questions.[67] D. S. 21060 was a resounding success in halting hyperinflation, but economic recovery has been slow. Annual GDP growth in the period from 1987 to 1990 averaged 2.5 percent, but GDP growth per capita continues to be negative. Private-sector investment is stagnant, and the formal economy remains depressed.

What conclusions can be drawn about the role of money doctors and the conditions that facilitate neoliberal economic experiments from this "thicker" description of the Bolivian experience? Certainly, this story suggests that the experiment hinged on much more than arriving at the right technical prescriptions ("getting the numbers right," in the parlance of economists). The NEP was a complicated exercise in politics, psychology, and social control.[68] Moreover, it was an experiment that owed much to accommodations by international actors and Bolivia's involvement in the drug trade.

The simultaneity of crises during the Siles government—economic, social, and political—produced a "breakpoint" in Bolivian history, a moment that opened up actors to the possibilities of effecting fundamental changes in the way Bolivia worked.[69] The idea of turning Bolivia away from state-centered economics was not a "new" idea. As I have shown, arguments about the failure of the populist state had been circulating since the 1950s. What was new was that, by 1985, the idea had found a social and political base in an emerging coalition of business leaders, conservative technocrats, and center-right politicians. With populist and leftist formulas discredited during the Siles administration, the neoliberal coalition was poised to take advantage of popular support for dramatic measures to end the crisis.

Committed to the ideological principles underlying the NEP and bent on carving out his place in Bolivian history, President Víctor Paz Estenssoro proved to be a deft political manager of the neoliberal experiment. Selective uses of force combined with intermittent offers of "dialogue" kept the already weakened labor movement off balance and unable to mount any effective resistance to D. S. 21060. Once in motion, the application of the neoliberal program only further weakened Bolivian trade unionism, and the political pact between the MNR and the ADN eclipsed Congress as a potential obstacle to the implementation of the program.

Maintaining consensus and cohesion inside the economic team also kept domestic opponents at bay. The cabinet change of January 1986, which brought Sánchez and Cariaga on board, and Sachs's incorporation into the team assured lucidity and commitment in the administration of the NEP. Sánchez de Lozada and Sachs developed a close working relationship. Like many economists, Sachs did indeed think of himself as a "doctor" administering painful, but necessary treatments.[70] His technical expertise, "medicalized" discourse, and Harvard pedigree all worked to reinforce the team's belief in the course it had chosen. Like Eder, Sachs constantly reassured his colleagues that the program was viable and necessary.

The pyschological conviction of the team fueled its imperviousness to pleas from civil groups to modify the program. Self-confidence and toughness became the stylistic signatures of the economic team.[71] The projection of "toughness" was important not just for fending off domestic lobbies but also for rehabilitating the image of the Bolivian government among influential international actors and making Bolivia's requests for financial support and special treatment more palatable.

In the style of earlier money doctors such as Kemmerer and Eder, Sachs played a variety of roles. He performed—as economists frequently do—a ritual function, baptizing the program that Bolivians (some of whom, like Sánchez de Lozada, were not professional economists) had already developed.[72] Sachs's involvement gave proof to the international community that the government's program was "economically correct" and committed. Sachs went on to become an official storyteller, or "spin doctor," of the Bolivian experience, propagating the idea that what had happened in Bolivia could and should be replayed in Kraków, Moscow, and points beyond.[73]

The sheer complexity of Bolivia's story, however, should give pause to money doctors seeking to replicate that "success" in other venues. Domestic critics of the Sachs Plan for Poland were quick to point to the pitfalls in generalizing the Bolivian experience. As one Polish analyst observed, "I would love to see Bolivia. I'm sure it's lovely, very exotic. I just don't want to see Bolivia *here*." The analyst went on to underscore the differing political and structural conditions in Latin America and Eastern Europe and the problems inherent in applying generic formulas to vastly differing realities.[74]

More reflection on the peculiarities of particular cases may do political scientists as well as economists some good. The Bolivian economic experiment was a fragile edifice built on an extraordinary convergence of factors. It was facilitated by the presence of a domestic support coalition; the skills of a machiavellian political manager; the exhaustion of civil society through a preceding crisis; the availability of alternatives in the informal sector of the economy (including opportunities afforded by Bolivia's position in the international drug trade); and the willingness of foreign governments and multilateral institutions to provide financial aid and tolerate deviation from orthodoxy on the debt issue.

In short, Bolivia's economic experiment hung on a set of circumstances that no money doctor, politician, or international agency could recreate with ease. Moreover, the experiment came at some cost to democratic political development. Describing the NEP's implementation, one leading government official admitted privately, "We behaved like authoritarian pigs." Reading grand lessons from Bolivia's story may be risky business, both for money doctors and the countries subjected to a Bolivian-style experiment.

Notes

1. This essay draws on research from a forthcoming book on neoliberal coalitions in the central Andes written by the author and James M. Malloy.

2. The term "neoliberal experiment" is used to denote policies that combine orthodox stabilization measures (for example, currency devaluation and price increases) with long-term reforms to restructure the economy by reducing the role of the state and subjecting economic activity to market forces. This definition is put forth by Alejandro Foxley in *Latin American Experiments in Neoconservative Economics* (Berkeley: University of California Press, 1983), 15–17. Foxley, however, preferred to use "neoconservative" rather than the Spanish "neoliberal" for English-speaking readers. For further discussion of the neoliberal experiments in the Southern Cone see Joseph Ramos, *Neoconservative Economics in the Southern Cone of Latin America* (Baltimore: Johns Hopkins University Press, 1986).

3. For such characterization see, for example, Robert E. Norton, "The American Out to Save Poland," *Fortune*, 29 January 1990, 129–131 (reprinted in this volume as "Jeff Sachs—Doctor Debt"); and Mary-Ann Bendel, "Poland's Mr. Fix-It," *Best of Business Quarterly* (Fall 1991): 8–13.

4. John Sedgwick, "The World of Doctor Debt," *Boston Magazine*, May 1991, 63–65, 107–108.

5. Economist Paul Krugman in Norton, "The American," 129.

6. For a much less sanguine view of Sachs's record see Jon Weiner, "Capitalist Shock Therapy," *The Nation*, 25 June 1990.

7. Any "economist-centered" approach to explaining policy runs the risk of missing the pivotal role played by other actors—the politicians, bureaucrats, interest groups, and mass public. For a discussion of the problem see Peter A. Hall, "Introduction," in *The Political Power of Economic Ideas: Keynesianism across Nations*, ed. Peter Hall (Princeton: Princeton University Press, 1989), 8–10.

8. For the definitive work on the Kemmerer missions see Paul W. Drake, *The Money Doctor in the Andes: The Kemmerer Missions, 1923–1933* (Durham, NC: Duke University Press, 1989). For a shorter overview see Barry Eichengreen, "House Calls of the Money Doctor: The Kemmerer Missions to Latin America, 1917–1933," reprinted in this volume.

9. For an overview of the findings of foreign missions in Bolivia see Gontrán Carranza Fernández, *El proceso histórico de la planificación en Bolivia* (La Paz: Editorial de la Universidad Mayor de San Andres, 1982).

10. See United Nations, "Mission of Technical Assistance to Bolivia," *Report of the United Nations Mission of Technical Assistance to Bolivia* (New York: United Nations, 1951).

11. For a discussion of the role of foreign technocrats in Bolivia see George Jackson Eder, *Inflation and Development in Latin America: A Case History of Inflation and Stabilization in Bolivia* (Ann Arbor, Michigan: Bureau of Business Research, Graduate School of Business Administration, University of Michigan, 1968), 473–486. Also see Robert J. Alexander, *The Bolivian National Revolution* (New Brunswick, NJ: Rutgers University Press, 1958), 242–270.

12. For an analysis of the Bolivian Revolution see James M. Malloy, *Bolivia: The Uncompleted Revolution* (Pittsburgh: University of Pittsburgh Press, 1970); James M. Malloy and Richard Thorn, eds., *Beyond the Revolution: Bolivia since 1952* (Pittsburgh: University of Pittsburgh Press, 1971); and James Dunkerley, *Rebellion in the Veins: Political Struggle in Bolivia, 1952–1982* (London: Verso, 1984).

13. For a comprehensive discussion of U.S. aid see James W. Wilkie, *The Bolivian Revolution and U.S. Aid since 1952* (Los Angeles: Latin American Center, University of California at Los Angeles, 1969).

14. The quotation is taken from the report authored by Zondag; see "U.S. Operations Mission to Bolivia," *Problems in the Economic Development of Bolivia* (La Paz: United States Operation Mission to Bolivia, 1956), 212. The illness metaphor continues to be a popular one among economists; it naturally conjures up a justification for aggressive intervention by experts—a "shock treatment" by money doctors. In an interview, Sachs reinvoked the image. Justifying the shock approach in Bolivia and Poland, Sachs argued, "When a guy comes into the emergency room and his heart's stopped, you just rip open the sternum and you don't worry about the scars that you leave. The idea is to get the guy's heart beating again. And you make a bloody mess. But you don't have any choice"; see Lawrence Weschler, "A Grand Experiment," *New Yorker*, 13 November 1989, 77. Susan Sontag has pointed to the dangers of using the imagery of illness in political discourse. See her *Illness as Metaphor and Aid and Its Metaphors* (New York: Anchor Books, 1990), 83. For an insightful analysis of the uses of metaphor and storytelling by economists see Donald N. McCloskey, *If You're So Smart: The Narrative of Economic Expertise* (Chicago: University of Chicago Press, 1990).

15. Eder had an undergraduate economics degree and a law degree. In addition to having previous experience in government as chief of the Latin American section of the U.S. Bureau of Foreign and Domestic Commerce from 1926 to 1932, Eder worked as an attorney for ITT in New York and Buenos Aires. In the 1960s, Eder taught at the School of Business Administration at the University of Michigan and authored several books that included his detailed account of Bolivian stabilization. Eder was one of the more eclectic money doctors—he also authored romance novels under the nom de plume Jackson Read. See *Who's Who in America 1990–1991* (Wilmette, IL: Marquis's Who's Who, Macmillan Directory Division, 1990), 917.

16. Eder, *Stabilization*, 87–88.

17. Ibid., 87–89.

18. At several points in his book, Eder notes his attempts to bolster the spirits of government officials. He describes President Siles as having bouts of depression and how he constantly tried to reassure Siles about the importance of pursuing the stabilization program. On one occasion, Eder recruited the papal nuncio to provide spiritual solace. See Eder, *Stabilization*, 153.

19. Malloy, *Bolivia*, 302.

20. The brutal conditions of everyday life in the tin-mining communities and the political repression experienced by miners is described by June Nash, *We Eat*

the Mines and the Mines Eat Us: Dependency and Exploitation in Bolivia's Tin Mines (New York: Columbia University Press, 1979). Also see Domitila Barrios de Chugara and Moema Viezzer, *Let Me Speak! Testimony of Domitila, a Woman of the Bolivian Mines*, trans. Victoria Ortiz (New York: Monthly Review Press, 1978).

21. Banzer's economic policies are discussed in Jerry R. Ladman, "The Political Economy of the 'Economic Miracle' of the Banzer Regime," in *Modern-Day Bolivia: Legacy of the Revolution and Prospects for the Future*, ed. Jerry R. Ladman (Tempe, AZ: Center for Latin American Studies, Arizona State University, 1982), 321–43.

22. At the time of the Musgrave mission, Carlos Calvo was the minister of finance and David Blanco was undersecretary of fiscal and tax policy. Juan Cariaga was the Bolivian coordinator of the mission. The findings were published in English; see Richard Musgrave, ed., *Fiscal Reform in Bolivia: Final Report of the Bolivian Mission on Tax Reform* (Cambridge, MA: International Tax Program, Harvard Law School, 1981).

23. For a discussion see Robert Devlin, *Debt and Crisis in Latin America: The Supply Side of the Story* (Princeton: Princeton University Press, 1989); and Oscar Ugarteche, *El estado deudor: Economia política de la deuda, Peru y Bolivia 1968–1984* (Lima: Instituto de Estudios Peruanos, 1986).

24. The document is reprinted in Confederación de Empresarios Privados de Bolivia (CEPB), *Pensamiento de la empresa privada (Documentos emitidos de febrero 1977 a marzo 1981)* (La Paz: Confederación de Empresarios Privados de Bolivia), 142–162.

25. See the "Memoria anual 1980–81" reprinted in the CEPB's *Pensamiento (1977–82)*, 82.

26. The proposals were published as "Lineamientos y Proposiciones de la Empresa Privada para un programa de Recuperación Económica," on 12 June 1984. The text is reproduced in Confederación de Empresarios Privados, *Pensamiento y acción de la empresa privada 1982–1985* (La Paz: CEPB, 1985), 301–313.

27. For a discussion of the development of the medium mining sector see Manuel E. Contreras and Mario Napoleon Pacheco, *Medio siglo de la minería mediana en Bolivia 1939–1989* (La Paz: Biblioteca Minera Boliviana, 1989).

28. The statements are found in "Conclusiones de la Comisión Económica," from "Encuentro Nacional de la Libre Empresa, La Paz, 5–6 de mayo de 1983." The documents are reprinted in *Pensamiento (1982–1985)*, 291.

29. The "resurrection of civil society" in political transitions is discussed by Guillermo O'Donnell and Philippe Schmitter, *Tentative Conclusions about Uncertain Democracies* (Baltimore: Johns Hopkins University Press, 1986), 48–56.

30. For an examination of the role of business in political transition see Catherine Conaghan, "Retreat to Democracy: Business and Political Transition in Bolivia and Ecuador," in *Democratic Transition and Consolidation in Southern Europe, Latin America, and Southeast Asia*, ed. Diane Ethier (London: Macmillan and Company, 1990), 73–90.

31. For a review of the packages see Juan Antonio Morales, *Precios, salarios, y política economíca durante la alta inflación boliviana de 1982 a 1985* (La Paz: Instituto Latinoamericano de Investigaciones Sociales, 1987), 44–45.

32. Figures are taken from Juan Antonio Morales, "Inflation Stabilization in Bolivia," in *Inflation Stabilization: The Experience of Israel, Argentina, Brazil,*

Bolivia, and Mexico, ed. Michael Bruno et al. (Cambridge: MIT Press, 1988), 306–346.

33. Morales, *Precios*, 63.

34. In contrast, there were 31 industrial disputes in 1981. In the following year, there were 301. Data is from James W. Wilkie, ed., *Statistical Abstract of Latin America*, Vol. 28 (Los Angeles: UCLA Latin American Center Publications, 1990).

35. Figures taken from Roberto Laserna, "La protesta territorial (La acción colectiva regional y urbana en una coyuntura de crisis democrática)" in *Crisis, democracia y conflicto social: La acción colectiva en Bolivia: 1982–1985*, ed. Roberto Laserna (Cochabamba: CERES, 1985), 203–252. By 1984, public disturbances were so chronic and widespread that the newspaper *Presencia* was publishing a daily schedule of the events entitled, "Agenda de paros, huelgas, emergencias, and ultimatums" (Agenda of Stoppages, Strikes, Emergencies, and Ultimatums).

36. Siles's statement is taken from Arturo Núñez del Prado, "Bolivia: Inflación y democracia," *Pensamiento iberoamericano* 9 (2d semestre: 1986), 274. In describing Siles's attitudes during the 1956 program, Eder also notes Siles's dismay at the thought of having to use force to implement the program. See Eder, *Stabilization*, 173.

37. For further discussion of the Siles period see James M. Malloy and Eduardo Gamarra, *Revolution and Reaction: Bolivia 1964–1985* (New Brunswick, NJ: Transaction, 1988), 157–200.

38. For a look at the campaign discourse see Ronald Grebe López et al., *¿Que ofrecen los candidatos? Elecciones 1985* (La Paz: ERBOL, 1985).

39. See Michael Bruno and Jeffrey Sachs, *Economics of Worldwide Stagflation* (Cambridge: Harvard University Press, 1985).

40. Biographical data on Sachs is from Mark Blaug, ed., *Who's Who in Economics: A Biographical Dictionary of Major Economists 1700–1986* (Cambridge: MIT Press, 1986), 741–742.

41. Interview, Juan Cariaga, 17 February 1986, La Paz.

42. Telephone interview, Jeffrey Sachs, 2 October 1992.

43. Interview, Gonzalo Sánchez de Lozada, 22 February 1986, La Paz.

44. While ADN leaders later characterized Paz's economic program as a "transfer of technology" from the ADN to the MNR, Sánchez de Lozada maintains that his team never had access to the actual draft of the ADN-Sachs plan. Interviews with Gonzalo Sánchez de Lozada, 22 February 1986 and 29 May 1988, La Paz. Sachs does not dispute this, although other sources indicate that a draft of the Sachs plan was available to the team.

45. Interview, 22 February 1986, La Paz.

46. Gonzalo Sánchez de Lozada, "La nueva política económica," *Foro Económico* 5 (September 1985): 6.

47. For further discussion of the NEP see Morales, "Inflation Stabilization in Bolivia." Also see Juan Cariaga, "Bolivia," in *Latin American Adjustment: How Much Has Happened?*, ed. John Williamson (Washington, DC: Institute for International Economics, 1990), 41–53. For Sachs's description see Jeffrey Sachs, "The Bolivian Hyperinflation and Stabilization," *American Economic Review*, 77, 2 (1987): 279–283.

48. Paz reportedly confined his cabinet ministers to one room for the duration of the twenty-four-hour meeting and disconnected the telephones to ensure that

details of the program would not be linked to opposition groups. In his discussion of the stabilization program, James Dunkerley correctly notes that the government's efforts to describe the program as a "New Economic Policy" never gained public acceptance; instead, the popular slang for the program referred to the decree number, simply *veintiuno zero sesenta* (twenty-one zero sixty). See his "Political Transition and Economic Stabilization: Bolivia, 1982–89," in *Political Suicide and Other Essays*, ed. James Dunkerley (London: Verso, 1992), 209–210.

49. Quotations from speech are taken from Federico Aguilo, *Estado de sitio: Apuntes para la historia de las jornadas septembrinas de 1985 en Bolivia* (Cochabamba: Asamblea Permanente de Derechos Humanos, 1985), 20–21.

50. See, for example, "Cronología de violencia," *Informe "R"* 6, 114 (April 1986).

51. For a detailed account of the events see "Por la vida y por la paz! Los caminantes de la patria," *Informe "R"* 6, 118 (September 1986).

52. Interview, Sánchez de Lozada, 22 February 1986.

53. Figures are cited in Morales, "Inflation Stabilization in Bolivia," 328.

54. Both letters were published in *Hoy*, 27 March 1986. The protest letter to Sachs was signed by high-profile cabinet members of the Siles government, including Flavio Machicado, Arturo Núñez del Prado, and José Ortiz Mercado.

55. *Hoy*, 20 August 1986. Serrate Reich was a politically ambitious, persistent critic of the economic team. *Hoy* heavily publicized the reports that an array of government officials, including members of the economic team, received "salary supplements" from international organizations even as they were prescribing salary austerity for everyone else. The documents and news reports are found in Carlos Serrate Reich, *Interpelación al neoliberalism* (La Paz: Empresa Editora Siglo, 1989).

56. An unflattering depiction of Sachs's participation in the meeting appeared in *Hoy*, 13 August 1986.

57. "The Harvard Debt Doctor's Controversial Cure," *Time*, 6 November 1989, 66.

58. Sánchez de Lozada went on to win the MNR's presidential nomination for the 1990 race. He narrowly won the popular vote, but a political pact between the MIR and the ADN resulted in the election of Jaime Paz Zamora of the MIR in the Congress. For an analysis of the political phenomenon of *gonismo* see Carlos Toranzo Roca, "Los rasgos de la nueva derecha boliviana," in Carlos F. Toranzo Roca and Mario Arrieta Abdalla, *Nueva derecha y desproletarización en Bolivia* (La Paz: UNITAS-ILDIS, 1989), 58–75.

59. For a discussion of the "deproletarianizing" and "repeasantizing" effects of the NEP on the labor force see Toranzo and Arrieta, *Nueva derecha*. For a fascinating look at the life of "relocalized" miners in La Paz see Godofredo Sandoval and M. Fernanda Sostres, *La ciudad prometida: Pobladores y organizaciones sociales en El Alto* (La Paz: ILDIS, Systema, 1989), 147–173.

60. See The Economist Intelligence Unit, *Bolivia: Country Profile 1991–92* (London: Business International, 1991), 9–10.

61. Fondo Social de Emergencia, "Estadísticas básicas," 18 April 1988, La Paz (photocopy).

62. For a recent overview of the literature on the Bolivian drug trade see Mario De Franco and Ricardo Godoy, "The Economic Consequences of Cocaine Production in Bolivia: Historical, Local, and Macroeconomic Perspectives," *Journal of Latin American Studies*, 24, 2 (May 1992): 375–406.

63. Figure is cited in Jeffrey Sachs, "Comprehensive Debt Retirement: The Bolivian Example," *Brookings Papers on Economic Activity* 2 (1988): 711.

64. Juan Antonio Morales and Jeffrey D. Sachs, "Bolivia's Economic Crisis," in *Developing Country Debt and Economic Performance*, Vol. 2 (Chicago: National Bureau of Economic Research, University of Chicago Press, 1990), 254.

65. Sachs developed a formal model illustrating how debt relief could be conceptualized as the rational and best choice for creditors and debtors. For the model see his "Debt Overhang of Developing Countries, in *Debt, Stabilization, and Development*, 91–95. For a brief look at his argument see Jeffrey Sachs, "How to Save the Third World," *The New Republic*, 28 October 1985, 20–22.

66. For an analysis of the Brady Plan by Jeffrey Sachs see "Making the Brady Plan Work," *Foreign Affairs* 68, 3 (Summer 1989): 87–104.

67. For the most part, the government of Jaime Paz Zamora has continued the policy lines of the NEP. The next presidential and congressional elections are scheduled for 1993. For an analysis of pending economic problems see Juan Antonio Morales, "Bolivia's Post-Stabilization Problems," Documento de Trabajo no. 08/90, junio de 1990, Instituto de Investigaciones Socioeconomicas (La Paz: Universidad Católica Boliviana).

68. The dynamics described in the Bolivian case (that is, the insulation of the economic team and the role of the preceding crisis) have parallels in other recent attempts at neoliberal economic reforms. See, for example, John Waterbury, "The Heart of the Matter? Public Enterprises and the Adjustment Process," in *The Politics of Economic Adjustment*, ed. Stephan Haggard and Robert Kaufman (Princeton: Princeton University Press, 1992); also see "Introduction" and "Conclusions" by Joan Nelson in *Economic Crisis and Policy Choice: The Politics of Adjustment in the Third World*, ed. Joan Nelson (Princeton: Princeton University Press, 1990), 3–32, 321–361. For a comparative discussion of neoliberal experiments in Bolivia, Peru, and Ecuador see Catherine Conaghan et al., "Business and the 'Boys': The Politics of Neoliberalism in the Central Andes," *Latin American Research Review*, no. 2 (Spring 1990): 3–30.

69. This notion of a "breakpoint" that provides the opportunity for new ideas to inform policymakers is taken from G. John Ikenberry's analysis of foreign policy decision making; see "A World Economy Restored: Expert Consensus and the Anglo-American Postwar Settlement," *International Organization* 46, 1 (Winter 1992): 289–321.

70. Sachs described himself in the following way: "I consider myself like a clinician. I've seen lots of patients, read lots of case histories. Like a doctor, I know what's good and what's bad"; Margaret Stein, "Jeffrey Sachs," *M Inc* 8 (September 1991): 136. See also the previously cited statement in note 13.

71. The projection of toughness seems to be standard stylistic fare among neoliberal economic teams. For a discussion of the distinctive style that developed in the orthodox team headed by José Martínez de Hoz in Argentina in the 1970s, see Julie M. Taylor, "Technocracy and National Identity: Attitudes toward Economic Policy," in *From Military Rule to Liberal Democracy in Argentina*, ed. Monica Peralta-Ramos and Carlos H. Waisman (Boulder: Westview, 1987), 131–146. The style and cohesion of economic teams are also discussed in a forthcoming book by Conaghan and Malloy.

72. For a fascinating discussion of the ritual and legitimating functions of economists see John Markoff and Veronica Montecinos, "The Irresistible Rise of

Economists," paper presented to the World Congress of Sociology, July 1990, Madrid.

73. Sachs assumed a much higher public profile in his subsequent forays into money doctoring. In Poland, he made the case for shock treatment in a televised speech in front of the parliament. As his first hands-on case of money doctoring, Bolivia has become a primary referrent for Sachs in his international advising of other countries.

74. Weschler, "A Grand Experiment." For further discussion of the controversies surrounding the Sachs Plan in Poland see Lawrence Weschler, "Shock," *New Yorker*, 10 December 1990, 86–136. Sachs does acknowledge the constraints posed by political circumstances in the unfolding of market reform programs. See his analysis of the Polish case, "Building a Market Economy in Poland," *Scientific American* 266 (March 1992): 34–40. Sachs does not say much, however, about how economic restructuring should be modified in the absense of optimal political conditions.

Suggested Readings

This bibliography concentrates on major books in English. Highly technical studies, especially in economics, are not included. For an introduction to modernization and dependency theories, see Peter F. Klaren and Thomas J. Bossert, eds., *Promise of Development: Theories of Change in Latin America* (Boulder, 1986). The landmark statement on dependency is Fernando Henrique Cardoso and Enzo Faletto, *Dependency and Development in Latin America* (Berkeley, 1979). On hegemony theories, important texts are Robert Gilpin, *The Political Economy of International Relations* (Princeton, 1987); Robert O. Keohane, *After Hegemony: Cooperation and Discord in the World Political Economy* (Princeton, 1984); and the Kindleberger book on the Great Depression noted below.

For general coverage of foreign advisers, see Merle Curti and Kendall Birr, *Prelude to Point Four: American Technical Missions Overseas, 1838–1938* (Madison, 1954); and Lauchlin Currie, *The Role of Economic Advisers in Developing Countries* (Westport, 1981). On the international roles and risks of foreign capital, a good starting place is Charles Lipson, *Standing Guard: Protecting Foreign Capital in the Nineteenth and Twentieth Centuries* (Berkeley, 1985).

The best sources on foreign investments in Latin America are provided by Carlos Marichal, *A Century of Debt Crises in Latin America: From Independence to the Great Depression, 1820–1930* (Princeton, 1989); and Barbara Stallings, *Banker to the Third World: U.S. Portfolio Investment in Latin America, 1900–1986* (Berkeley, 1987). Other key studies of lending experiences prior to the 1970s, especially during the 1920s–1930s debt cycle, include Max Winkler, *Investments of United States Capital in Latin America* (Boston, 1928); John T. Madden et al., *America's Experience as a Creditor Nation* (New York, 1937); Cleona Lewis, *America's Stake in International Investments* (Washington, DC, 1938); J. Fred Rippy, *British Investment in Latin America, 1822–1949* (Minneapolis, 1959); and United Nations, Department of Economic and Social Affairs, *Foreign Capital in Latin America* (New York, 1955) and *External Financing in Latin America* (New York, 1965). For banking, William C. Phelps, *The Foreign Expansion of American Banks: American Branch Banking Abroad* (New York, 1927) is recommended.

To explore the 1930s debt crisis, an excellent anthology is Rosemary Thorp, ed., *Latin America in the 1930s: The Role of the Periphery in World Crisis* (London, 1984). For an influential interpretation of the global crash, see Charles P. Kindleberger, *The World in Depression, 1929–1939* (Berkeley, 1975).

On the 1980s debt crisis, there are scads of books. In addition to the Stallings volume mentioned above, six good studies to begin with include Richard E. Feinberg and Valeriana Kallab, eds., *Adjustment Crisis in the Third World* (New Brunswick, 1984); Miguel S. Wionczek, ed., *Politics and Economics of External Debt Crisis: The Latin American Experience* (Boulder, 1985); Miles Kahler, ed., *The Politics of International Debt* (Ithaca, 1986); Pedro-Pablo Kuczynski, *Latin American Debt: A Twentieth Century Fund Book* (Baltimore, 1988); Robert Devlin, *Debt and Crisis in Latin America: The Supply Side of the Story* (Princeton, 1989); and Barry Eichengreen and Peter Lindert, eds., *The International Debt Crisis in Historical Perspective* (Cambridge, 1990).

More emphasis on the internal repercussions of the debt crisis can be found in Jonathan Hartlyn and Samuel A. Morley, eds., *Latin American Political Economy: Financial Crisis and Political Change* (Boulder, 1986); Rosemary Thorp and Laurence Whitehead, eds., *Latin American Debt and the Adjustment Crisis* (Pittsburgh, 1987); Barbara Stallings and Robert Kaufman, eds., *Debt and Democracy in Latin America* (Boulder, 1989); Howard Handelman and Werner Baer, eds., *Paying the Costs of Austerity in Latin America* (Boulder, 1989); Joan M. Nelson, ed., *Economic Crisis and Policy Choice: The Politics of Adjustment in Developing Countries* (Princeton, 1990); and Stephen Haggard and Robert Kaufman, eds., *The Politics of Economic Adjustment: International Constraints, Distributive Conflicts, and the State* (Princeton, 1992).

The impulses and parameters of U.S. expansionism are treated in broad compass in Emily S. Rosenberg, *Spreading the American Dream: American Economic and Cultural Expansion, 1890–1945* (New York, 1982); also insightful is her article "Foundations of United States International Financial Power: Gold Standard Diplomacy, 1900–1905," *Business History Review* 59 (Summer 1985): 169–202. Classic criticism of the early decades of U.S. commercial and financial expansion can be found in William Appleman Williams, *The Tragedy of American Diplomacy*, rev. ed. (New York, 1972). A more positive assessment is offered by Herbert Feis, *The Diplomacy of the Dollar: First Era, 1919–1932* (Baltimore, 1950). See also Joseph S. Tulchin, *The Aftermath of War: World War I and U.S. Policy toward Latin America* (New York, 1971).

There is a vast literature on U.S. colonialism and interventionism from the 1890s to the 1920s. Despite the cascade of recent publications on U.S.

incursions in the Caribbean and Central America, the most comprehensive information for the early period can still be found in the patriotic paean of Samuel Flagg Bemis, *The Latin American Policy of the United States: An Historical Interpretation* (New York, 1943). For a survey from the 1780s to the 1980s, see Walter LaFeber, *Inevitable Revolutions: The United States in Central America* (New York, 1984).

Other books of general utility on U.S. invasions in the Caribbean basin include, chronologically, Dana G. Munro, *Intervention and Dollar Diplomacy in the Caribbean, 1900–1921* (Princeton, 1964) and *The United States and the Caribbean Republics, 1921–1933* (Princeton, 1974); Whitney T. Perkins, *Constraint of Empire: The United States and Caribbean Interventions* (Westport, 1981); and Lester D. Langley, *The Banana Wars: An Inner History of American Empire, 1900–1934* (Lexington, 1983). On particular countries, see R. R. Hill, *Fiscal Intervention in Nicaragua* (New York, 1933); Bruce J. Calder, *The Impact of Intervention: The Dominican Republic during the U.S. Occupation of 1916–1924* (Austin, 1984); and Louis A. Pérez, Jr., *Cuba under the Platt Amendment, 1902–1934* (Pittsburgh, 1986).

The most thorough coverage of Edwin Kemmerer's operations in South America is found in Paul W. Drake, *The Money Doctor in the Andes: The Kemmerer Missions, 1923–1933* (Durham, 1989). Those missions are placed in context by Robert N. Seidel, "Progressive Pan Americanism: Development and United States Policy toward South America, 1906–1931" (Ph.D. diss., Cornell University, 1973). Kemmerer's expedition to Ecuador is examined by Linda Alexander Rodríguez, *The Search for Public Policy: Regional Politics and Government Finances in Ecuador, 1830–1940* (Berkeley, 1985), and to South Africa by Bruce R. Dalgaard, "South Africa's Impact on Britain's Return to Gold, 1925" (Ph.D. diss., University of Illinois, 1976). The money doctor's own views can be sampled in Edwin W. Kemmerer, "Economic Advisory Work for Governments," *Economic Review* 17, no. 1 (March 1927): 1–12. To see how central banks engaged in similar international economic restructuring, read Richard Hemmig Meyer, *Bankers' Diplomacy: Monetary Stabilization in the Twenties* (New York, 1970).

The International Monetary Fund has attracted a large body of literature, including J. Keith Horsefield, ed., *The International Monetary Fund, 1945–1965: Twenty Years of International Monetary Cooperation*, 3 vols. (Washington, DC, 1969); Cheryl Payer, *The Debt Trap: The IMF and the Third World* (New York, 1974); Margaret Garritsen de Vries, *International Monetary Fund, 1966–1971: The System under Stress*, 2 vols. (Washington, DC, 1976); John Williamson, ed., *IMF Conditionality* (Washington, DC, 1983); and Tony Killick et al., *The Quest for Economic Stabilisation: The IMF and the Third World* (London, 1984). Two books focus on the Latin

American experience: Rosemary Thorp and Laurence Whitehead, *Inflation and Stabilisation in Latin America* (New York, 1979); and Manuel Pastor, Jr., *The International Monetary Fund and Latin America: Economic Stabilization and Class Conflict* (Boulder, 1987).

On the Chicago Boys, the most important study is by Juan Gabriel Valdés, *La Escuela de Chicago: Operación Chile* (Buenos Aires, 1989). One of the few analyses in English comes from Philip J. O'Brien, "The New Leviathan: The Chicago School and the Chilean Regime, 1973–1980," *Occasional Papers* 38 (University of Glasgow, Institute of Latin American Studies, 1982). The Chicago Boys are one of several important issues treated by Eduardo Silva, "Capitalist Coalitions and Economic Policymaking in Authoritarian Chile, 1973–1988" (Ph.D. diss., University of California, San Diego, 1991).

To learn more about the views and accomplishments of Jeffrey D. Sachs, see three publications by him: *Developing Country Debt and Economic Performance* (Chicago, 1989): "How to Save the Third World," *New Republic* (October 28, 1985): 20–22; and "Making the Brady Plan Work," *Foreign Affairs* 68, no. 3 (Summer 1989): 87–104. Also useful is an article by John Sedgwick, "The World of Doctor Debt," *Boston Magazine* (May 1991): 63–65, 107–8.